I've lost some weight. Here's *World Trigger* vol

—Daisuke Ashih

Daisuke Ashihara began his manga career at t
27 when his manga *Room 303* won second pla
75th Tezuka Awards. His first series, *Super Dog*
began serialization in *Weekly Shonen Jump*
World Trigger is his second serialized work i
Shonen Jump. He is also the author of sever
works, including the one-shots *Super Dog*
Trigger Keeper and *Elite Agent Jin*.

WORLD TRIGGER

WORLD TRIGGER VOL. 16
SHONEN JUMP Manga Edition

STORY AND ART BY DAISUKE ASHIHARA

Translation/Toshikazu Aizawa
Touch-Up Art & Lettering/Annaliese Christman
Design/Sam Elzway
Editor/Marlene First

Printed in the U.S.A.

Published by VIZ Media, LLC
P.O. Box 77010
San Francisco, CA 94107

10 9 8 7 6 5 4 3 2 1
First printing, July 2017

www.viz.com

THE WORLD'S
MOST POPULAR MANGA

www.shonenjump.com

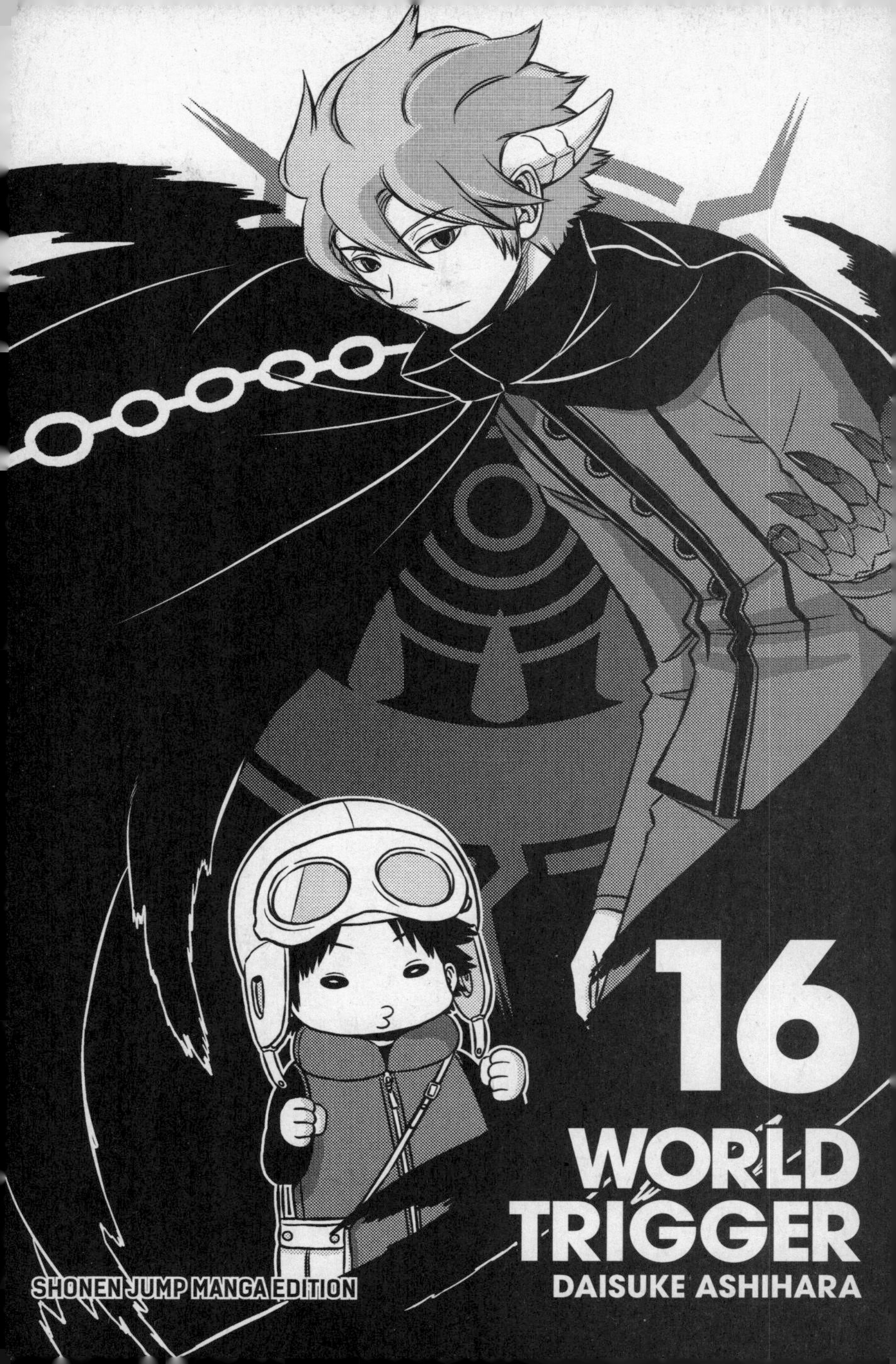
16
WORLD TRIGGER
SHONEN JUMP MANGA EDITION
DAISUKE ASHIHARA

WORLD TRIGGER DATA BASE

Invasion NEIGHBOR

Invaders from another dimension that enter Mikado City through Gates. Most "Neighbors" here are Trion soldiers built for war. The Neighbors who actually live on the other side of the Gates are human, like Yuma.

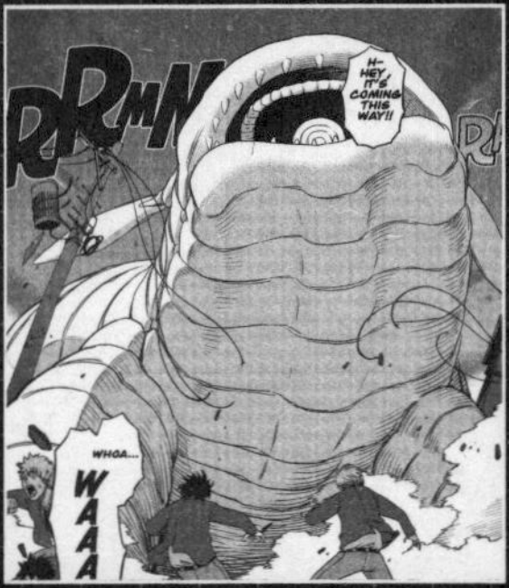
RRMN
H-HEY, IT'S COMING THIS WAY!!
WHOA...
WAAA
Trion soldier built for war.

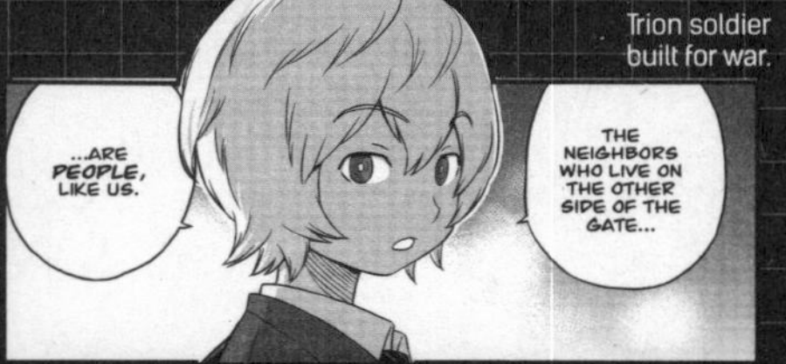
THE NEIGHBORS WHO LIVE ON THE OTHER SIDE OF THE GATE...
...ARE PEOPLE, LIKE US.

GALOPOULA

One of the two countries that are Aftokrator's subordinates. They invaded under orders from Aftokrator.

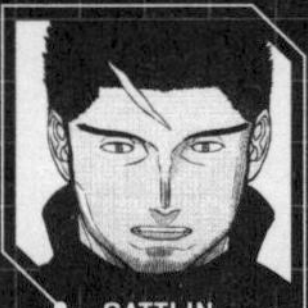
GATTLIN

Captain. He uses a claw-shaped Trigger named Vasilissa.

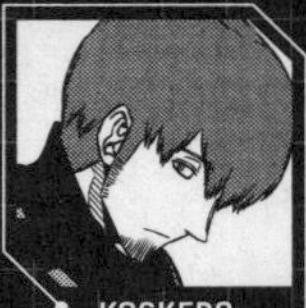
KOSKERO

Vice captain. He uses a liquid Trigger named Nikokyra.

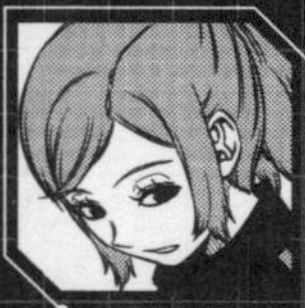
WEN SAW

She uses a Trigger that copies herself named Servitora.

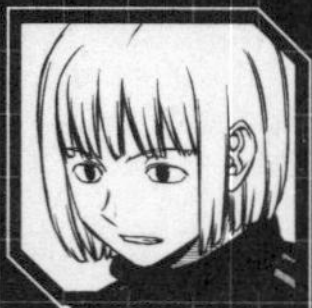
REGHINDETZ

He encounters Hyuse while being in charge of diverting Meeden's troops.

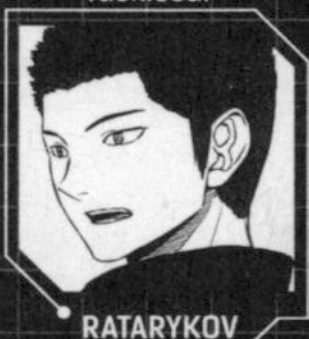
RATARYKOV

He uses a circular flying Trigger named Despinis.

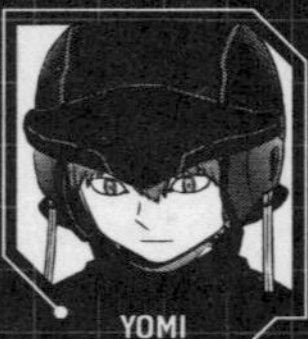
YOMI

Operator. His side effect is Absolute Parallel Simultaneous Cerebration.

Trion Soldiers

Rhodokhroun, a subordinate nation of Aftokrator, provided them with 200 Dogs and 95 Idras, making a strong force capable of going to war.

Idra

▶ A humanoid Trion Soldier made for group combat. Capable of programing detailed combat tactics.

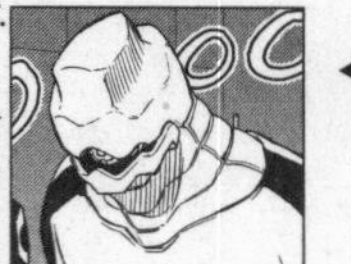

Dog

▶ Dog-type Trion soldiers. There are several varieties such as recon, combat support, and charging.

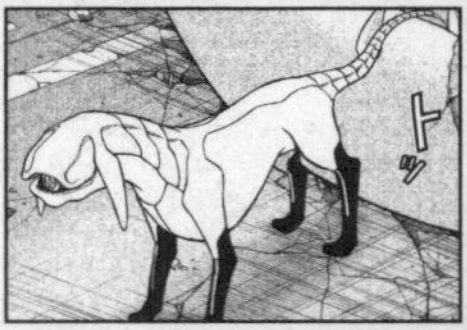

BORDER

An agency founded to protect the city's peace from Neighbors. Agents are classified as follows: C-Rank for trainees, B-Rank for main forces, A-Rank for elites and S-Rank for those with Black Triggers. A-Rank squads get to go on away missions to Neighbor worlds.

Resistance

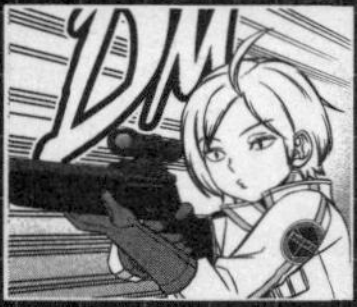

C-Rank: Izuho

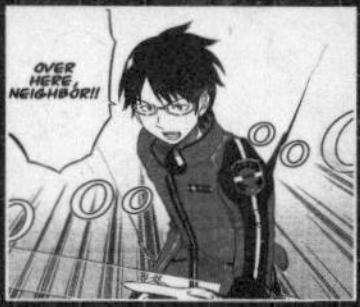
OVER HERE, NEIGHBOR!!

B-Rank: Osamu

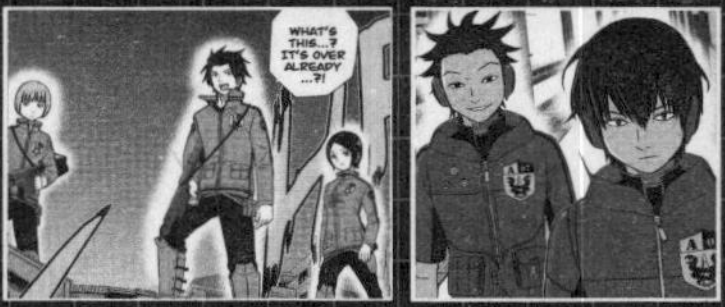
WHAT'S THIS...? IT'S OVER ALREADY ...?!

A-Rank: Arashiyama Squad, Miwa Squad

Trigger

A technology created by Neighbors to manipulate Trion. Used mainly as weapons, Triggers come in various types. Border classifies them into three groups: Attacker, Gunner, and Sniper.

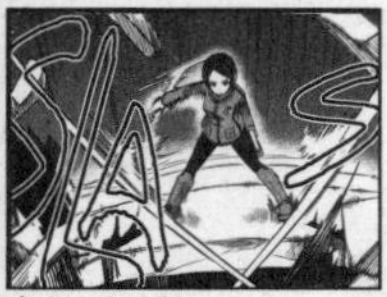

▲Attacker Trigger

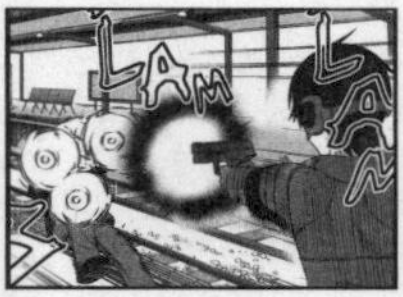

▲Gunner Trigger

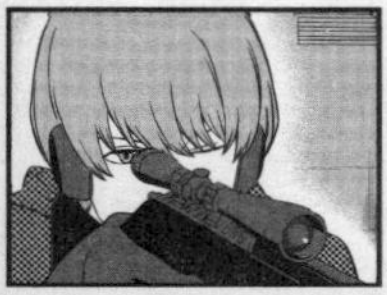

◀Sniper Trigger

Black Trigger

A special Trigger created when a skilled user pours their entire life force and Trion into a Trigger. Outperforms regular Triggers, but the user must be compatible with the personality of the creator, meaning only a few people can use any given Black Trigger.

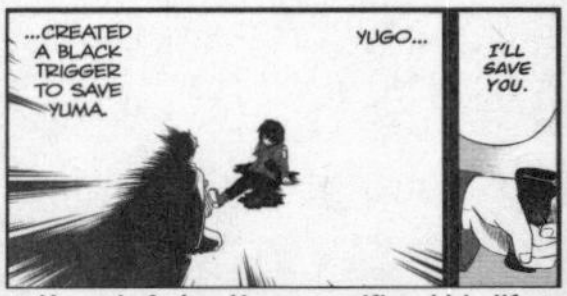
I'LL SAVE YOU.
YUGO...
...CREATED A BLACK TRIGGER TO SAVE YUMA.

▲Yuma's father Yugo sacrificed his life to create a Black Trigger and save Yuma.

STORY

About four years ago, a Gate connecting to another dimension opened in Mikado City, leading to the appearance of invaders called Neighbors. After the establishment of the Border Defence Agency, people were able to return to their normal lives.

Osamu Mikumo is a junior high student who meets Yuma Kuga, a Neighbor. Yuma is targeted for capture by Border, but Tamakoma branch agent Yuichi Jin steps in to help. He convinces Yuma to join Border instead, then gives his Black Trigger to HQ in exchange for Yuma's enlistment. Now Osamu, Yuma and Osamu's friend Chika work towards making A-Rank together.

Aftokrator, the largest military nation in the Neighborhood, begins another large-scale invasion!! Border succeeds in driving them back, but over thirty C-Rank trainees are kidnapped in the process. Border implements more plans for away missions to retrieve the missing Agents.

Osamu's squad, Tamakoma-2, enters the Rank Wars for a chance to be chosen for away missions. The fifth round is about to begin when Border HQ comes under attack by Galopoula, Aftokrator's subordinate nation. As the battle is coming to a close, Hyuse meets up with Reghindetz!

WORLD TRIGGER CHARACTERS

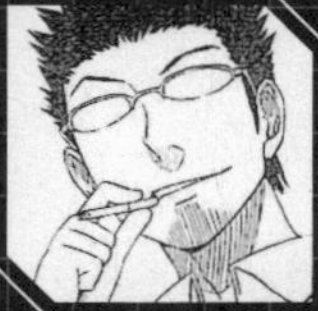

TAKUMI RINDO

Tamakoma Branch Director.

TAMAKOMA BRANCH

Understanding toward Neighbors. Considered divergent from Border's main philosophy.

TAMAKOMA-2

Tamakoma's B-Rank squad, aiming to get promoted to A-Rank.

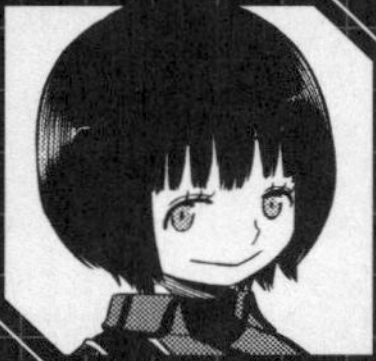

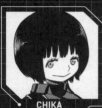

CHIKA AMATORI

Osamu's childhood friend. She has high Trion levels.

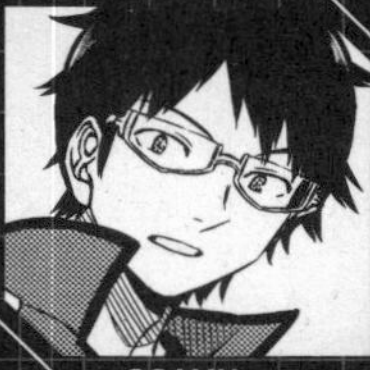

OSAMU MIKUMO

Ninth-grader who's compelled to help those in trouble. Captain of Tamakoma-2 (Mikumo squad).

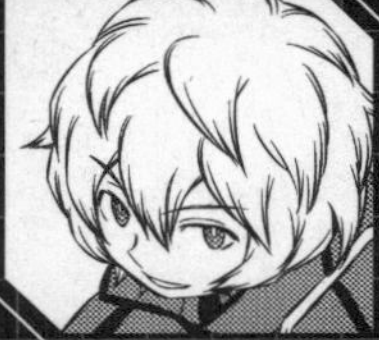

YUMA KUGA

A Neighbor who carries a Black Trigger.

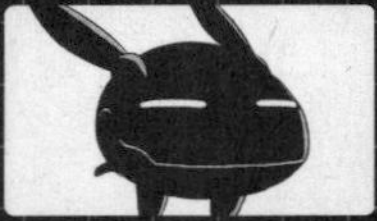

REPLICA

Yuma's chaperone. Missing after recent invasion.

TAMAKOMA-1

Tamakoma's A-Rank squad.

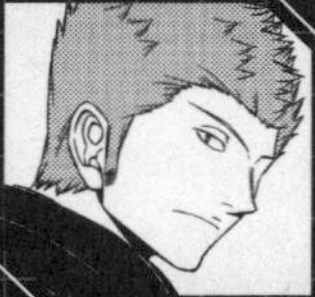

REIJI KIZAKI

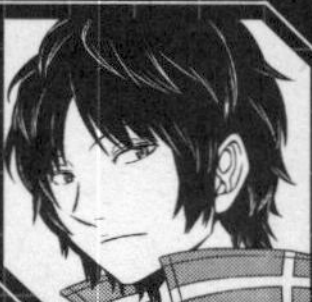

KYOSUKE KARASUMA

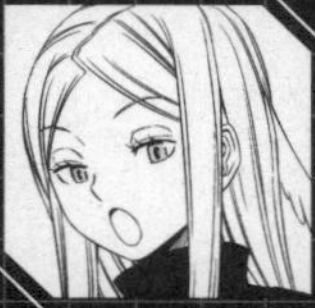

KIRIE KONAMI

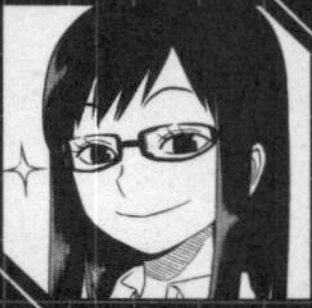

SHIORI USAMI

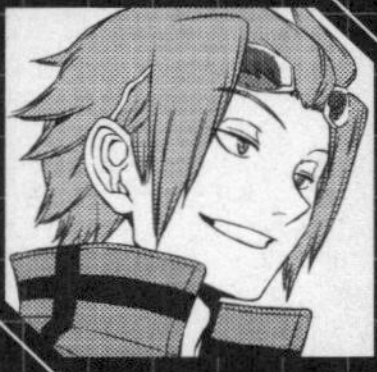

YUICHI JIN

Former S-Rank Black Trigger user. His Side Effect lets him see the future.

KATORI SQUAD

B-Rank #9 Squad operating out of Border HQ.

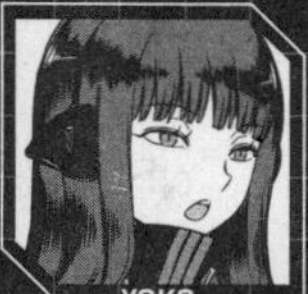

YOKO KATORI

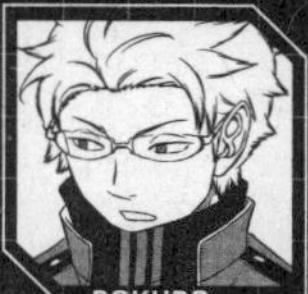

ROKURO WAKAMURA

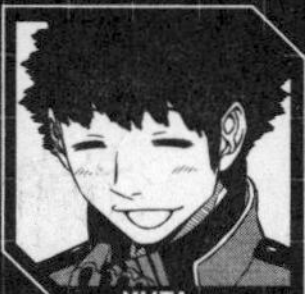

YUTA MIURA

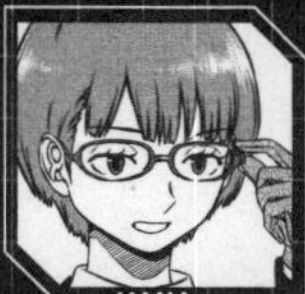

HANA SOMEI

KAKIZAKI SQUAD

B-Rank #13 Squad operating out of Border HQ. Squad has two all-rounders.

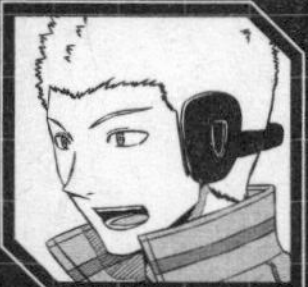

KUNIHARU KAKIZAKI

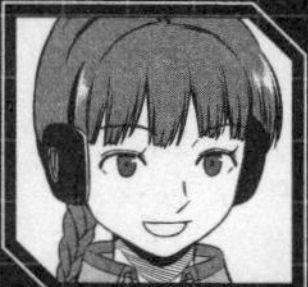

FUMIKA TERUYA

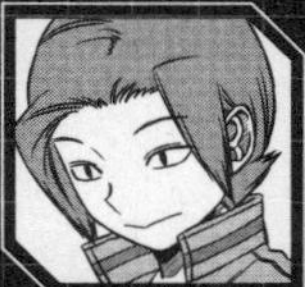

KOTARO TOMOE

B-RANK AGENTS

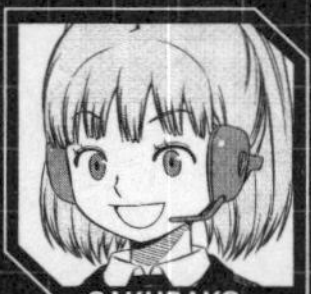

SAKURAKO TAKETOMI

Operator for B-Rank #16 Ebina Squad.

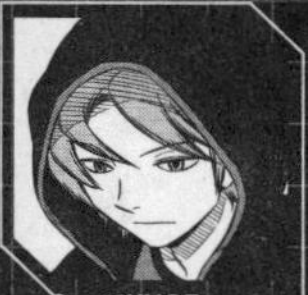

HYUSE

Neighbor from Aftokrator left behind in the invasion.

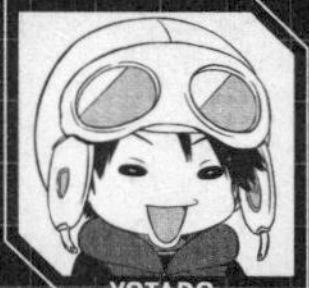

YOTARO RINDO

Tamakoma Branch kid.

A-RANK AGENTS

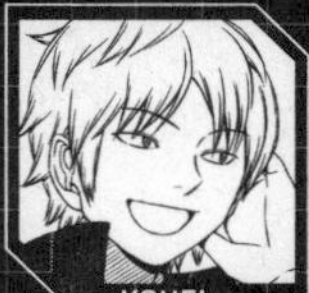

KOHEI IZUMI

Shooter from A-Rank #1 Tachikawa Squad.

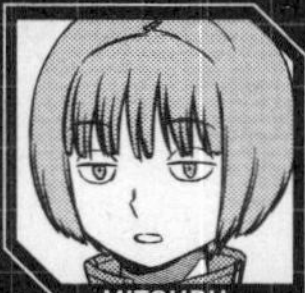

MITSURU TOKIEDA

All-Rounder from A-Rank #5 Arashiyama Squad.

BORDER HQ

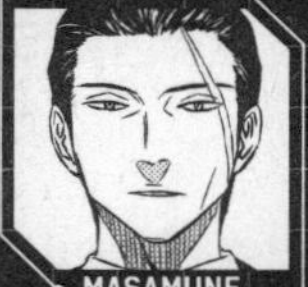

MASAMUNE KIDO

HQ Commander

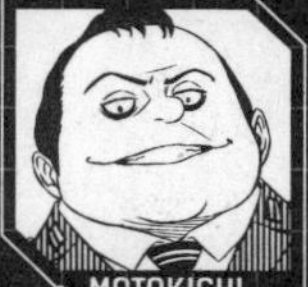

MOTOKICHI KINUTA

R&D Director

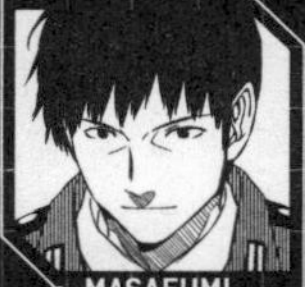

MASAFUMI SHINODA

HQ Directora and Defense commander.

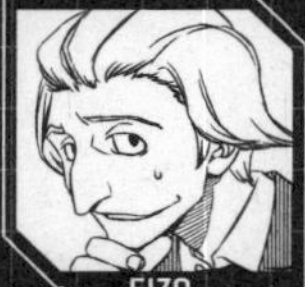

EIZO NETSUKI

PR Director

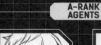

WORLD TRIGGER

CONTENTS

16

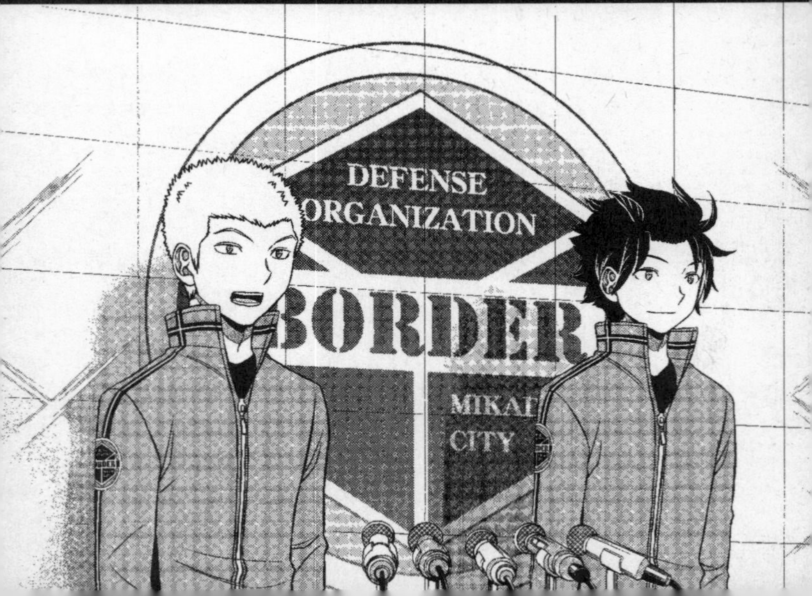

DEFENSE ORGANIZATION
BORDER
CITY

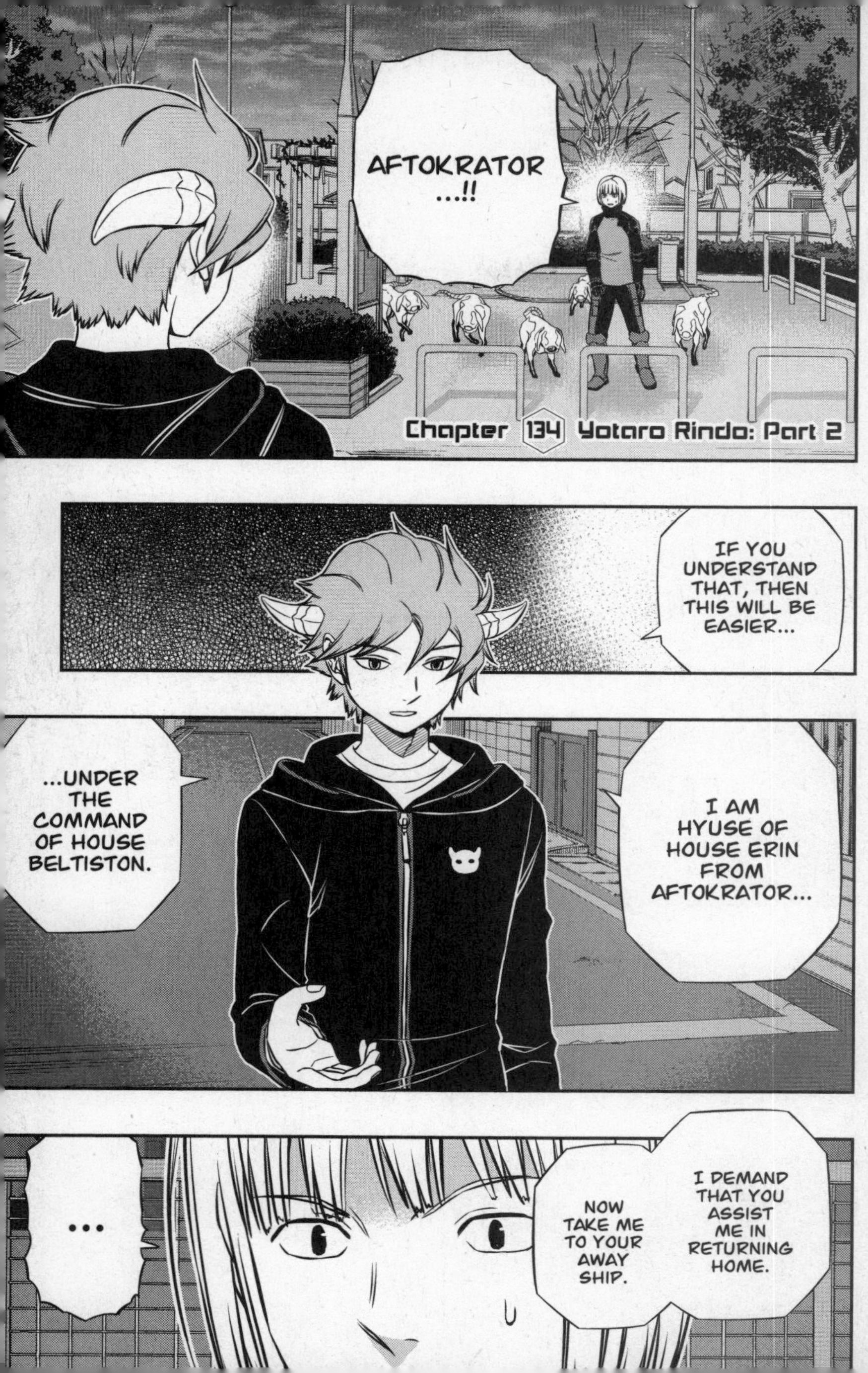
AFTOKRATOR ...!!
Chapter 134 Yotaro Rindo: Part 2
IF YOU UNDERSTAND THAT, THEN THIS WILL BE EASIER...
I AM HYUSE OF HOUSE ERIN FROM AFTOKRATOR...
...UNDER THE COMMAND OF HOUSE BELTISTON.
I DEMAND THAT YOU ASSIST ME IN RETURNING HOME.
NOW TAKE ME TO YOUR AWAY SHIP.
...

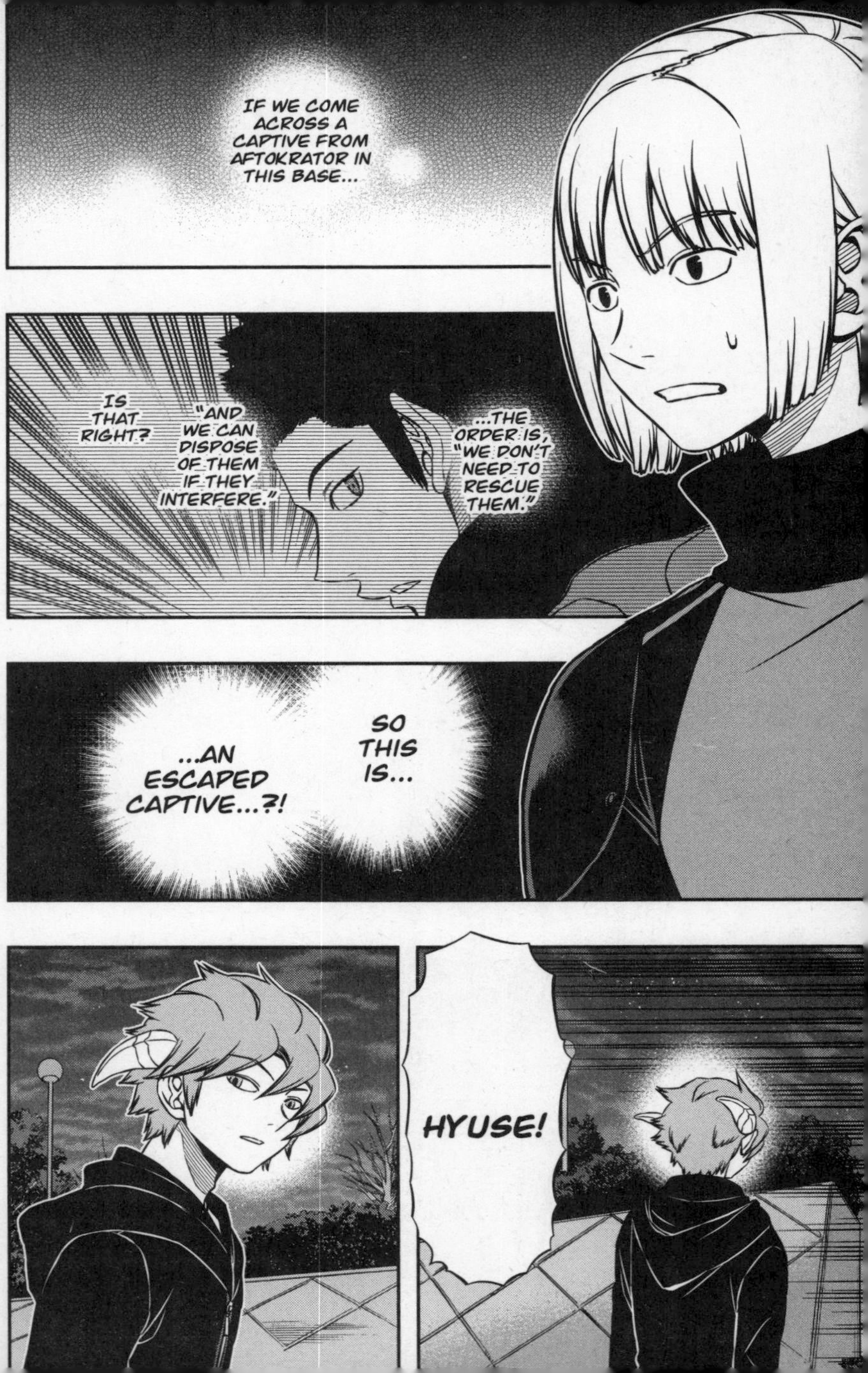
IF WE COME ACROSS A CAPTIVE FROM AFTOKRATOR IN THIS BASE...
...THE ORDER IS, "WE DON'T NEED TO RESCUE THEM."
"AND WE CAN DISPOSE OF THEM IF THEY INTERFERE."
IS THAT RIGHT?
SO THIS IS...
...AN ESCAPED CAPTIVE...?!
HYUSE!

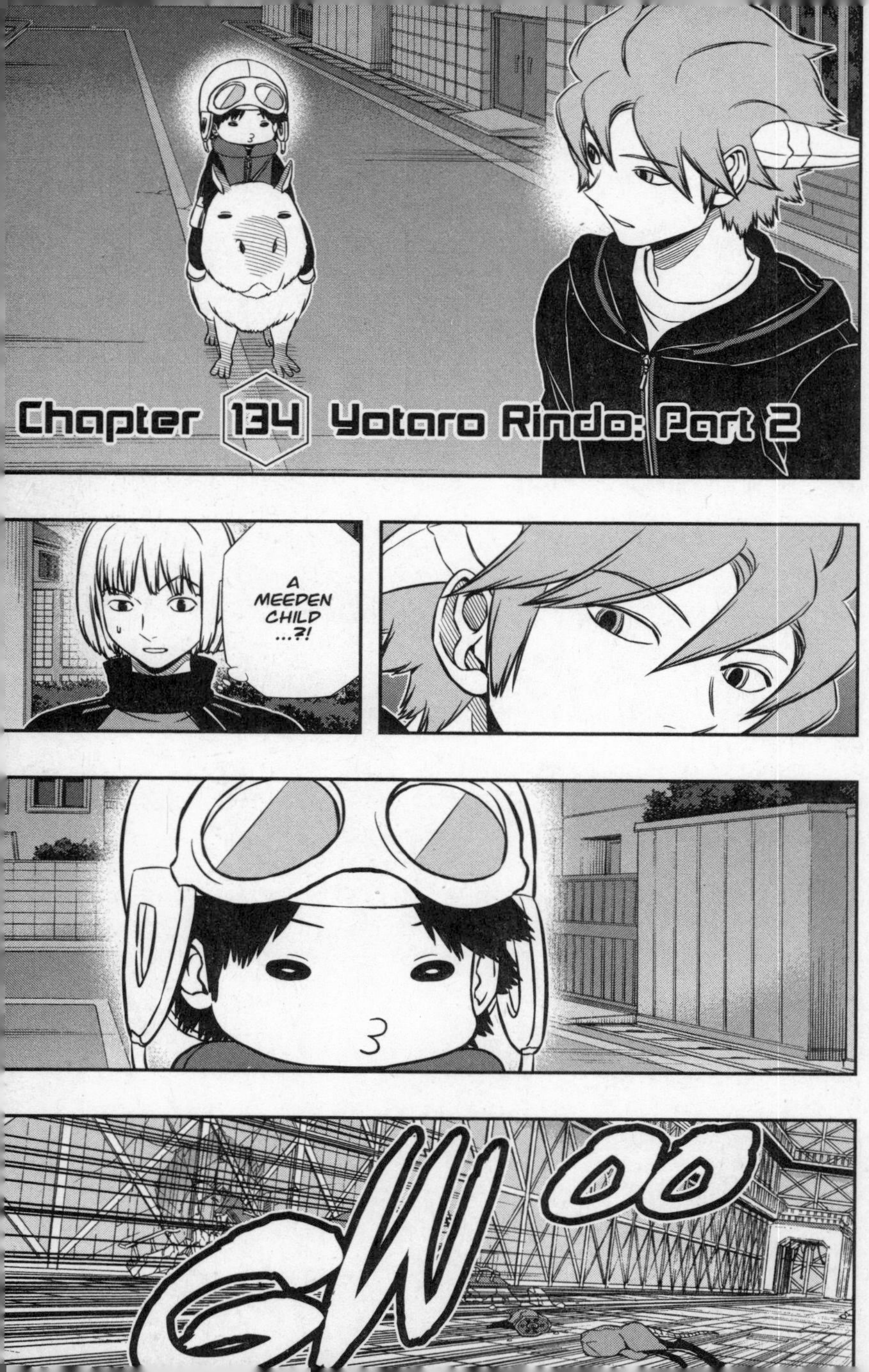

Chapter 134 Yotaro Rindo: Part 2
A MEEDEN CHILD ...?!

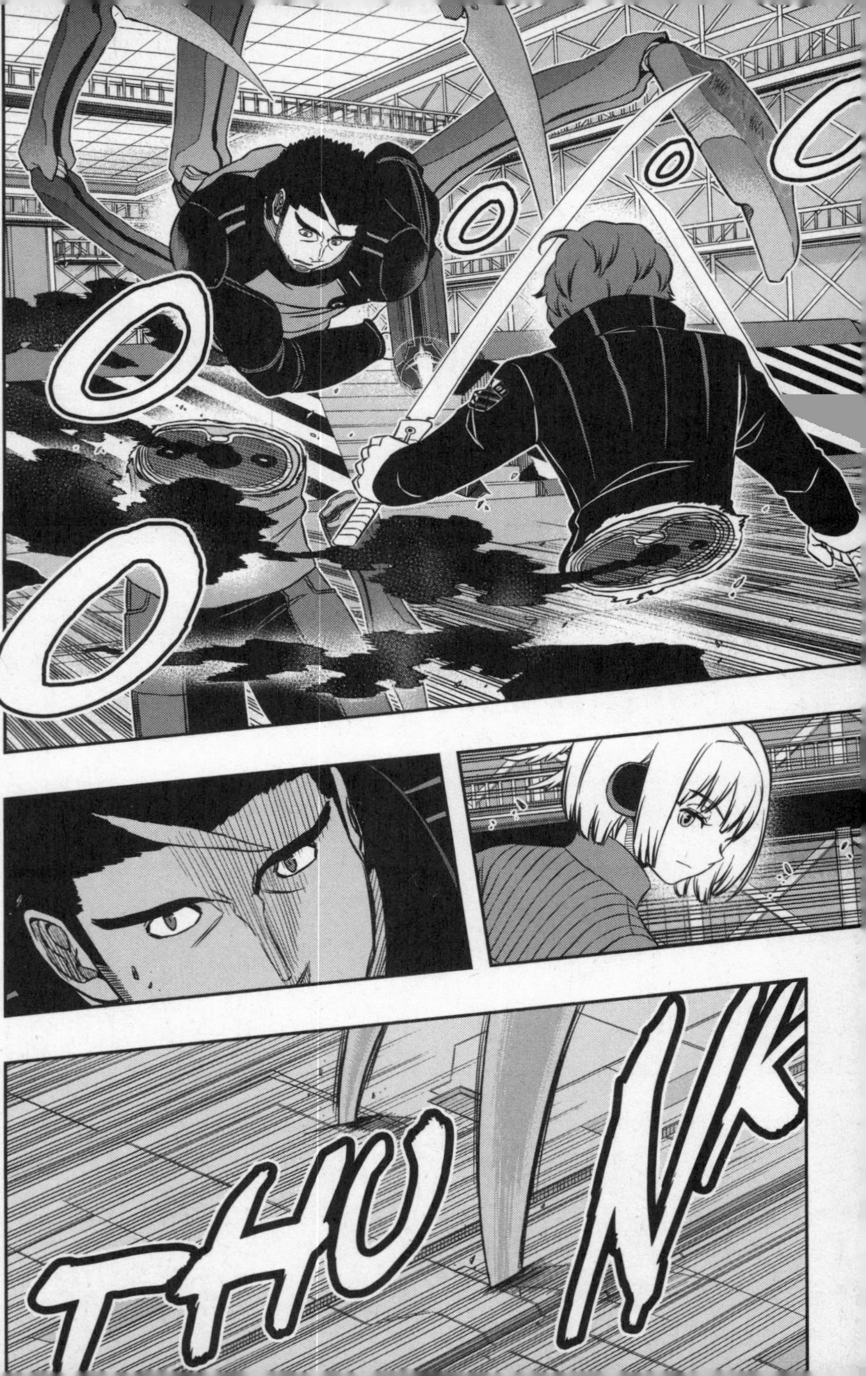
OOOOOO
THUNK

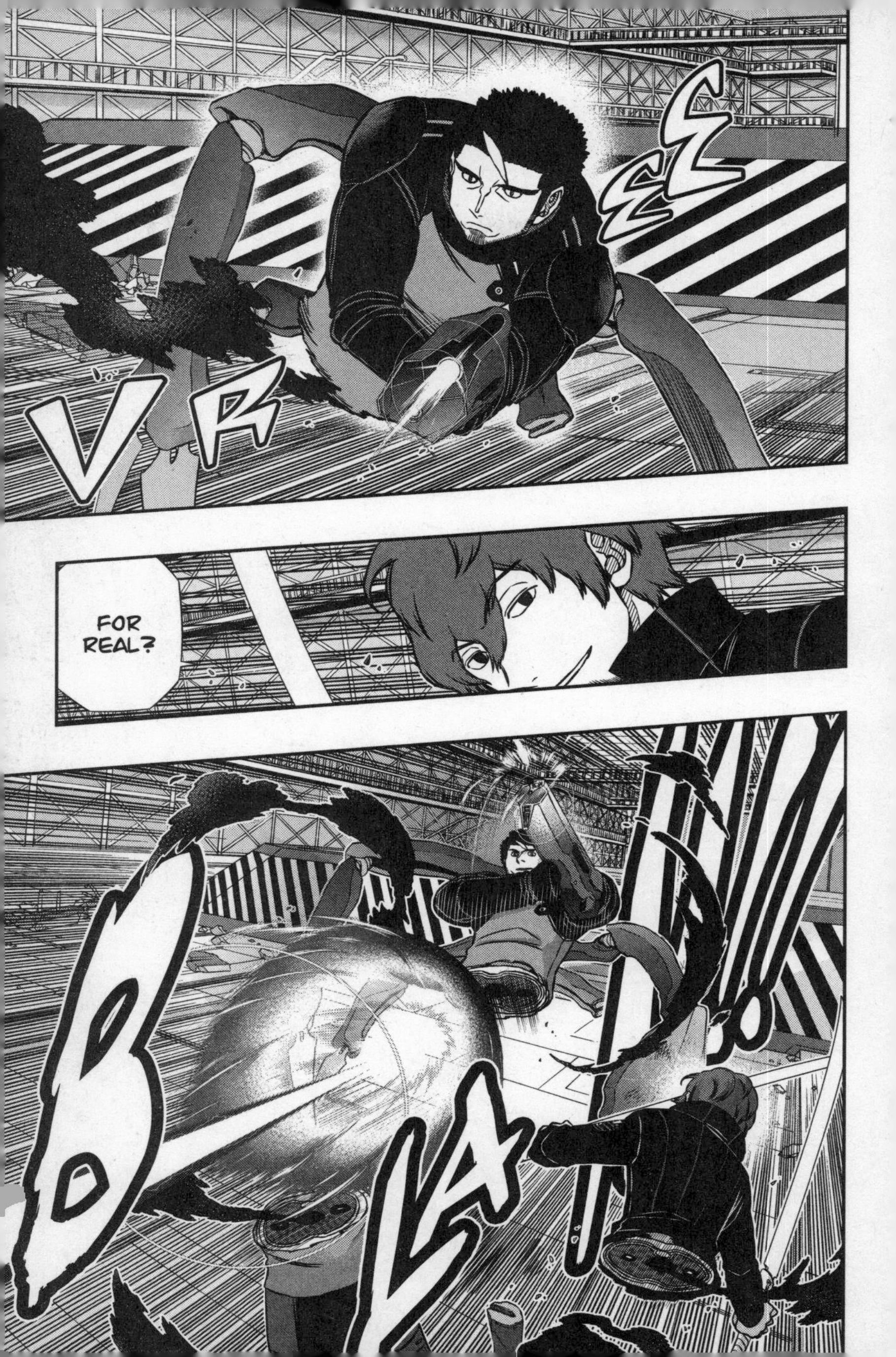
VR
FOR REAL?

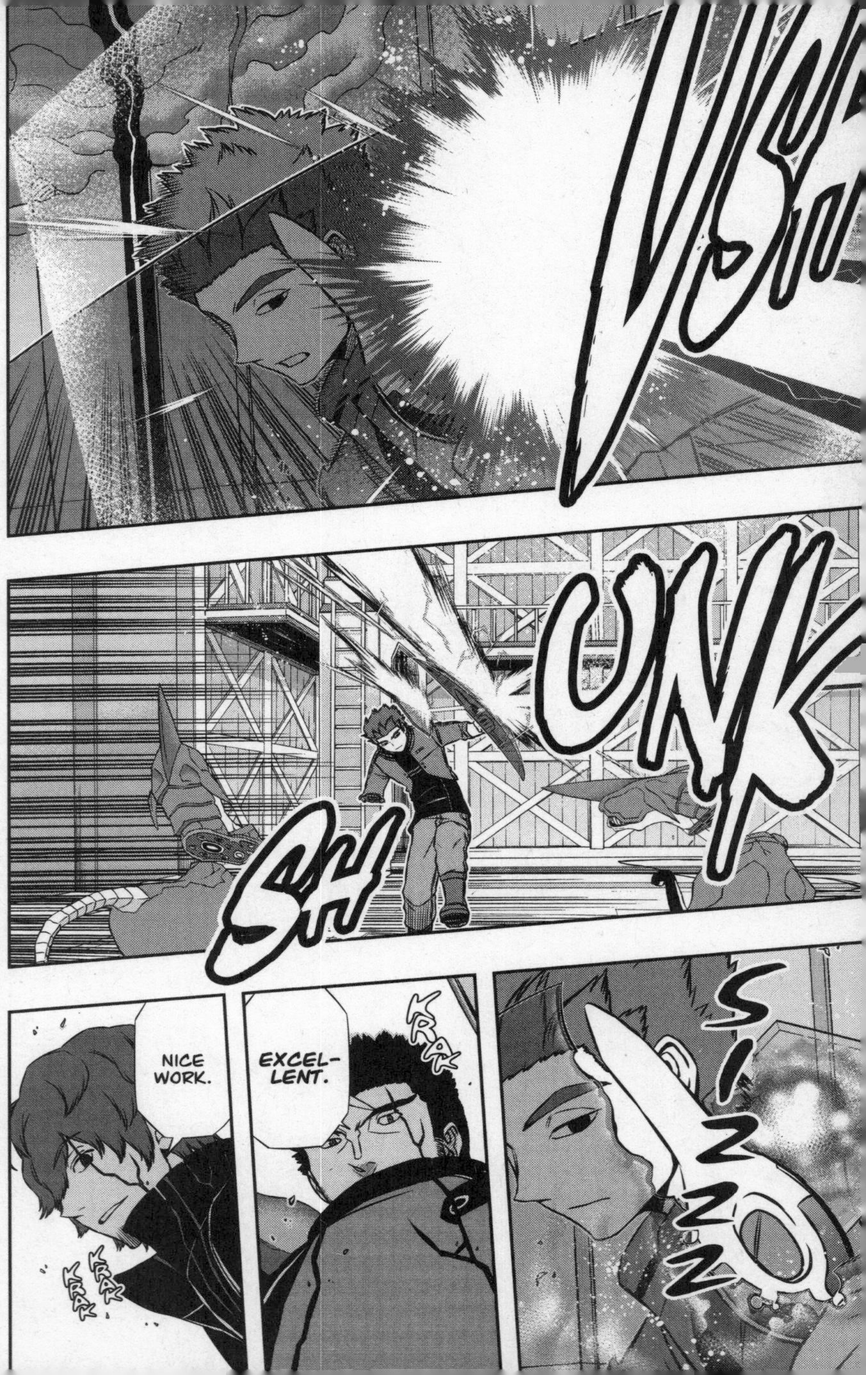

UNK
SH
SIZZZ
KRAK
EXCEL-LENT.
NICE WORK.
KRAK KRAK

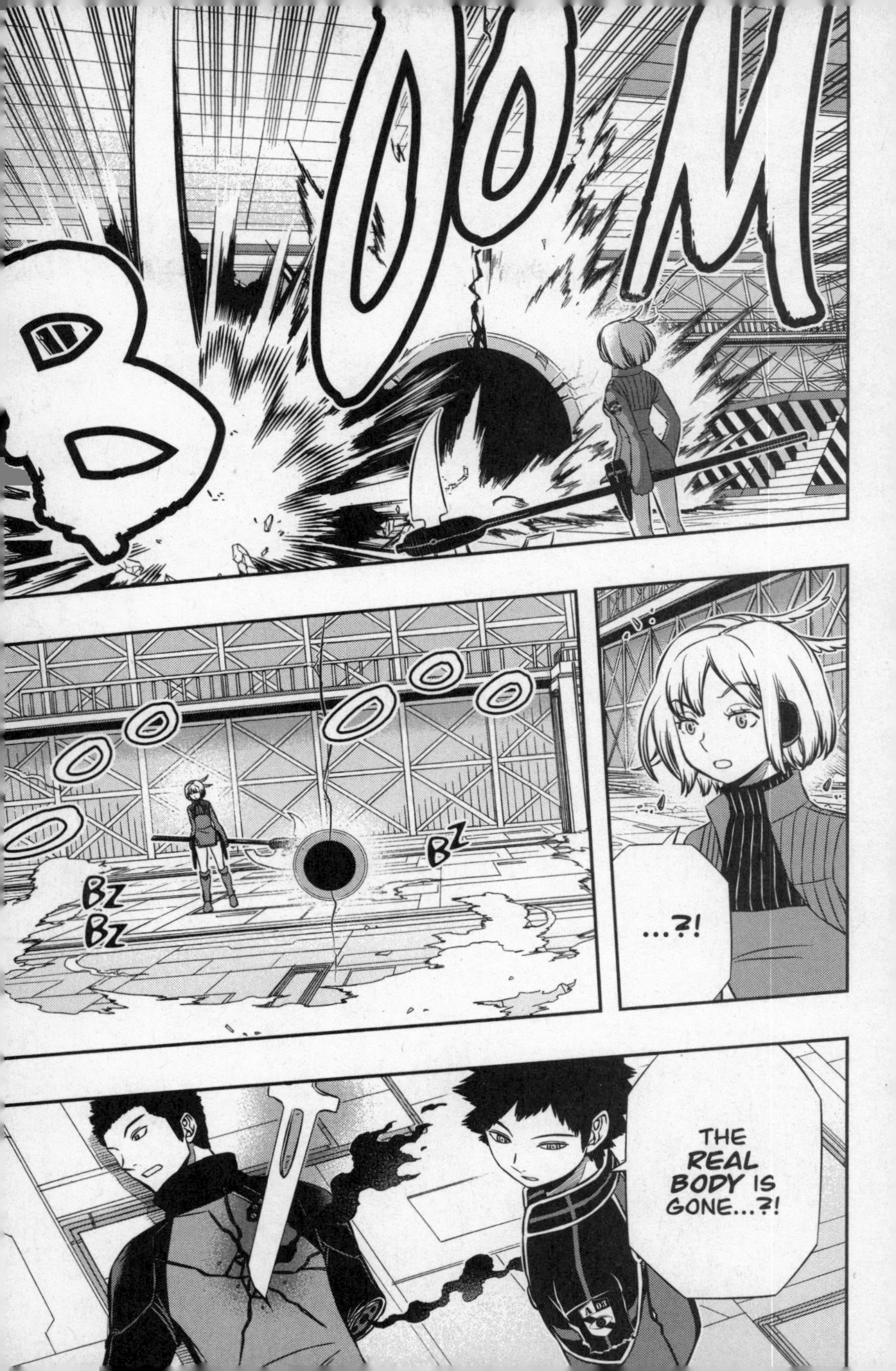
BOOM
...?!
BZ
BZ BZ
THE REAL BODY IS GONE...?!

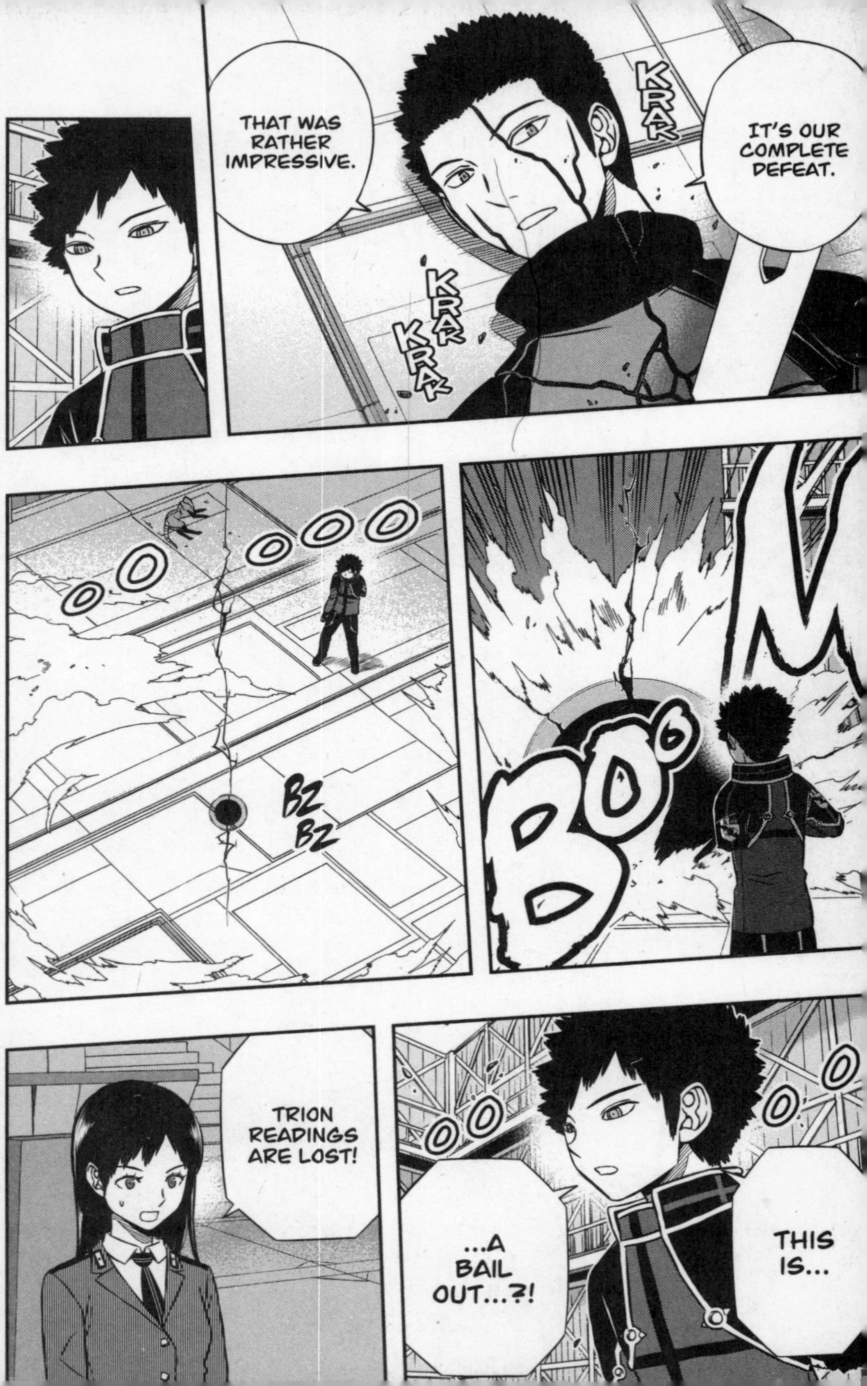
IT'S OUR COMPLETE DEFEAT.
KRAK
THAT WAS RATHER IMPRESSIVE.
KRAK KRAK
BOOM
BZ BZ
THIS IS...
...A BAIL OUT...?!
TRION READINGS ARE LOST!

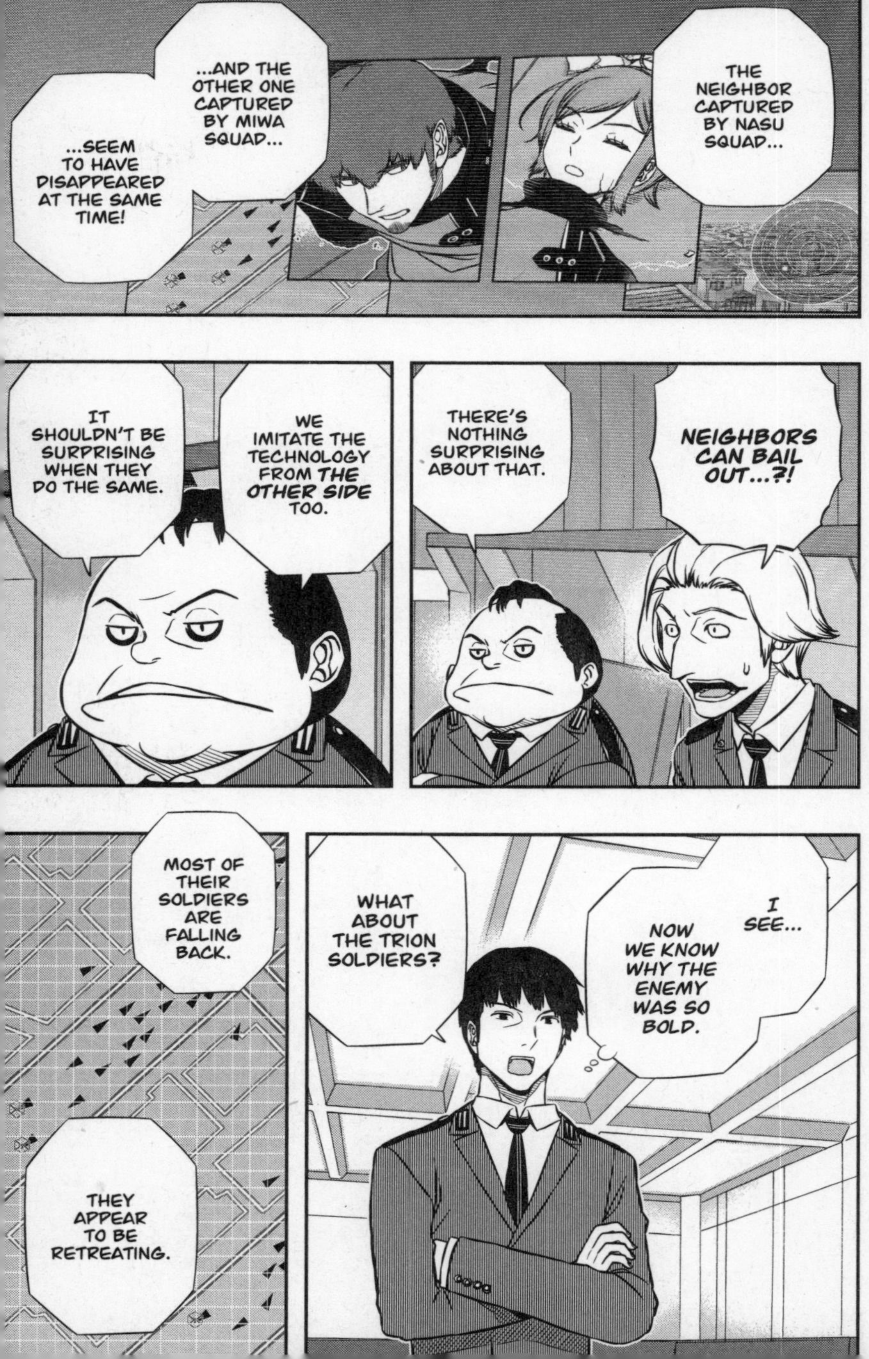
THE NEIGHBOR CAPTURED BY NASU SQUAD...
...AND THE OTHER ONE CAPTURED BY MIWA SQUAD...
...SEEM TO HAVE DISAPPEARED AT THE SAME TIME!
NEIGHBORS CAN BAIL OUT...?!
THERE'S NOTHING SURPRISING ABOUT THAT.
WE IMITATE THE TECHNOLOGY FROM THE OTHER SIDE TOO.
IT SHOULDN'T BE SURPRISING WHEN THEY DO THE SAME.
I SEE...
NOW WE KNOW WHY THE ENEMY WAS SO BOLD.
WHAT ABOUT THE TRION SOLDIERS?
MOST OF THEIR SOLDIERS ARE FALLING BACK.
THEY APPEAR TO BE RETREATING.

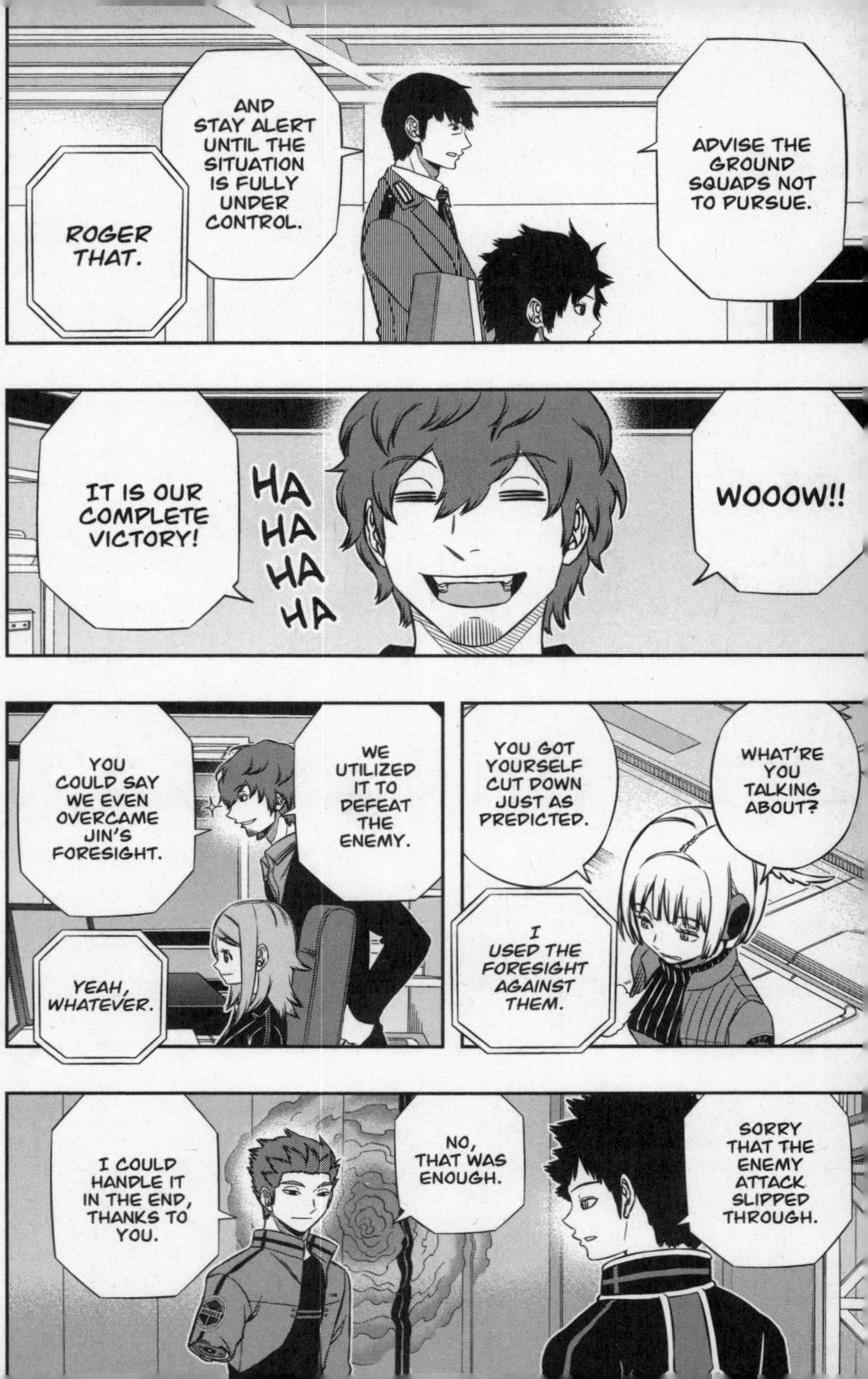
ADVISE THE GROUND SQUADS NOT TO PURSUE.
AND STAY ALERT UNTIL THE SITUATION IS FULLY UNDER CONTROL.
ROGER THAT.
WOOOW!!
HA HA HA HA
IT IS OUR COMPLETE VICTORY!
WHAT'RE YOU TALKING ABOUT?
YOU GOT YOURSELF CUT DOWN JUST AS PREDICTED.
I USED THE FORESIGHT AGAINST THEM.
WE UTILIZED IT TO DEFEAT THE ENEMY.
YOU COULD SAY WE EVEN OVERCAME JIN'S FORESIGHT.
YEAH, WHATEVER.
SORRY THAT THE ENEMY ATTACK SLIPPED THROUGH.
NO, THAT WAS ENOUGH.
I COULD HANDLE IT IN THE END, THANKS TO YOU.

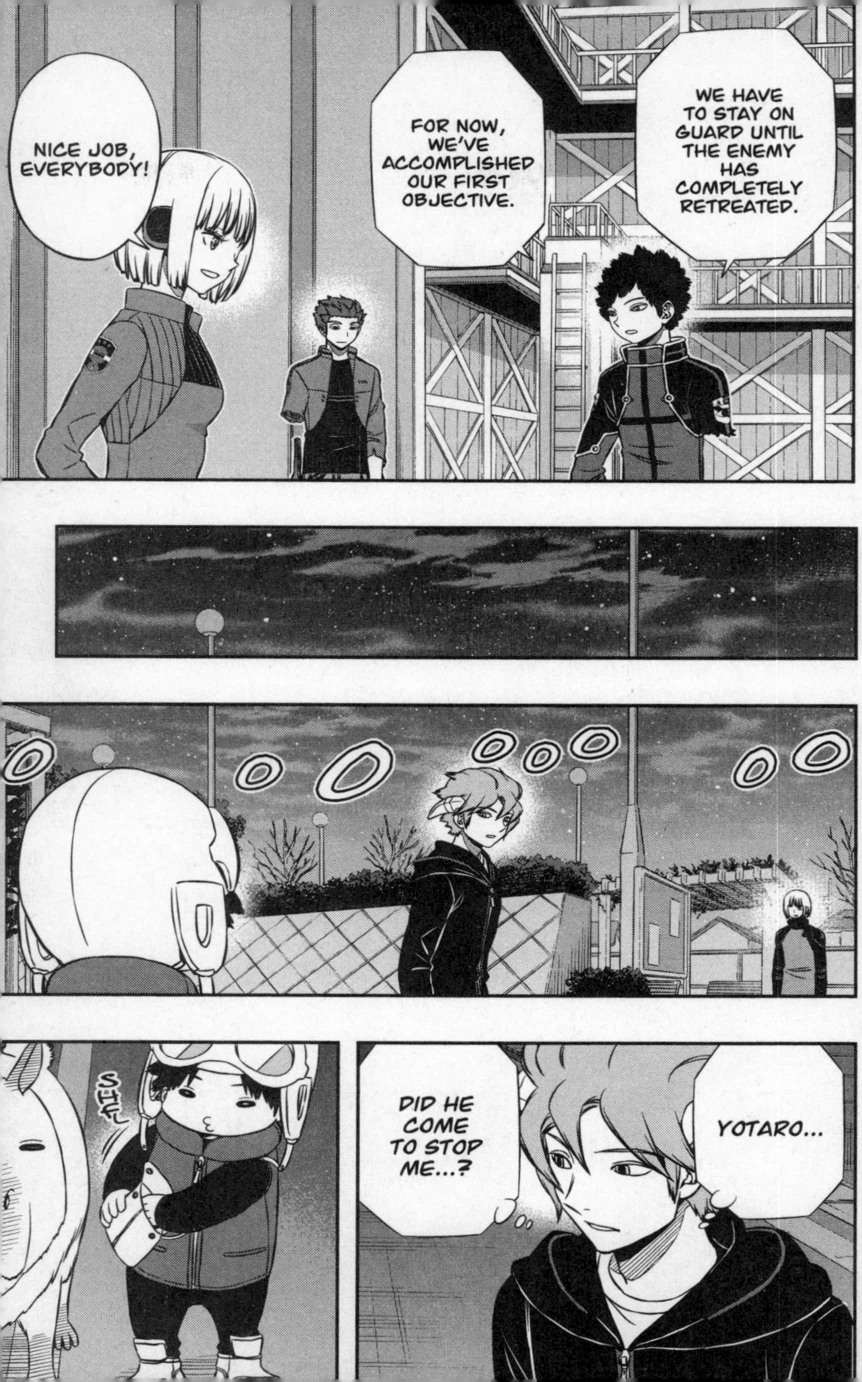
WE HAVE TO STAY ON GUARD UNTIL THE ENEMY HAS COMPLETELY RETREATED.
FOR NOW, WE'VE ACCOMPLISHED OUR FIRST OBJECTIVE.
NICE JOB, EVERYBODY!
YOTARO...
DID HE COME TO STOP ME...?
SHFL

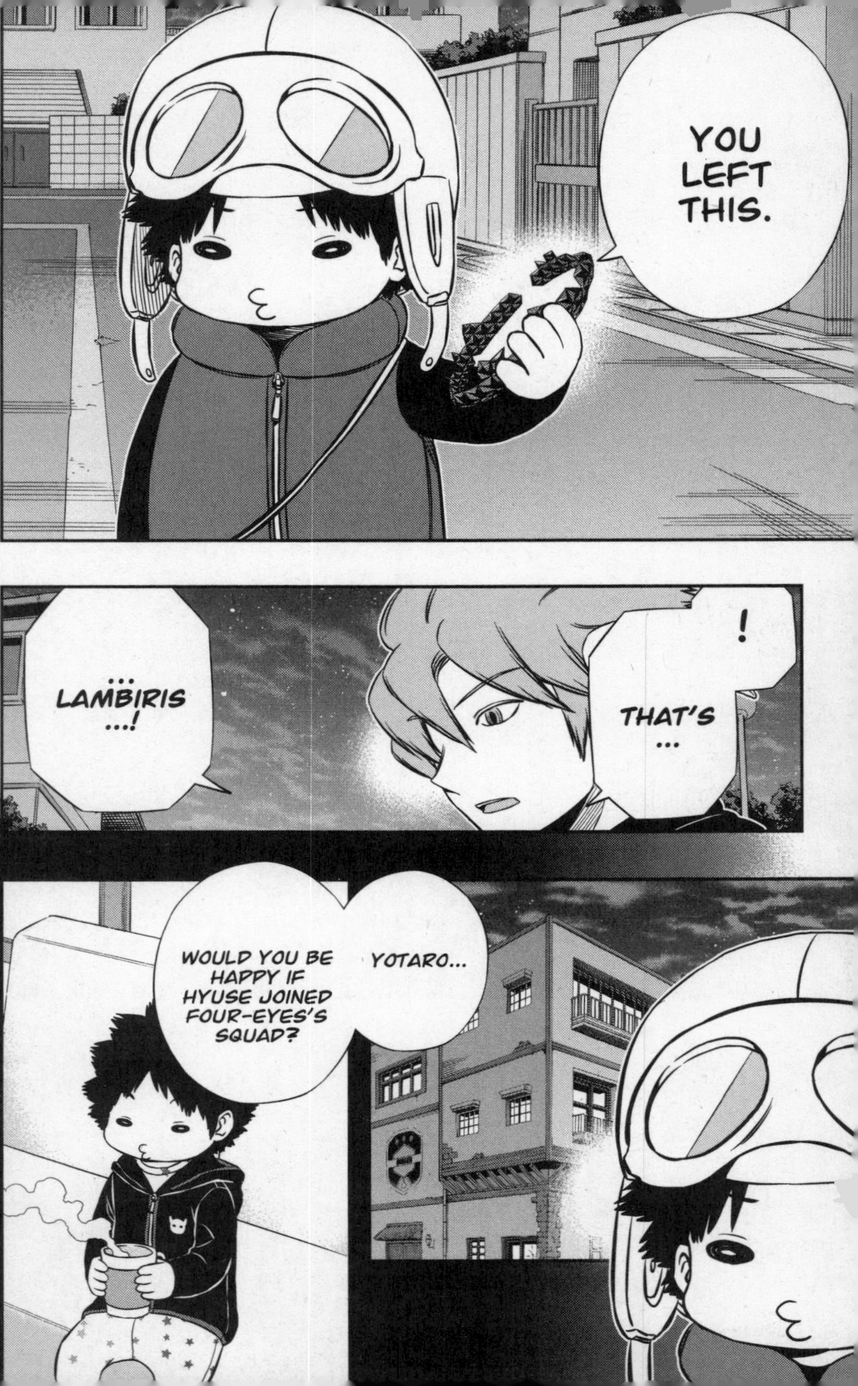
YOU LEFT THIS.
!
THAT'S ...
... LAMBIRIS ...!
YOTARO...
WOULD YOU BE HAPPY IF HYUSE JOINED FOUR-EYES'S SQUAD?

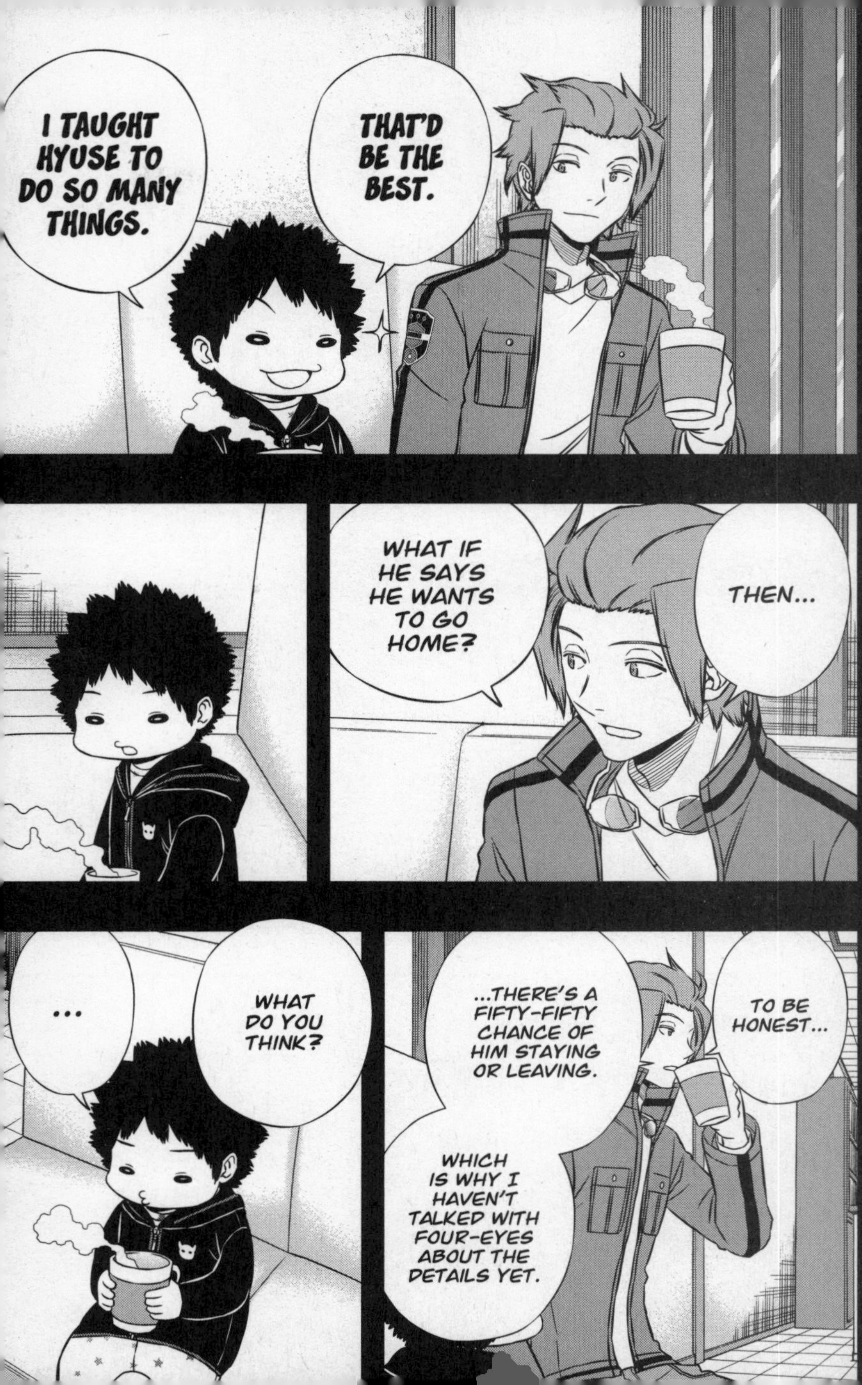
THAT'D BE THE BEST.
I TAUGHT HYUSE TO DO SO MANY THINGS.
THEN...
WHAT IF HE SAYS HE WANTS TO GO HOME?
TO BE HONEST...
...THERE'S A FIFTY-FIFTY CHANCE OF HIM STAYING OR LEAVING.
WHICH IS WHY I HAVEN'T TALKED WITH FOUR-EYES ABOUT THE DETAILS YET.
WHAT DO YOU THINK?
...

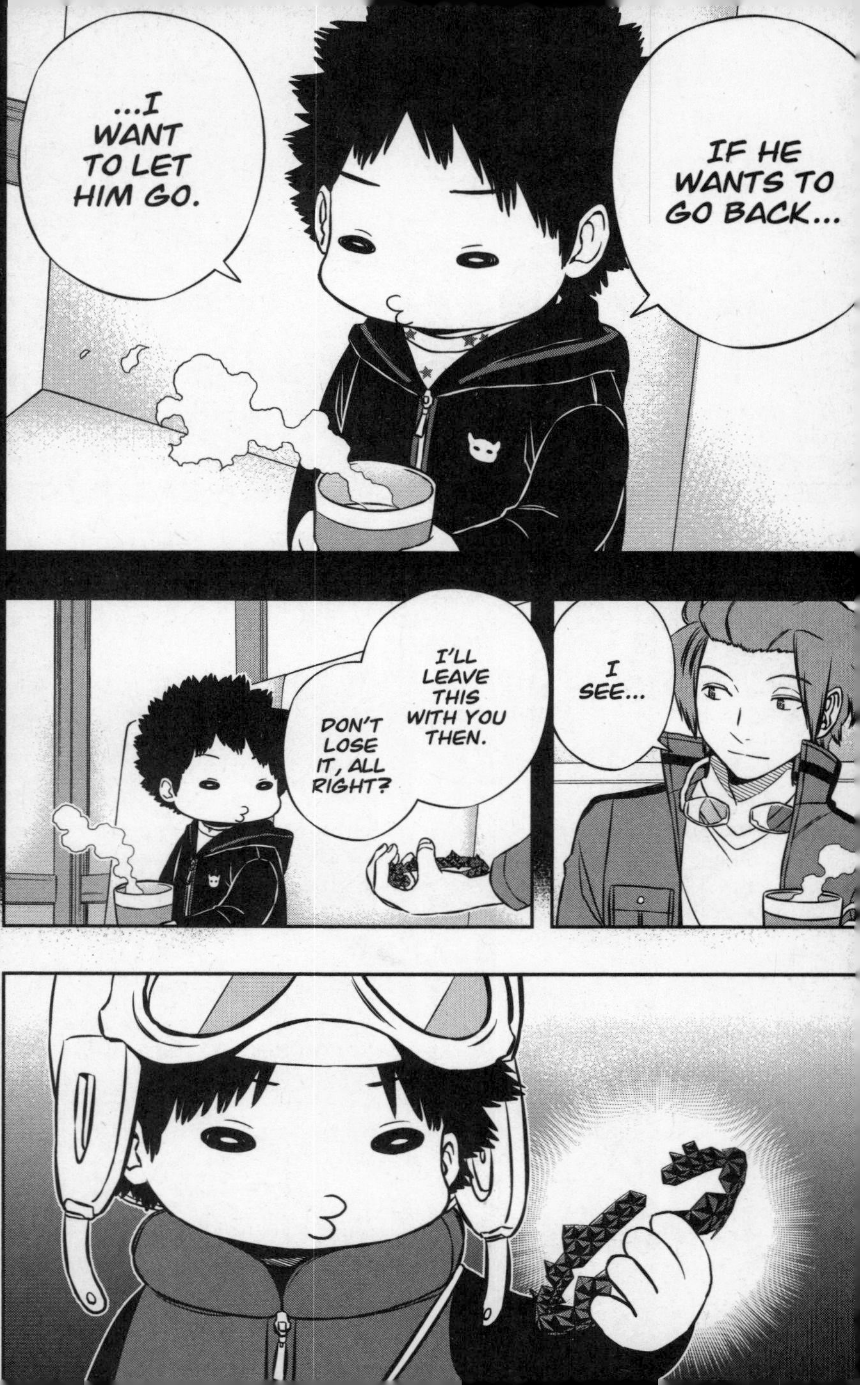
IF HE WANTS TO GO BACK...
...I WANT TO LET HIM GO.
I SEE...
I'LL LEAVE THIS WITH YOU THEN.
DON'T LOSE IT, ALL RIGHT?

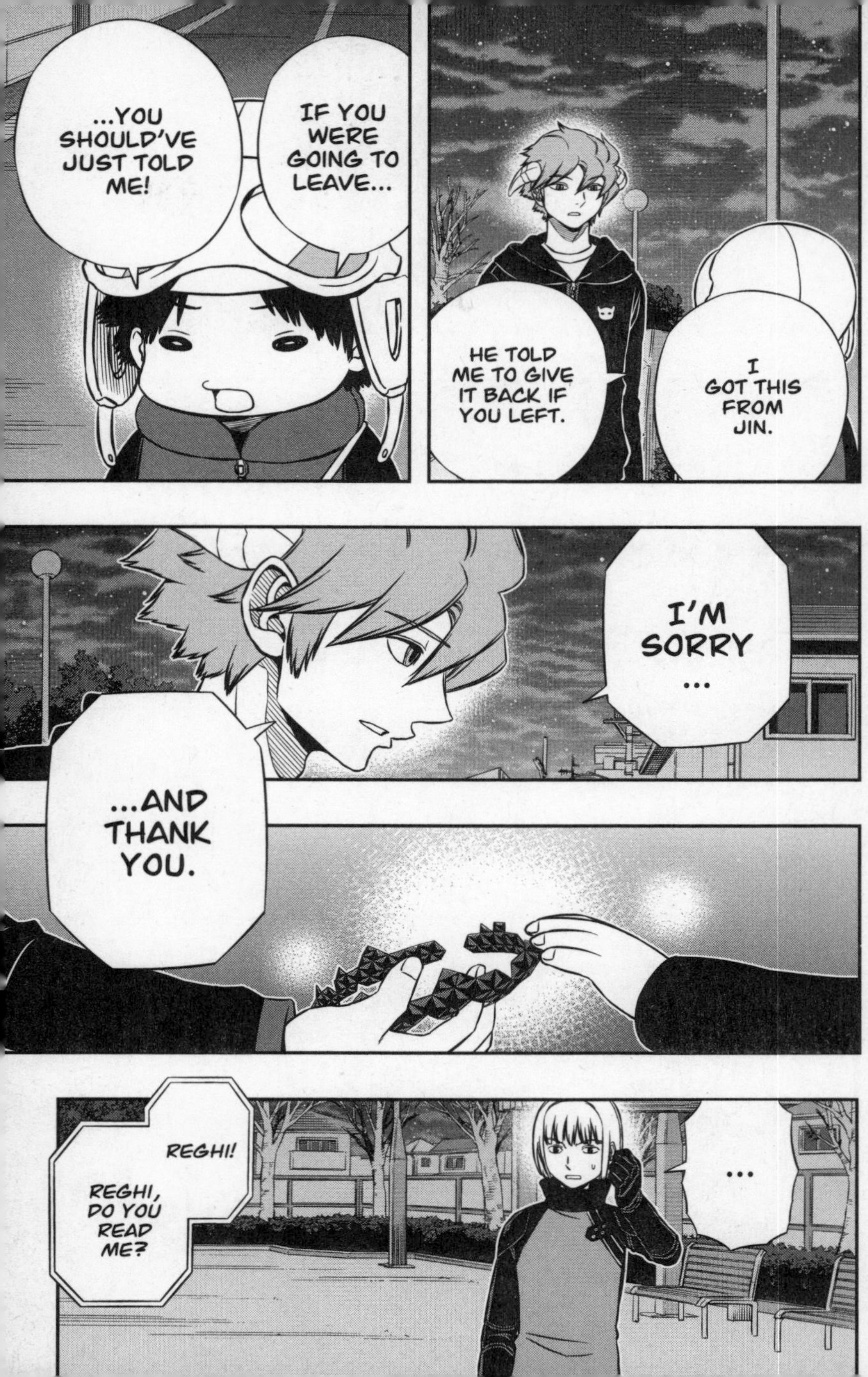
I GOT THIS FROM JIN.
HE TOLD ME TO GIVE IT BACK IF YOU LEFT.
IF YOU WERE GOING TO LEAVE...
...YOU SHOULD'VE JUST TOLD ME!
I'M SORRY ...
...AND THANK YOU.
...
REGHI!
REGHI, DO YOU READ ME?

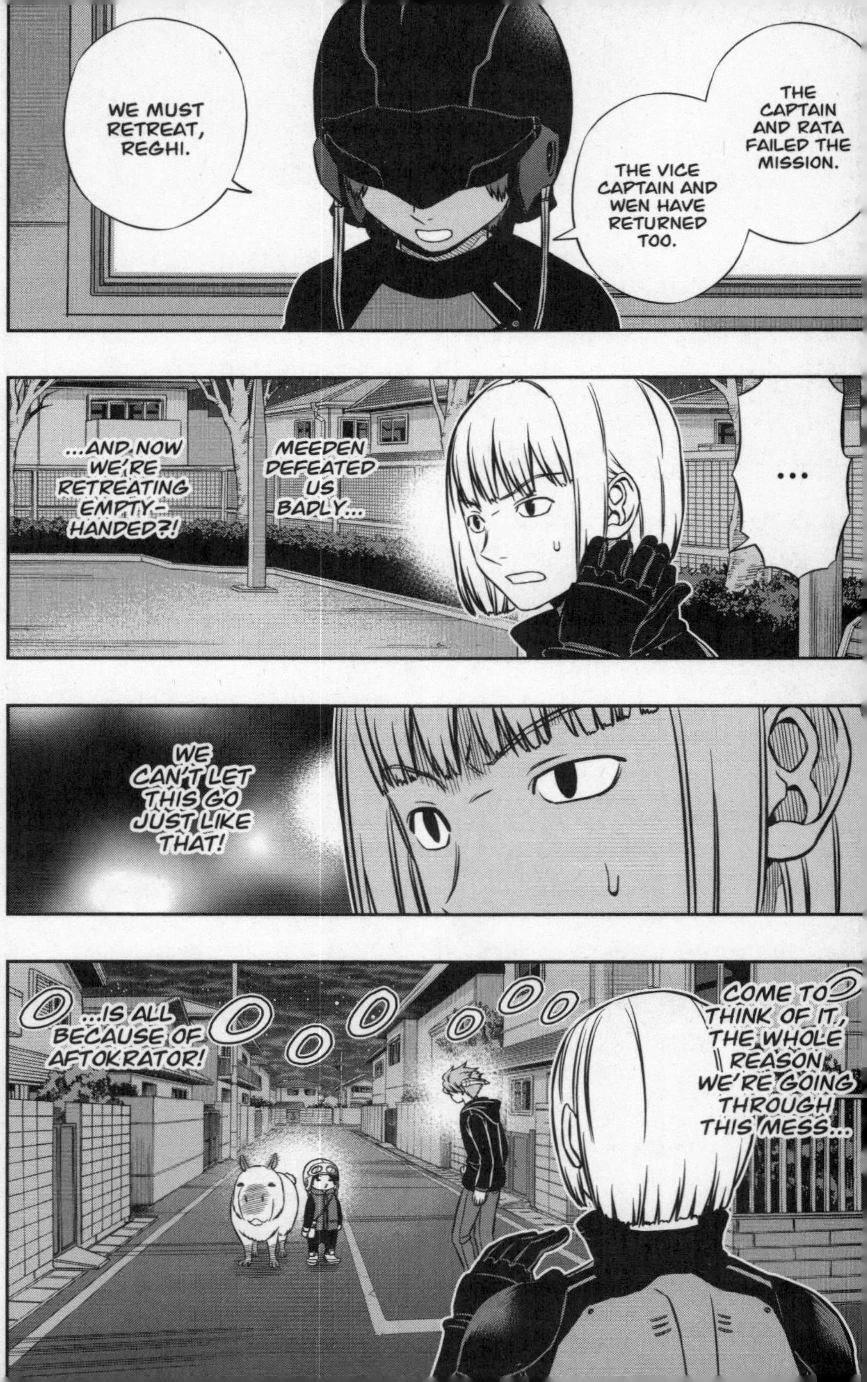
THE CAPTAIN AND RATA FAILED THE MISSION.
THE VICE CAPTAIN AND WEN HAVE RETURNED TOO.
WE MUST RETREAT, REGHI.
...
MEEDEN DEFEATED US BADLY...
...AND NOW WE'RE RETREATING EMPTY-HANDED?!
WE CAN'T LET THIS GO JUST LIKE THAT!
COME TO THINK OF IT, THE WHOLE REASON WE'RE GOING THROUGH THIS MESS...
...IS ALL BECAUSE OF AFTOKRATOR!

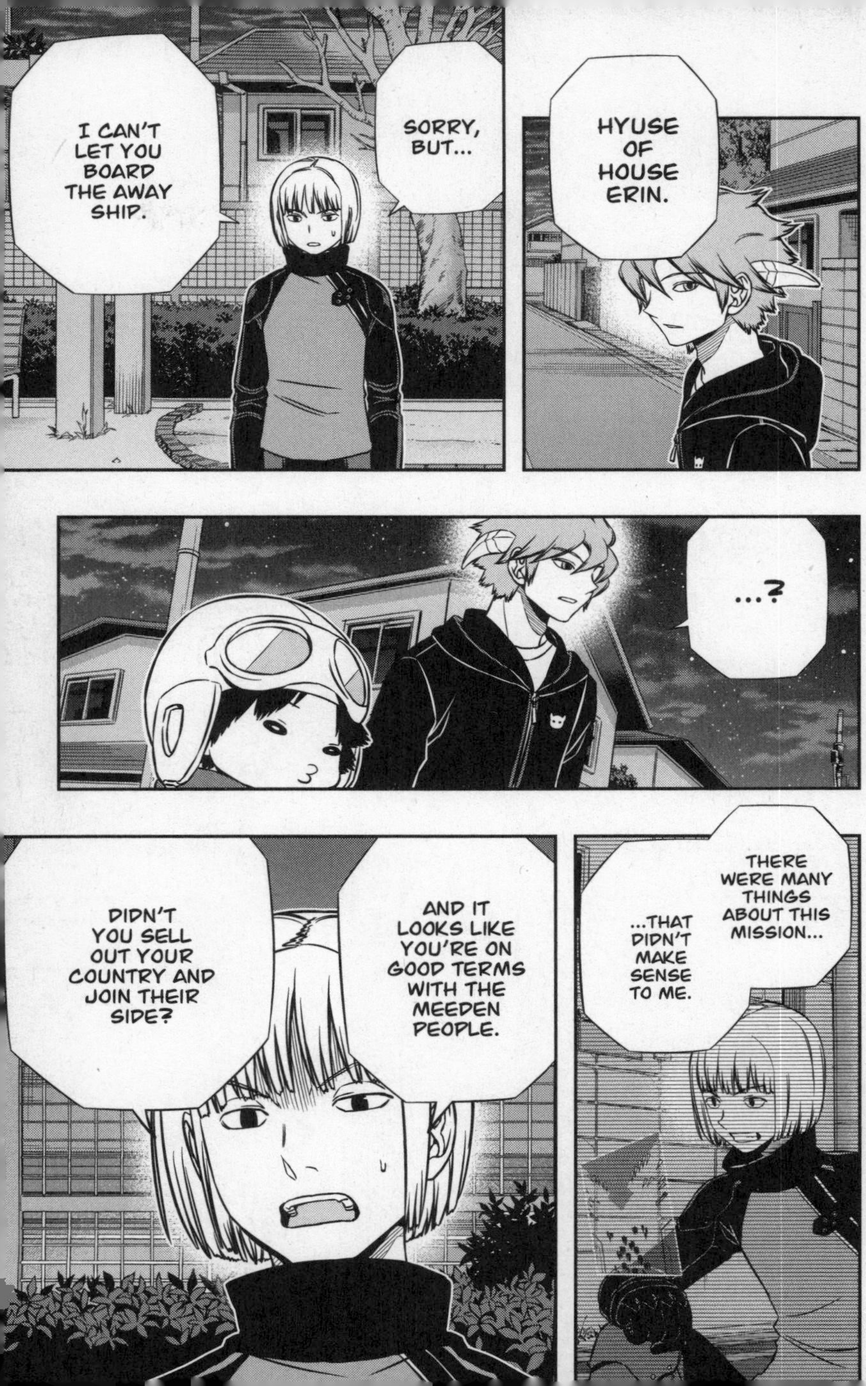
HYUSE OF HOUSE ERIN.
SORRY, BUT...
I CAN'T LET YOU BOARD THE AWAY SHIP.
...?
THERE WERE MANY THINGS ABOUT THIS MISSION...
...THAT DIDN'T MAKE SENSE TO ME.
AND IT LOOKS LIKE YOU'RE ON GOOD TERMS WITH THE MEEDEN PEOPLE.
DIDN'T YOU SELL OUT YOUR COUNTRY AND JOIN THEIR SIDE?

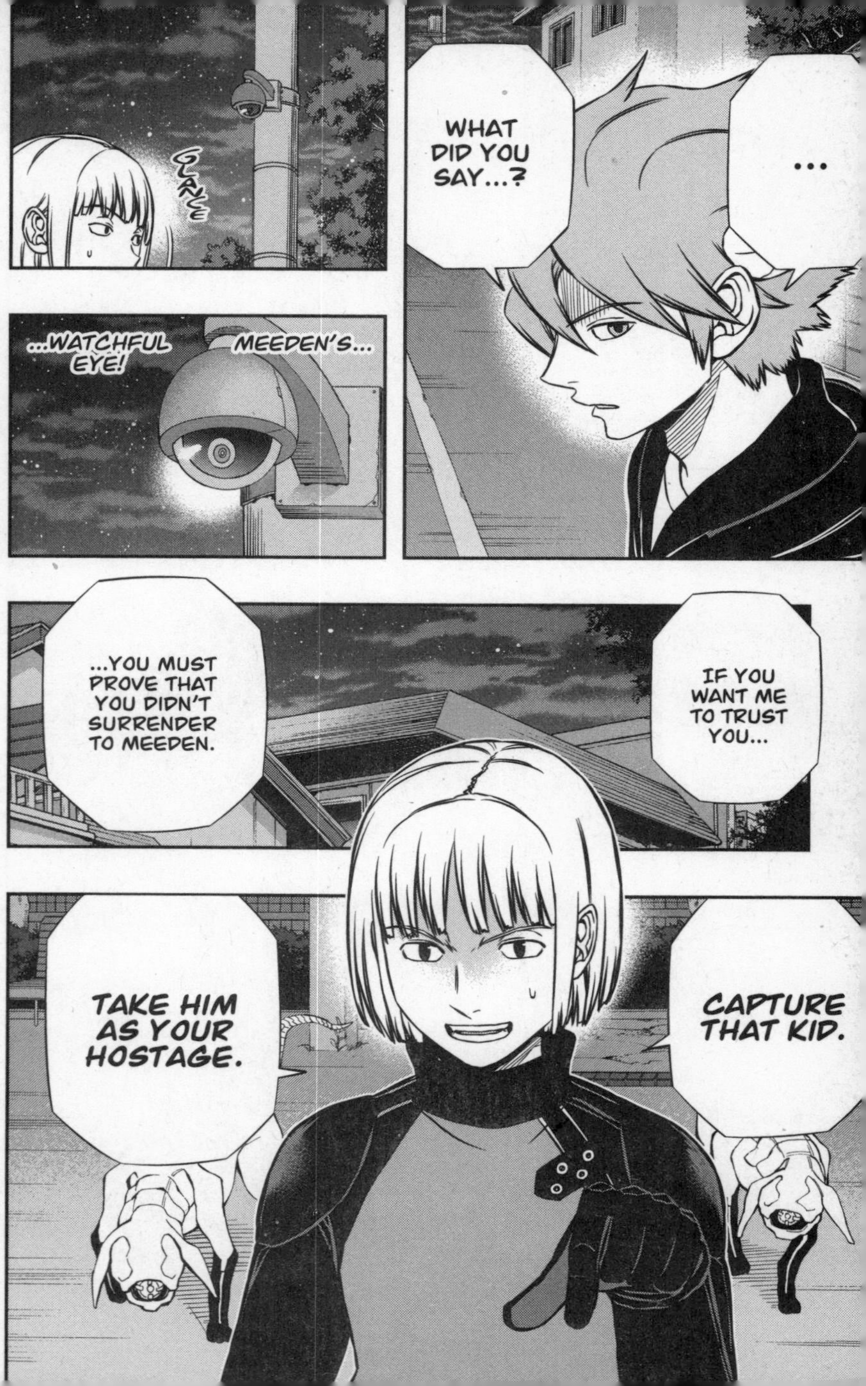
...
WHAT DID YOU SAY...?
GLANCE
MEEDEN'S...
...WATCHFUL EYE!
IF YOU WANT ME TO TRUST YOU...
...YOU MUST PROVE THAT YOU DIDN'T SURRENDER TO MEEDEN.
CAPTURE THAT KID.
TAKE HIM AS YOUR HOSTAGE.

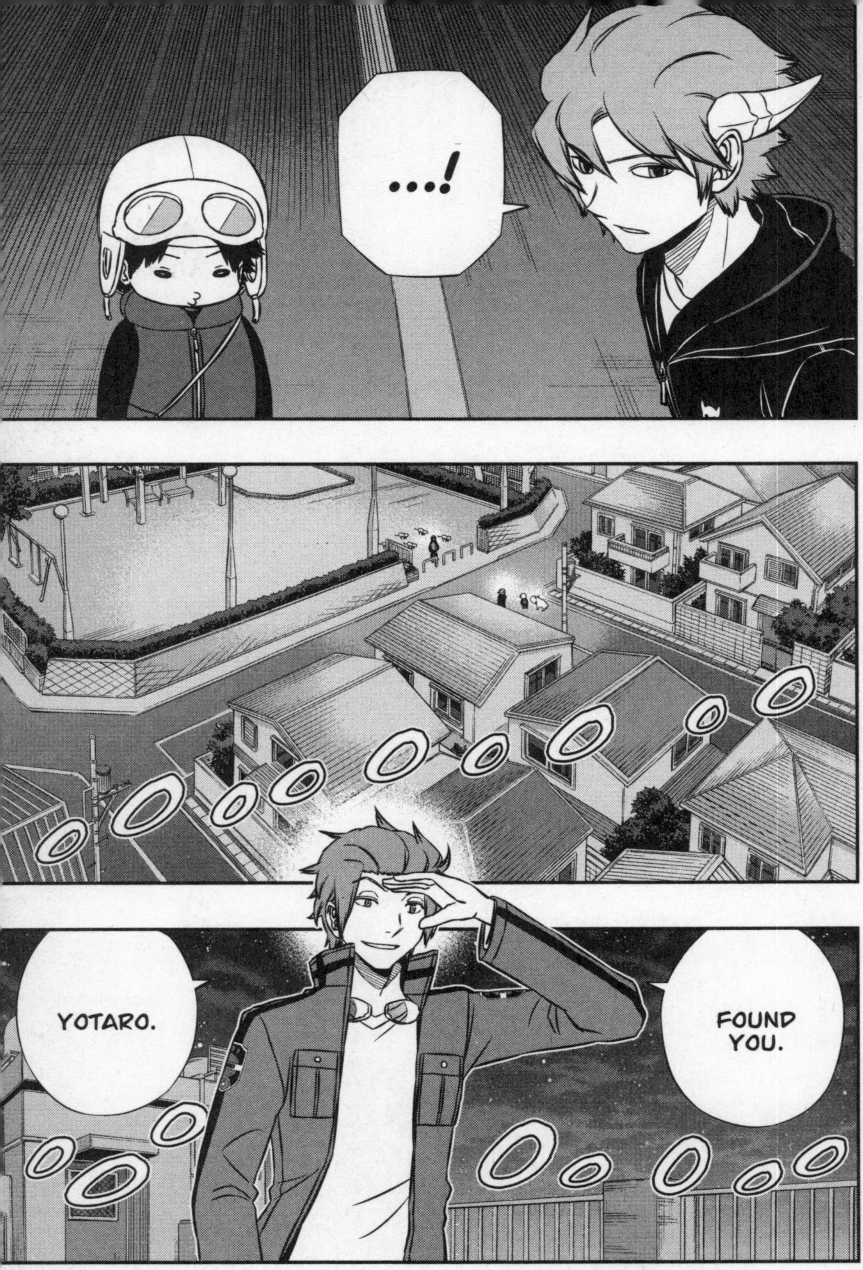
...!
FOUND YOU.
YOTARO.

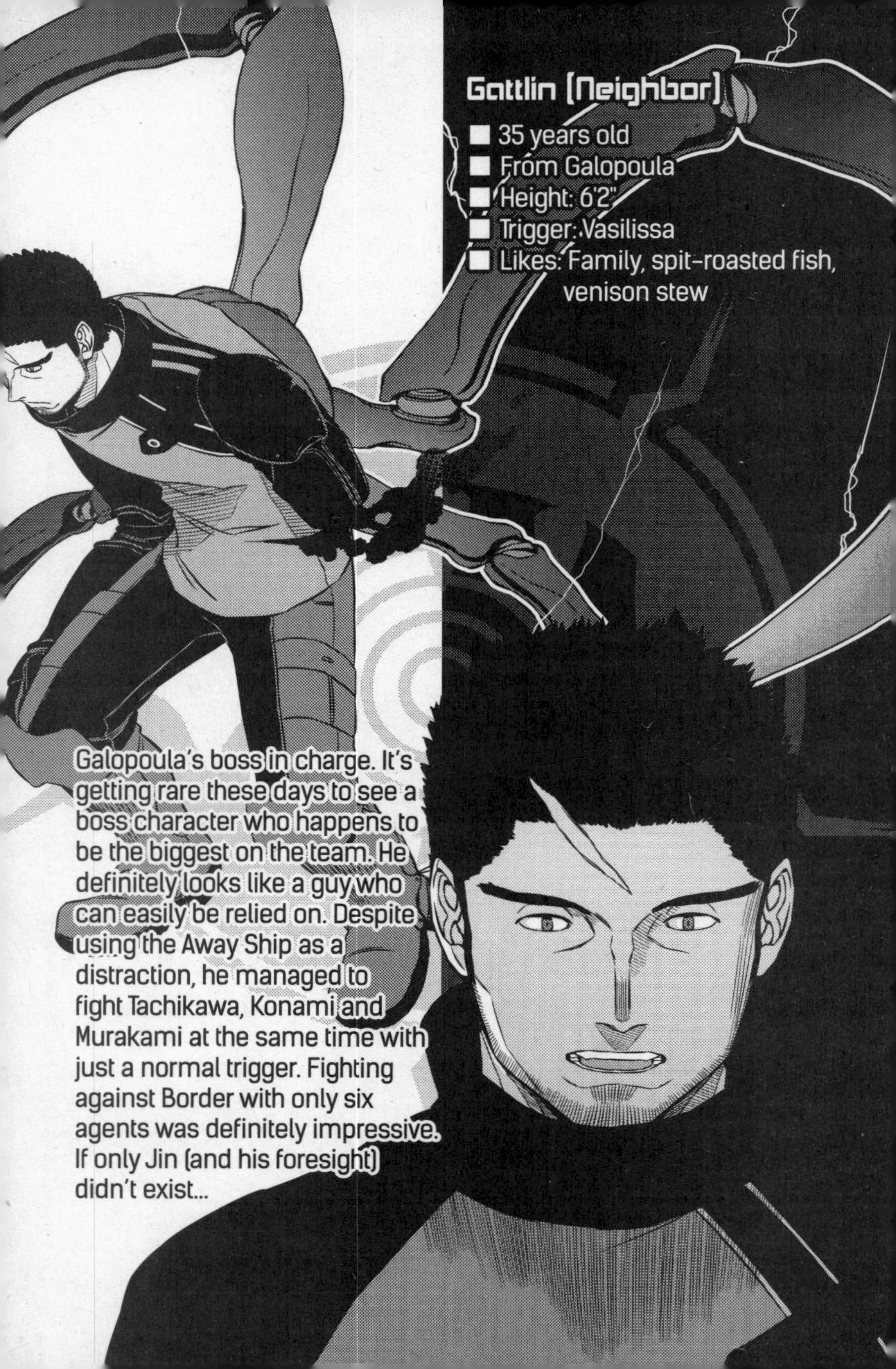

Gattlin (Neighbor)

- 35 years old
- From Galopoula
- Height: 6'2"
- Trigger: Vasilissa
- Likes: Family, spit-roasted fish, venison stew

Galopoula's boss in charge. It's getting rare these days to see a boss character who happens to be the biggest on the team. He definitely looks like a guy who can easily be relied on. Despite using the Away Ship as a distraction, he managed to fight Tachikawa, Konami and Murakami at the same time with just a normal trigger. Fighting against Border with only six agents was definitely impressive. If only Jin (and his foresight) didn't exist...

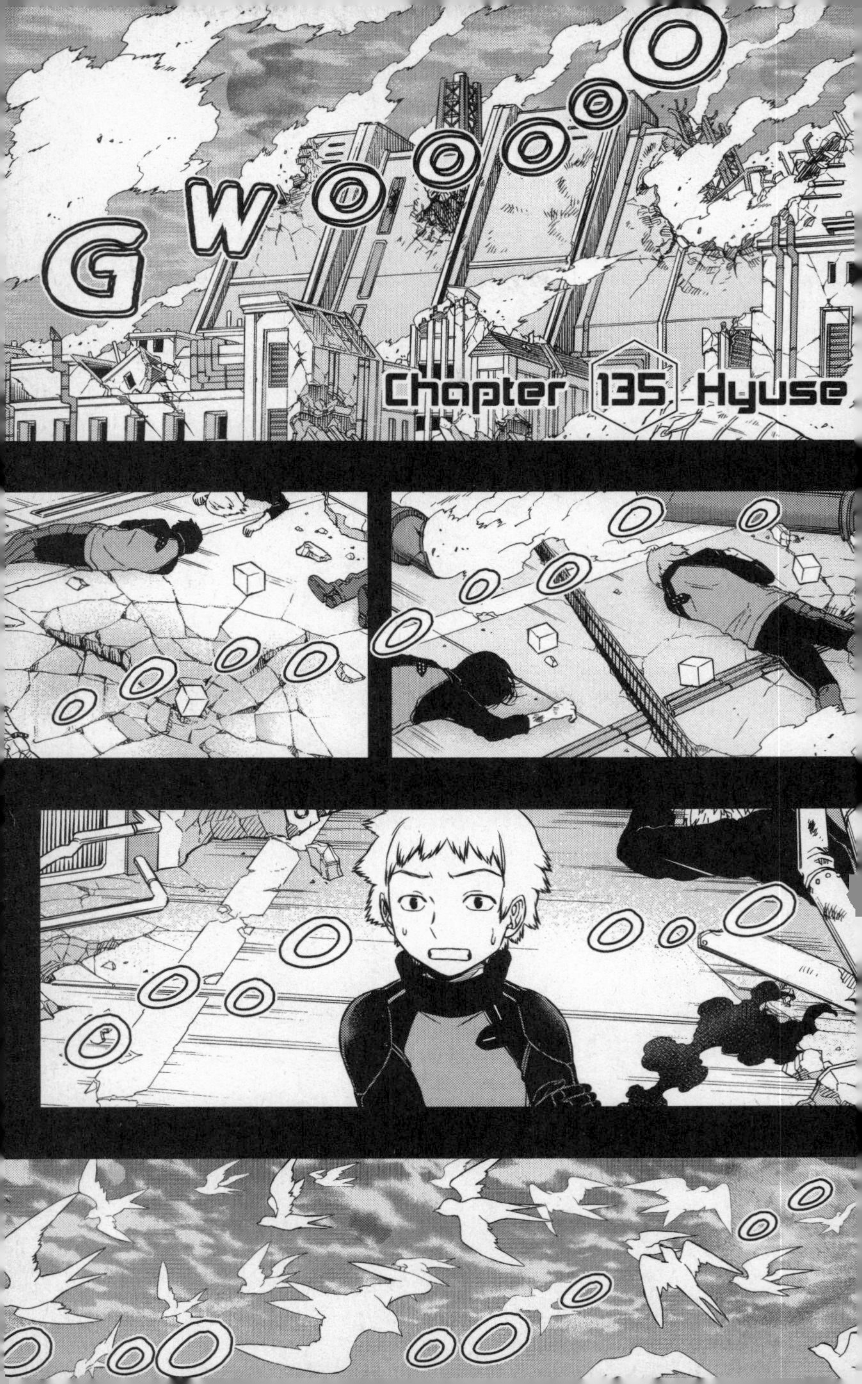
GWOOOOOO
Chapter 135 Hyuse

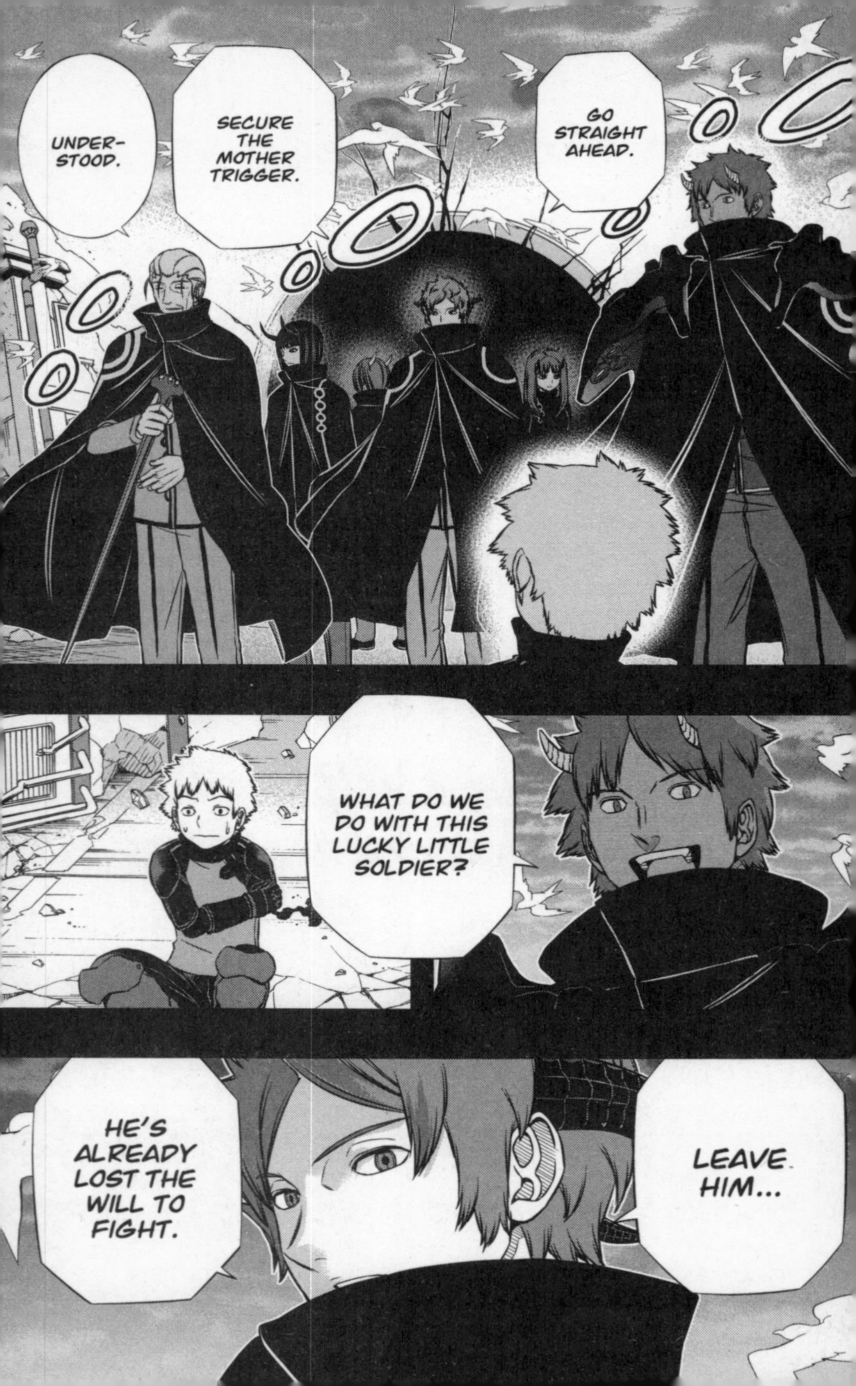
GO STRAIGHT AHEAD.
SECURE THE MOTHER TRIGGER.
UNDER-STOOD.
WHAT DO WE DO WITH THIS LUCKY LITTLE SOLDIER?
LEAVE HIM...
HE'S ALREADY LOST THE WILL TO FIGHT.

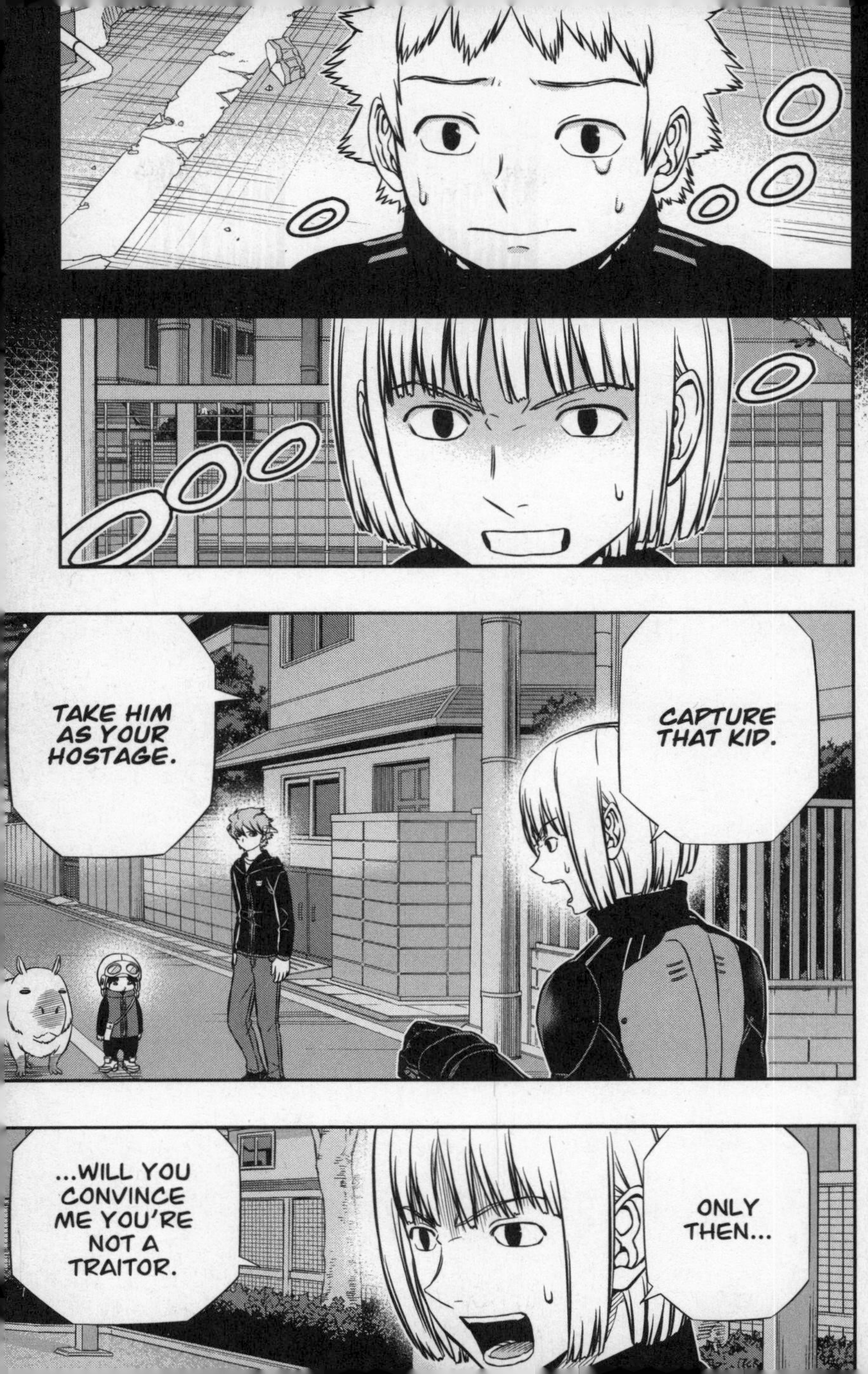
CAPTURE THAT KID.
TAKE HIM AS YOUR HOSTAGE.
ONLY THEN...
...WILL YOU CONVINCE ME YOU'RE NOT A TRAITOR.

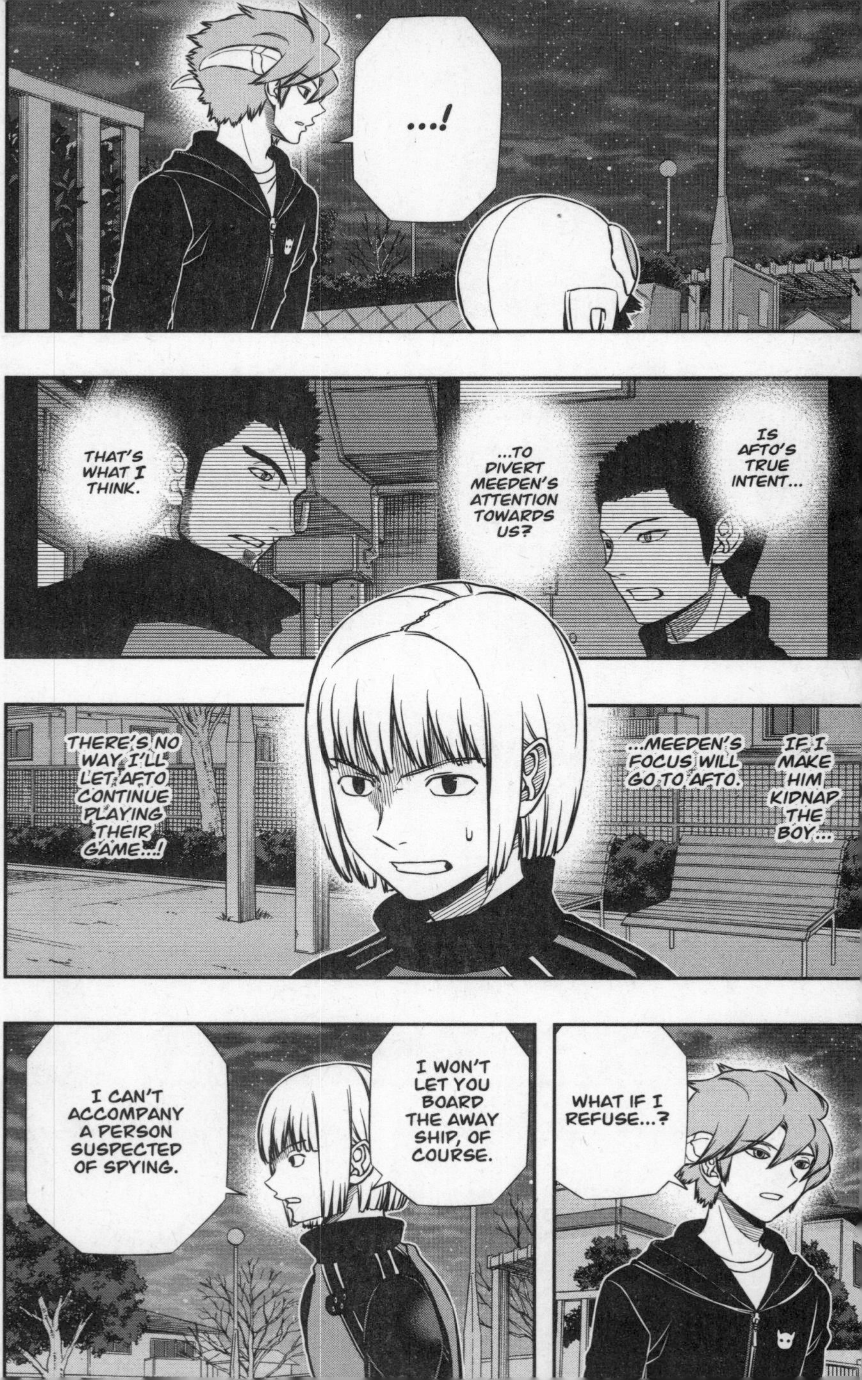
...!
IS AFTO'S TRUE INTENT...
...TO DIVERT MEEDEN'S ATTENTION TOWARDS US?
THAT'S WHAT I THINK.
IF I MAKE HIM KIDNAP THE BOY...
...MEEDEN'S FOCUS WILL GO TO AFTO.
THERE'S NO WAY I'LL LET AFTO CONTINUE PLAYING THEIR GAME...!
WHAT IF I REFUSE...?
I WON'T LET YOU BOARD THE AWAY SHIP, OF COURSE.
I CAN'T ACCOMPANY A PERSON SUSPECTED OF SPYING.

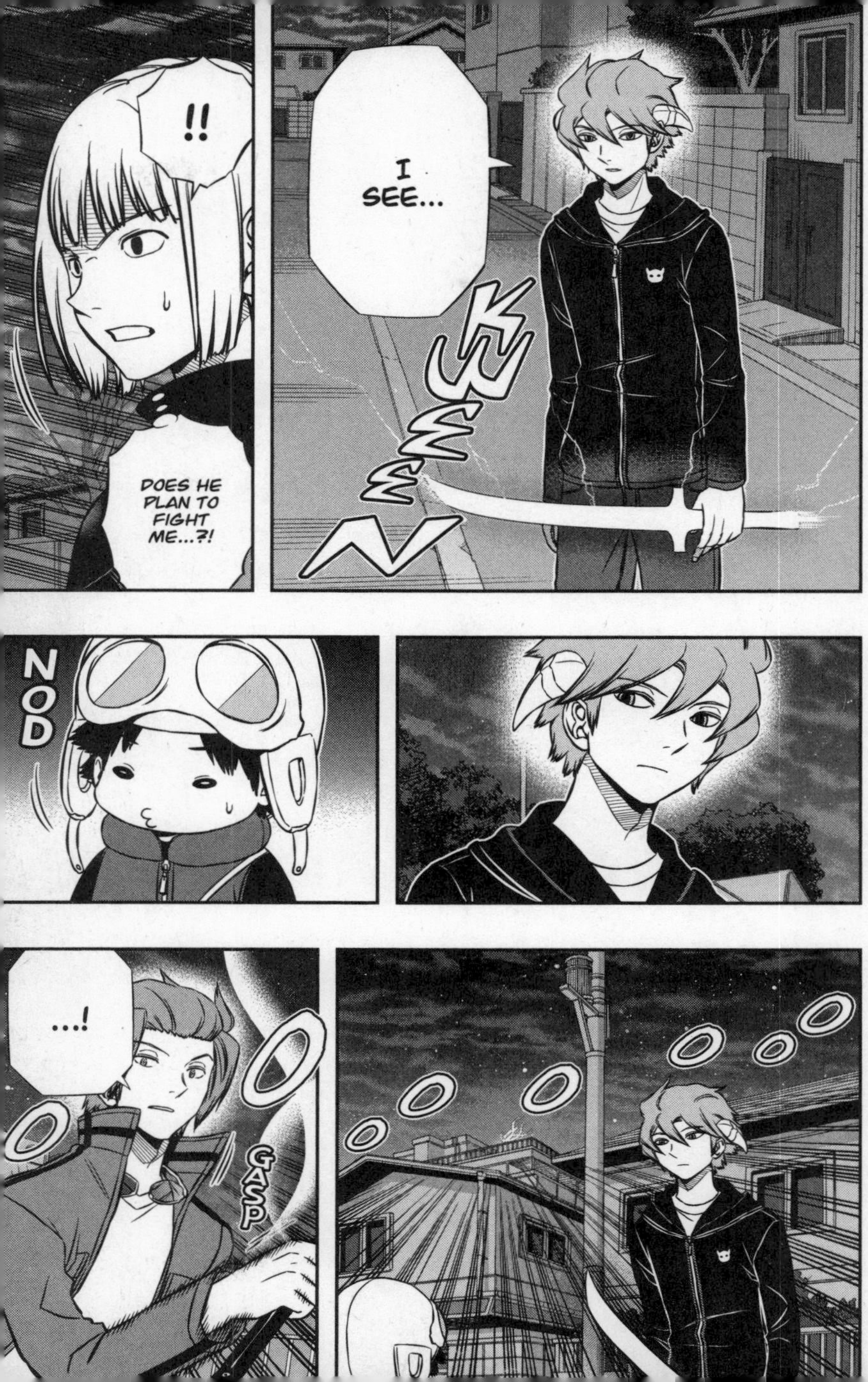
I SEE...
KYEEEN
!!
DOES HE PLAN TO FIGHT ME...?!
NOD
...!
GASP

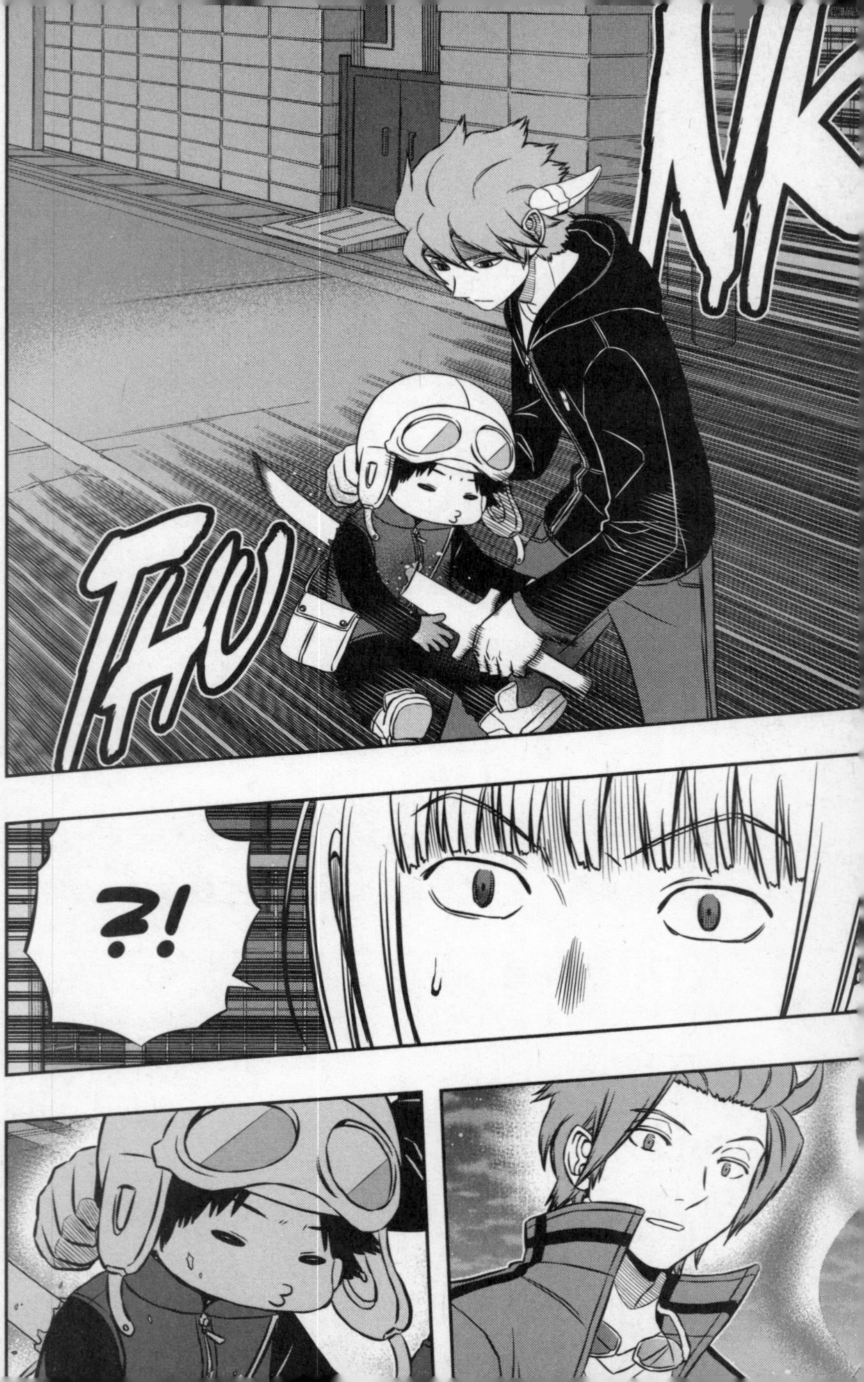
THU
NK
?!

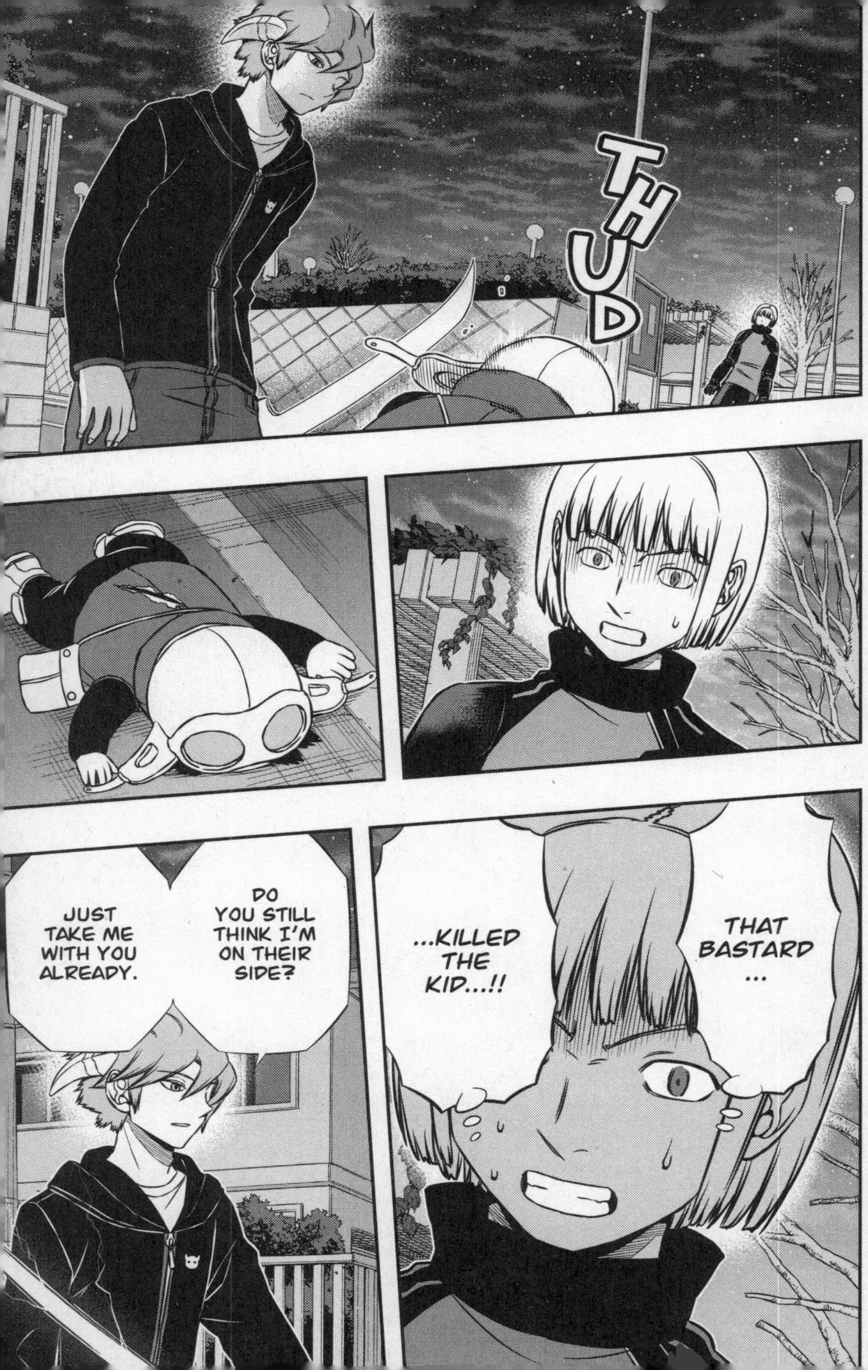
THUD
THAT BASTARD ...
...KILLED THE KID...!!
DO YOU STILL THINK I'M ON THEIR SIDE?
JUST TAKE ME WITH YOU ALREADY.

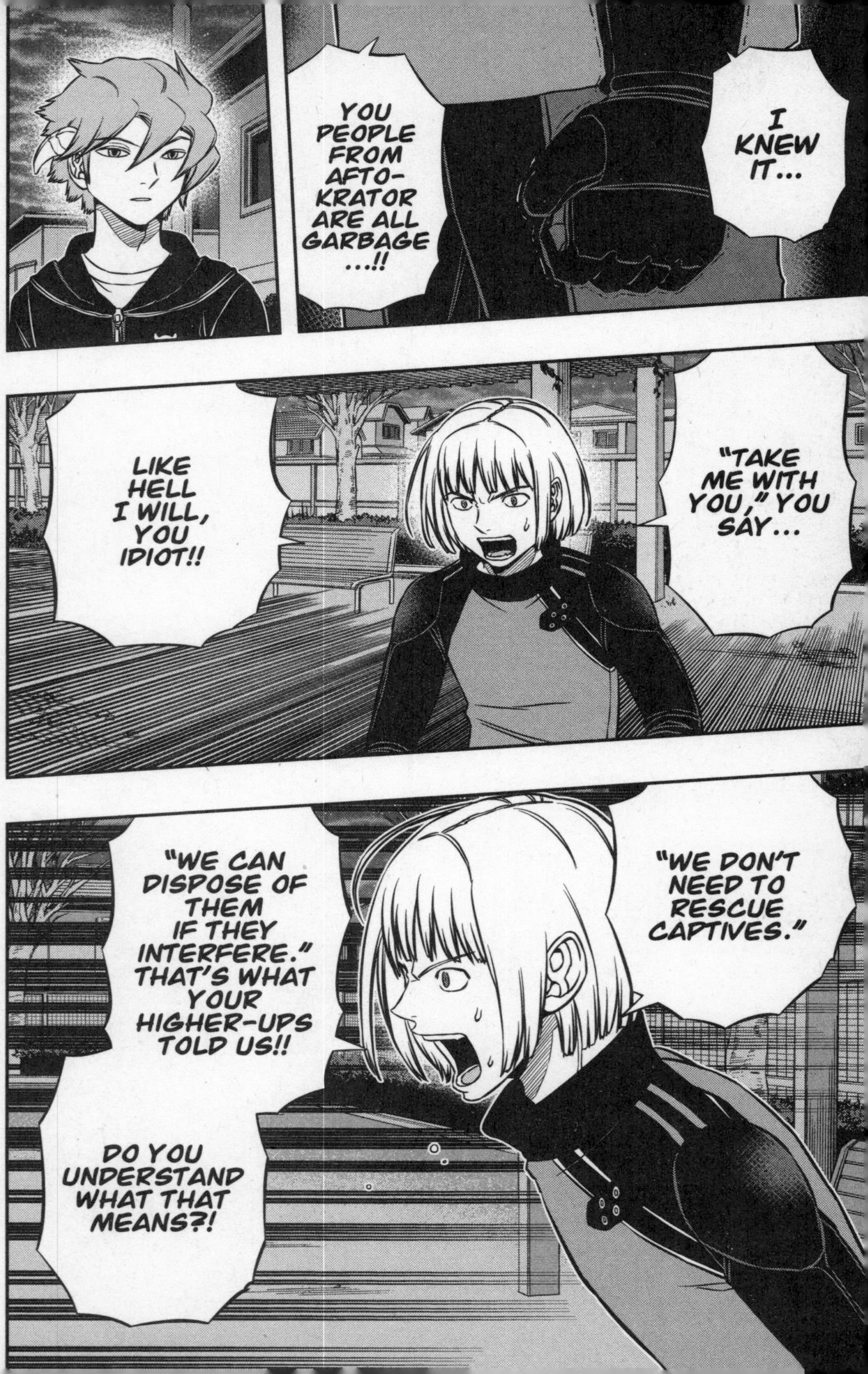
I KNEW IT...
YOU PEOPLE FROM AFTO-KRATOR ARE ALL GARBAGE...!!
"TAKE ME WITH YOU," YOU SAY...
LIKE HELL I WILL, YOU IDIOT!!
"WE DON'T NEED TO RESCUE CAPTIVES."
"WE CAN DISPOSE OF THEM IF THEY INTERFERE." THAT'S WHAT YOUR HIGHER-UPS TOLD US!!
DO YOU UNDERSTAND WHAT THAT MEANS?!

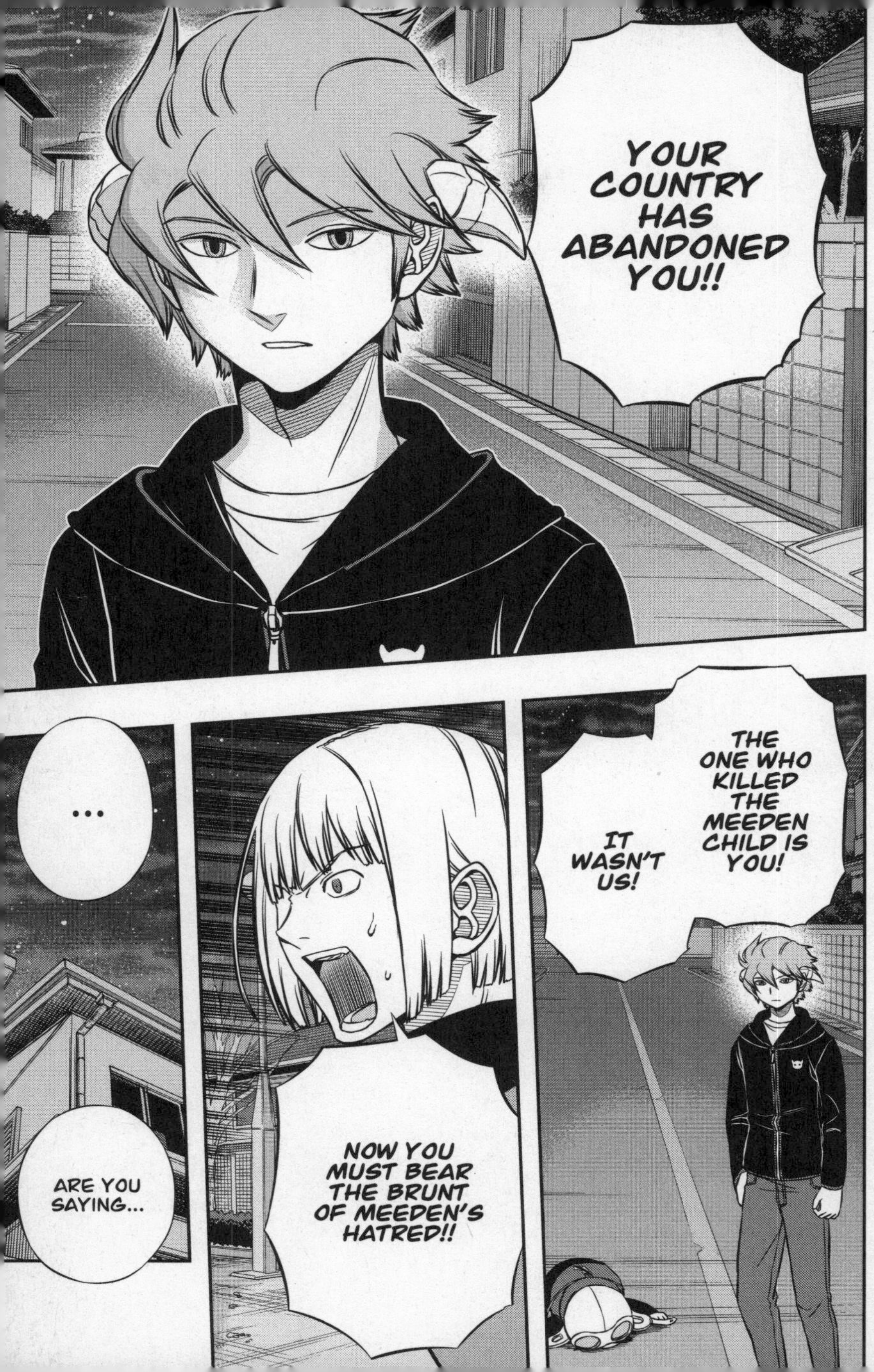
YOUR COUNTRY HAS ABANDONED YOU!!
THE ONE WHO KILLED THE MEEDEN CHILD IS YOU!
IT WASN'T US!
NOW YOU MUST BEAR THE BRUNT OF MEEDEN'S HATRED!!
...
ARE YOU SAYING...

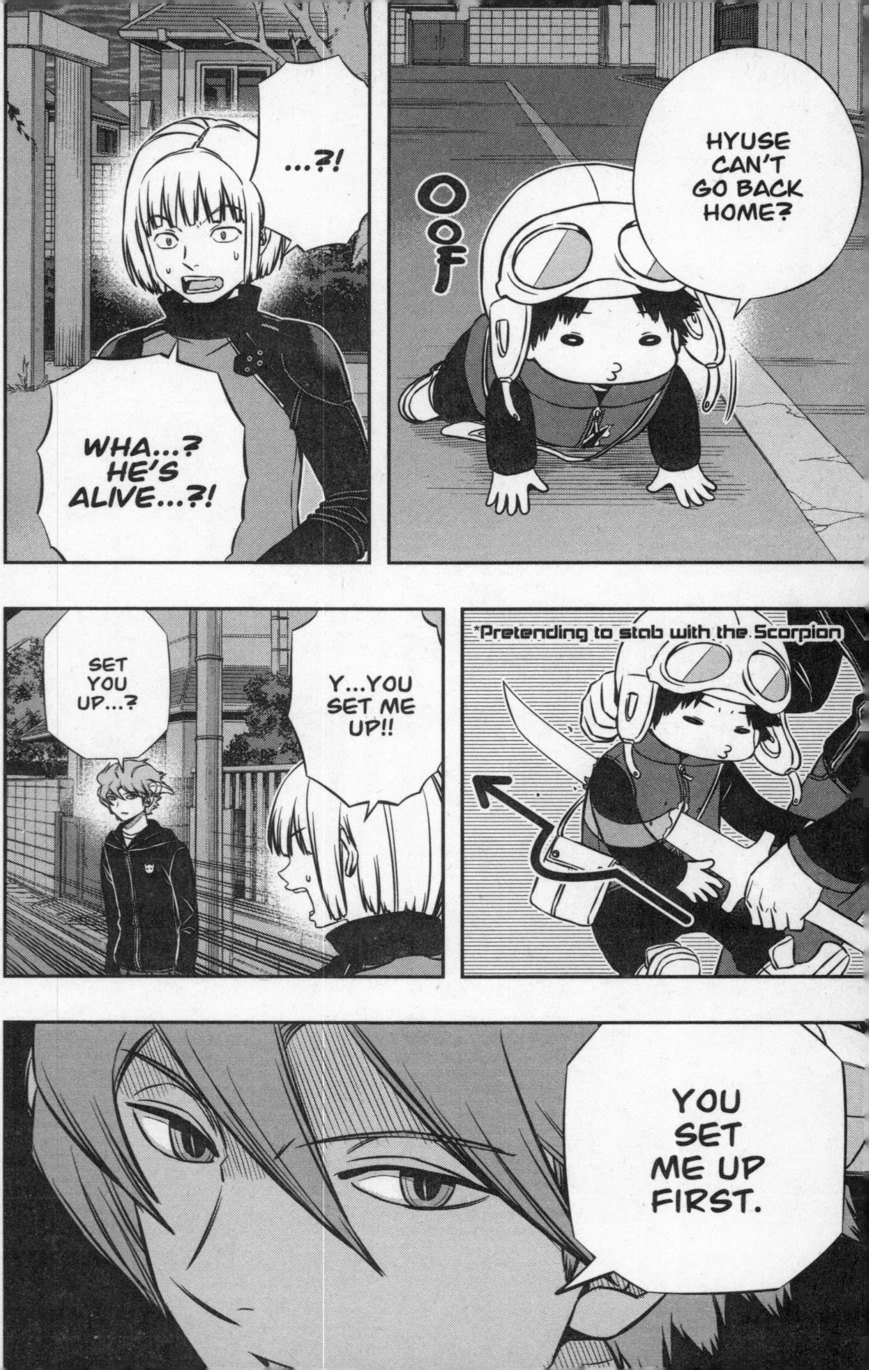
HYUSE CAN'T GO BACK HOME?
OOF
...?!
WHA...? HE'S ALIVE...?!
*Pretending to stab with the Scorpion
Y...YOU SET ME UP!!
SET YOU UP...?
YOU SET ME UP FIRST.

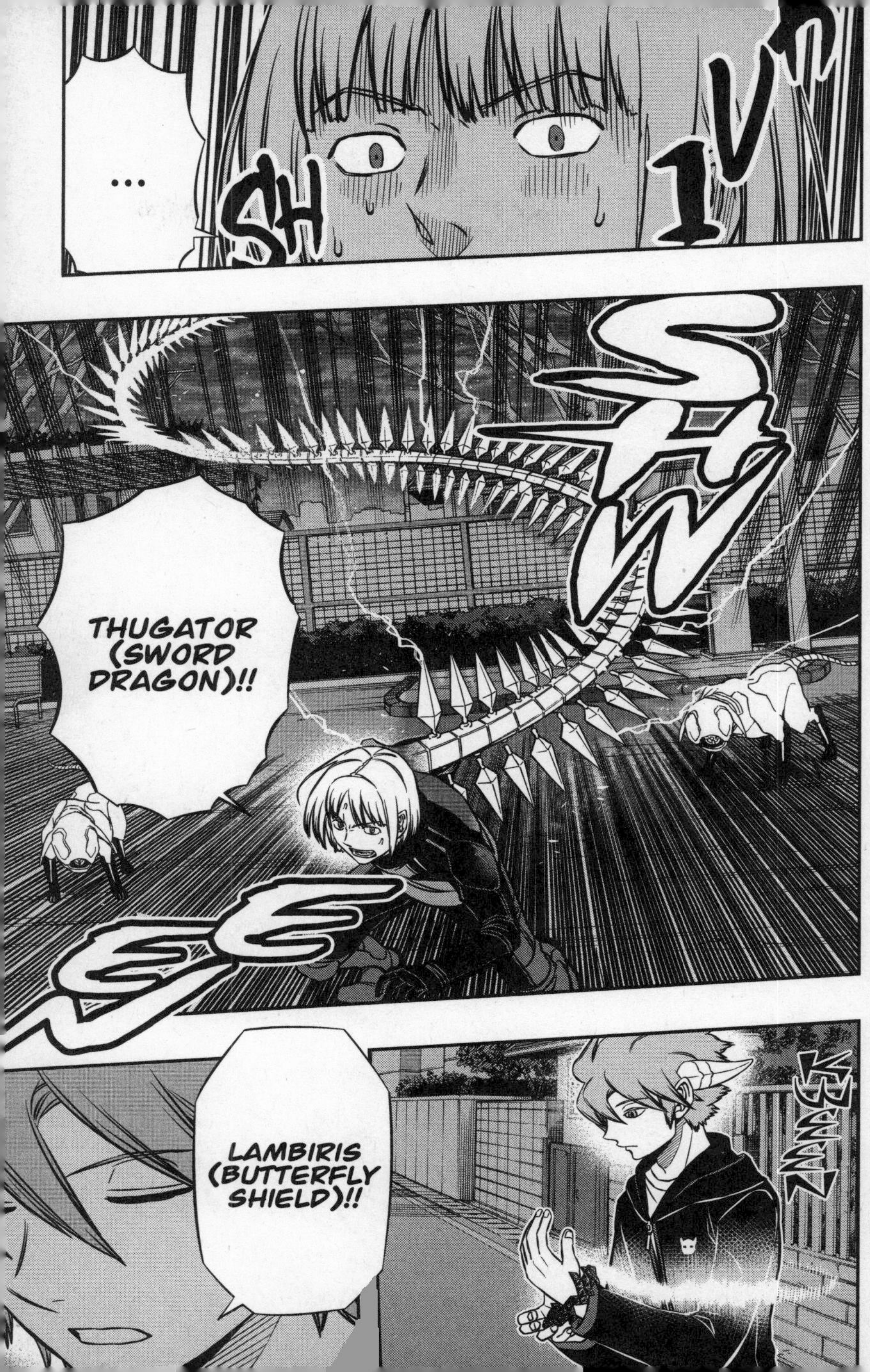
...
THUGATOR (SWORD DRAGON)!!
LAMBIRIS (BUTTERFLY SHIELD)!!

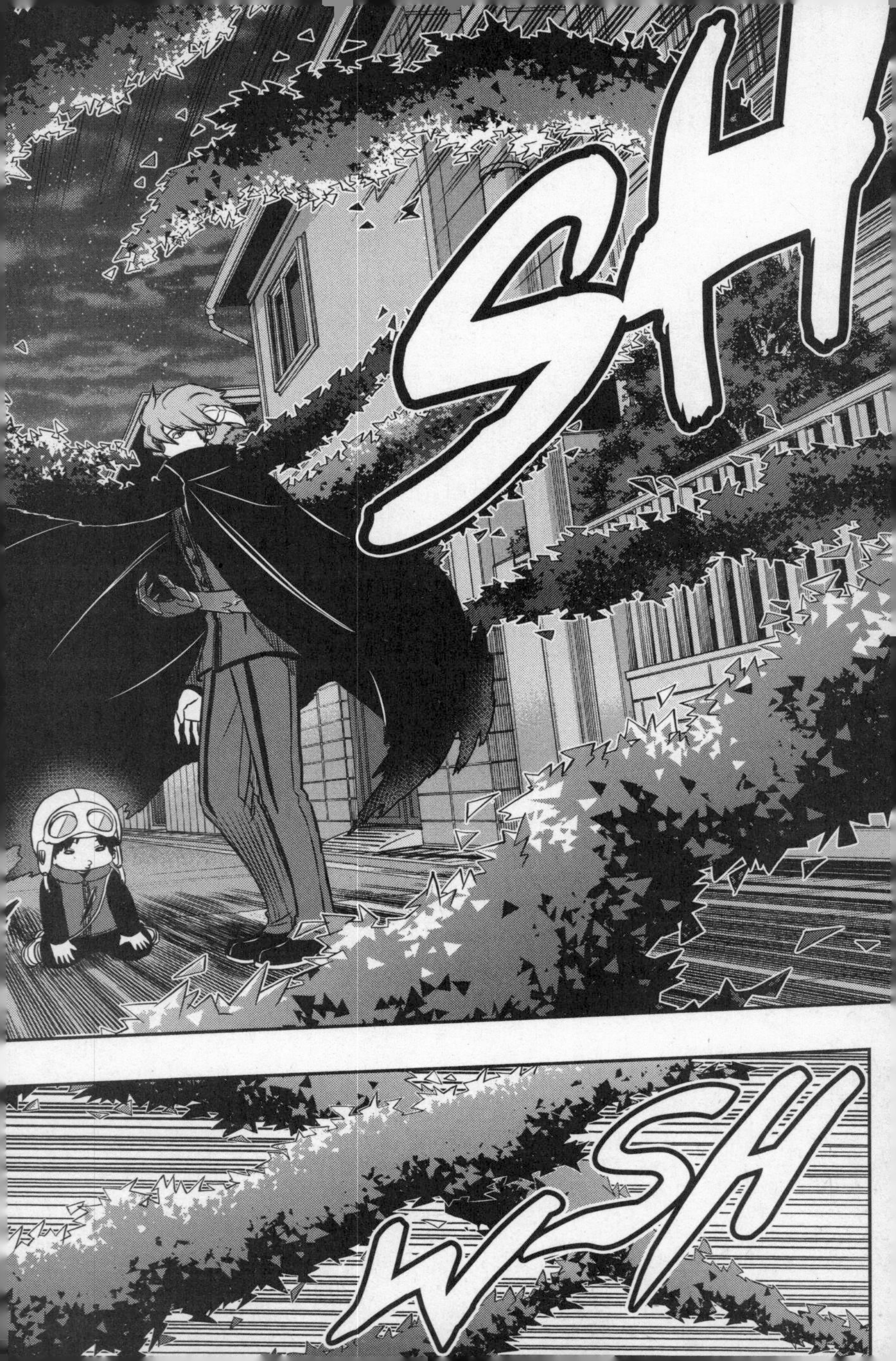
SH
WSH

READ THIS WAY

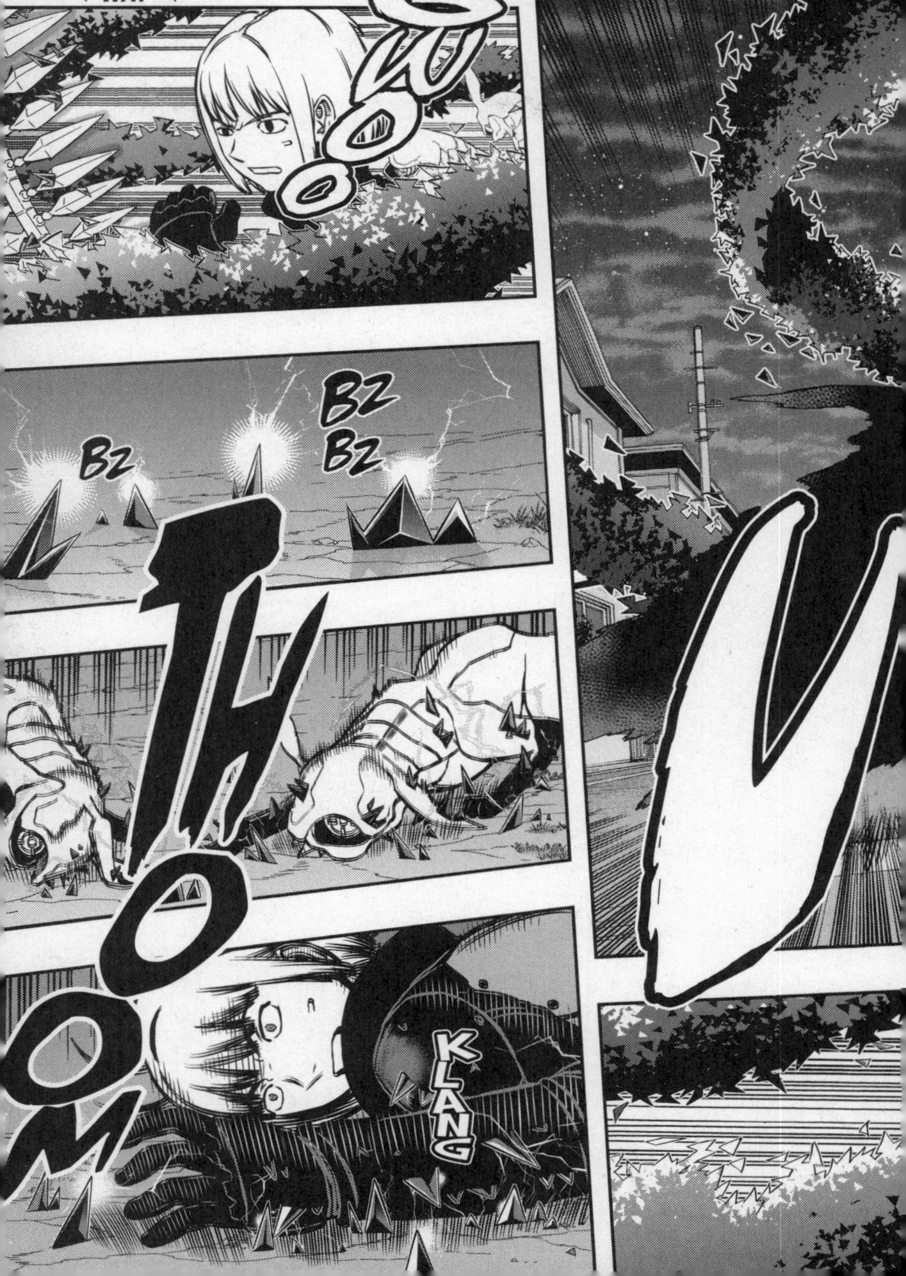

SWOO
BZ BZ
BZ
KLANG

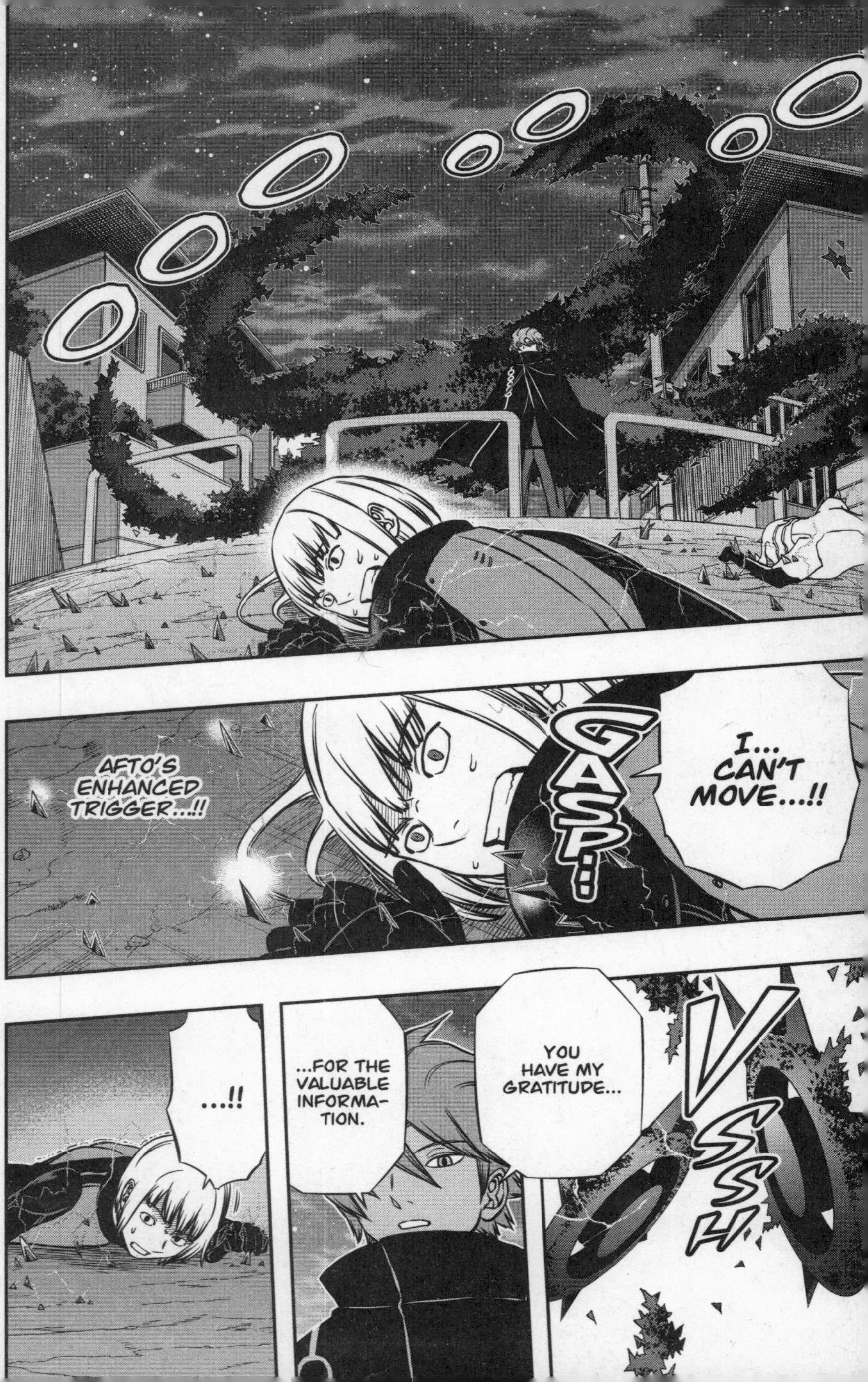

I... CAN'T MOVE...!!
GASP..
AFTO'S ENHANCED TRIGGER...!!
VSSH.
YOU HAVE MY GRATITUDE...
...FOR THE VALUABLE INFORMATION.
...!!

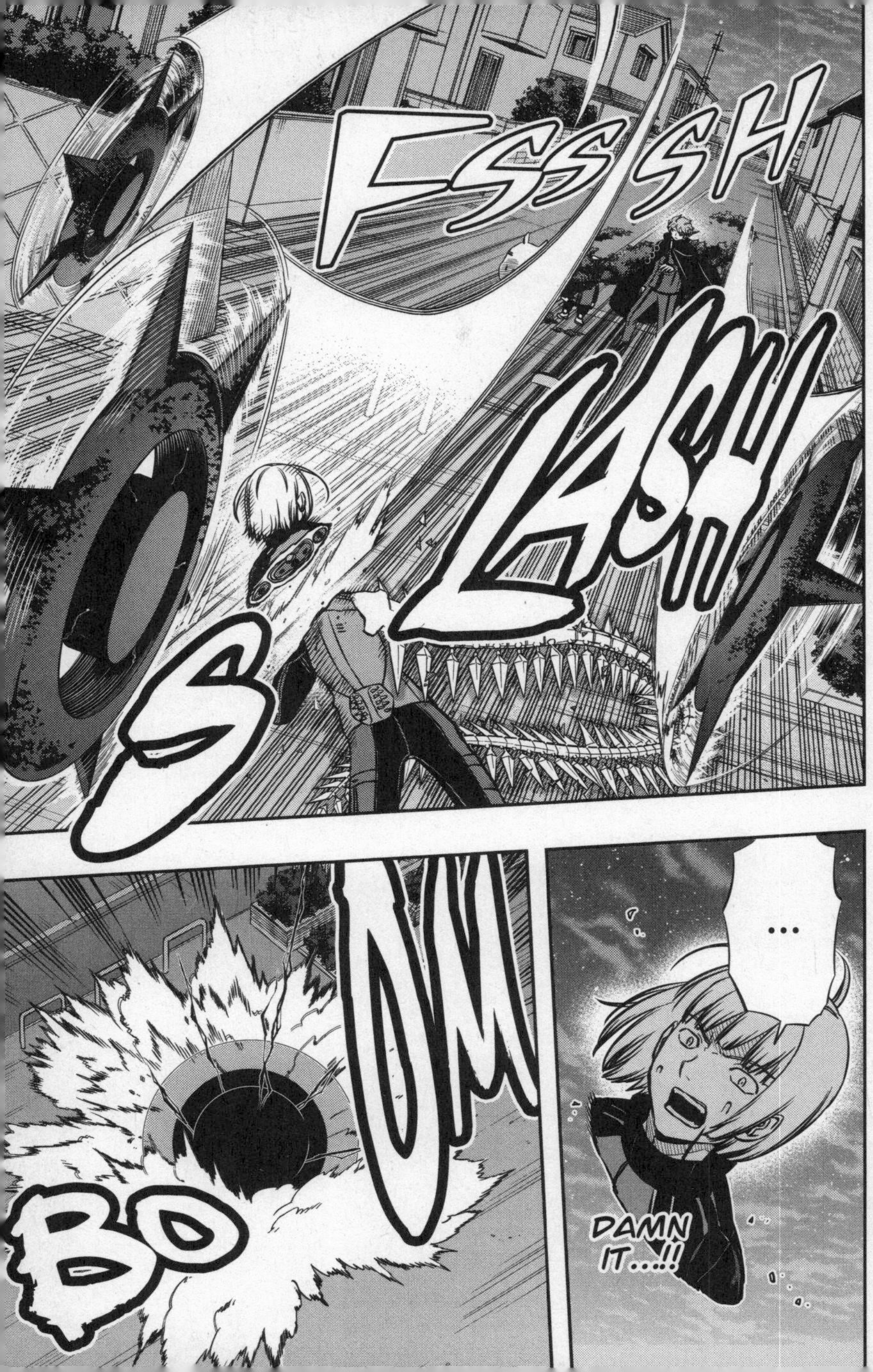
FSSSH
SLASH
...
DAMN IT...!!
BOOM

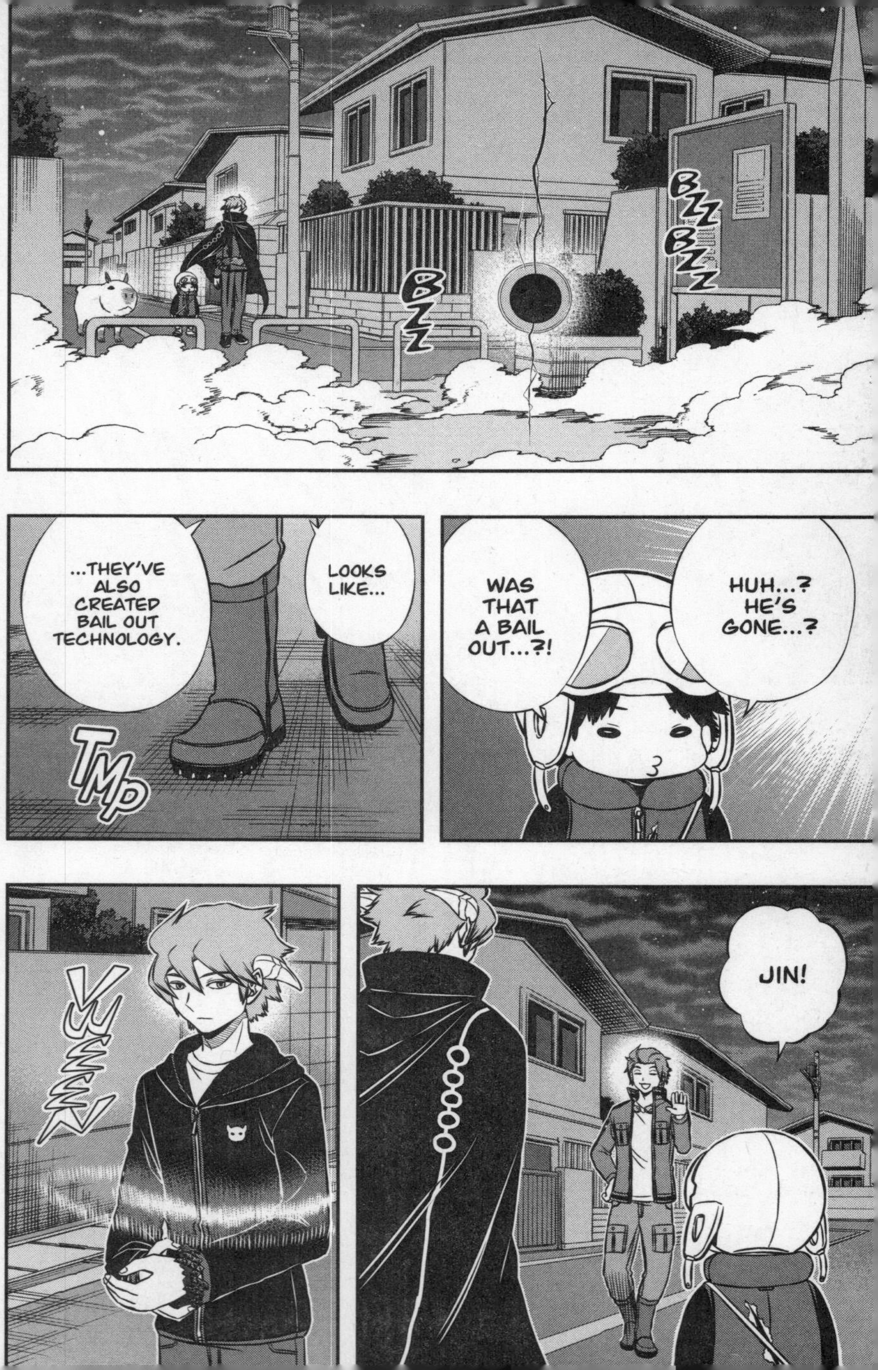
BZZ BZZ
BZZ
HUH...? HE'S GONE...?
WAS THAT A BAIL OUT...?!
LOOKS LIKE...
...THEY'VE ALSO CREATED BAIL OUT TECHNOLOGY.
TMP
JIN!
VWEEN

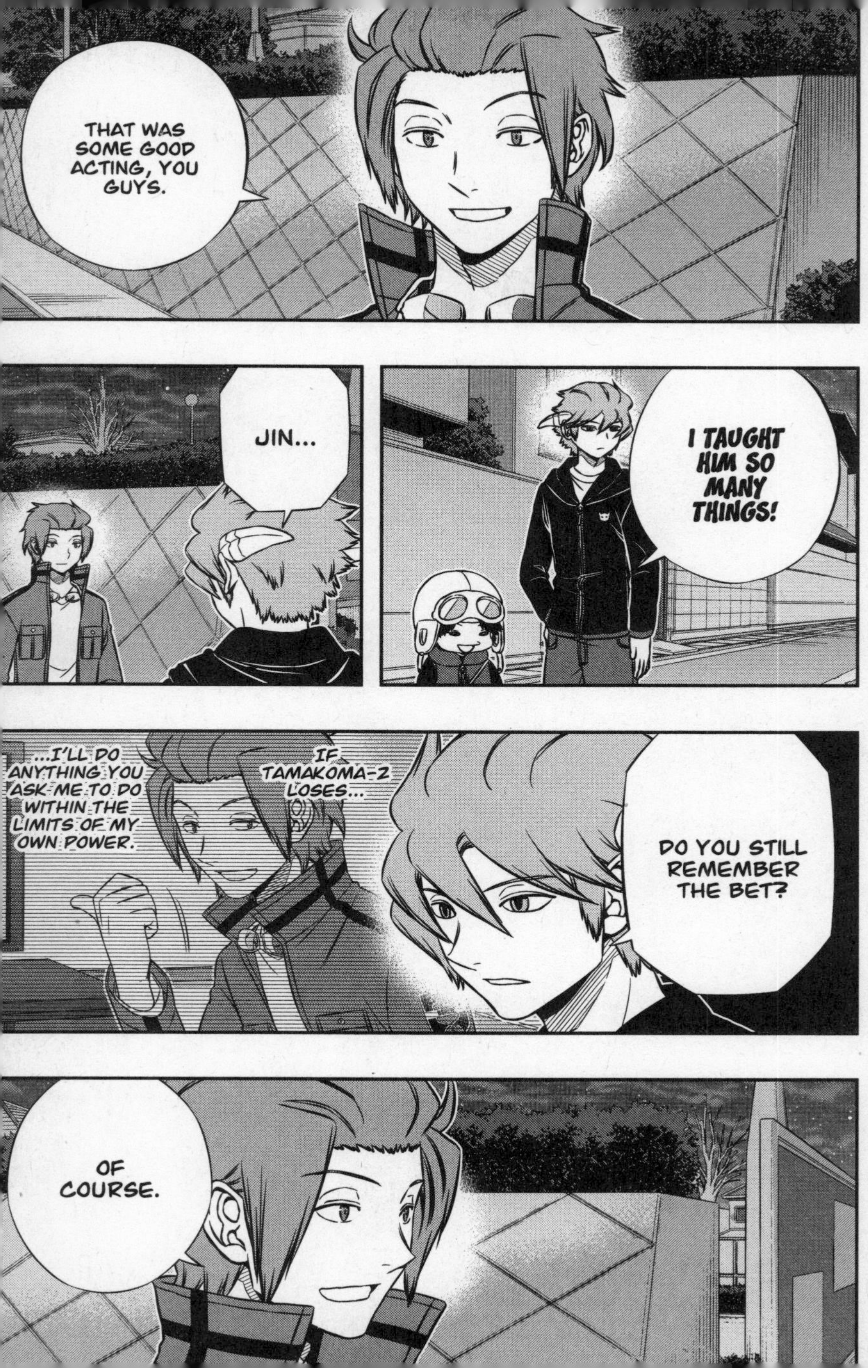
THAT WAS SOME GOOD ACTING, YOU GUYS.
I TAUGHT HIM SO MANY THINGS!
JIN...
DO YOU STILL REMEMBER THE BET?
IF TAMAKOMA-2 LOSES...
...I'LL DO ANYTHING YOU ASK ME TO DO WITHIN THE LIMITS OF MY OWN POWER.
OF COURSE.

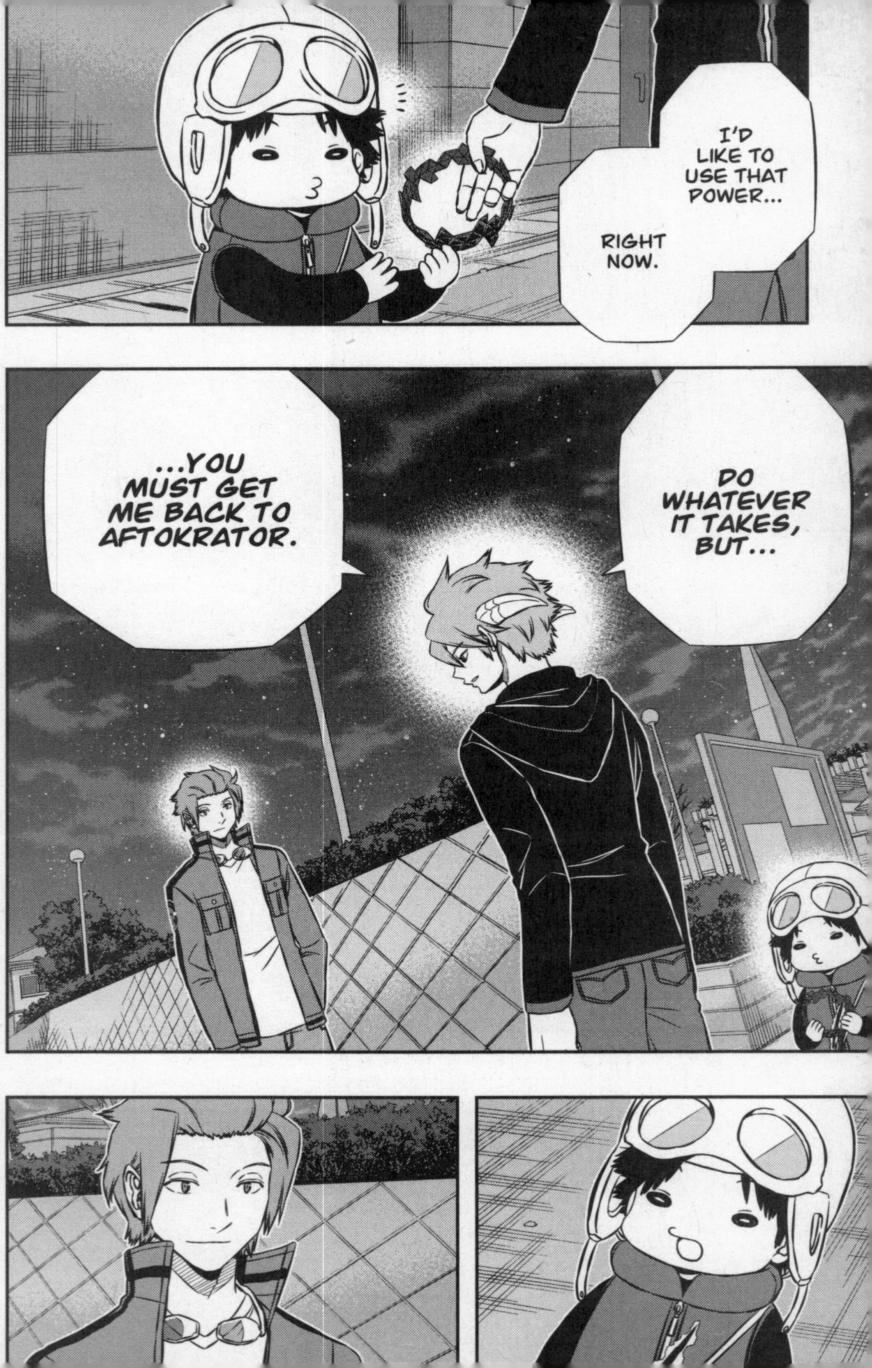
I'D LIKE TO USE THAT POWER...
RIGHT NOW.
DO WHATEVER IT TAKES, BUT...
...YOU MUST GET ME BACK TO AFTOKRATOR.

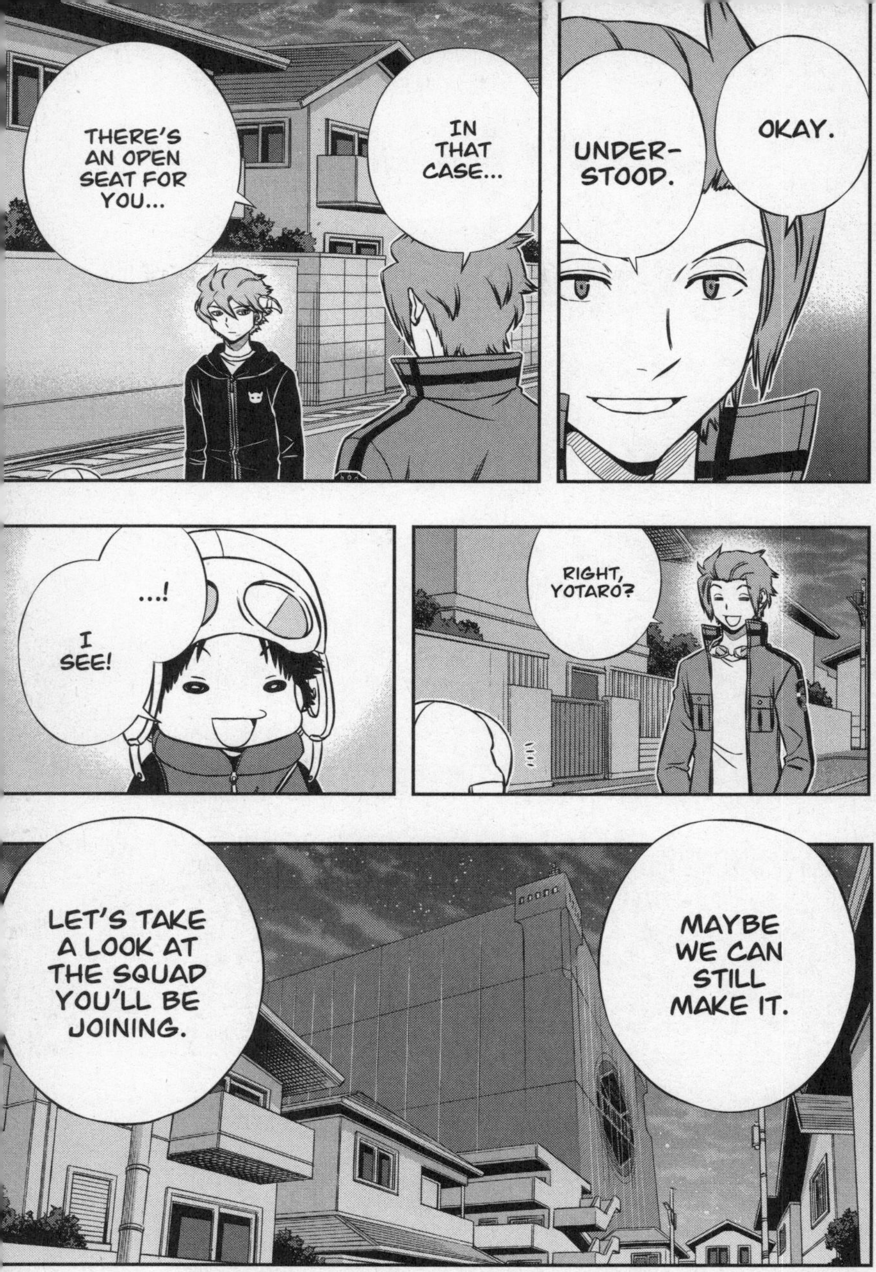
OKAY.
UNDER-STOOD.
IN THAT CASE...
THERE'S AN OPEN SEAT FOR YOU...
RIGHT, YOTARO?
...!
I SEE!
MAYBE WE CAN STILL MAKE IT.
LET'S TAKE A LOOK AT THE SQUAD YOU'LL BE JOINING.

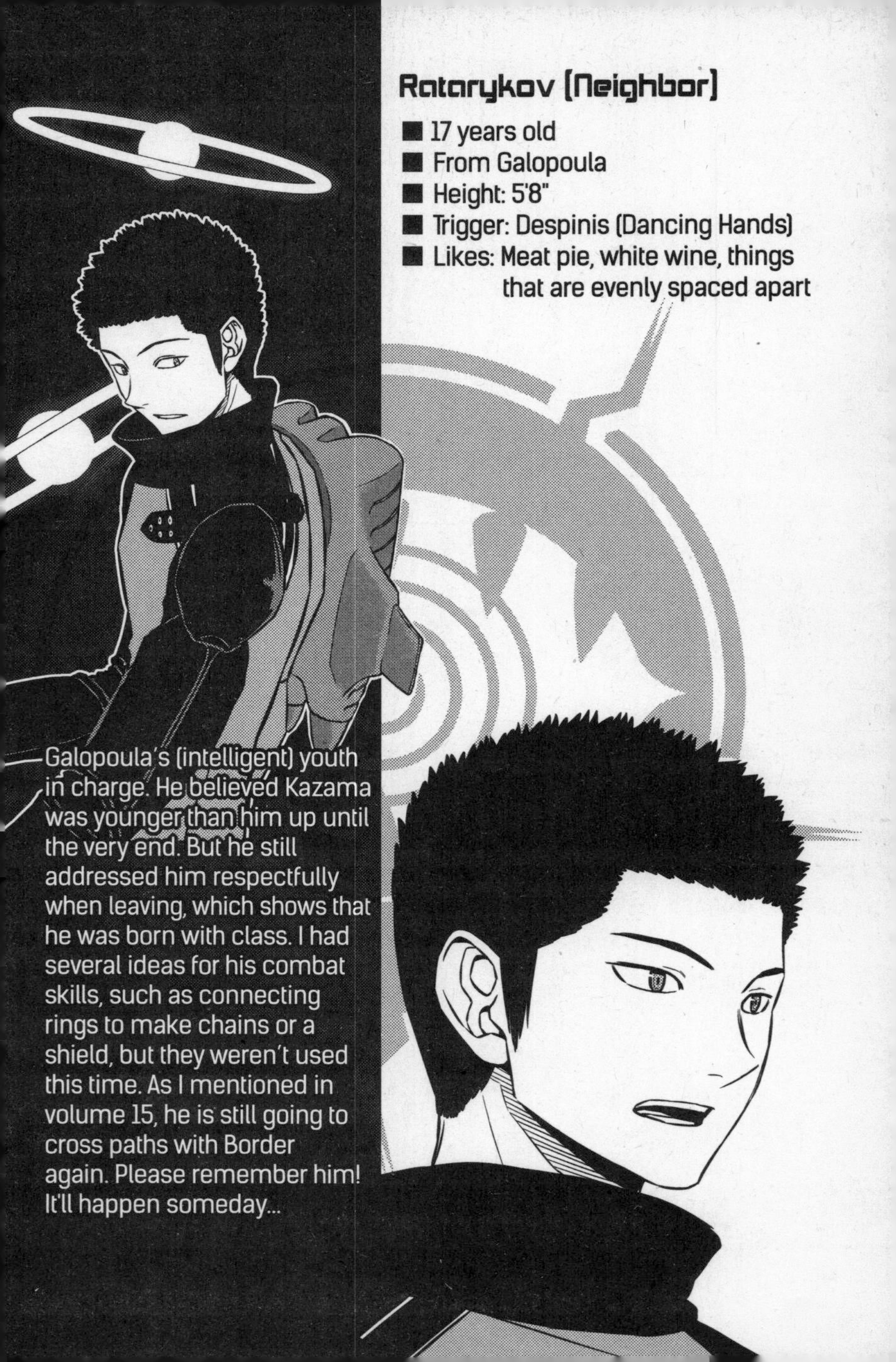

Ratarykov (Neighbor)

- 17 years old
- From Galopoula
- Height: 5'8"
- Trigger: Despinis (Dancing Hands)
- Likes: Meat pie, white wine, things that are evenly spaced apart

Galopoula's (intelligent) youth in charge. He believed Kazama was younger than him up until the very end. But he still addressed him respectfully when leaving, which shows that he was born with class. I had several ideas for his combat skills, such as connecting rings to make chains or a shield, but they weren't used this time. As I mentioned in volume 15, he is still going to cross paths with Border again. Please remember him! It'll happen someday...

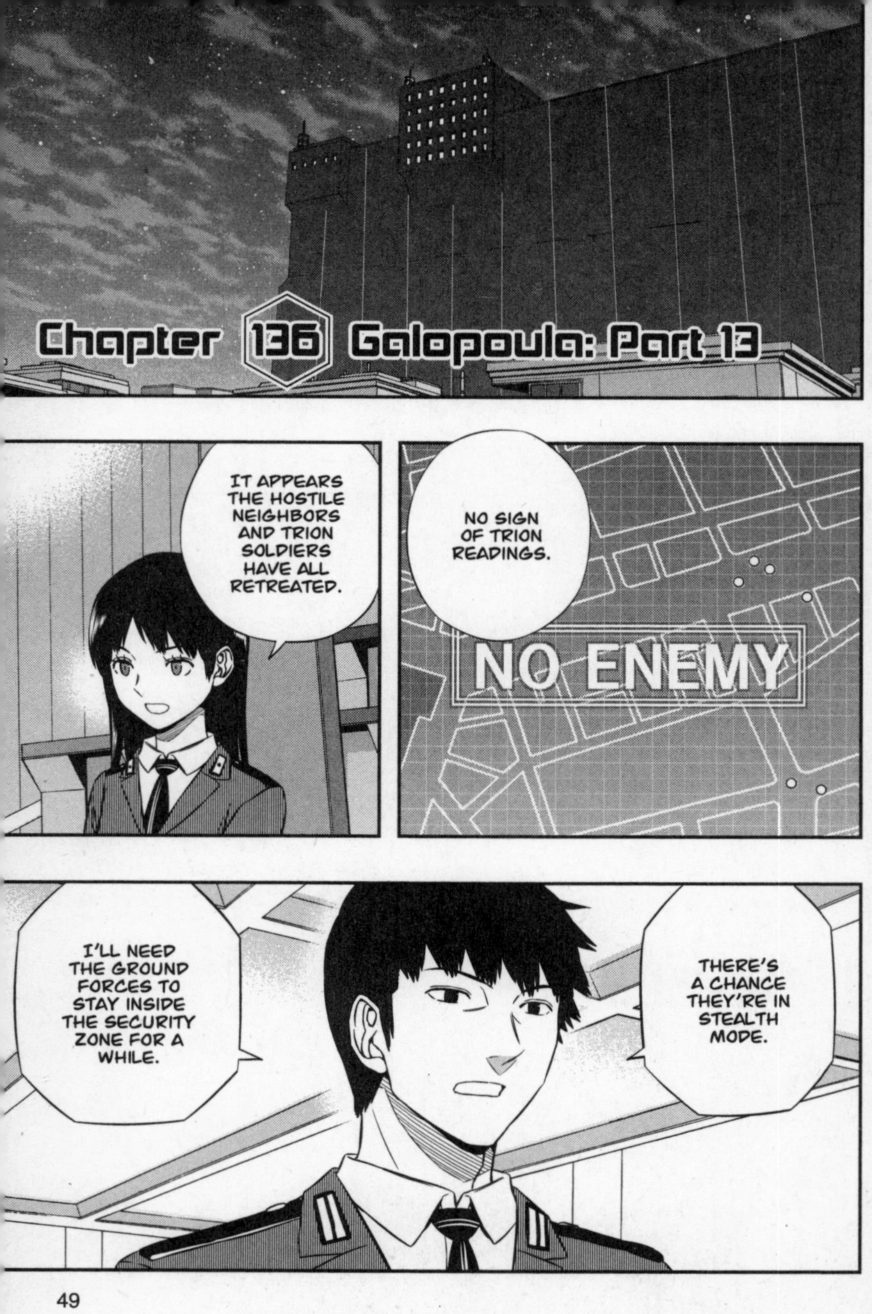
Chapter 136 Galopoula: Part 13
NO SIGN OF TRION READINGS.
NO ENEMY
IT APPEARS THE HOSTILE NEIGHBORS AND TRION SOLDIERS HAVE ALL RETREATED.
THERE'S A CHANCE THEY'RE IN STEALTH MODE.
I'LL NEED THE GROUND FORCES TO STAY INSIDE THE SECURITY ZONE FOR A WHILE.

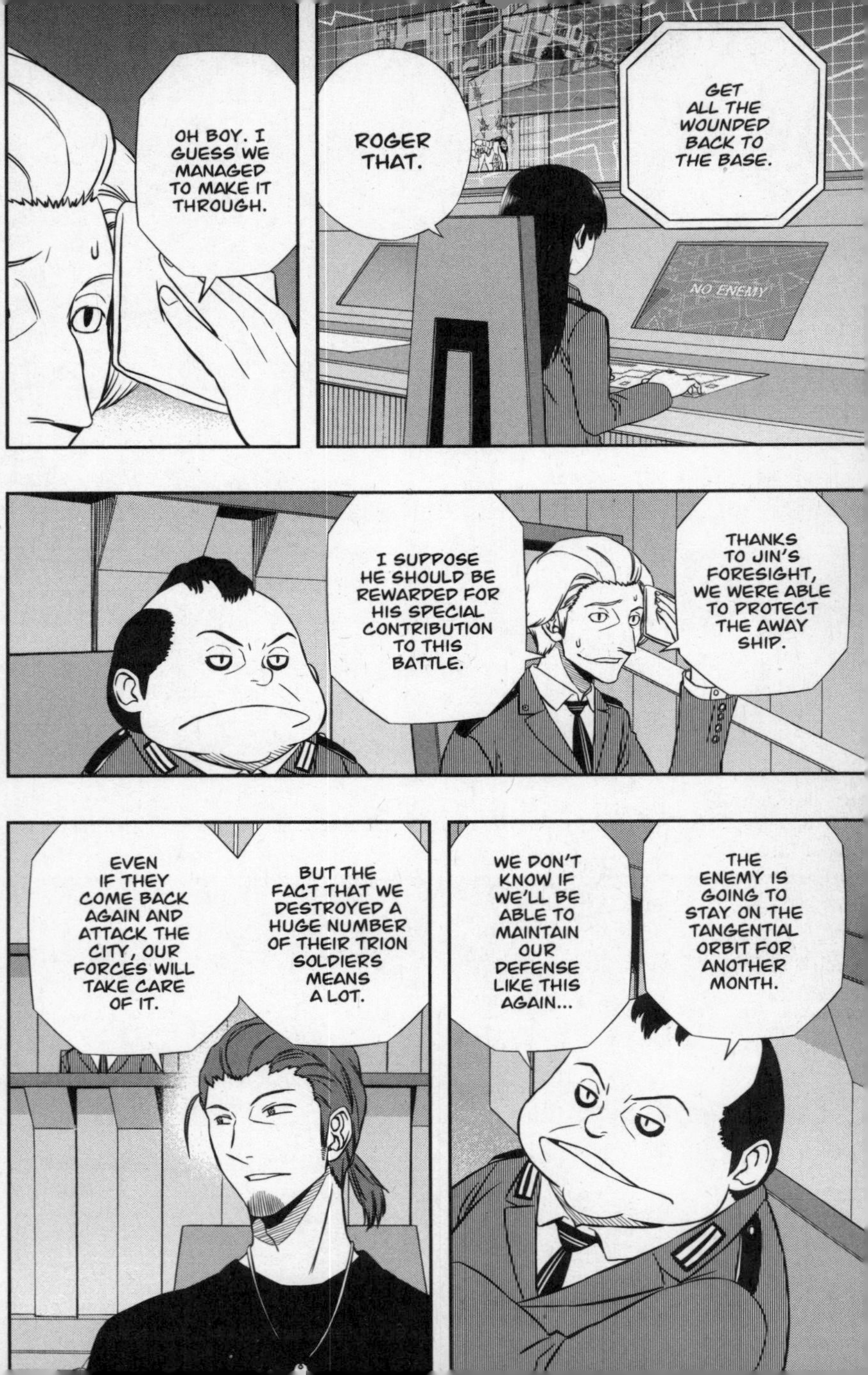
GET ALL THE WOUNDED BACK TO THE BASE.
ROGER THAT.
NO ENEMY
OH BOY. I GUESS WE MANAGED TO MAKE IT THROUGH.
THANKS TO JIN'S FORESIGHT, WE WERE ABLE TO PROTECT THE AWAY SHIP.
I SUPPOSE HE SHOULD BE REWARDED FOR HIS SPECIAL CONTRIBUTION TO THIS BATTLE.
THE ENEMY IS GOING TO STAY ON THE TANGENTIAL ORBIT FOR ANOTHER MONTH.
WE DON'T KNOW IF WE'LL BE ABLE TO MAINTAIN OUR DEFENSE LIKE THIS AGAIN...
BUT THE FACT THAT WE DESTROYED A HUGE NUMBER OF THEIR TRION SOLDIERS MEANS A LOT.
EVEN IF THEY COME BACK AGAIN AND ATTACK THE CITY, OUR FORCES WILL TAKE CARE OF IT.

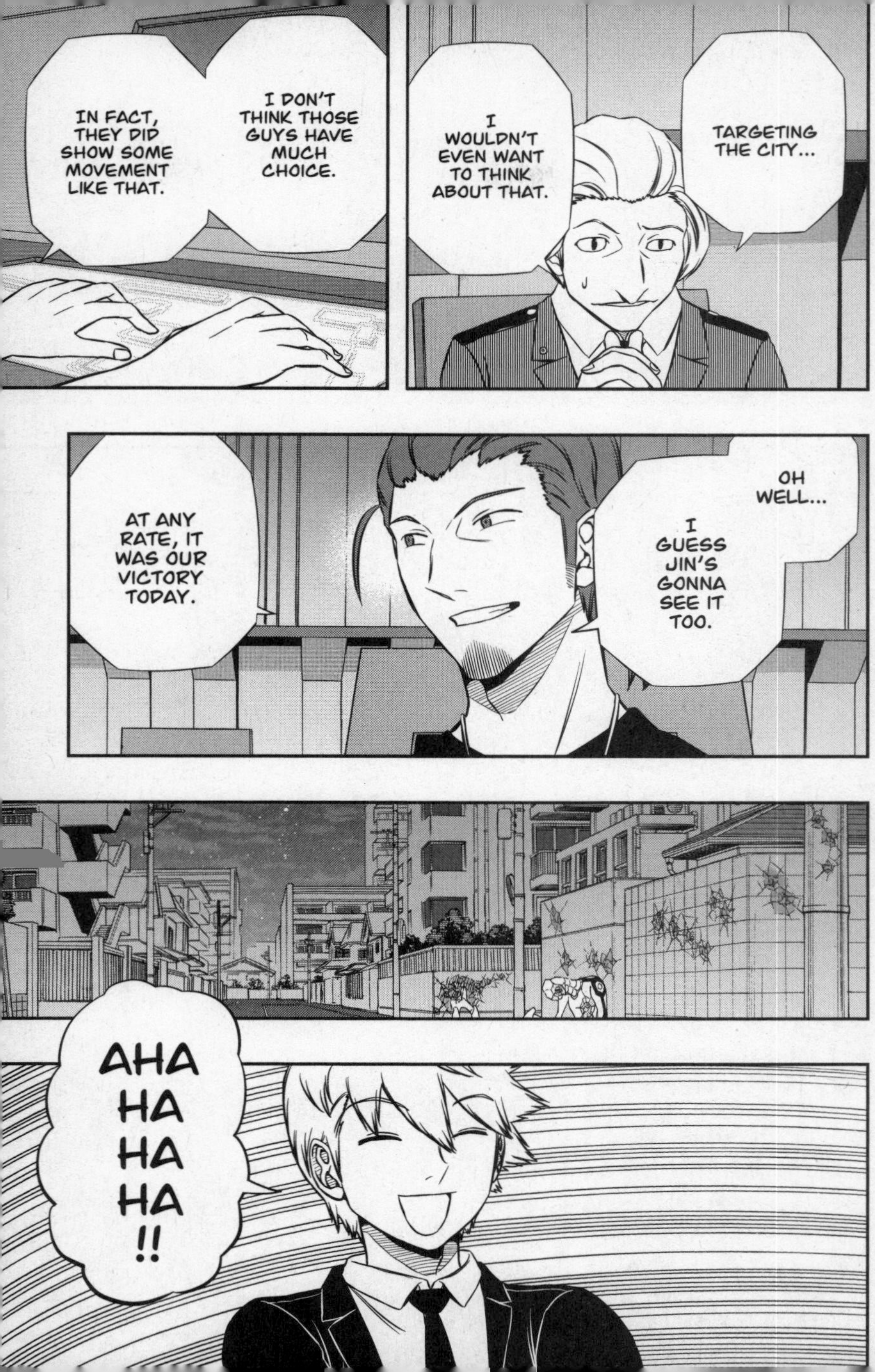
TARGETING THE CITY...
I WOULDN'T EVEN WANT TO THINK ABOUT THAT.
I DON'T THINK THOSE GUYS HAVE MUCH CHOICE.
IN FACT, THEY DID SHOW SOME MOVEMENT LIKE THAT.
OH WELL...
I GUESS JIN'S GONNA SEE IT TOO.
AT ANY RATE, IT WAS OUR VICTORY TODAY.
AHA HA HA HA!!

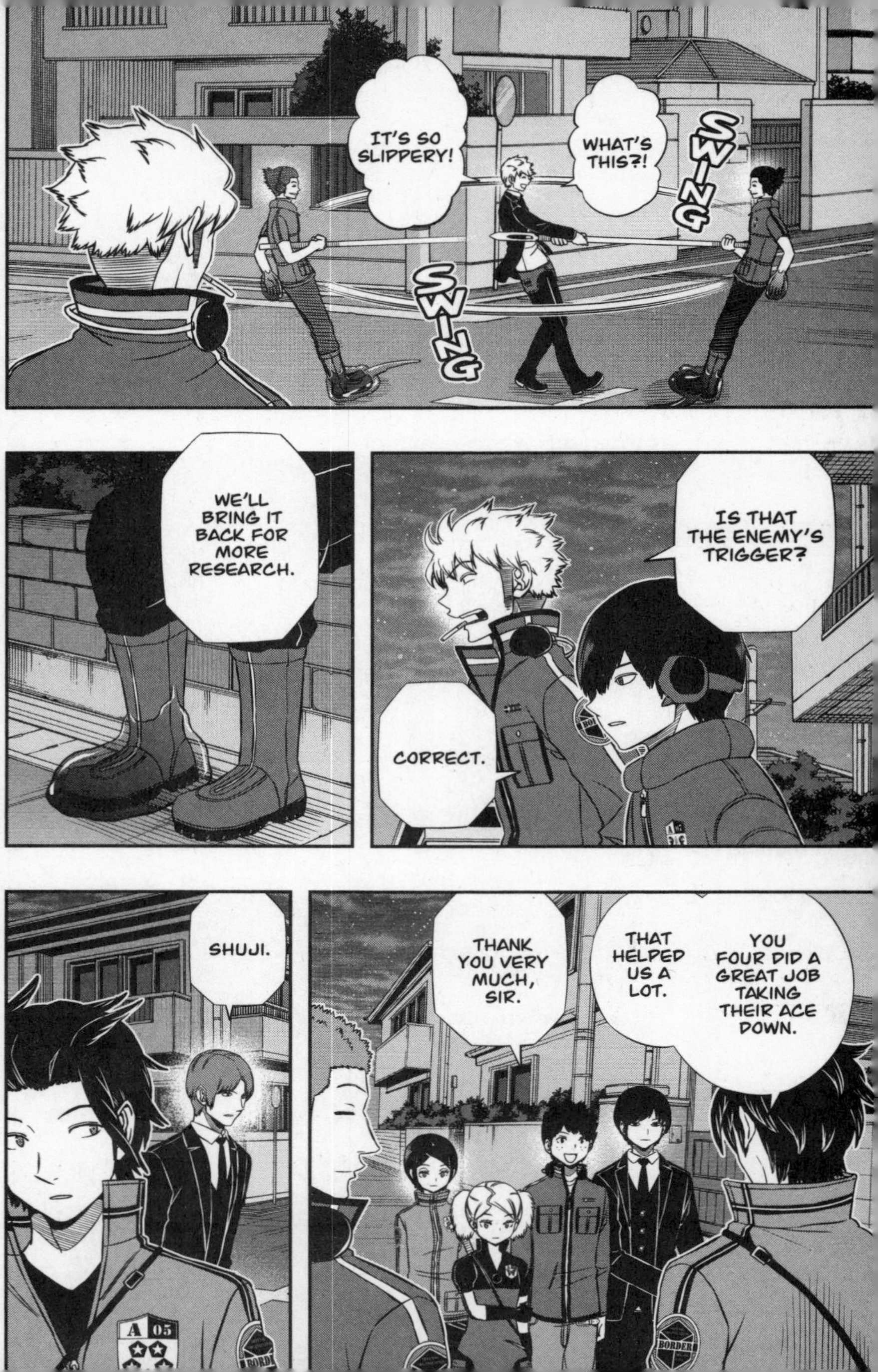
SWING
WHAT'S THIS?!
IT'S SO SLIPPERY!
SWING
IS THAT THE ENEMY'S TRIGGER?
CORRECT.
WE'LL BRING IT BACK FOR MORE RESEARCH.
YOU FOUR DID A GREAT JOB TAKING THEIR ACE DOWN.
THAT HELPED US A LOT.
THANK YOU VERY MUCH, SIR.
SHUJI.

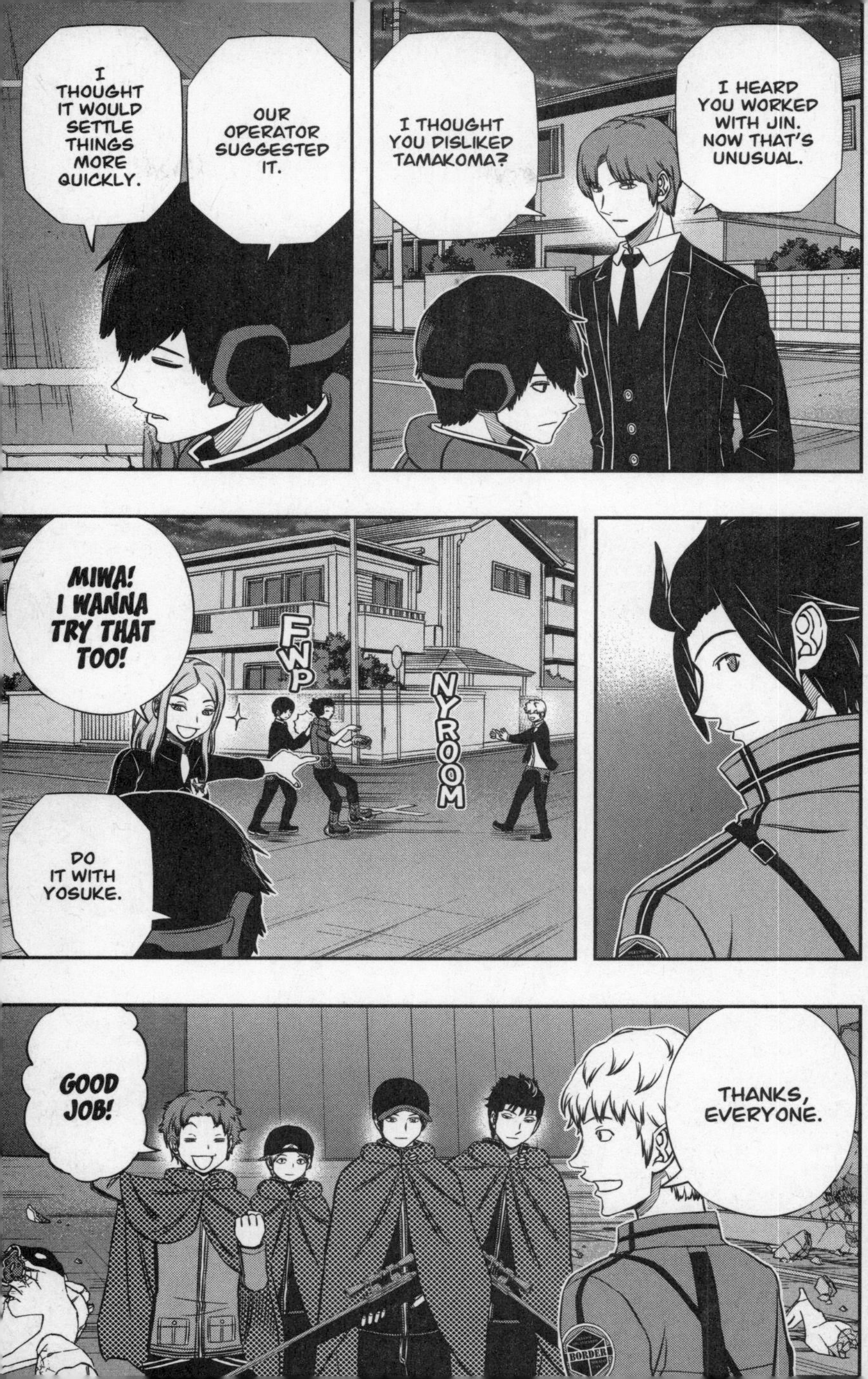
I HEARD YOU WORKED WITH JIN. NOW THAT'S UNUSUAL.
I THOUGHT YOU DISLIKED TAMAKOMA?
OUR OPERATOR SUGGESTED IT.
I THOUGHT IT WOULD SETTLE THINGS MORE QUICKLY.
MIWA! I WANNA TRY THAT TOO!
FWP
NYROOM
DO IT WITH YOSUKE.
THANKS, EVERYONE.
GOOD JOB!

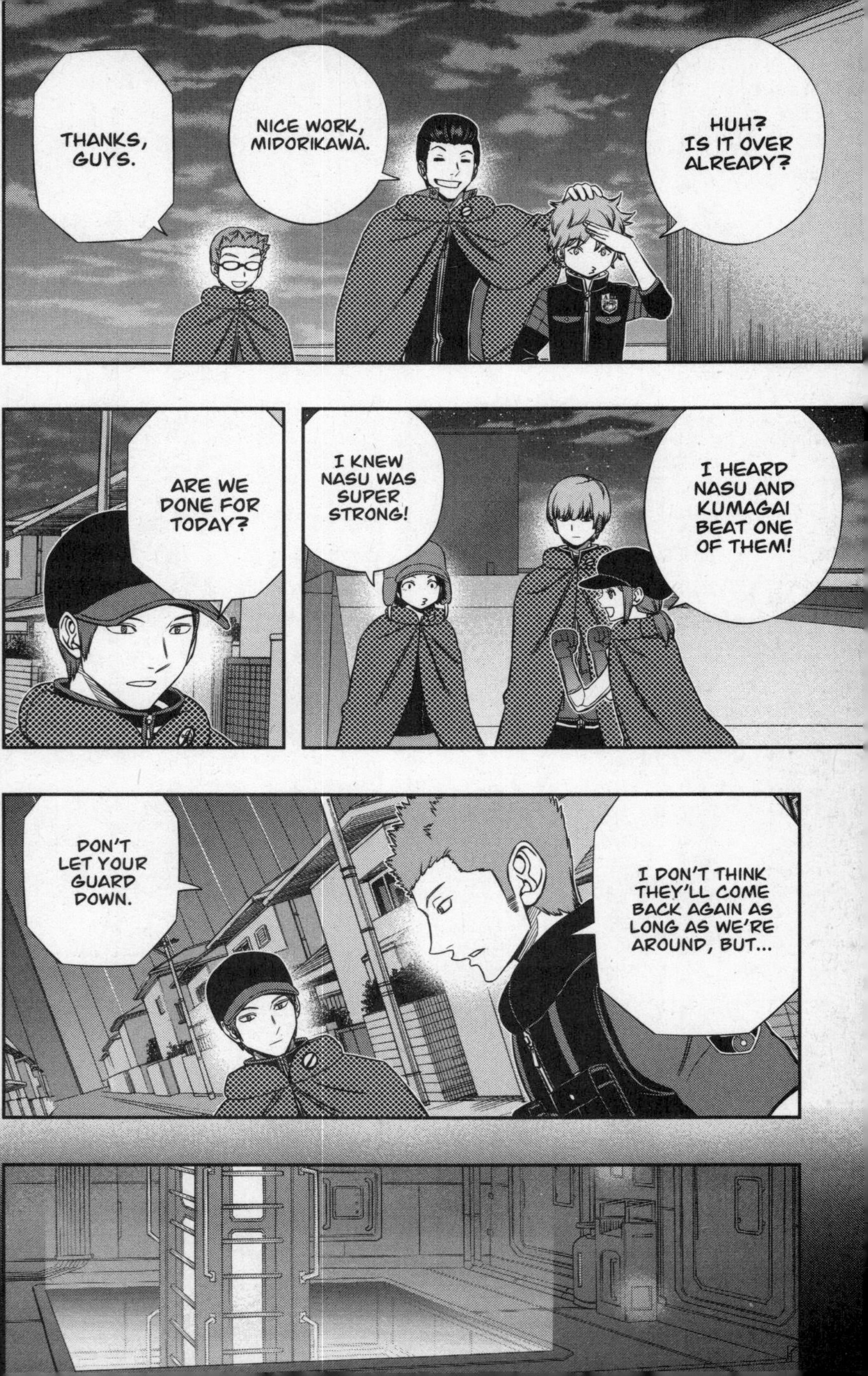
HUH? IS IT OVER ALREADY?
NICE WORK, MIDORIKAWA.
THANKS, GUYS.
I HEARD NASU AND KUMAGAI BEAT ONE OF THEM!
I KNEW NASU WAS SUPER STRONG!
ARE WE DONE FOR TODAY?
I DON'T THINK THEY'LL COME BACK AGAIN AS LONG AS WE'RE AROUND, BUT...
DON'T LET YOUR GUARD DOWN.

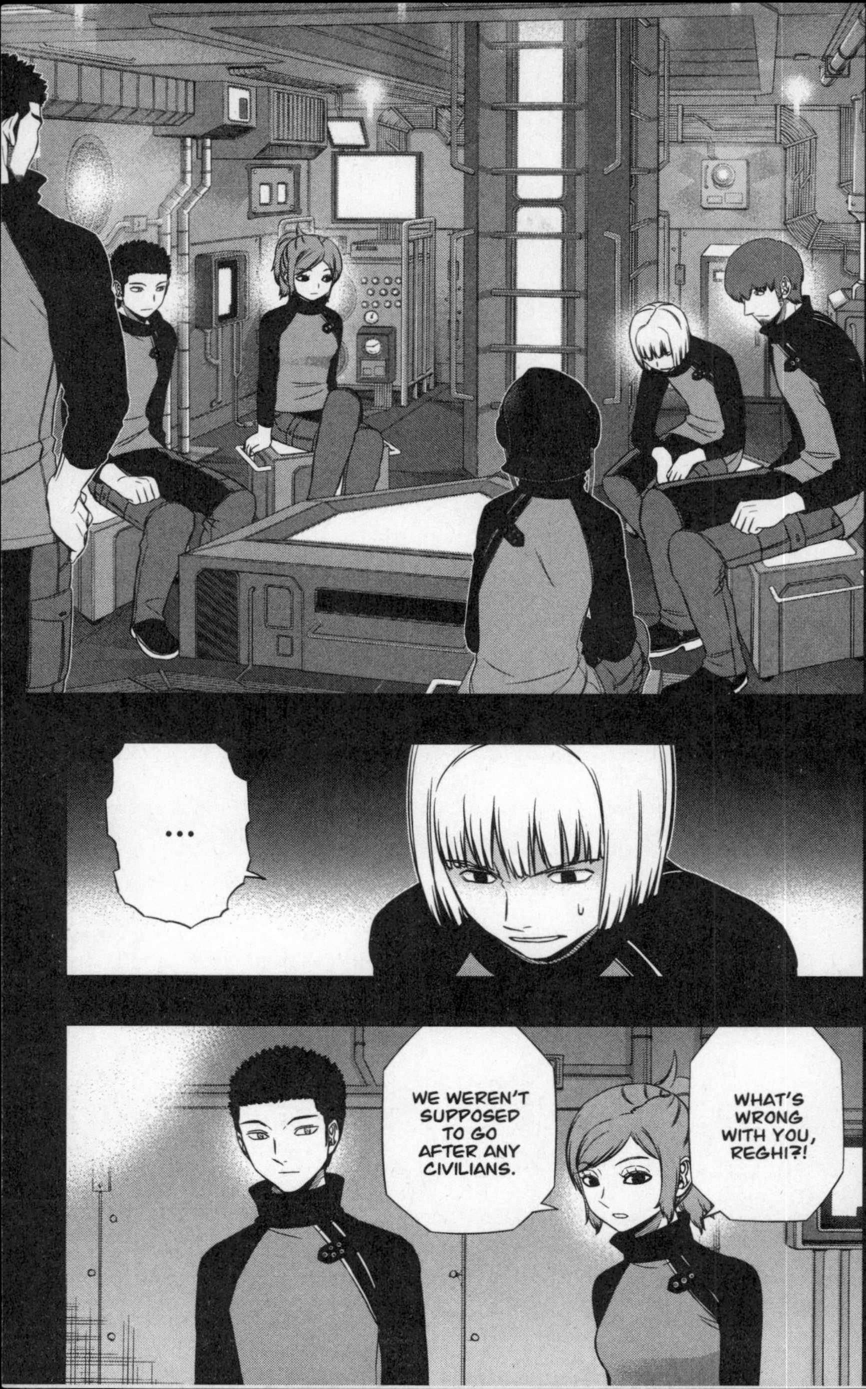
...
WHAT'S WRONG WITH YOU, REGHI?!
WE WEREN'T SUPPOSED TO GO AFTER ANY CIVILIANS.

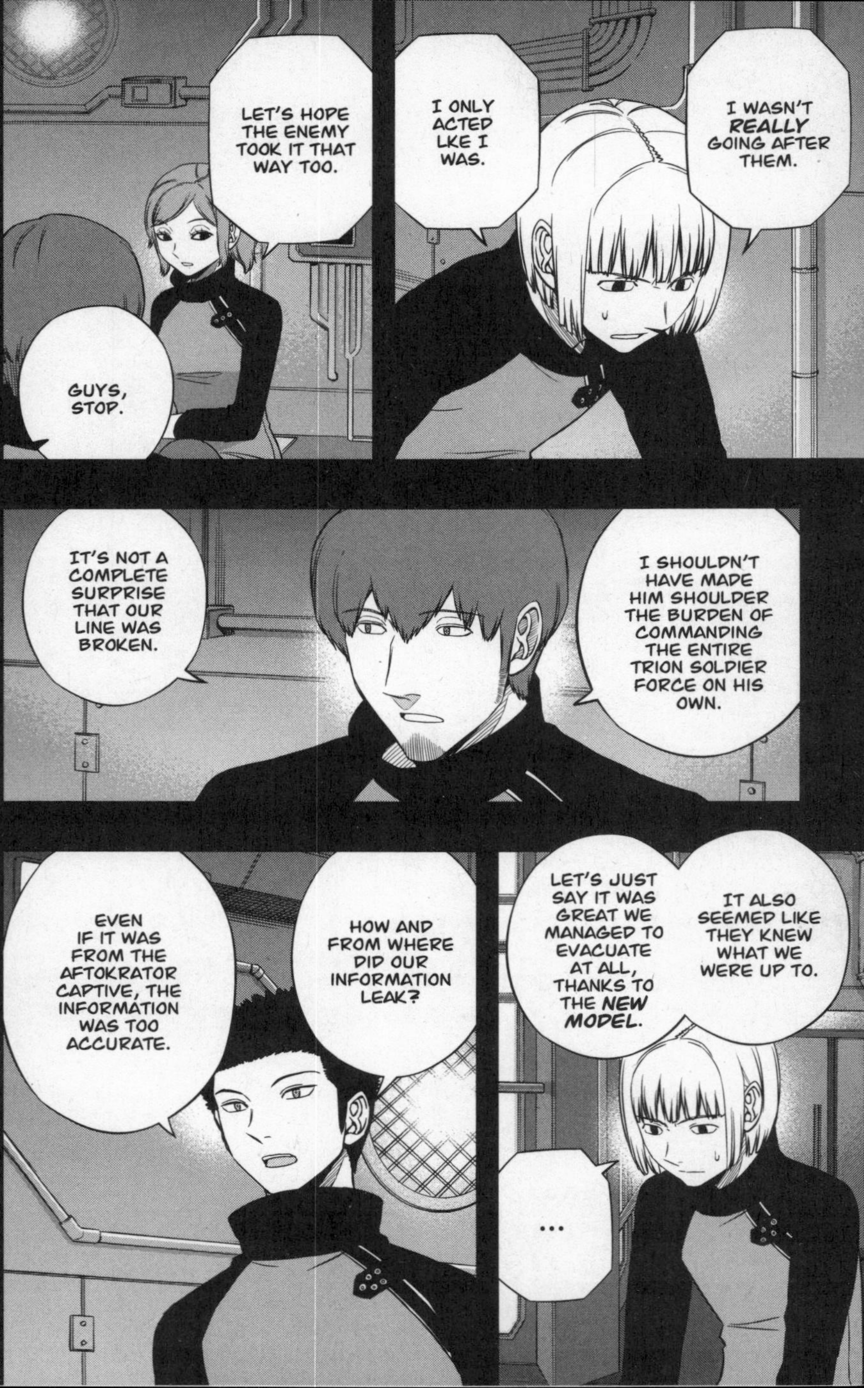

I WASN'T REALLY GOING AFTER THEM.
I ONLY ACTED LKE I WAS.
LET'S HOPE THE ENEMY TOOK IT THAT WAY TOO.
GUYS, STOP.
I SHOULDN'T HAVE MADE HIM SHOULDER THE BURDEN OF COMMANDING THE ENTIRE TRION SOLDIER FORCE ON HIS OWN.
IT'S NOT A COMPLETE SURPRISE THAT OUR LINE WAS BROKEN.
IT ALSO SEEMED LIKE THEY KNEW WHAT WE WERE UP TO.
LET'S JUST SAY IT WAS GREAT WE MANAGED TO EVACUATE AT ALL, THANKS TO THE NEW MODEL.
...
HOW AND FROM WHERE DID OUR INFORMATION LEAK?
EVEN IF IT WAS FROM THE AFTOKRATOR CAPTIVE, THE INFORMATION WAS TOO ACCURATE.

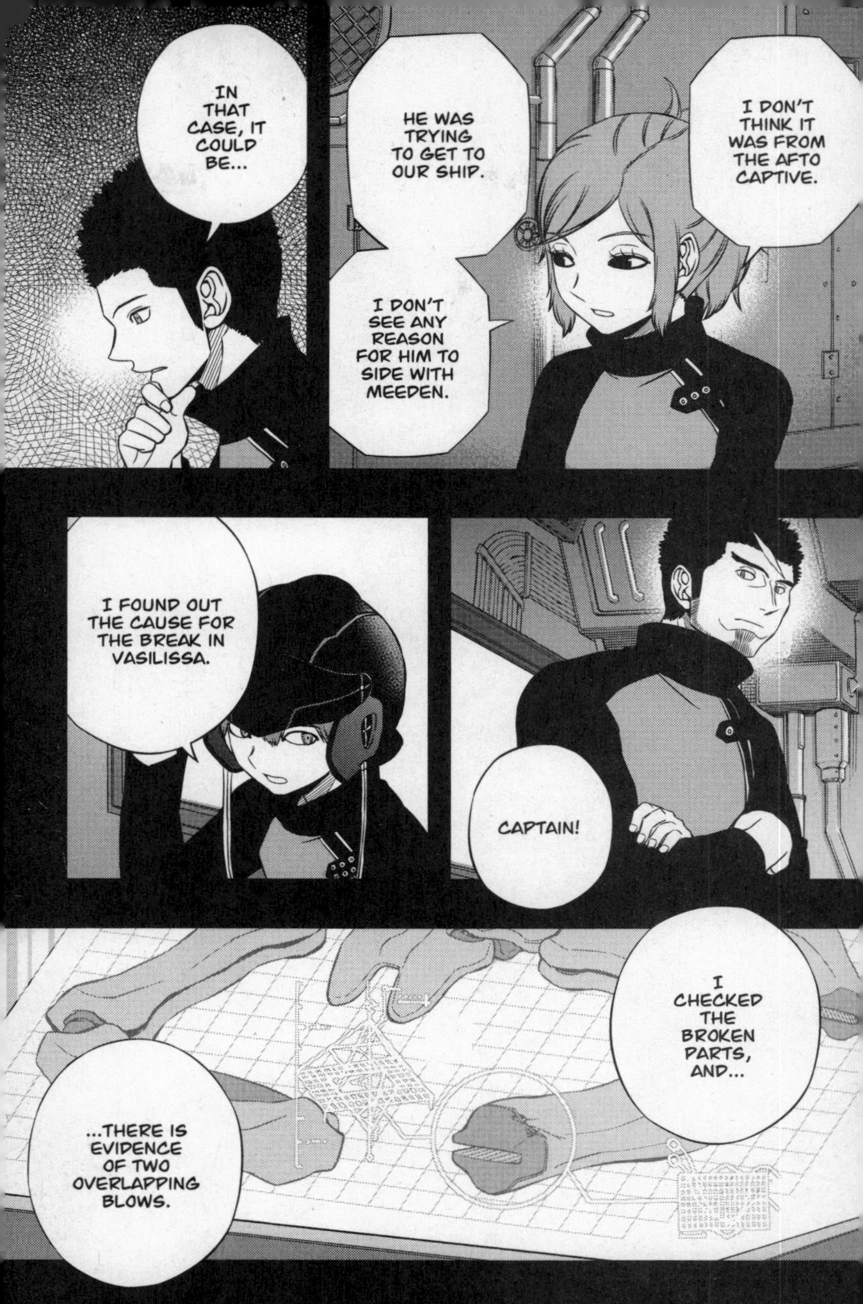
I DON'T THINK IT WAS FROM THE AFTO CAPTIVE.
HE WAS TRYING TO GET TO OUR SHIP.
I DON'T SEE ANY REASON FOR HIM TO SIDE WITH MEEDEN.
IN THAT CASE, IT COULD BE...
CAPTAIN!
I FOUND OUT THE CAUSE FOR THE BREAK IN VASILISSA.
I CHECKED THE BROKEN PARTS, AND...
...THERE IS EVIDENCE OF TWO OVERLAPPING BLOWS.

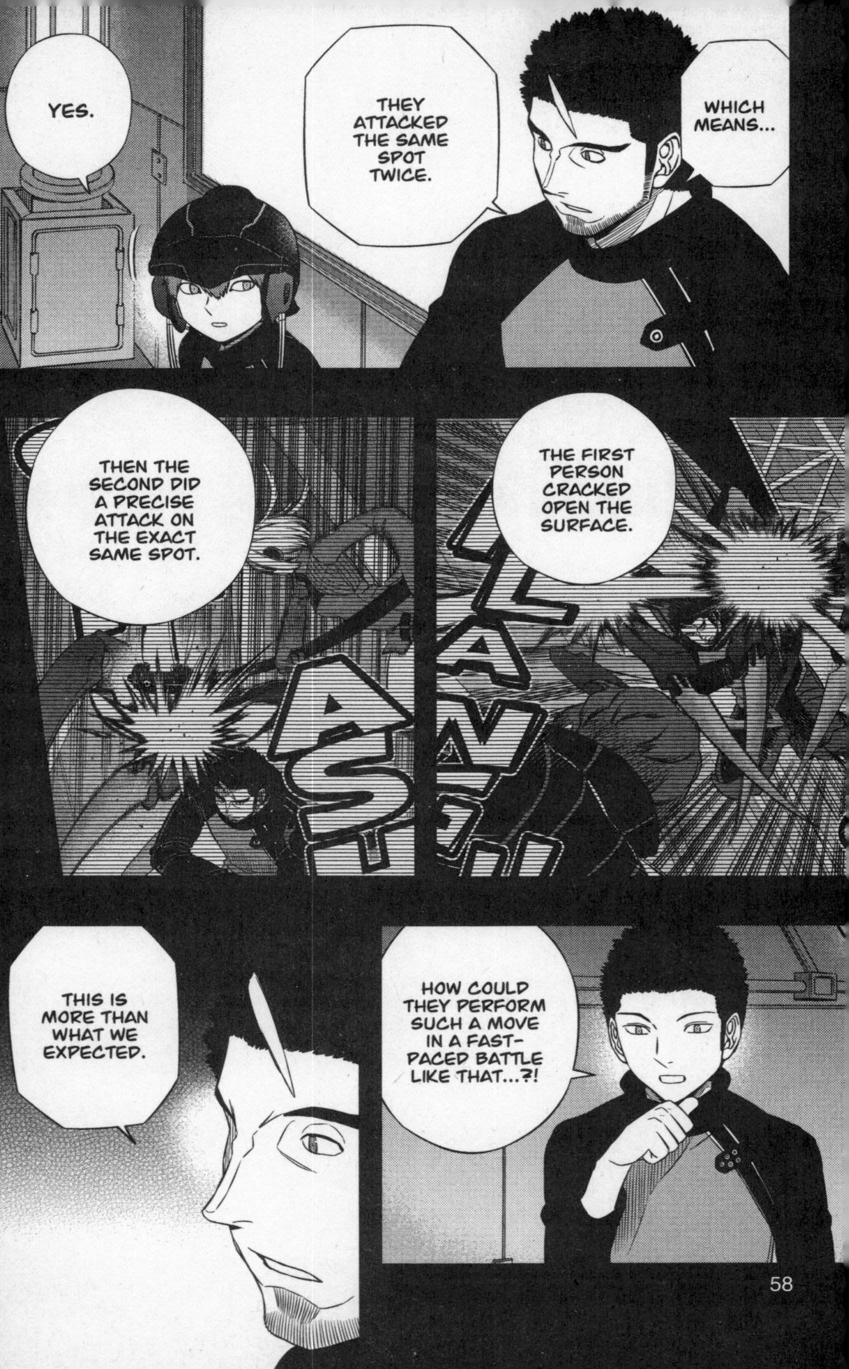
WHICH MEANS...
THEY ATTACKED THE SAME SPOT TWICE.
YES.
THE FIRST PERSON CRACKED OPEN THE SURFACE.
THEN THE SECOND DID A PRECISE ATTACK ON THE EXACT SAME SPOT.
HOW COULD THEY PERFORM SUCH A MOVE IN A FAST-PACED BATTLE LIKE THAT...?!
THIS IS MORE THAN WHAT WE EXPECTED.

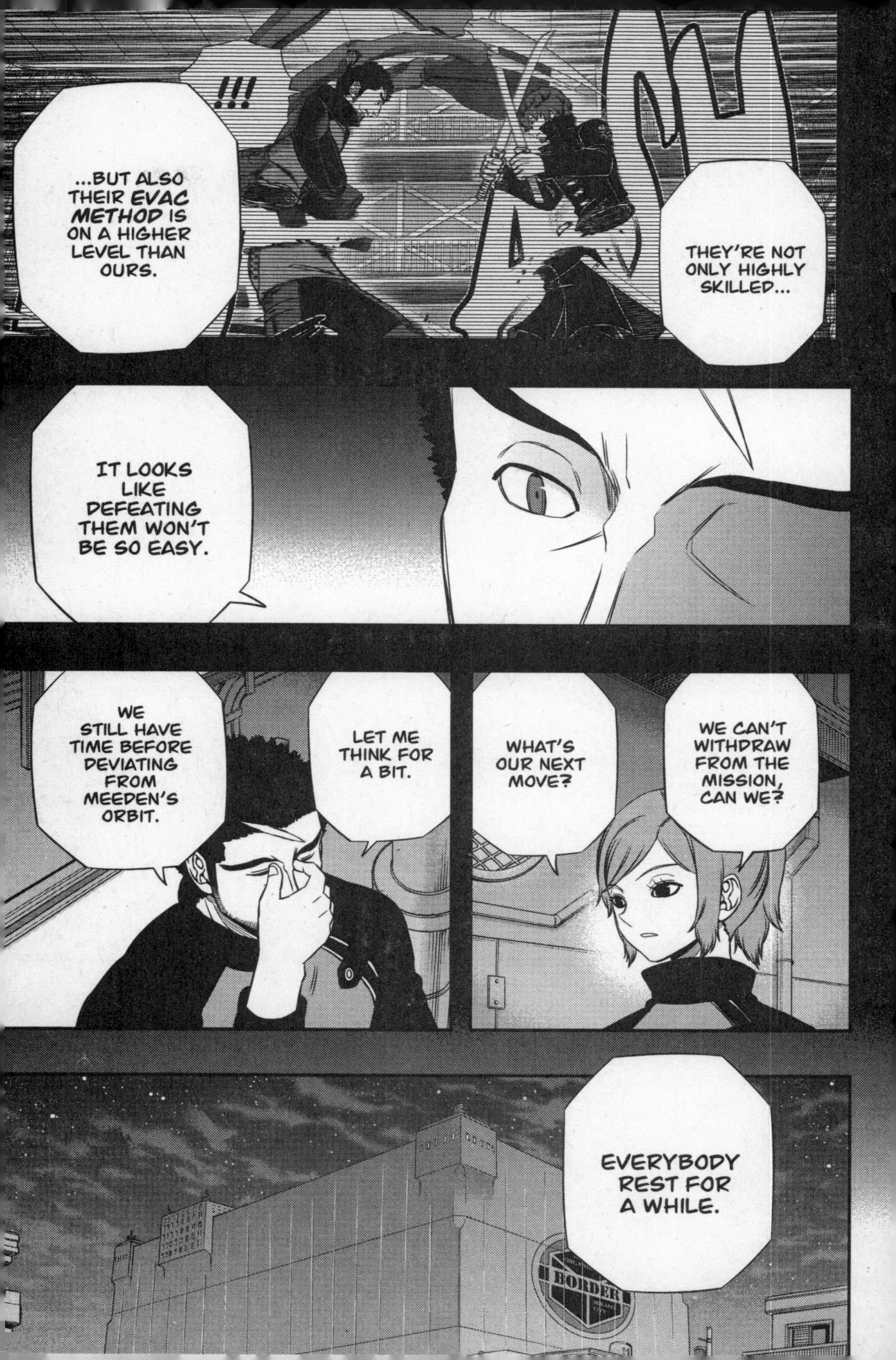
THEY'RE NOT ONLY HIGHLY SKILLED...
!!!
...BUT ALSO THEIR *EVAC METHOD* IS ON A HIGHER LEVEL THAN OURS.
IT LOOKS LIKE DEFEATING THEM WON'T BE SO EASY.
WE CAN'T WITHDRAW FROM THE MISSION, CAN WE?
WHAT'S OUR NEXT MOVE?
LET ME THINK FOR A BIT.
WE STILL HAVE TIME BEFORE DEVIATING FROM MEEDEN'S ORBIT.
EVERYBODY REST FOR A WHILE.
BORDER

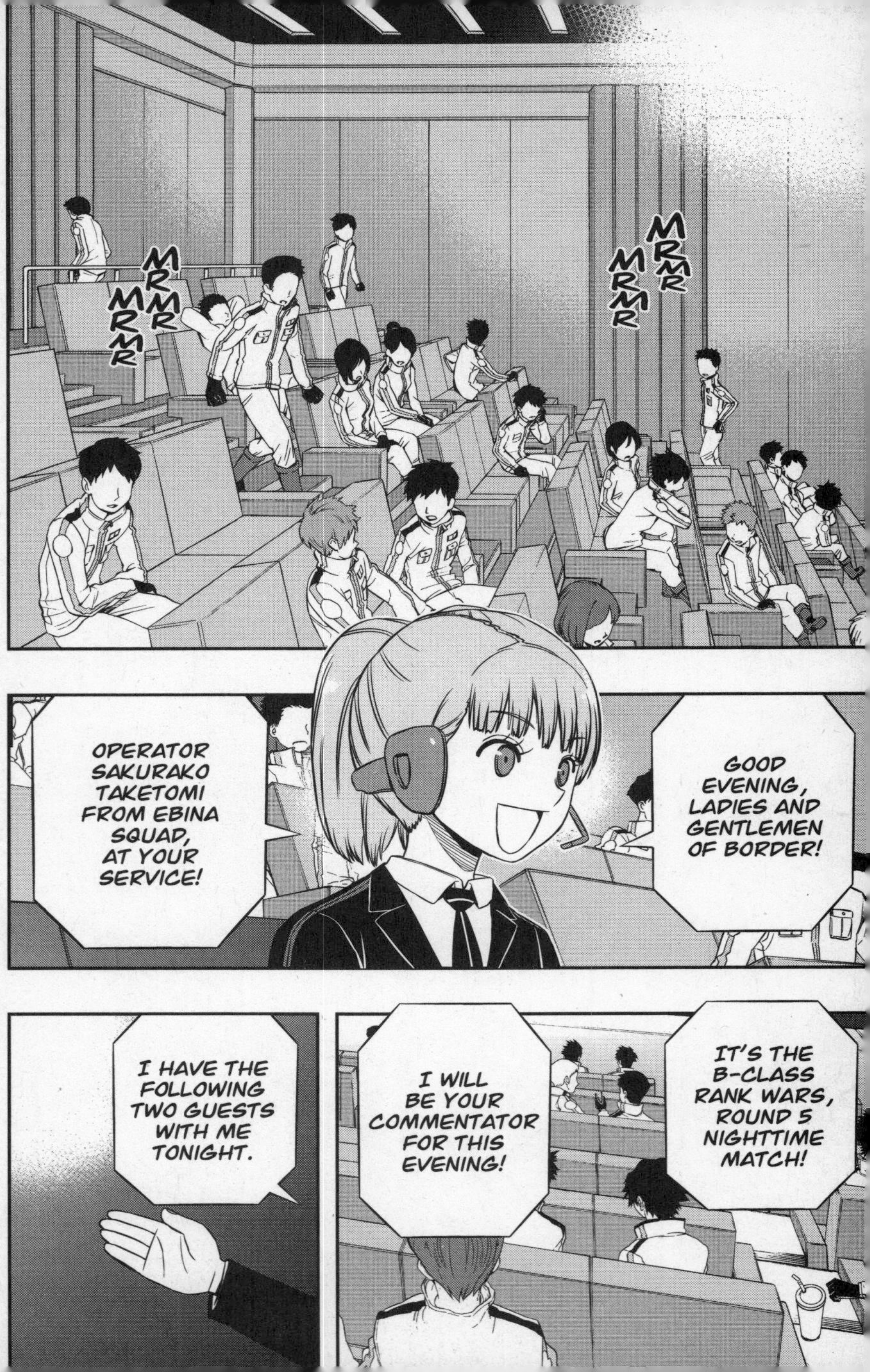
MRMR
MRMR
MRMR
MRMR
GOOD EVENING, LADIES AND GENTLEMEN OF BORDER!
OPERATOR SAKURAKO TAKETOMI FROM EBINA SQUAD, AT YOUR SERVICE!
IT'S THE B-CLASS RANK WARS, ROUND 5 NIGHTTIME MATCH!
I WILL BE YOUR COMMENTATOR FOR THIS EVENING!
I HAVE THE FOLLOWING TWO GUESTS WITH ME TONIGHT.

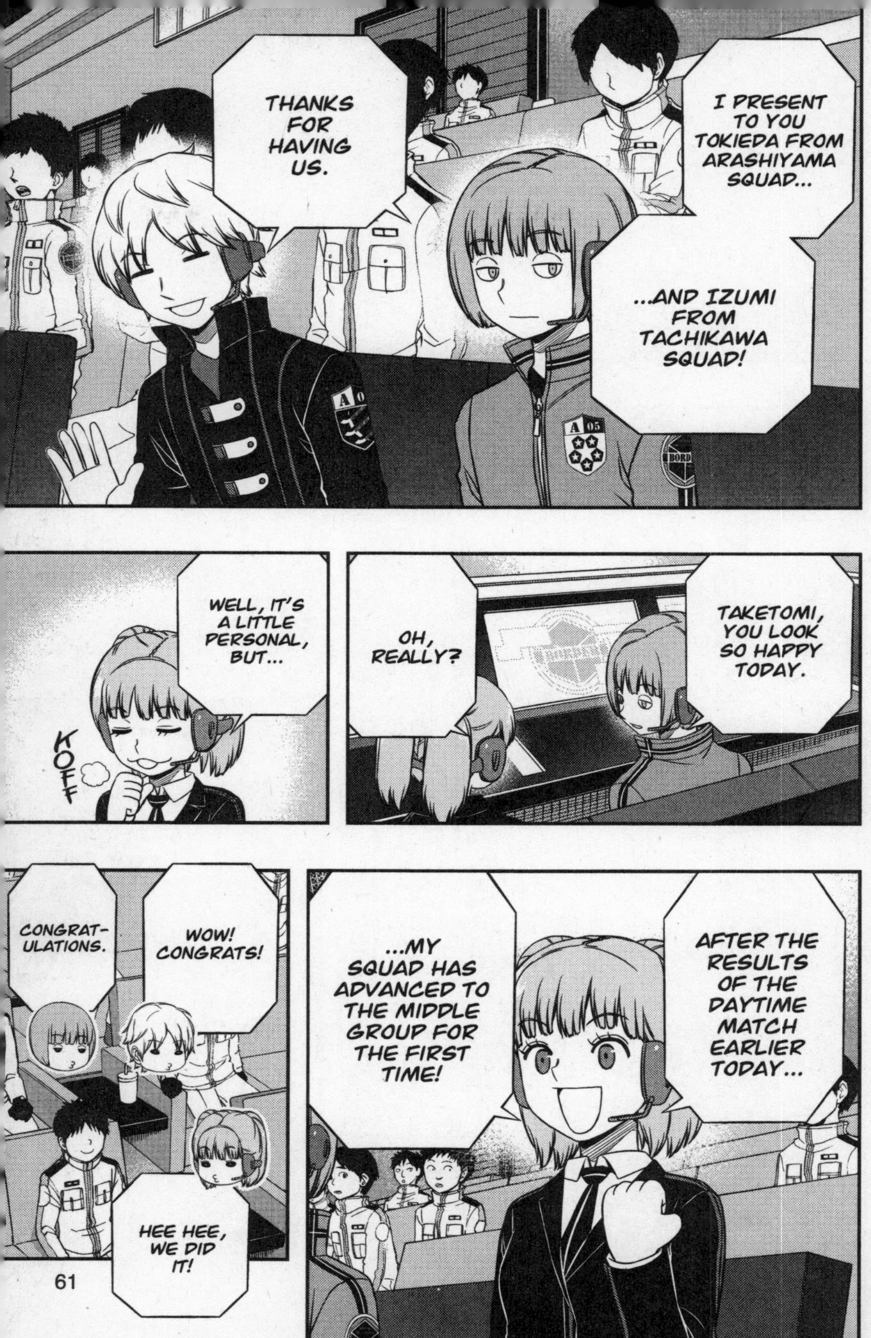
I PRESENT TO YOU TOKIEDA FROM ARASHIYAMA SQUAD...
...AND IZUMI FROM TACHIKAWA SQUAD!
THANKS FOR HAVING US.
TAKETOMI, YOU LOOK SO HAPPY TODAY.
OH, REALLY?
WELL, IT'S A LITTLE PERSONAL, BUT...
KOFF
AFTER THE RESULTS OF THE DAYTIME MATCH EARLIER TODAY...
...MY SQUAD HAS ADVANCED TO THE MIDDLE GROUP FOR THE FIRST TIME!
WOW! CONGRATS!
CONGRAT-ULATIONS.
HEE HEE, WE DID IT!

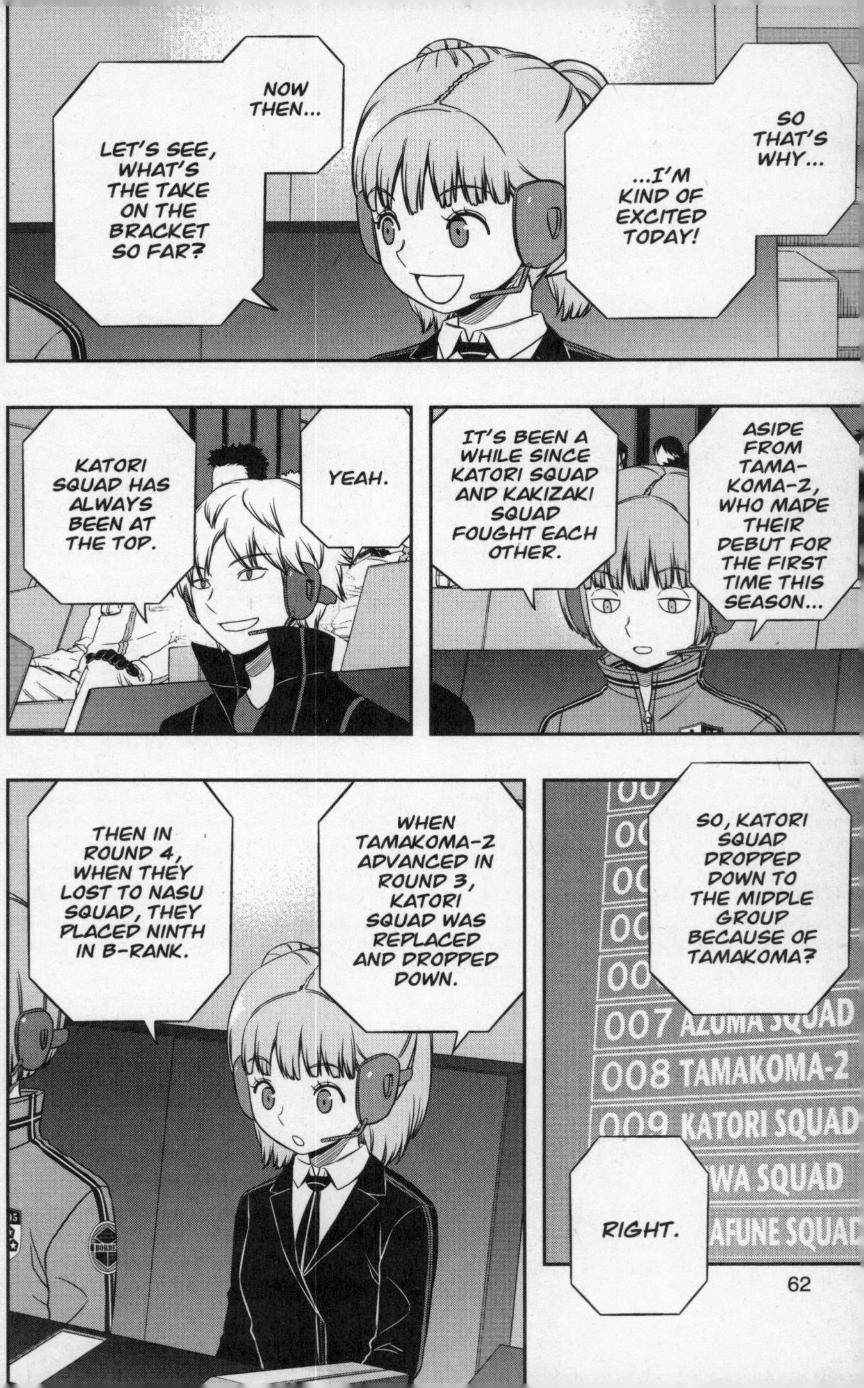
SO THAT'S WHY...
...I'M KIND OF EXCITED TODAY!
NOW THEN...
LET'S SEE, WHAT'S THE TAKE ON THE BRACKET SO FAR?
ASIDE FROM TAMA-KOMA-2, WHO MADE THEIR DEBUT FOR THE FIRST TIME THIS SEASON...
IT'S BEEN A WHILE SINCE KATORI SQUAD AND KAKIZAKI SQUAD FOUGHT EACH OTHER.
YEAH.
KATORI SQUAD HAS ALWAYS BEEN AT THE TOP.
SO, KATORI SQUAD DROPPED DOWN TO THE MIDDLE GROUP BECAUSE OF TAMAKOMA?
007 AZUMA SQUAD
008 TAMAKOMA-2
009 KATORI SQUAD
RIGHT.
WHEN TAMAKOMA-2 ADVANCED IN ROUND 3, KATORI SQUAD WAS REPLACED AND DROPPED DOWN.
THEN IN ROUND 4, WHEN THEY LOST TO NASU SQUAD, THEY PLACED NINTH IN B-RANK.

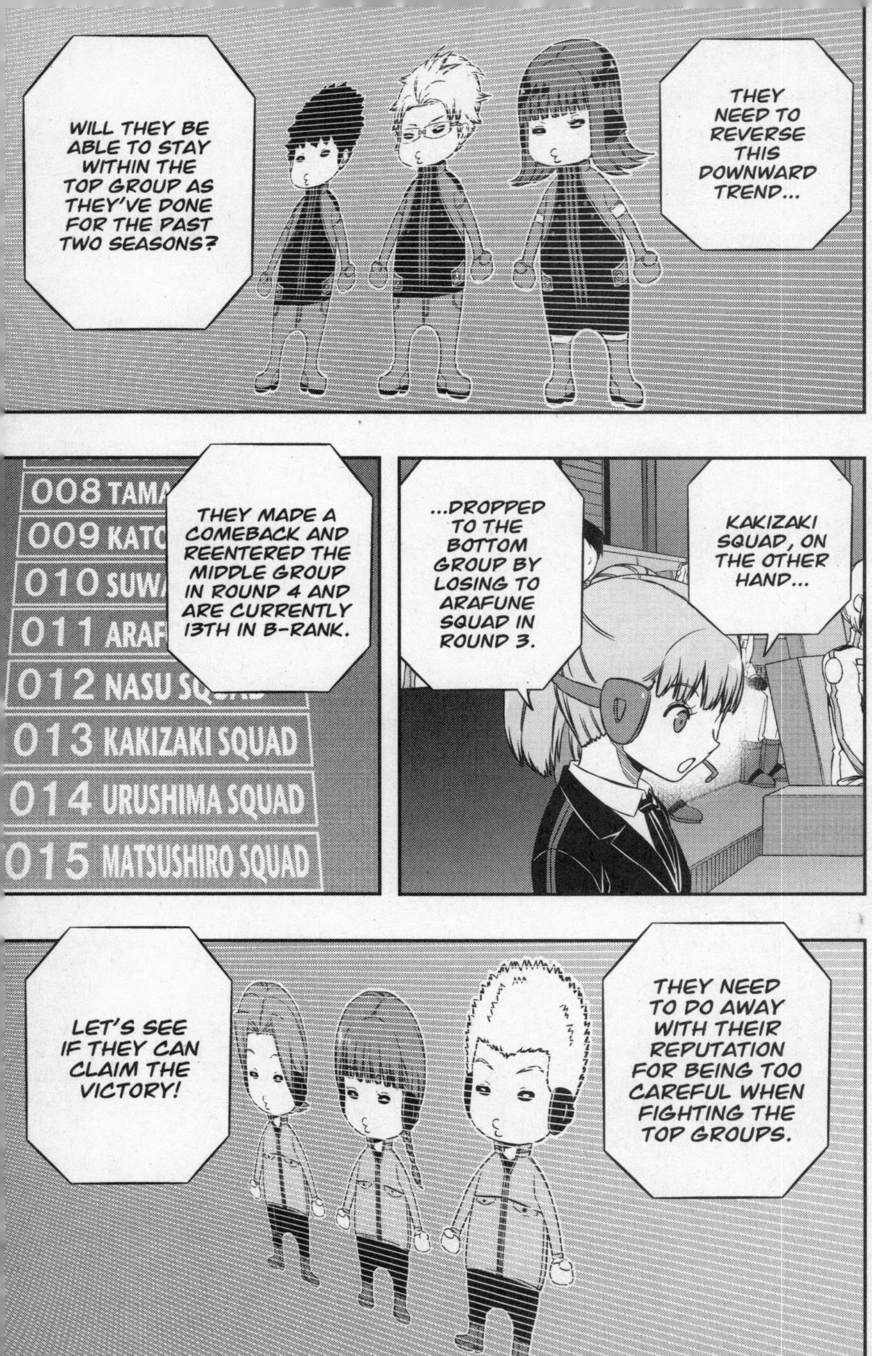
THEY NEED TO REVERSE THIS DOWNWARD TREND...
WILL THEY BE ABLE TO STAY WITHIN THE TOP GROUP AS THEY'VE DONE FOR THE PAST TWO SEASONS?
KAKIZAKI SQUAD, ON THE OTHER HAND...
...DROPPED TO THE BOTTOM GROUP BY LOSING TO ARAFUNE SQUAD IN ROUND 3.
THEY MADE A COMEBACK AND REENTERED THE MIDDLE GROUP IN ROUND 4 AND ARE CURRENTLY 13TH IN B-RANK.
012 NASU
013 KAKIZAKI SQUAD
014 URUSHIMA SQUAD
015 MATSUSHIRO SQUAD
THEY NEED TO DO AWAY WITH THEIR REPUTATION FOR BEING TOO CAREFUL WHEN FIGHTING THE TOP GROUPS.
LET'S SEE IF THEY CAN CLAIM THE VICTORY!

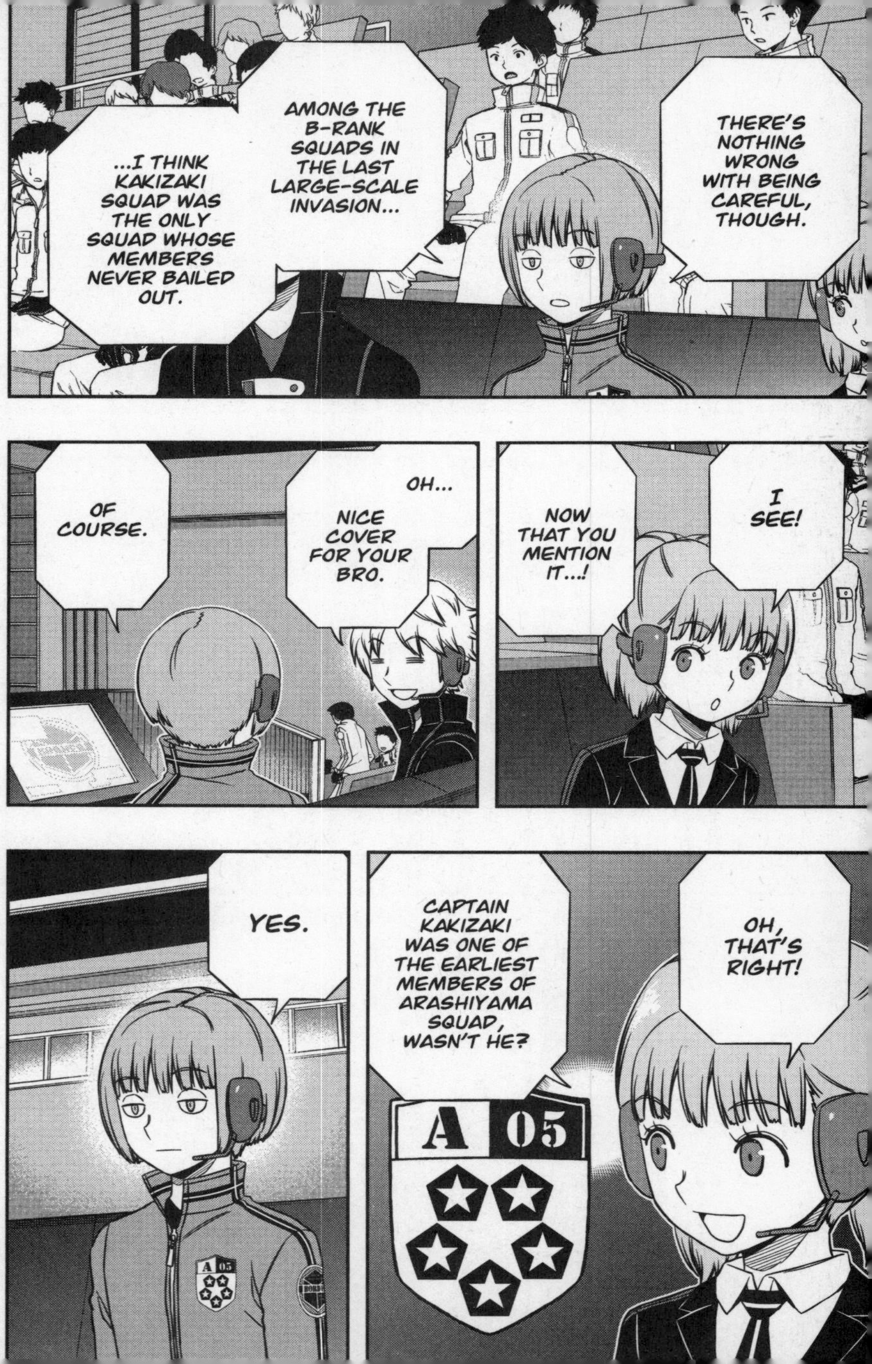
THERE'S NOTHING WRONG WITH BEING CAREFUL, THOUGH.
AMONG THE B-RANK SQUADS IN THE LAST LARGE-SCALE INVASION...
...I THINK KAKIZAKI SQUAD WAS THE ONLY SQUAD WHOSE MEMBERS NEVER BAILED OUT.
I SEE!
NOW THAT YOU MENTION IT...!
OH...
NICE COVER FOR YOUR BRO.
OF COURSE.
OH, THAT'S RIGHT!
CAPTAIN KAKIZAKI WAS ONE OF THE EARLIEST MEMBERS OF ARASHIYAMA SQUAD, WASN'T HE?
A 05
YES.

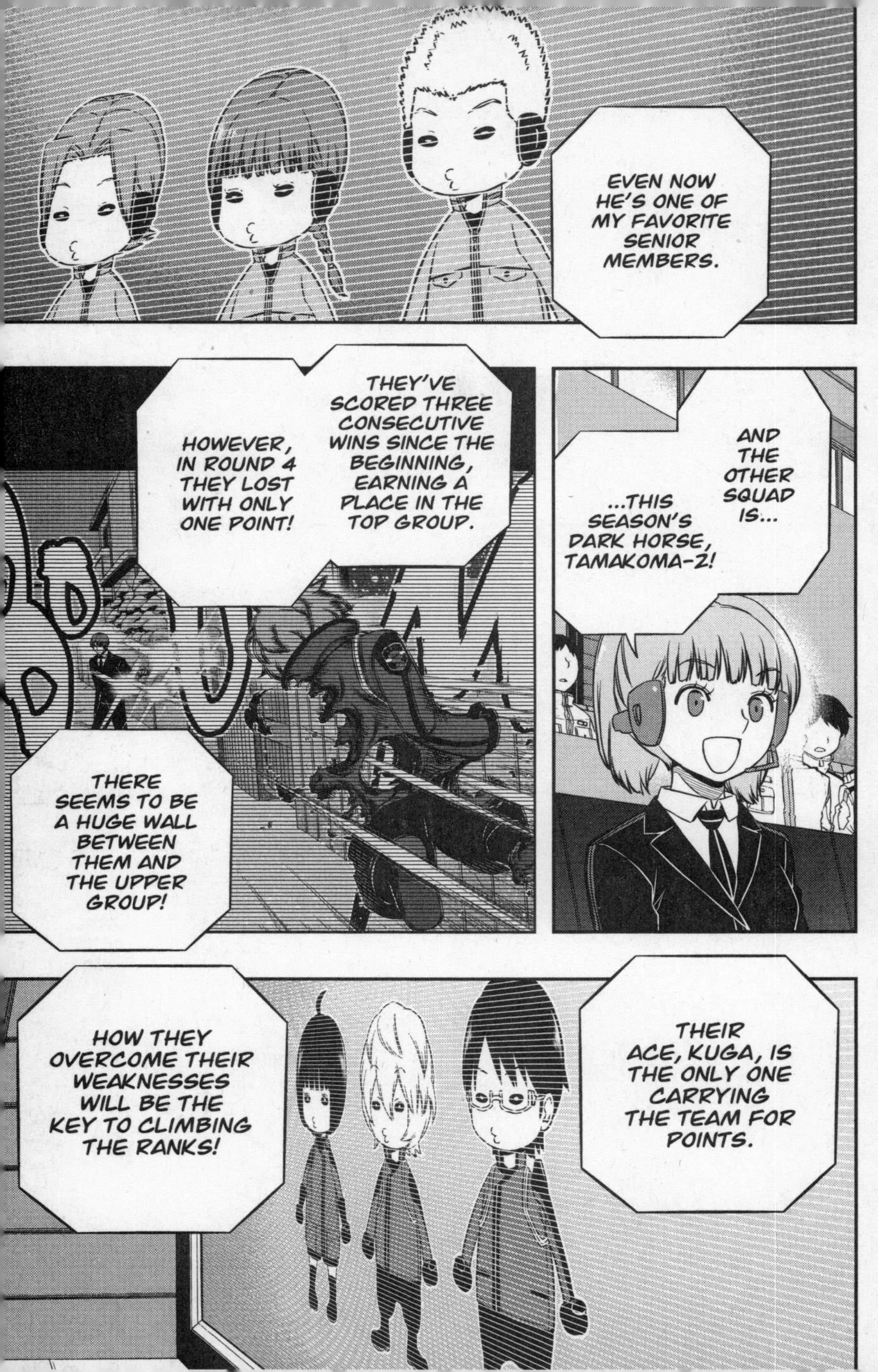
EVEN NOW HE'S ONE OF MY FAVORITE SENIOR MEMBERS.
AND THE OTHER SQUAD IS...
...THIS SEASON'S DARK HORSE, TAMAKOMA-2!
THEY'VE SCORED THREE CONSECUTIVE WINS SINCE THE BEGINNING, EARNING A PLACE IN THE TOP GROUP.
HOWEVER, IN ROUND 4 THEY LOST WITH ONLY ONE POINT!
THERE SEEMS TO BE A HUGE WALL BETWEEN THEM AND THE UPPER GROUP!
THEIR ACE, KUGA, IS THE ONLY ONE CARRYING THE TEAM FOR POINTS.
HOW THEY OVERCOME THEIR WEAKNESSES WILL BE THE KEY TO CLIMBING THE RANKS!

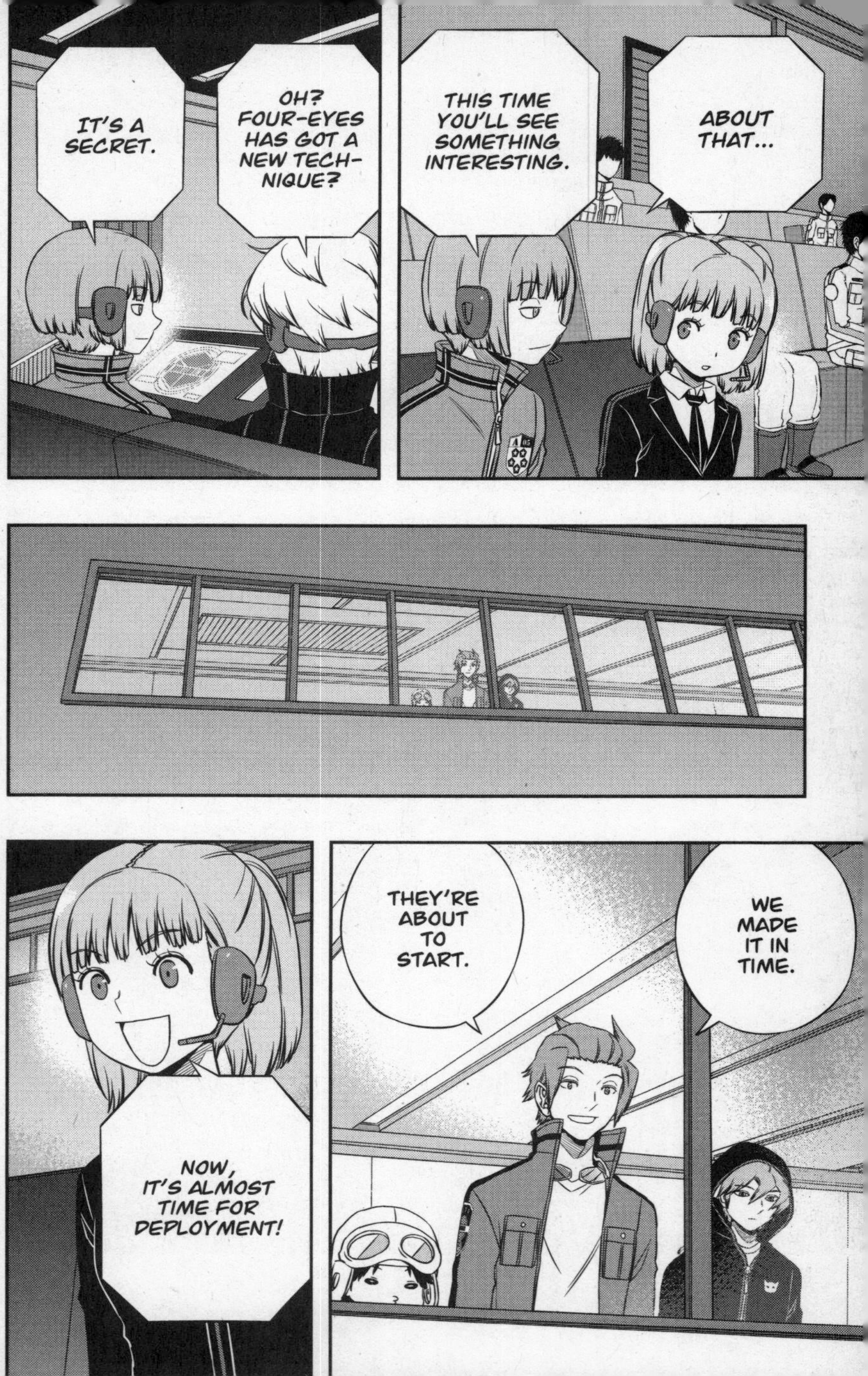
ABOUT THAT...
THIS TIME YOU'LL SEE SOMETHING INTERESTING.
OH? FOUR-EYES HAS GOT A NEW TECHNIQUE?
IT'S A SECRET.
WE MADE IT IN TIME.
THEY'RE ABOUT TO START.
NOW, IT'S ALMOST TIME FOR DEPLOYMENT!

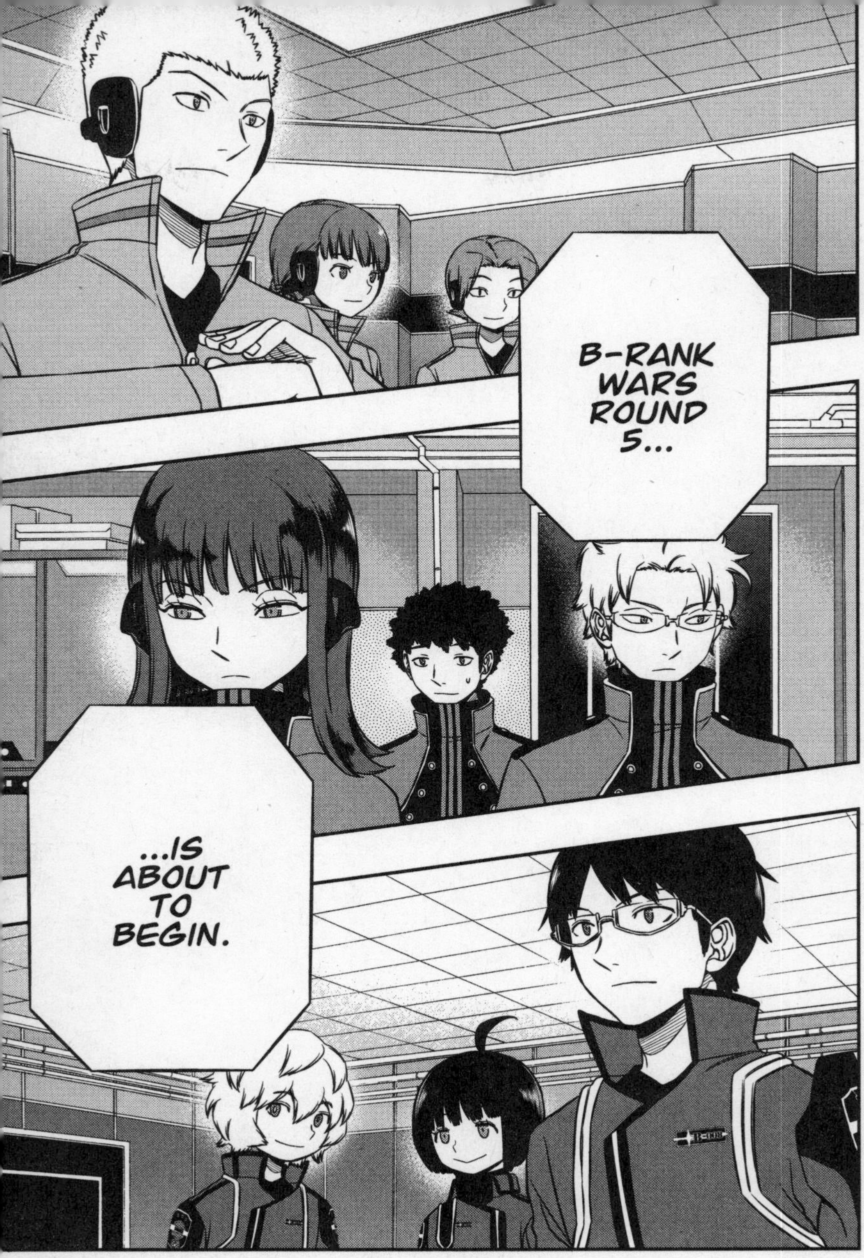
B-RANK WARS ROUND 5...
...IS ABOUT TO BEGIN.

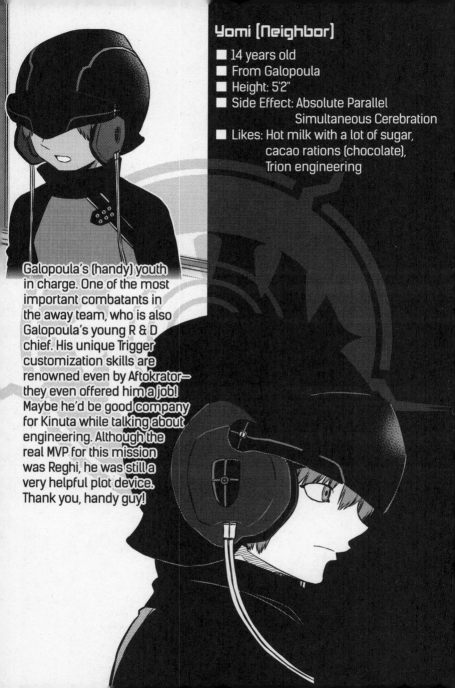

Yomi (Neighbor)

- 14 years old
- From Galopoula
- Height: 5'2"
- Side Effect: Absolute Parallel Simultaneous Cerebration
- Likes: Hot milk with a lot of sugar, cacao rations (chocolate), Trion engineering

Galopoula's (handy) youth in charge. One of the most important combatants in the away team, who is also Galopoula's young R & D chief. His unique Trigger customization skills are renowned even by Aftokrator— they even offered him a job! Maybe he'd be good company for Kinuta while talking about engineering. Although the real MVP for this mission was Reghi, he was still a very helpful plot device. Thank you, handy guy!

Tamakoma-2 Strategy Room

A few minutes earlier...

LET'S REVIEW THE OPPONENTS' STRATEGIES.

Chapter 137 Katori Squad

KATORI SQUAD...

...IS AN ACE-FOCUSED GROUP LIKE OURS.

THEIR ACE GETS MOST OF THE POINTS...

...AND THE OTHER TWO USE CHAMELEONS AS SUPPORT.

SUB TRIGGER   MAIN TRIGGER

SUB TRIGGER   MA

SUB TRIGGER   MAIN

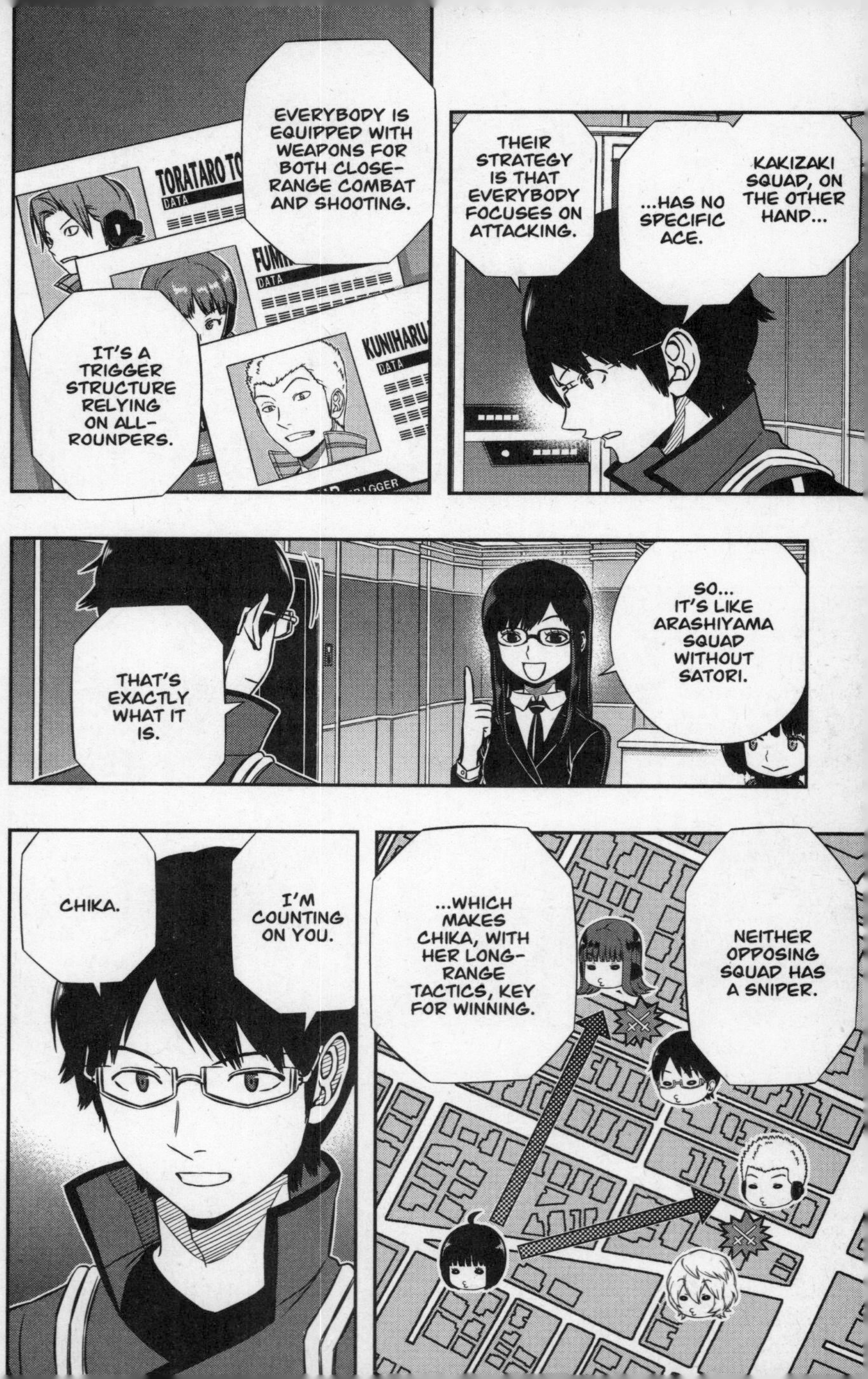
KAKIZAKI SQUAD, ON THE OTHER HAND...
...HAS NO SPECIFIC ACE.
THEIR STRATEGY IS THAT EVERYBODY FOCUSES ON ATTACKING.
EVERYBODY IS EQUIPPED WITH WEAPONS FOR BOTH CLOSE-RANGE COMBAT AND SHOOTING.
IT'S A TRIGGER STRUCTURE RELYING ON ALL-ROUNDERS.
SO... IT'S LIKE ARASHIYAMA SQUAD WITHOUT SATORI.
THAT'S EXACTLY WHAT IT IS.
NEITHER OPPOSING SQUAD HAS A SNIPER.
...WHICH MAKES CHIKA, WITH HER LONG-RANGE TACTICS, KEY FOR WINNING.
I'M COUNTING ON YOU.
CHIKA.

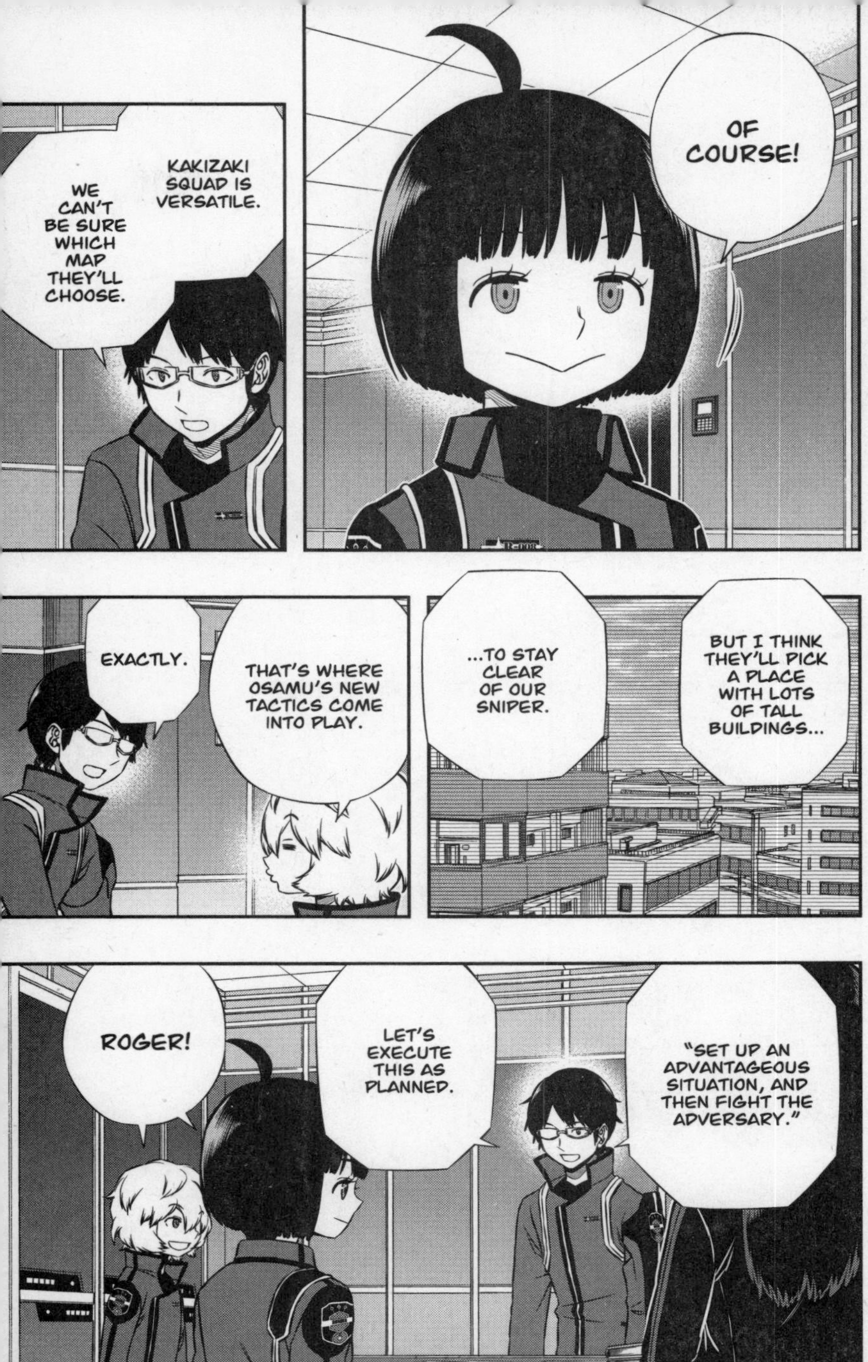
OF COURSE!
KAKIZAKI SQUAD IS VERSATILE.
WE CAN'T BE SURE WHICH MAP THEY'LL CHOOSE.
BUT I THINK THEY'LL PICK A PLACE WITH LOTS OF TALL BUILDINGS...
...TO STAY CLEAR OF OUR SNIPER.
THAT'S WHERE OSAMU'S NEW TACTICS COME INTO PLAY.
EXACTLY.
"SET UP AN ADVANTAGEOUS SITUATION, AND THEN FIGHT THE ADVERSARY."
LET'S EXECUTE THIS AS PLANNED.
ROGER!

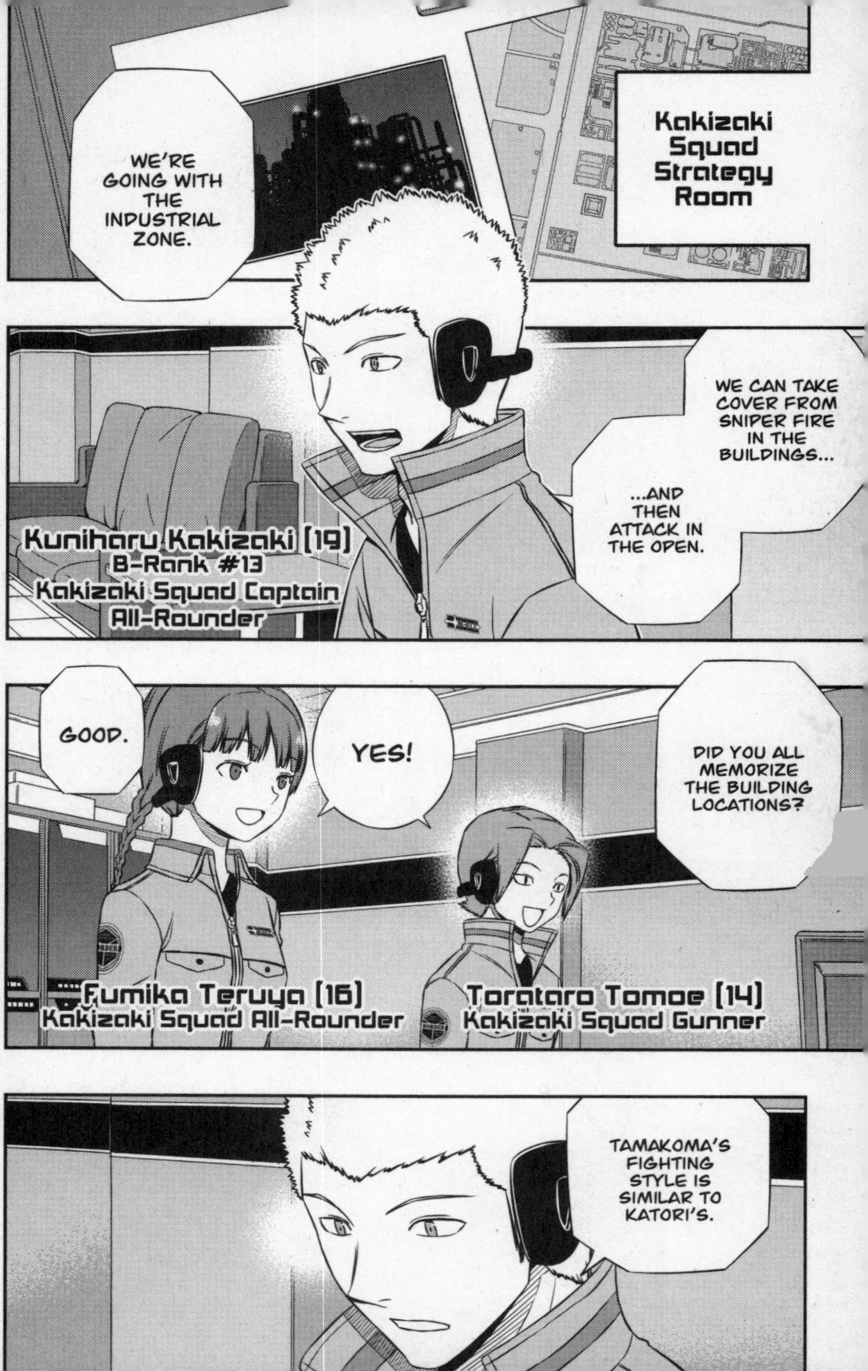
Kakizaki Squad Strategy Room
WE'RE GOING WITH THE INDUSTRIAL ZONE.
WE CAN TAKE COVER FROM SNIPER FIRE IN THE BUILDINGS...
...AND THEN ATTACK IN THE OPEN.
Kuniharu Kakizaki [19] B-Rank #13 Kakizaki Squad Captain All-Rounder
DID YOU ALL MEMORIZE THE BUILDING LOCATIONS?
YES!
GOOD.
Torataro Tomoe [14] Kakizaki Squad Gunner
Fumika Teruya [16] Kakizaki Squad All-Rounder
TAMAKOMA'S FIGHTING STYLE IS SIMILAR TO KATORI'S.

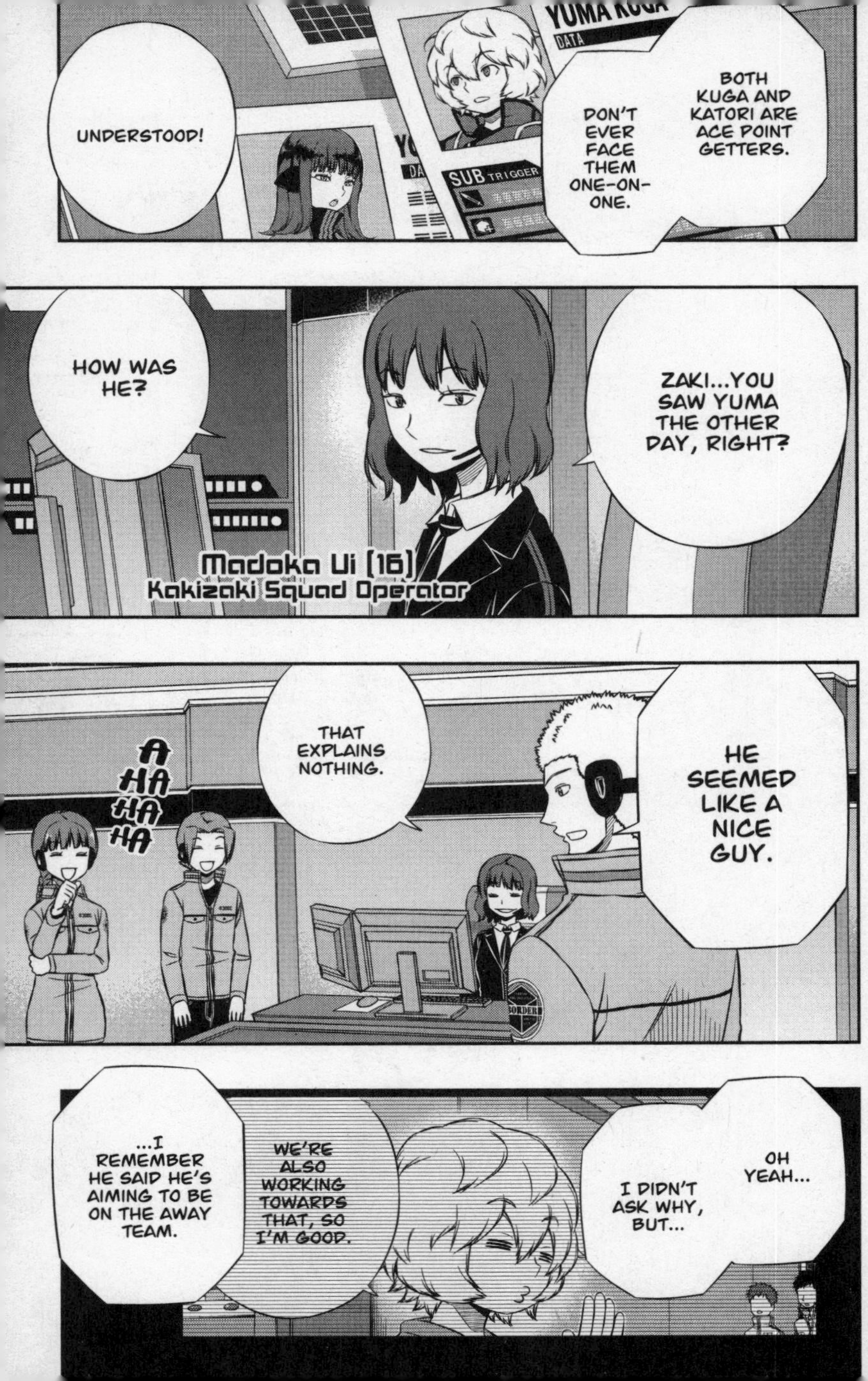
YUMA KUGA
DATA
SUB TRIGGER
BOTH KUGA AND KATORI ARE ACE POINT GETTERS.
DON'T EVER FACE THEM ONE-ON-ONE.
UNDERSTOOD!
ZAKI...YOU SAW YUMA THE OTHER DAY, RIGHT?
HOW WAS HE?
Madoka Ui (16)
Kakizaki Squad Operator
HE SEEMED LIKE A NICE GUY.
THAT EXPLAINS NOTHING.
AHAHAHAHA
BORDER
OH YEAH...
I DIDN'T ASK WHY, BUT...
...I REMEMBER HE SAID HE'S AIMING TO BE ON THE AWAY TEAM.
WE'RE ALSO WORKING TOWARDS THAT, SO I'M GOOD.

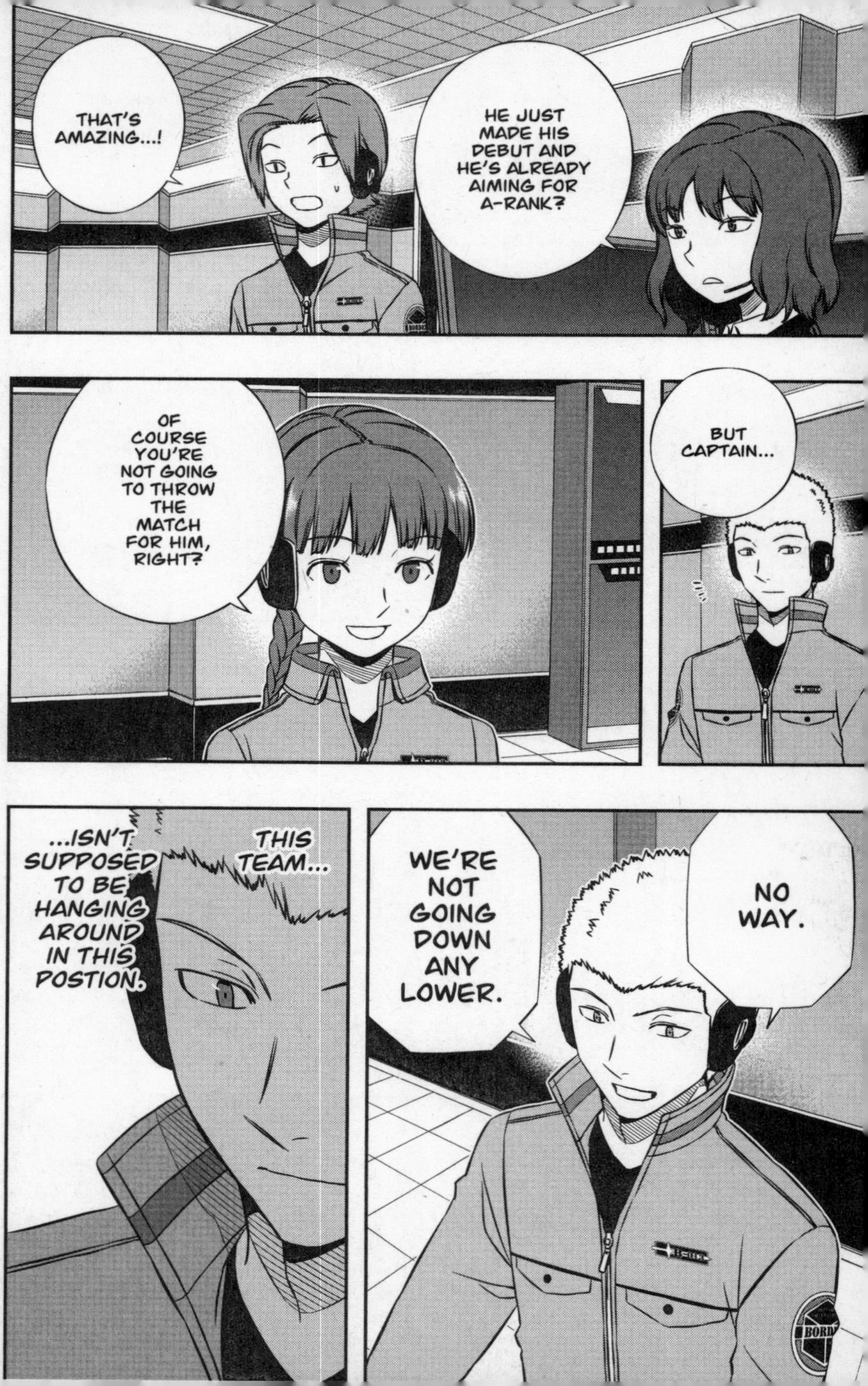
HE JUST MADE HIS DEBUT AND HE'S ALREADY AIMING FOR A-RANK?
THAT'S AMAZING...!
BUT CAPTAIN...
OF COURSE YOU'RE NOT GOING TO THROW THE MATCH FOR HIM, RIGHT?
NO WAY.
WE'RE NOT GOING DOWN ANY LOWER.
THIS TEAM...
...ISN'T SUPPOSED TO BE HANGING AROUND IN THIS POSTION.

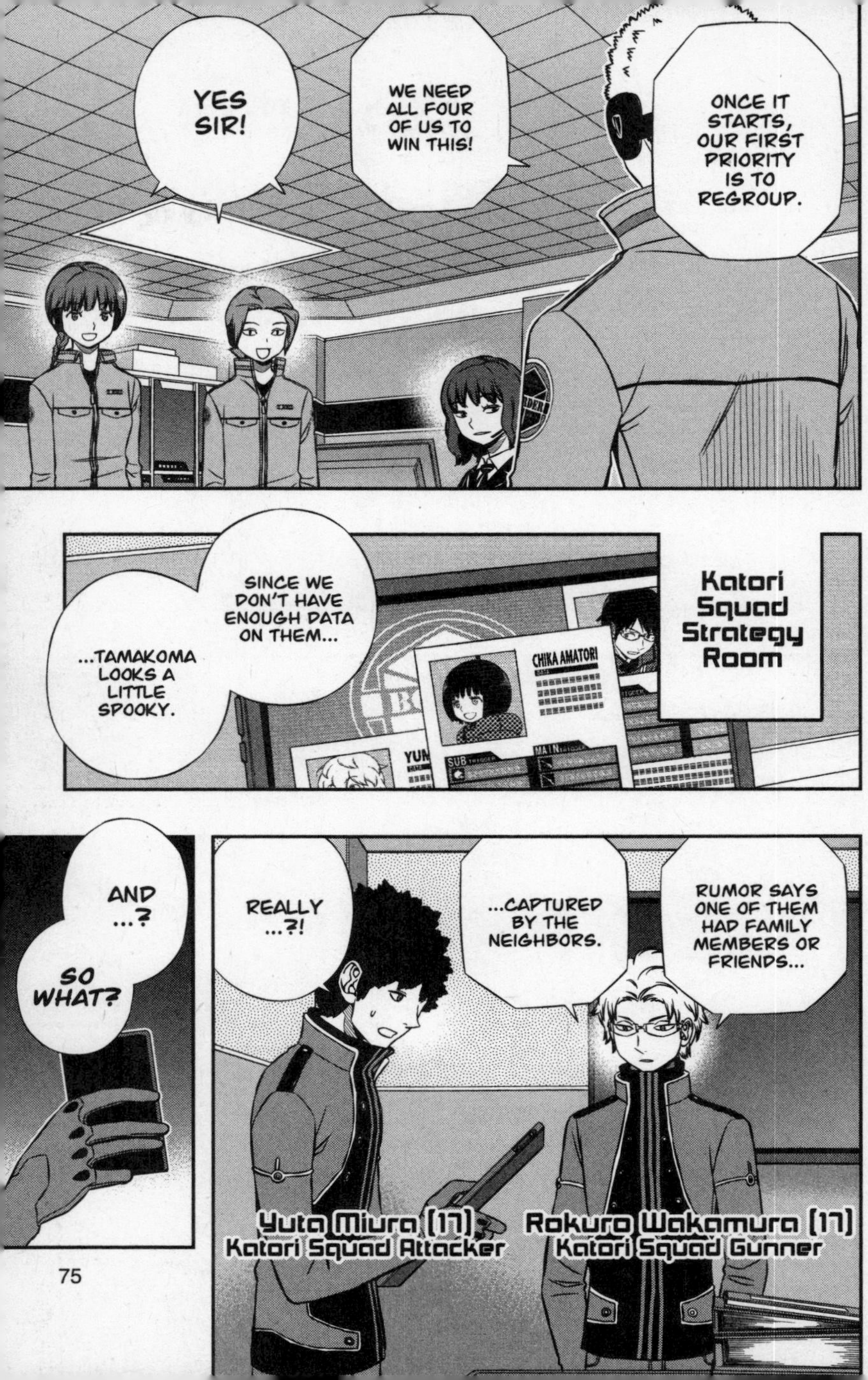
ONCE IT STARTS, OUR FIRST PRIORITY IS TO REGROUP.
WE NEED ALL FOUR OF US TO WIN THIS!
YES SIR!
Katori Squad Strategy Room
SINCE WE DON'T HAVE ENOUGH DATA ON THEM...
...TAMAKOMA LOOKS A LITTLE SPOOKY.
CHIKA AMATORI
RUMOR SAYS ONE OF THEM HAD FAMILY MEMBERS OR FRIENDS...
...CAPTURED BY THE NEIGHBORS.
REALLY ...?!
Rokuro Wakamura (17) Katori Squad Gunner
Yuta Miura (17) Katori Squad Attacker
AND ...?
SO WHAT?

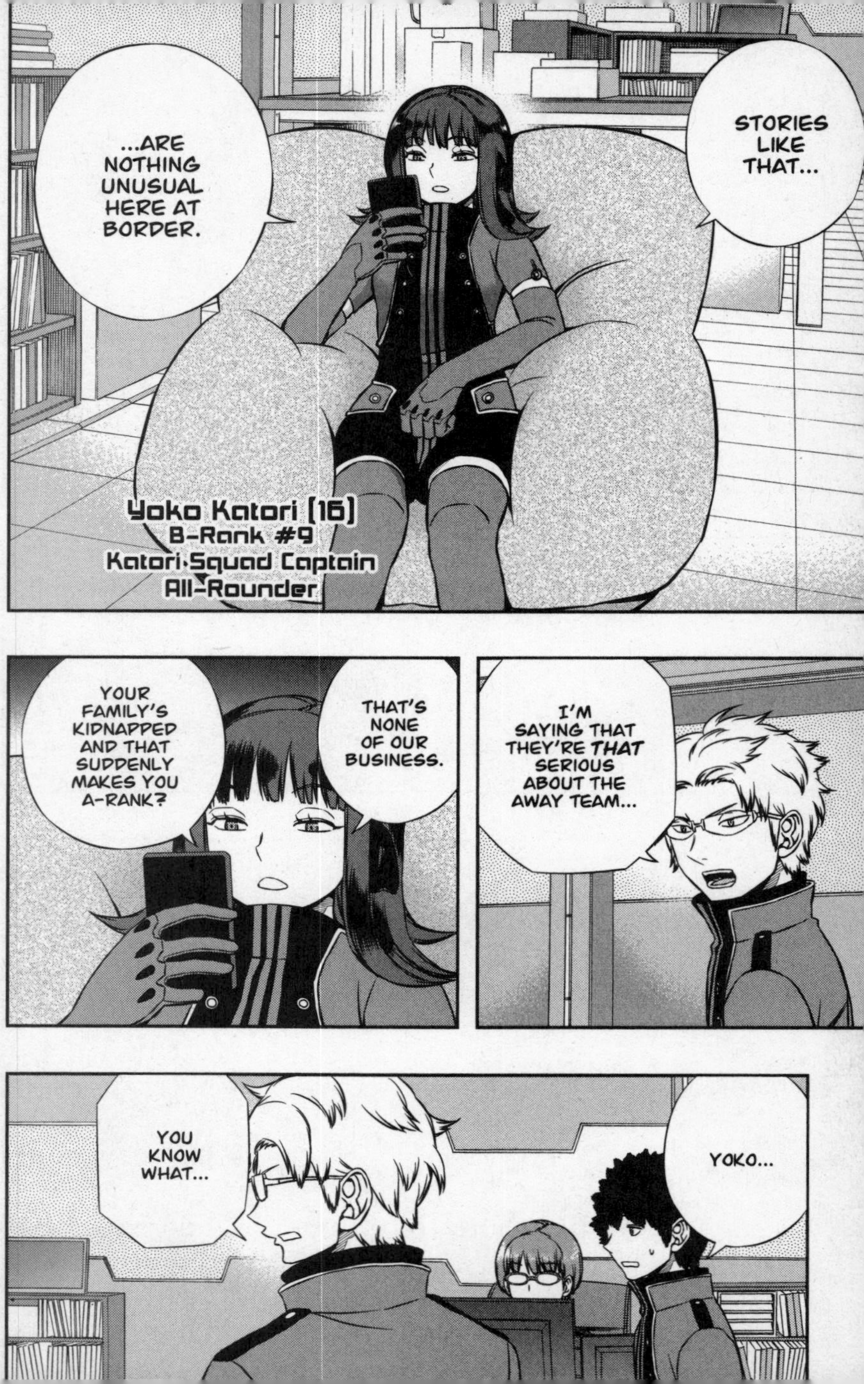
STORIES LIKE THAT...
...ARE NOTHING UNUSUAL HERE AT BORDER.
Yoko Katori (16)
B-Rank #9
Katori Squad Captain
All-Rounder
I'M SAYING THAT THEY'RE THAT SERIOUS ABOUT THE AWAY TEAM...
THAT'S NONE OF OUR BUSINESS.
YOUR FAMILY'S KIDNAPPED AND THAT SUDDENLY MAKES YOU A-RANK?
YOKO...
YOU KNOW WHAT...

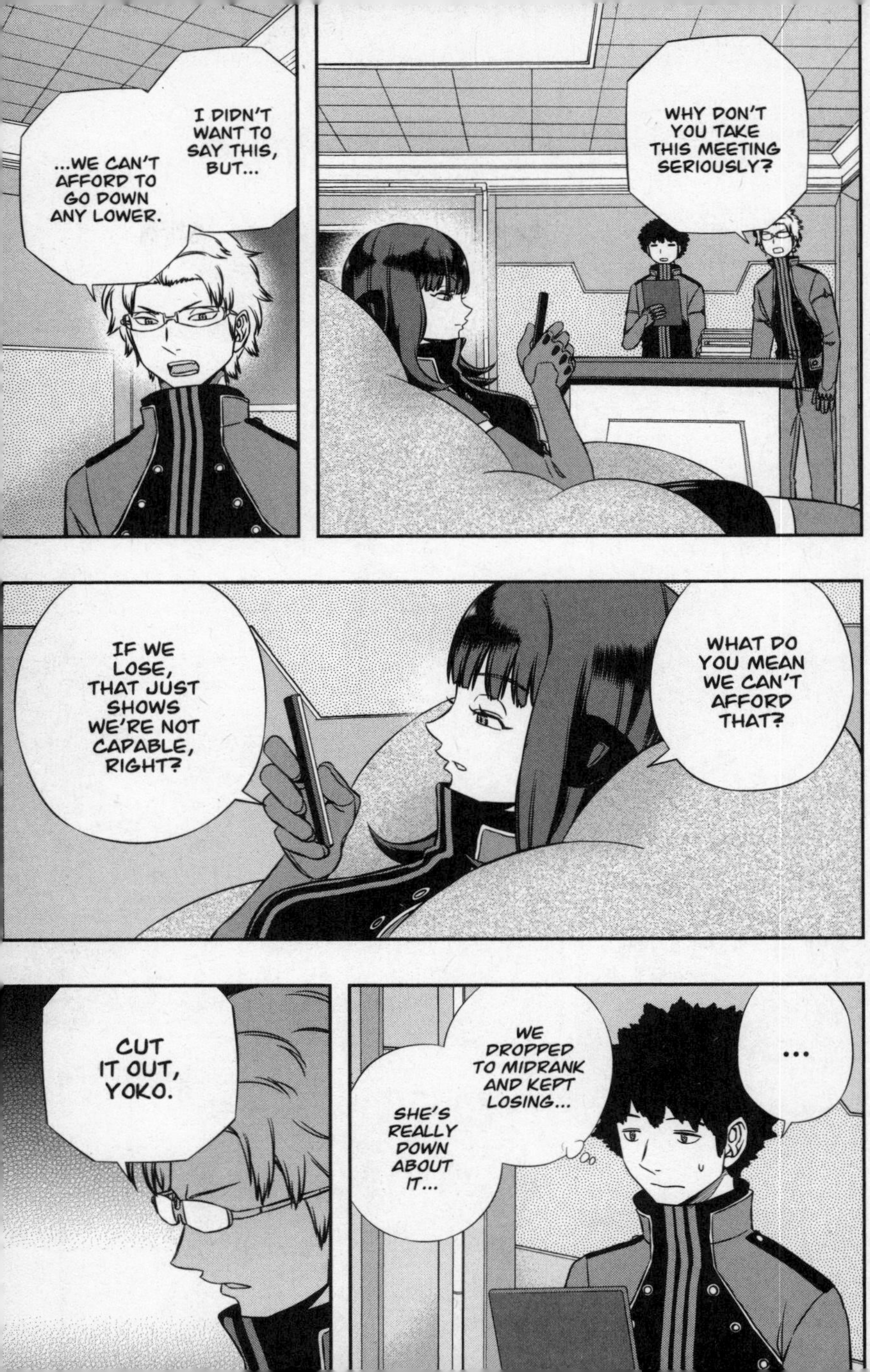
WHY DON'T YOU TAKE THIS MEETING SERIOUSLY?
I DIDN'T WANT TO SAY THIS, BUT...
...WE CAN'T AFFORD TO GO DOWN ANY LOWER.
WHAT DO YOU MEAN WE CAN'T AFFORD THAT?
IF WE LOSE, THAT JUST SHOWS WE'RE NOT CAPABLE, RIGHT?
...
WE DROPPED TO MIDRANK AND KEPT LOSING...
SHE'S REALLY DOWN ABOUT IT...
CUT IT OUT, YOKO.

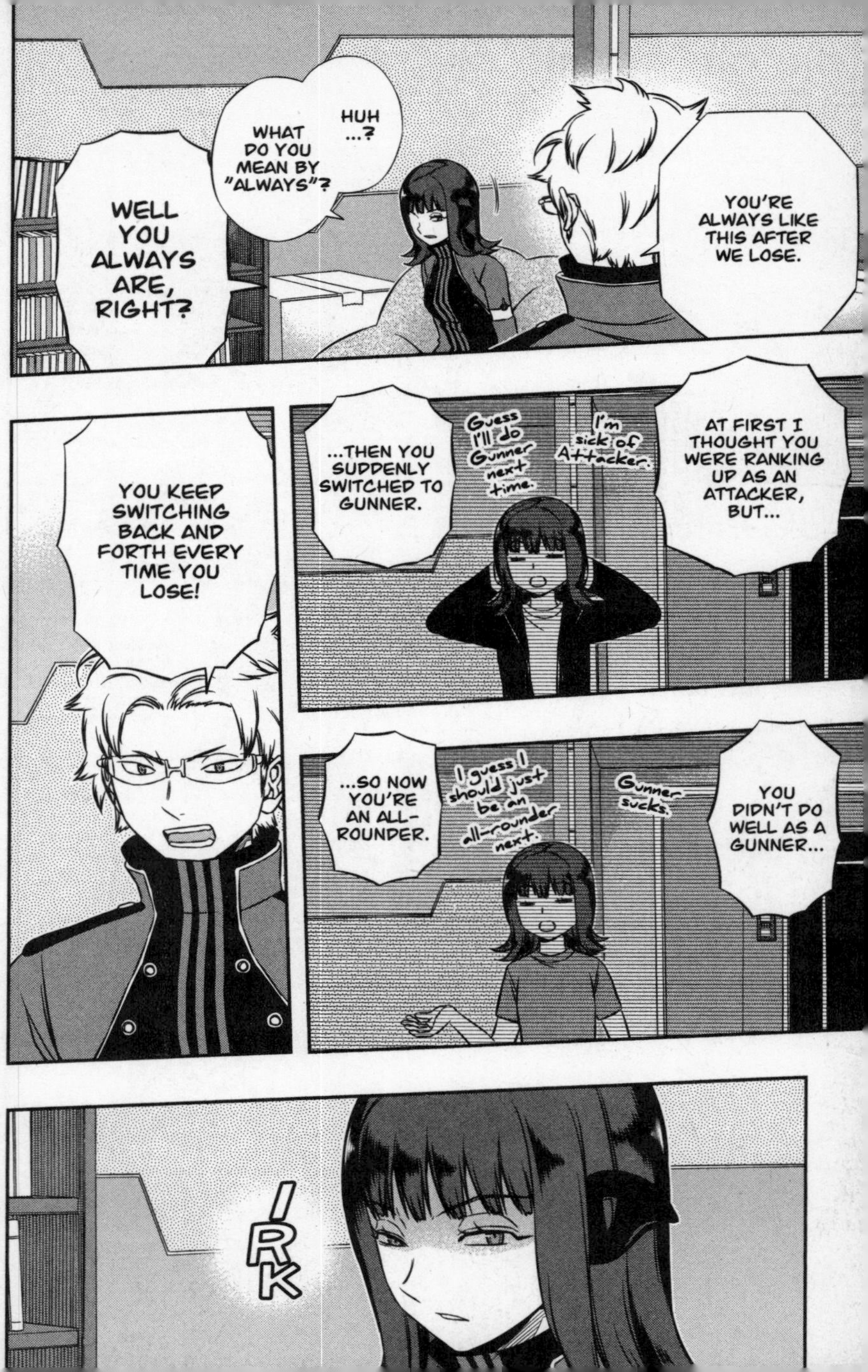
YOU'RE ALWAYS LIKE THIS AFTER WE LOSE.
HUH ...?
WHAT DO YOU MEAN BY "ALWAYS"?
WELL YOU ALWAYS ARE, RIGHT?
AT FIRST I THOUGHT YOU WERE RANKING UP AS AN ATTACKER, BUT...
I'm sick of Attacker.
Guess I'll do Gunner next time.
...THEN YOU SUDDENLY SWITCHED TO GUNNER.
YOU DIDN'T DO WELL AS A GUNNER...
Gunner sucks.
I guess I should just be an all-rounder next.
...SO NOW YOU'RE AN ALL-ROUNDER.
YOU KEEP SWITCHING BACK AND FORTH EVERY TIME YOU LOSE!
IRK

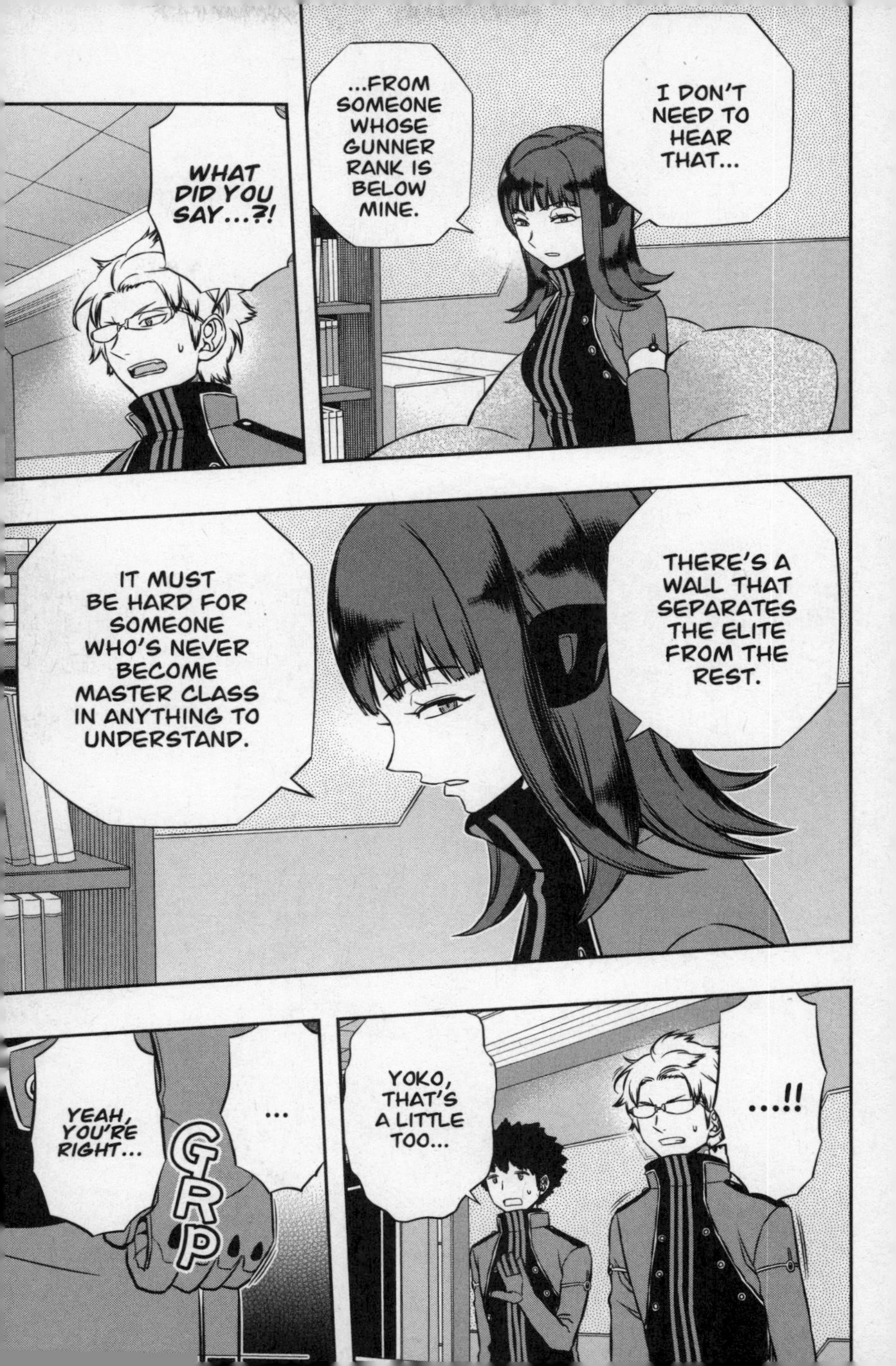
I DON'T NEED TO HEAR THAT...
...FROM SOMEONE WHOSE GUNNER RANK IS BELOW MINE.
WHAT DID YOU SAY...?!
THERE'S A WALL THAT SEPARATES THE ELITE FROM THE REST.
IT MUST BE HARD FOR SOMEONE WHO'S NEVER BECOME MASTER CLASS IN ANYTHING TO UNDERSTAND.
...!!
YOKO, THAT'S A LITTLE TOO...
...
GRP
YEAH, YOU'RE RIGHT...

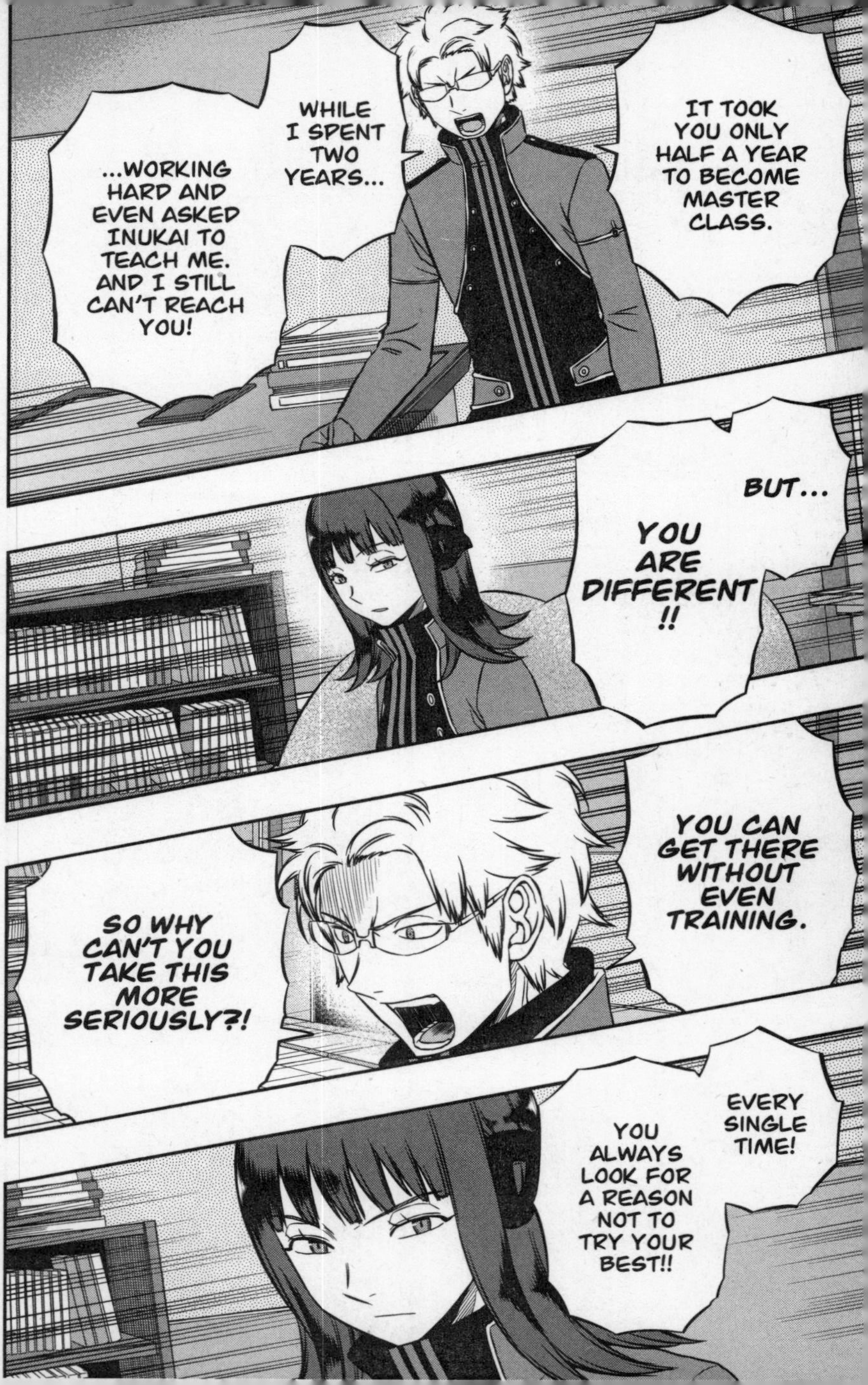
IT TOOK YOU ONLY HALF A YEAR TO BECOME MASTER CLASS.
WHILE I SPENT TWO YEARS...
...WORKING HARD AND EVEN ASKED INUKAI TO TEACH ME. AND I STILL CAN'T REACH YOU!
BUT...
YOU ARE DIFFERENT!!
YOU CAN GET THERE WITHOUT EVEN TRAINING.
SO WHY CAN'T YOU TAKE THIS MORE SERIOUSLY?!
EVERY SINGLE TIME!
YOU ALWAYS LOOK FOR A REASON NOT TO TRY YOUR BEST!!

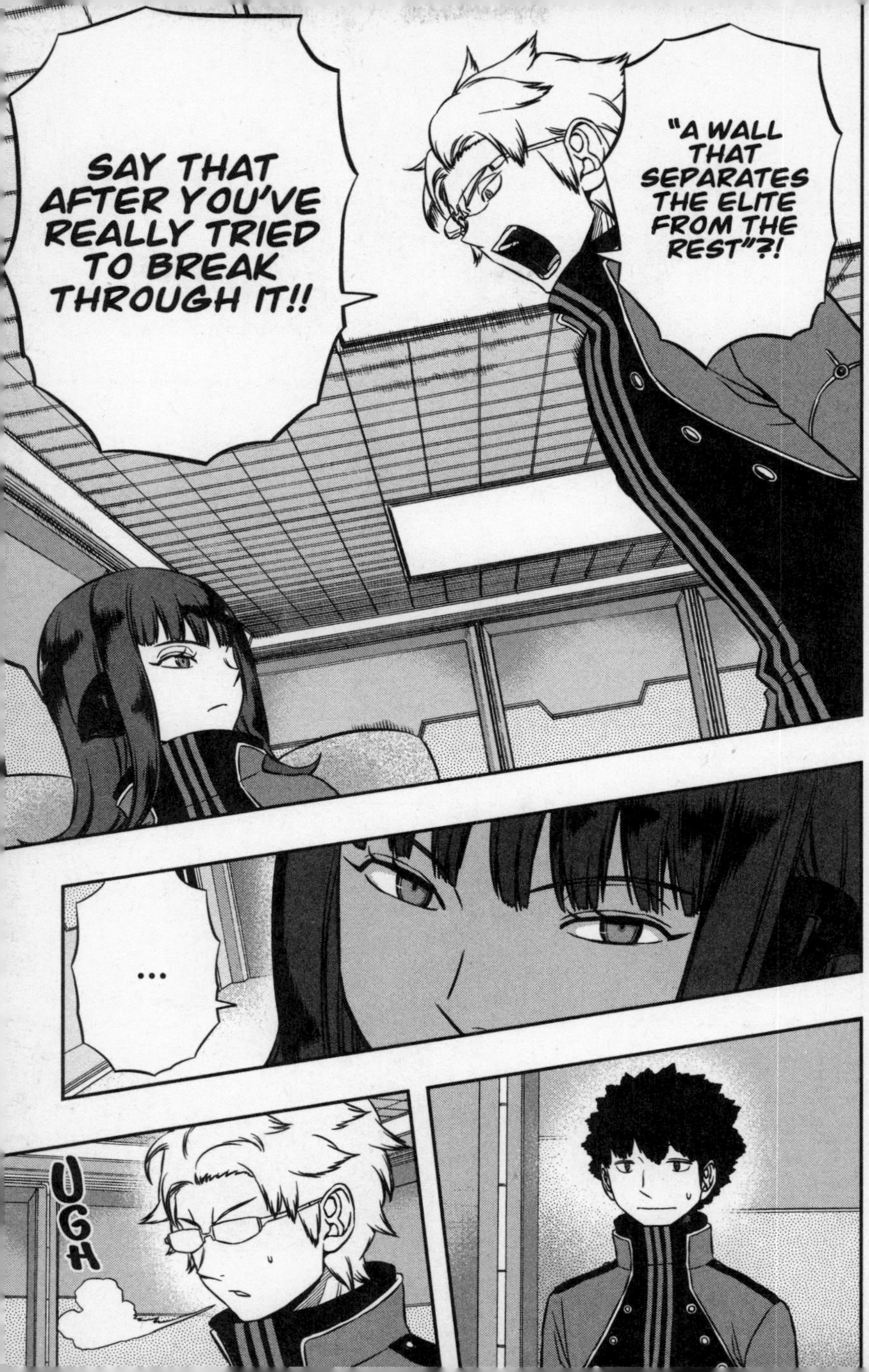
"A WALL THAT SEPARATES THE ELITE FROM THE REST"?!
SAY THAT AFTER YOU'VE REALLY TRIED TO BREAK THROUGH IT!!
...
UGH

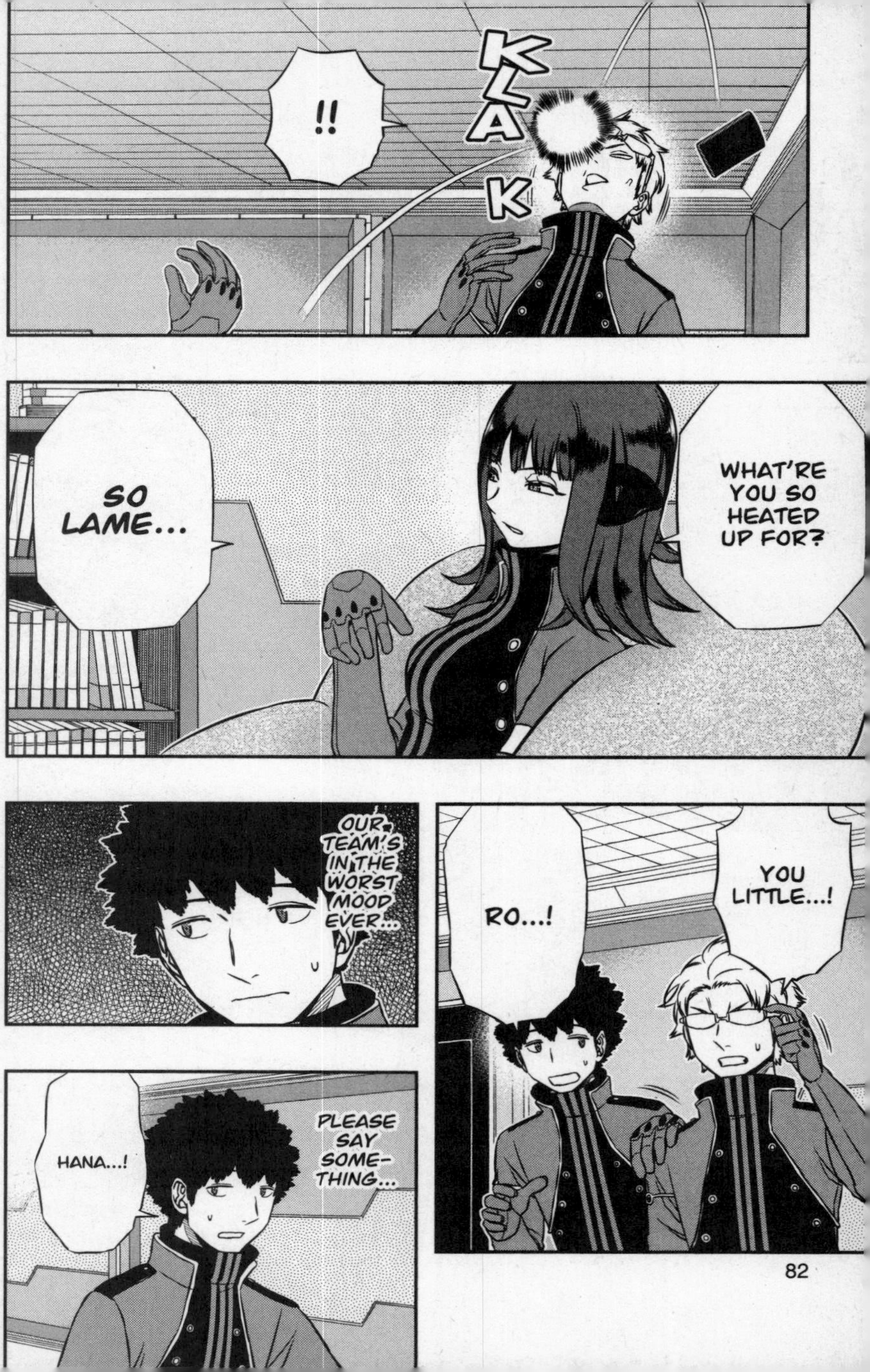
KLAK
!!
WHAT'RE YOU SO HEATED UP FOR?
SO LAME...
YOU LITTLE...!
RO...!
OUR TEAM'S IN THE WORST MOOD EVER...
PLEASE SAY SOME-THING...
HANA...!

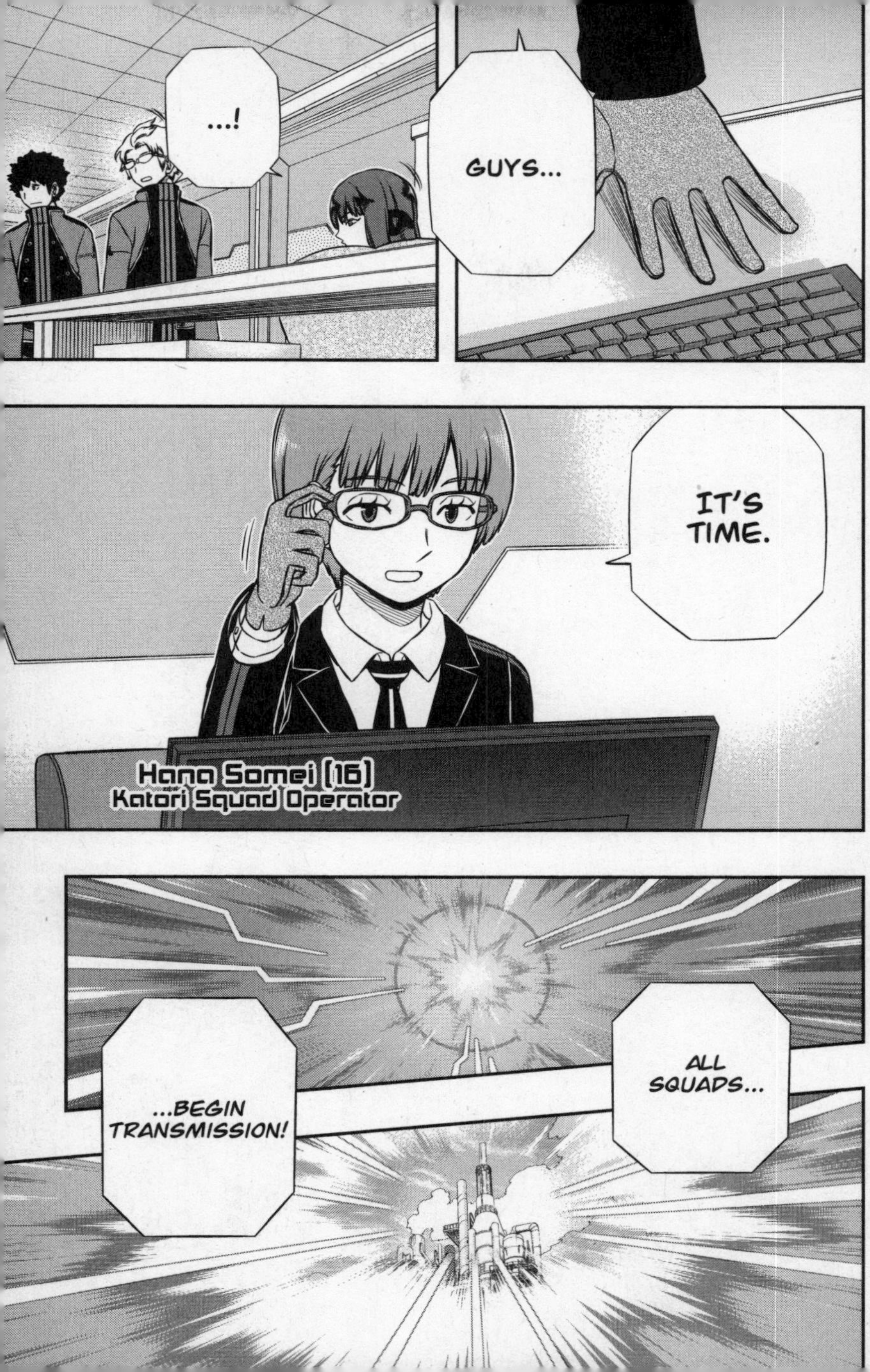
GUYS...
...!
IT'S TIME.
Hana Somei (16)
Katori Squad Operator
ALL SQUADS...
...BEGIN TRANSMISSION!

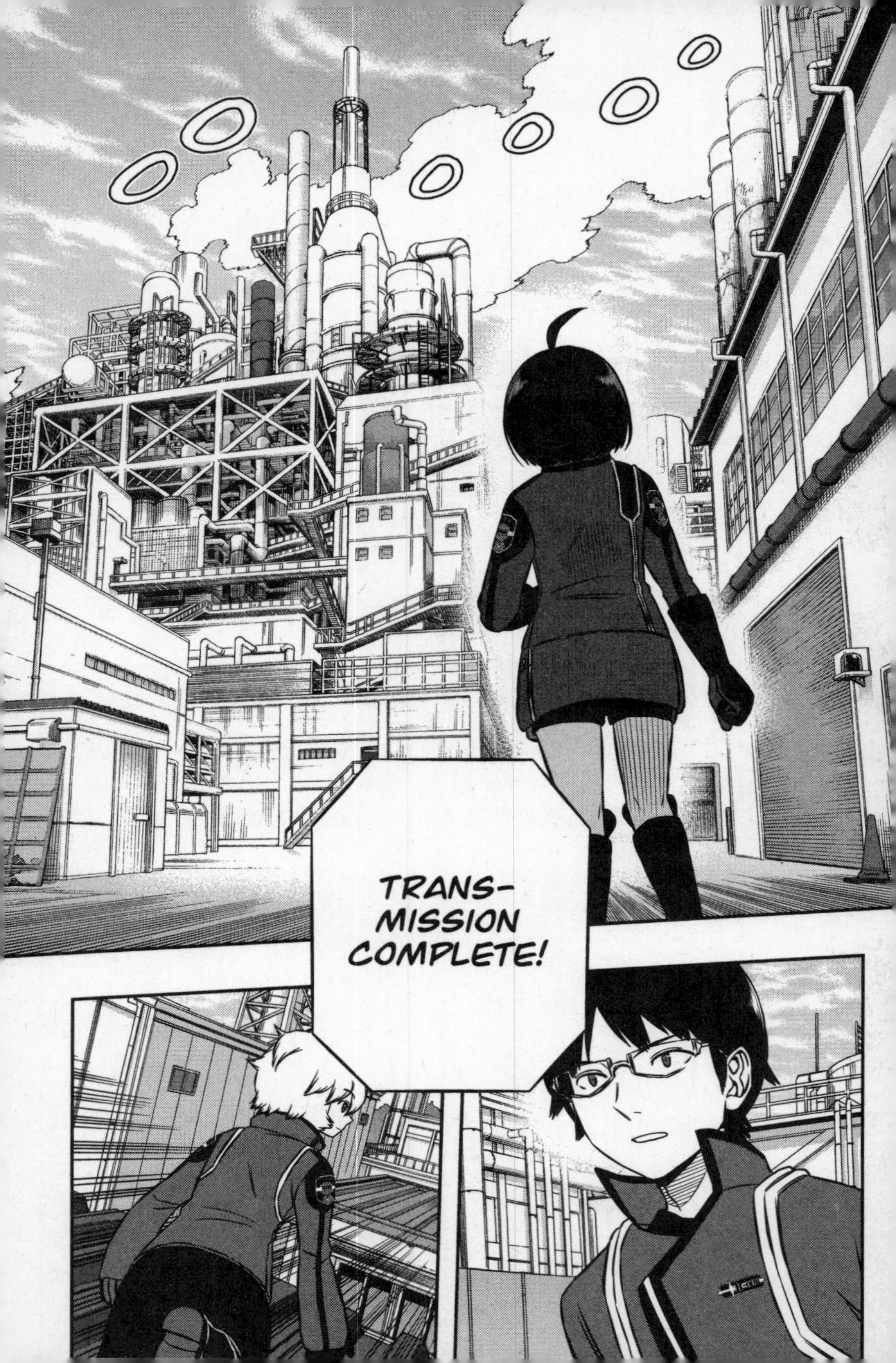
TRANS-MISSION COMPLETE!

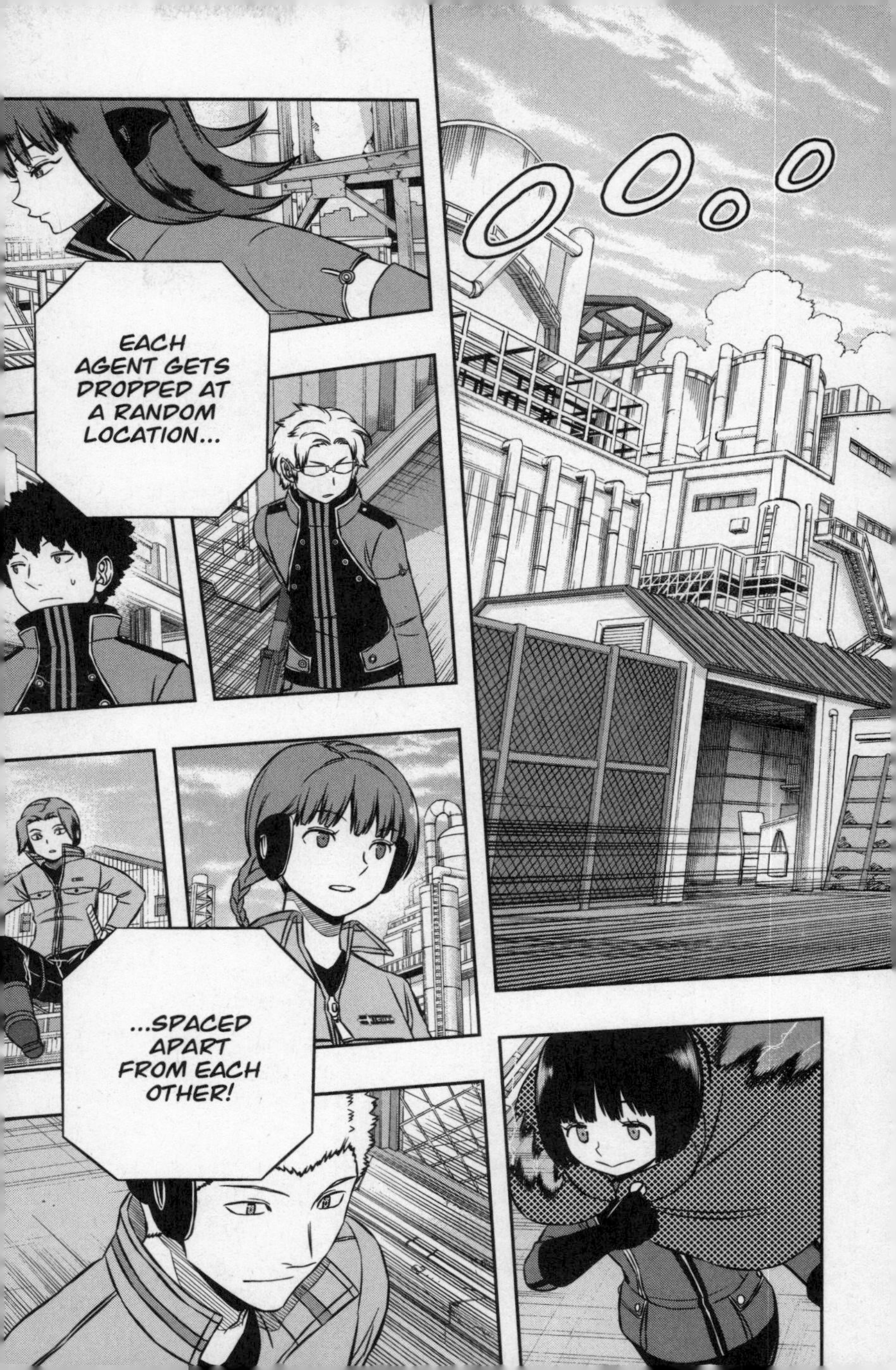
EACH AGENT GETS DROPPED AT A RANDOM LOCATION...
...SPACED APART FROM EACH OTHER!

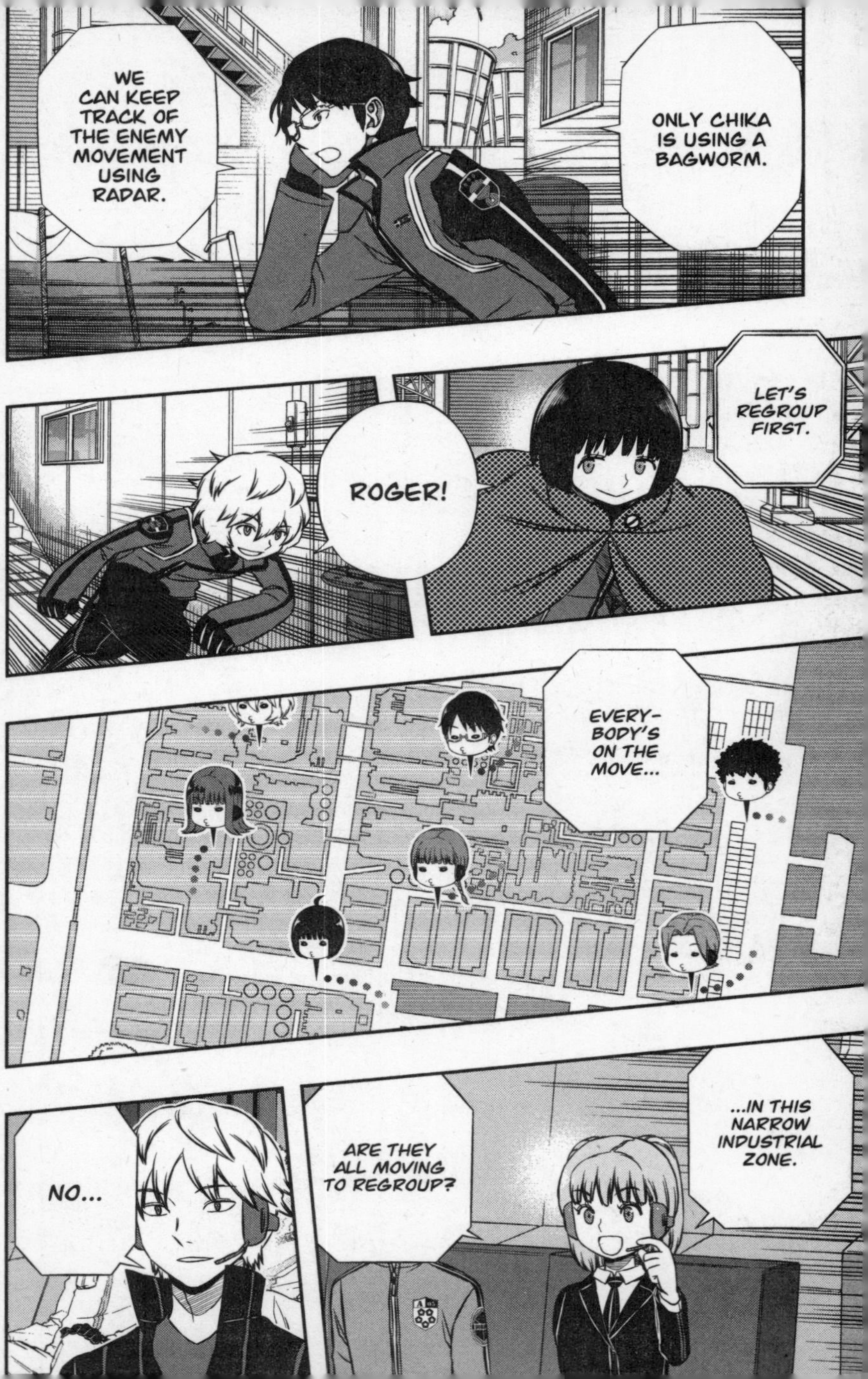

ONLY CHIKA IS USING A BAGWORM.
WE CAN KEEP TRACK OF THE ENEMY MOVEMENT USING RADAR.
LET'S REGROUP FIRST.
ROGER!
EVERY-BODY'S ON THE MOVE...
...IN THIS NARROW INDUSTRIAL ZONE.
ARE THEY ALL MOVING TO REGROUP?
NO...

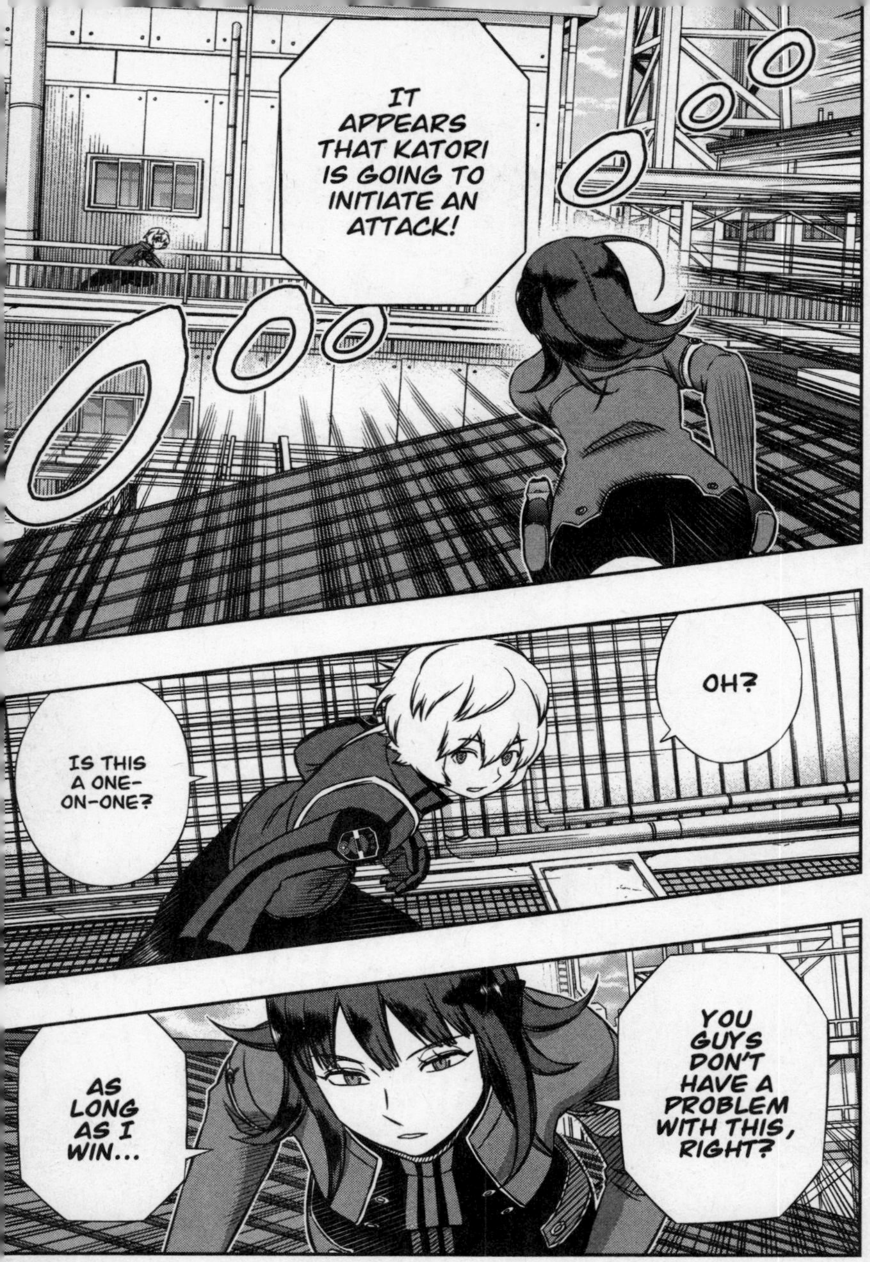
IT APPEARS THAT KATORI IS GOING TO INITIATE AN ATTACK!
OH?
IS THIS A ONE-ON-ONE?
YOU GUYS DON'T HAVE A PROBLEM WITH THIS, RIGHT?
AS LONG AS I WIN...

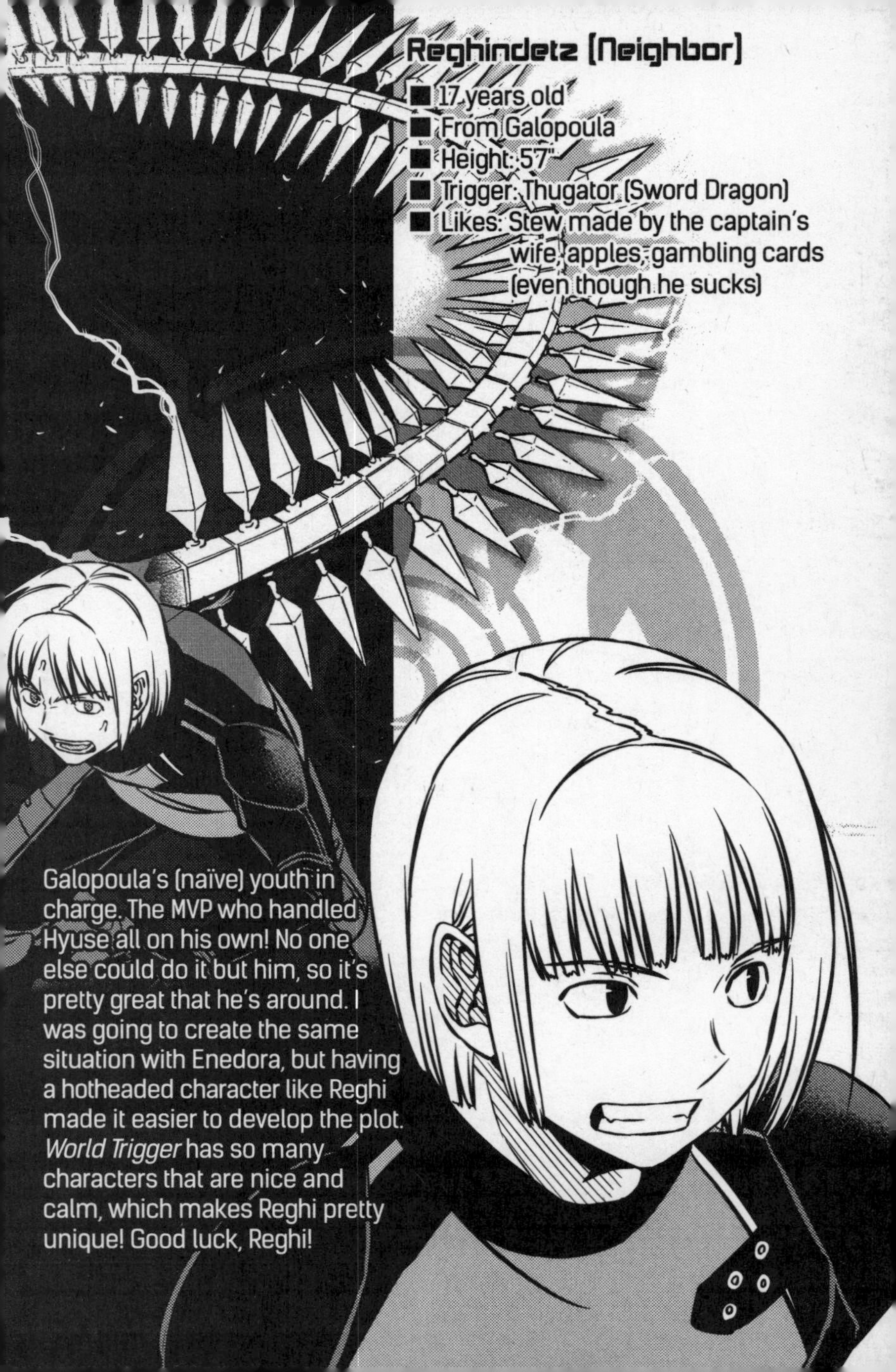

Reghindetz (Neighbor)

- 17 years old
- From Galopoula
- Height: 5'7"
- Trigger: Thugator (Sword Dragon)
- Likes: Stew made by the captain's wife, apples, gambling cards (even though he sucks)

Galopoula's (naïve) youth in charge. The MVP who handled Hyuse all on his own! No one else could do it but him, so it's pretty great that he's around. I was going to create the same situation with Enedora, but having a hotheaded character like Reghi made it easier to develop the plot. *World Trigger* has so many characters that are nice and calm, which makes Reghi pretty unique! Good luck, Reghi!

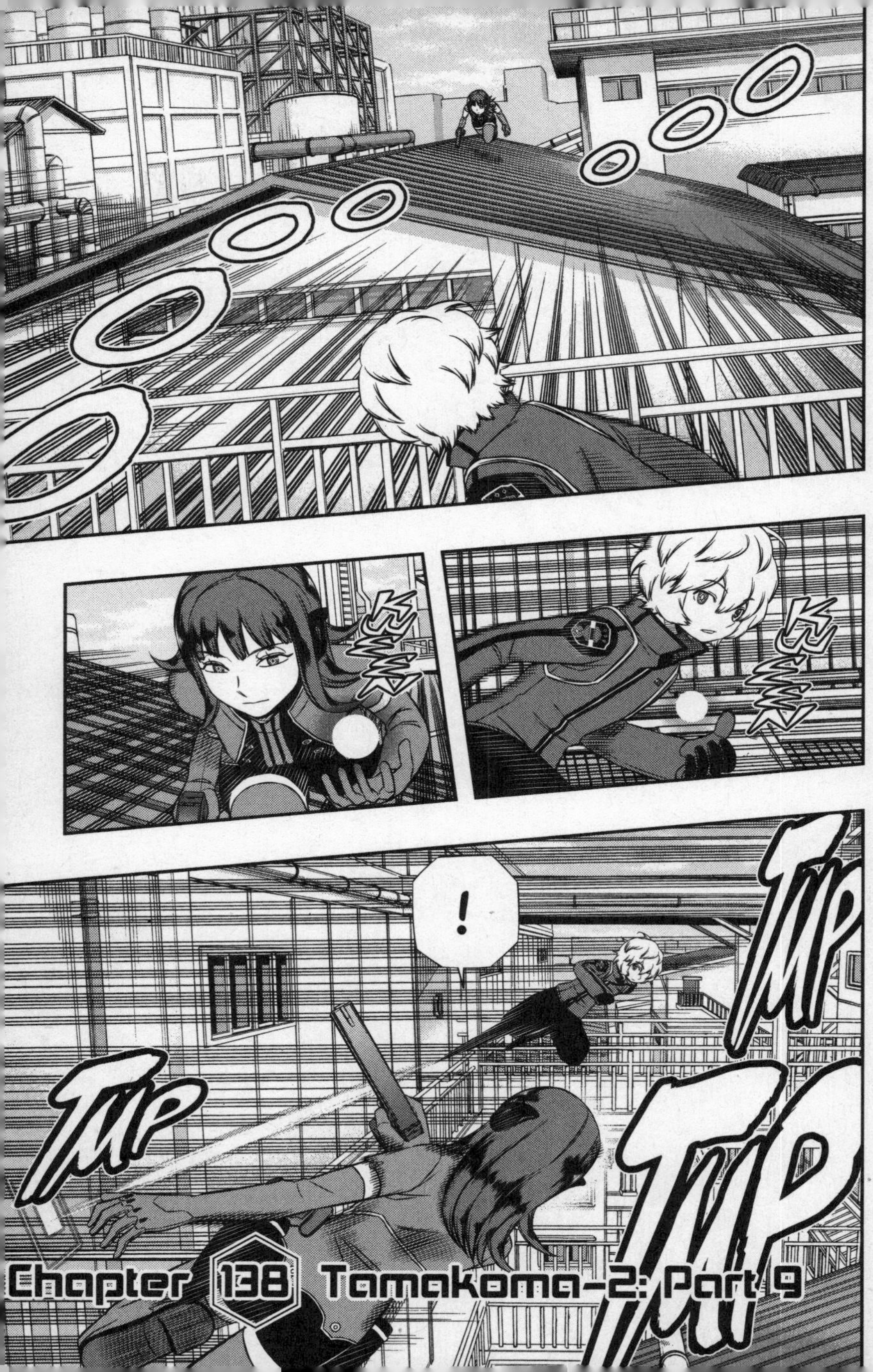
!
TMP
TMP
TMP
Chapter 138 Tamakoma-2: Part 9

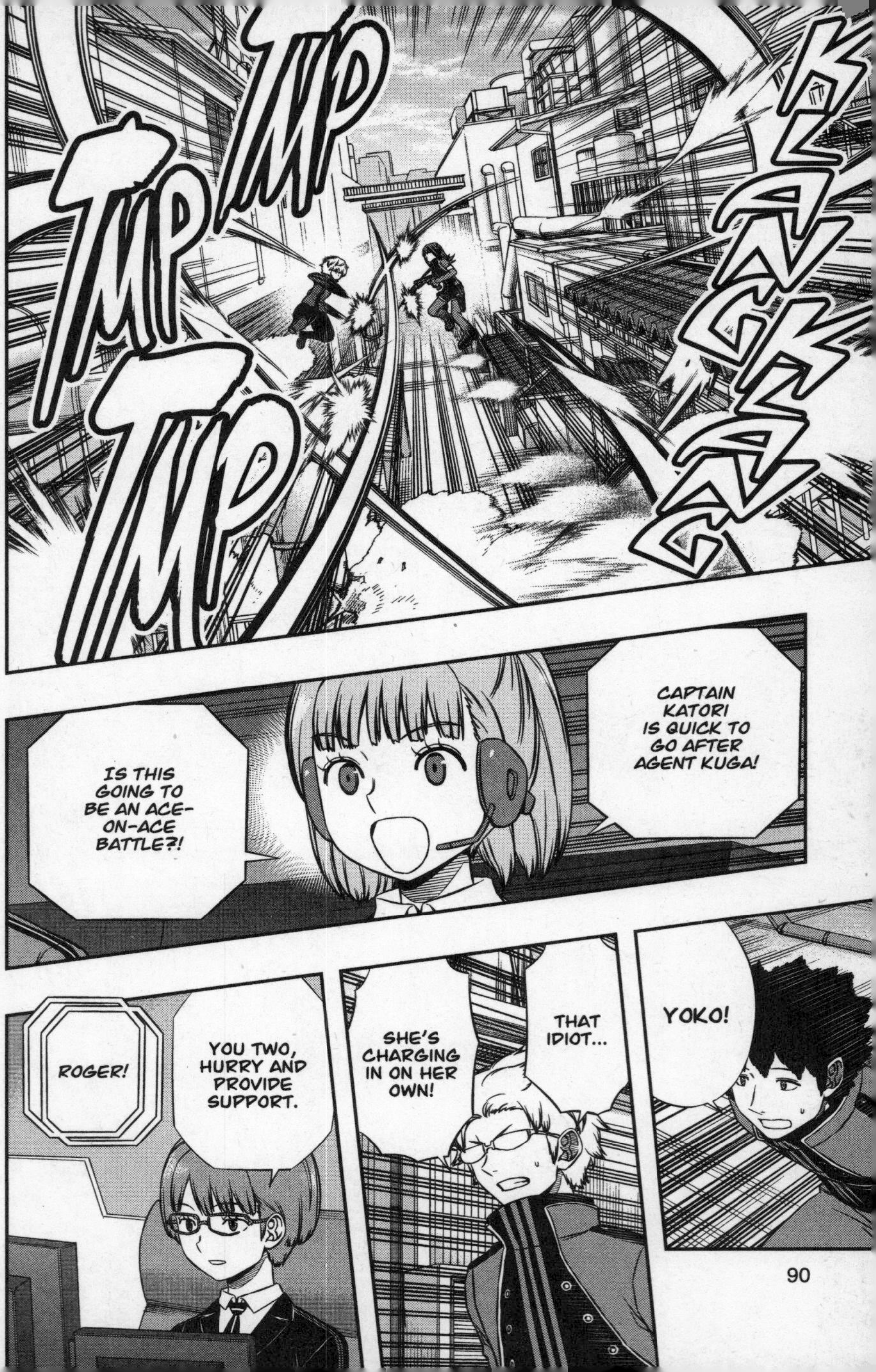
KLANGKANG
TMP TMP
TMP
CAPTAIN KATORI IS QUICK TO GO AFTER AGENT KUGA!
IS THIS GOING TO BE AN ACE-ON-ACE BATTLE?!
YOKO!
THAT IDIOT...
SHE'S CHARGING IN ON HER OWN!
YOU TWO, HURRY AND PROVIDE SUPPORT.
ROGER!

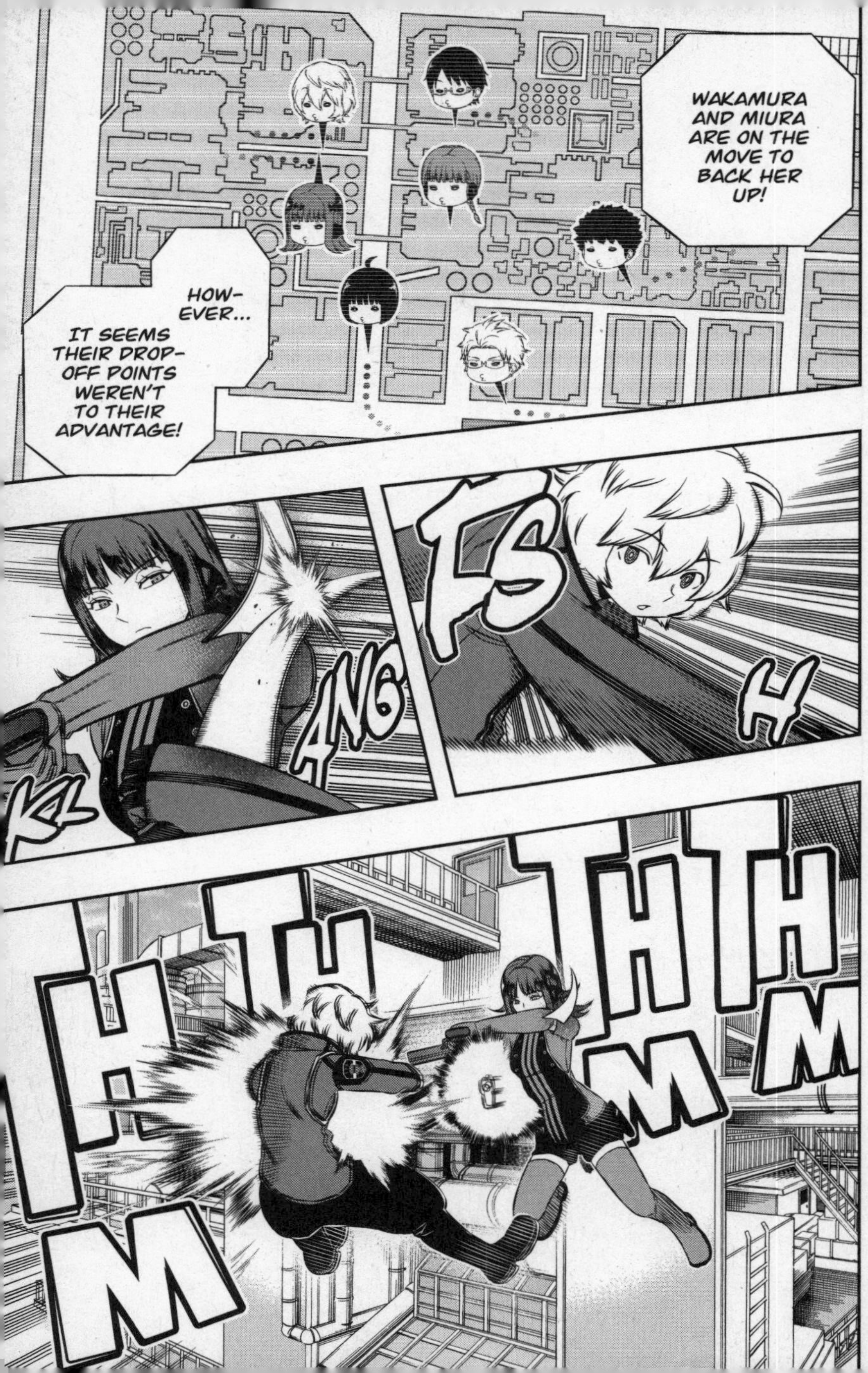
WAKAMURA AND MIURA ARE ON THE MOVE TO BACK HER UP!
HOW-EVER...
IT SEEMS THEIR DROP-OFF POINTS WEREN'T TO THEIR ADVANTAGE!
FS
H
ANG
KL
THTH
M
M
M
H
TH
H
M

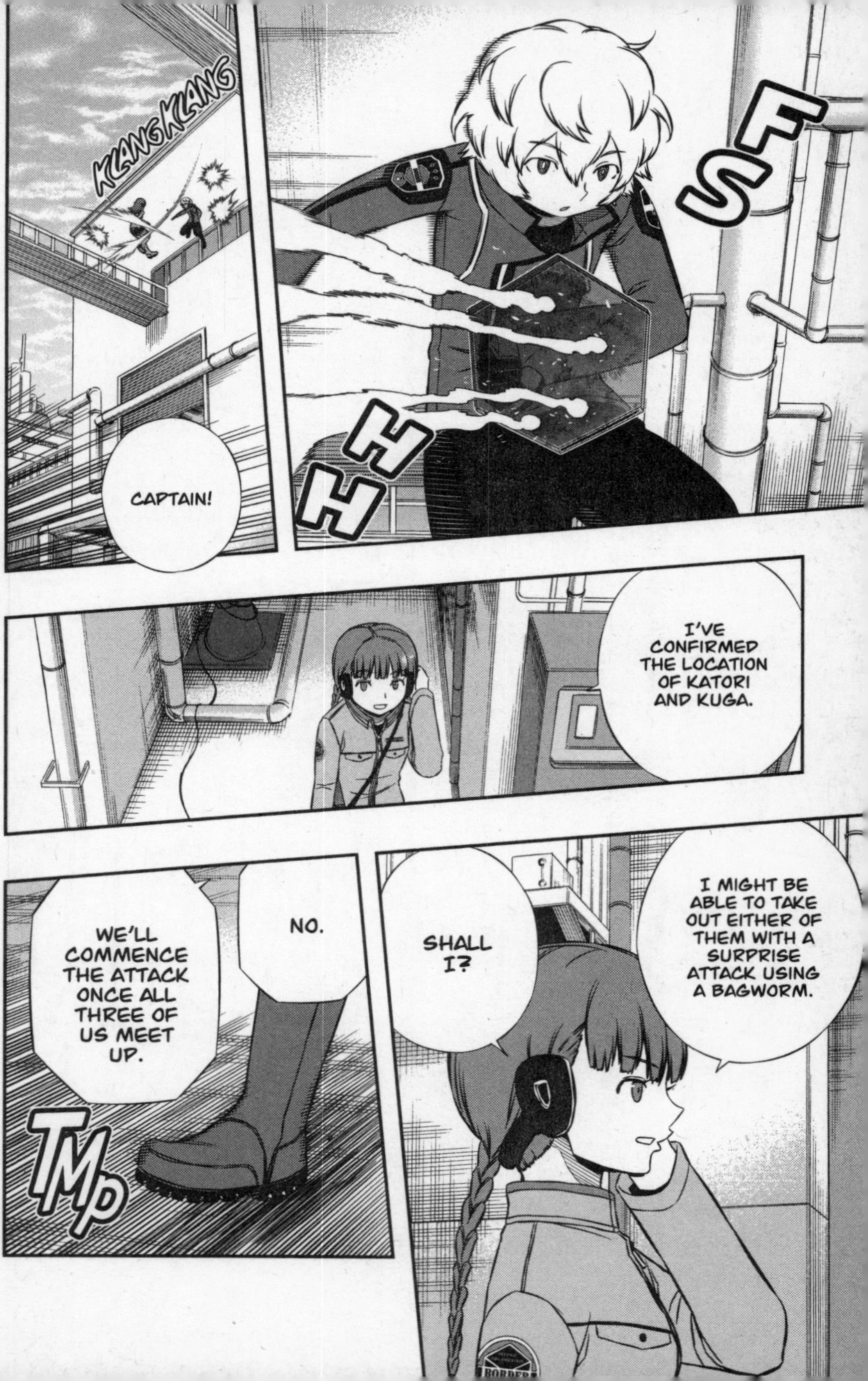
FS
HH
KLANG KLANG
CAPTAIN!
I'VE CONFIRMED THE LOCATION OF KATORI AND KUGA.
I MIGHT BE ABLE TO TAKE OUT EITHER OF THEM WITH A SURPRISE ATTACK USING A BAGWORM.
SHALL I?
NO.
WE'LL COMMENCE THE ATTACK ONCE ALL THREE OF US MEET UP.
TMP

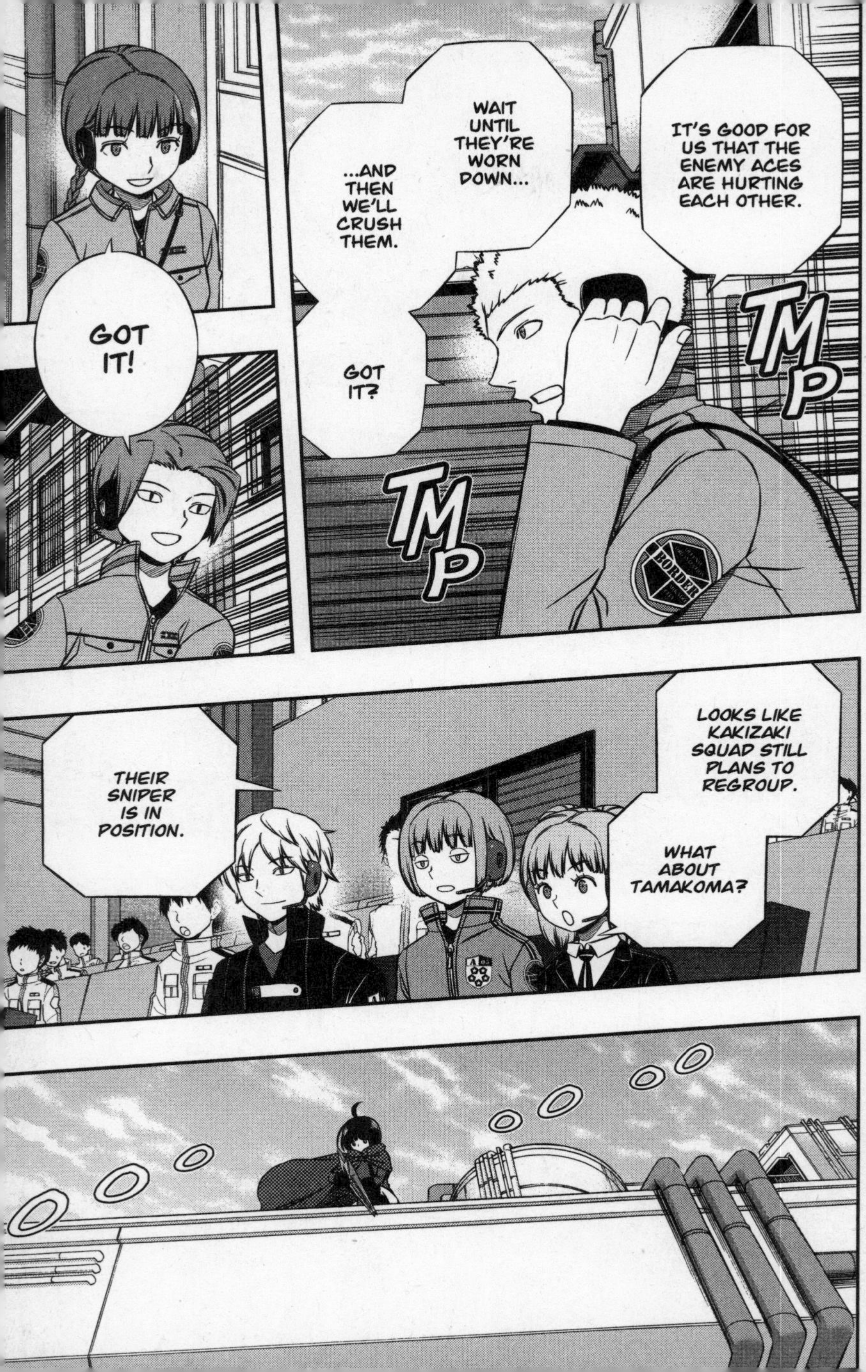
IT'S GOOD FOR US THAT THE ENEMY ACES ARE HURTING EACH OTHER.
WAIT UNTIL THEY'RE WORN DOWN...
...AND THEN WE'LL CRUSH THEM.
GOT IT?
TMP
TMP
GOT IT!
LOOKS LIKE KAKIZAKI SQUAD STILL PLANS TO REGROUP.
WHAT ABOUT TAMAKOMA?
THEIR SNIPER IS IN POSITION.

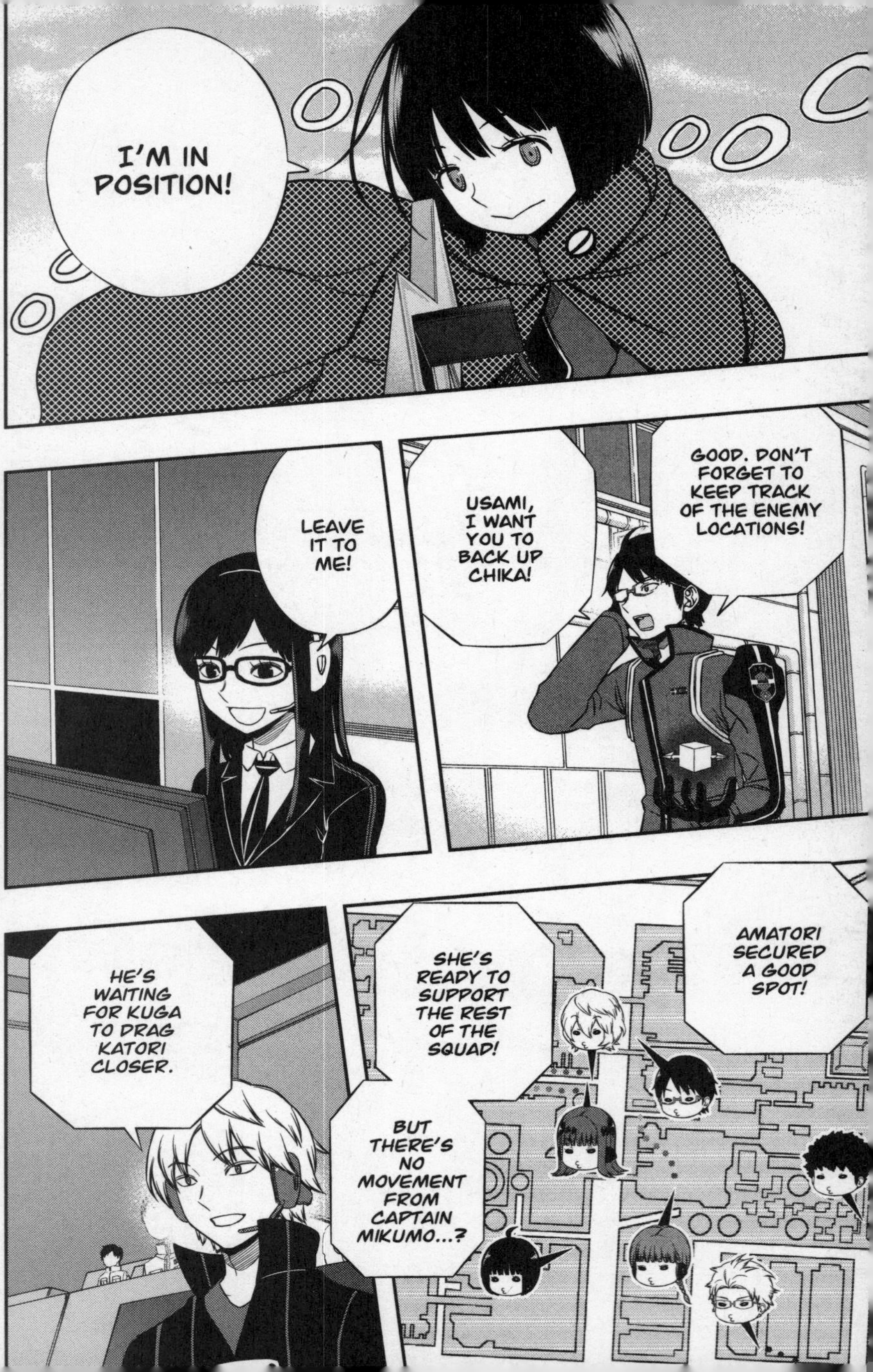
I'M IN POSITION!
GOOD. DON'T FORGET TO KEEP TRACK OF THE ENEMY LOCATIONS!
USAMI, I WANT YOU TO BACK UP CHIKA!
LEAVE IT TO ME!
AMATORI SECURED A GOOD SPOT!
SHE'S READY TO SUPPORT THE REST OF THE SQUAD!
BUT THERE'S NO MOVEMENT FROM CAPTAIN MIKUMO...?
HE'S WAITING FOR KUGA TO DRAG KATORI CLOSER.

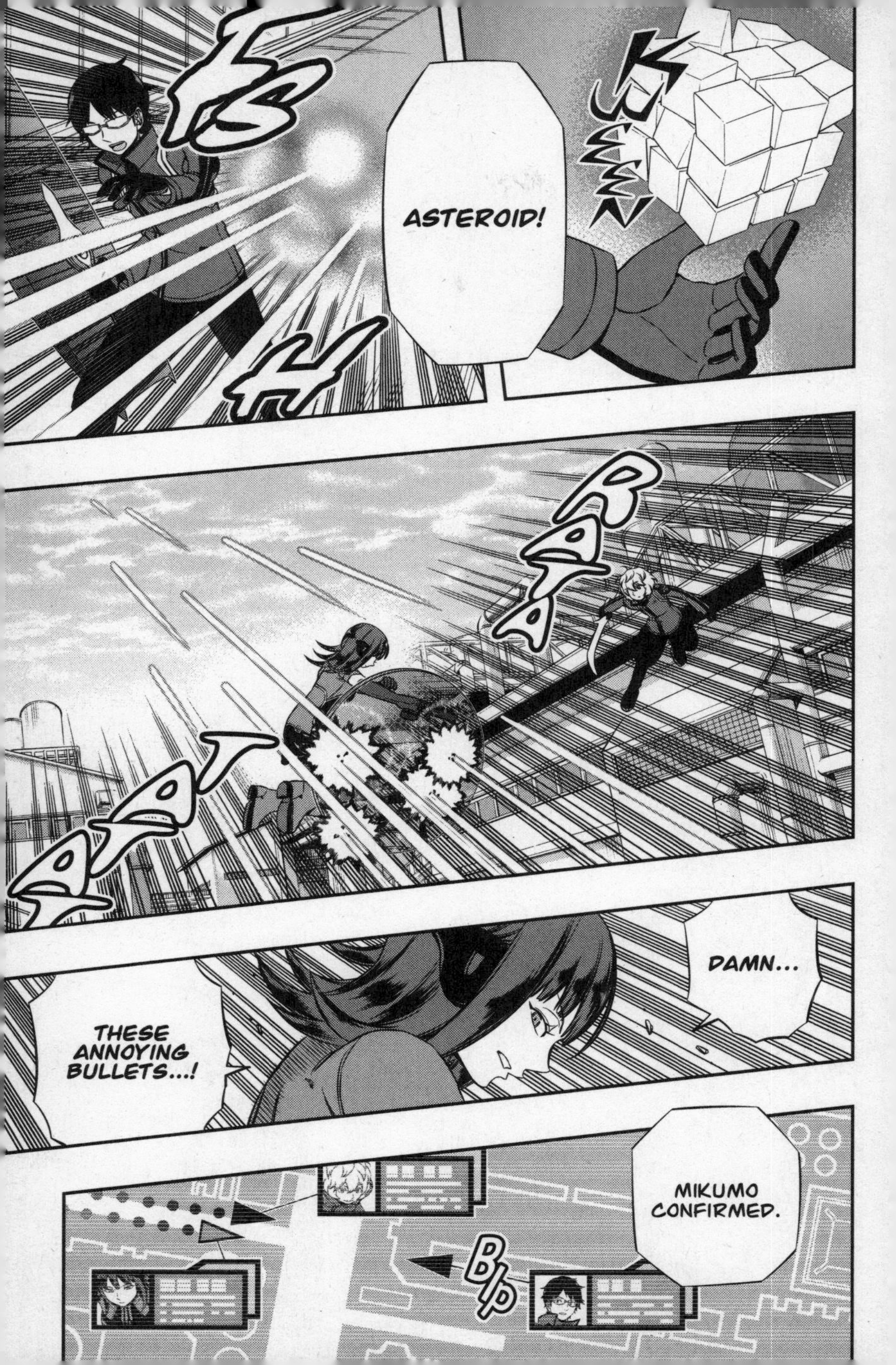
KWEEN
ASTEROID!
RATA
DAMN...
THESE ANNOYING BULLETS...!
MIKUMO CONFIRMED.
BIP

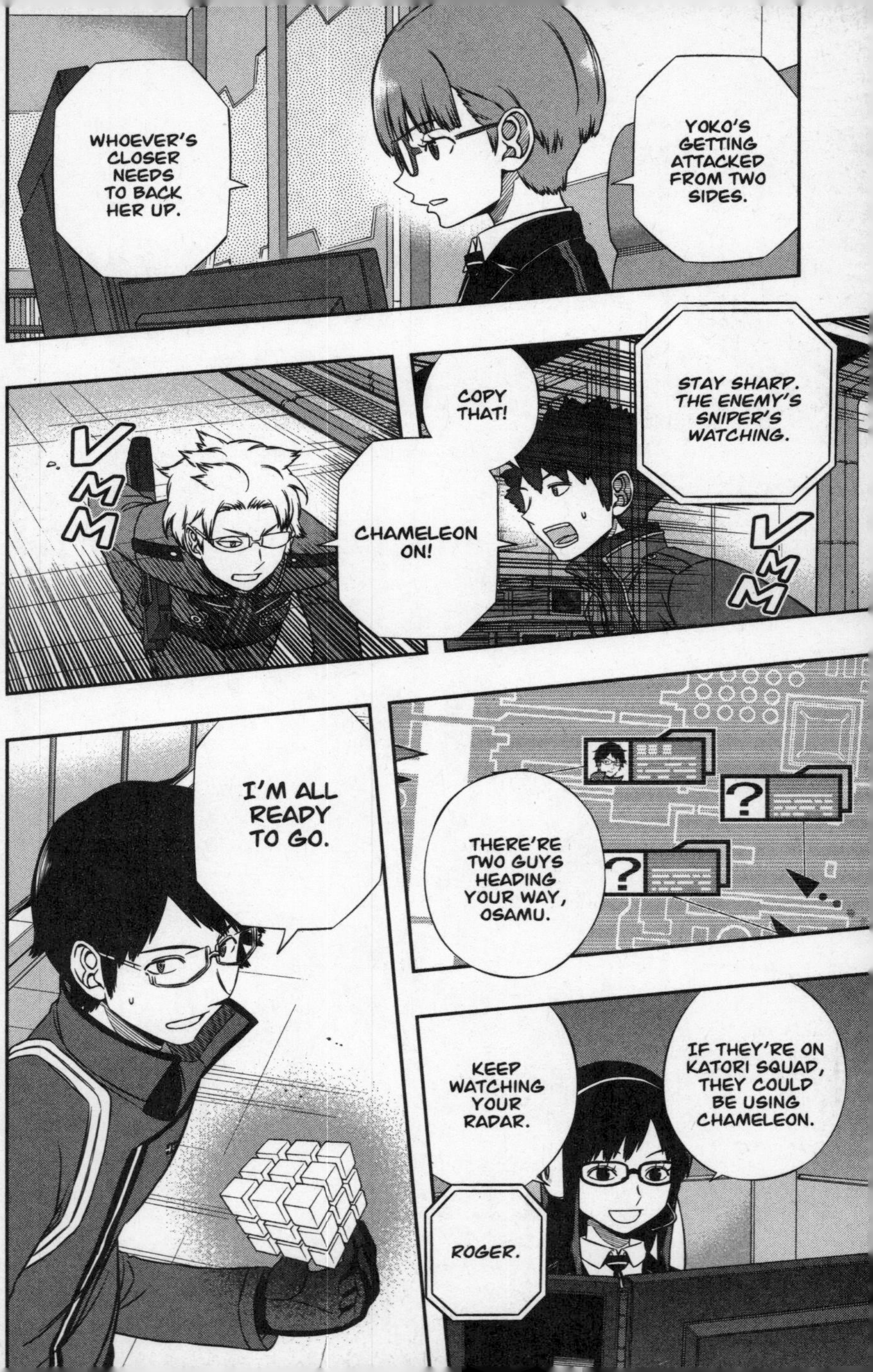
YOKO'S GETTING ATTACKED FROM TWO SIDES.
WHOEVER'S CLOSER NEEDS TO BACK HER UP.
STAY SHARP. THE ENEMY'S SNIPER'S WATCHING.
COPY THAT!
VMM
CHAMELEON ON!
VMM
THERE'RE TWO GUYS HEADING YOUR WAY, OSAMU.
IF THEY'RE ON KATORI SQUAD, THEY COULD BE USING CHAMELEON.
KEEP WATCHING YOUR RADAR.
ROGER.
I'M ALL READY TO GO.

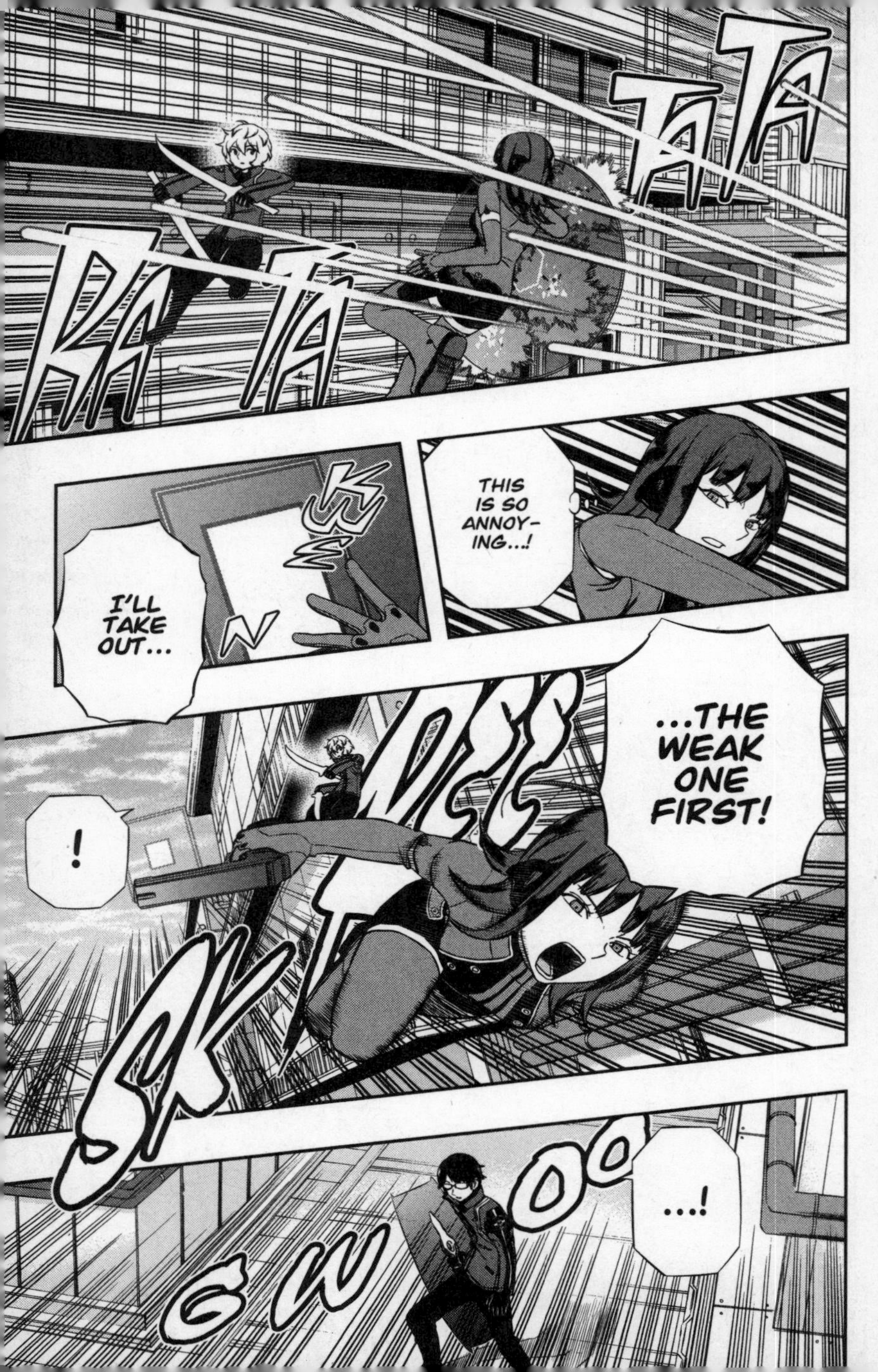
TA TA
KA TA
THIS IS SO ANNOY-ING...!
I'LL TAKE OUT...
...THE WEAK ONE FIRST!
!
...!
GWOOO

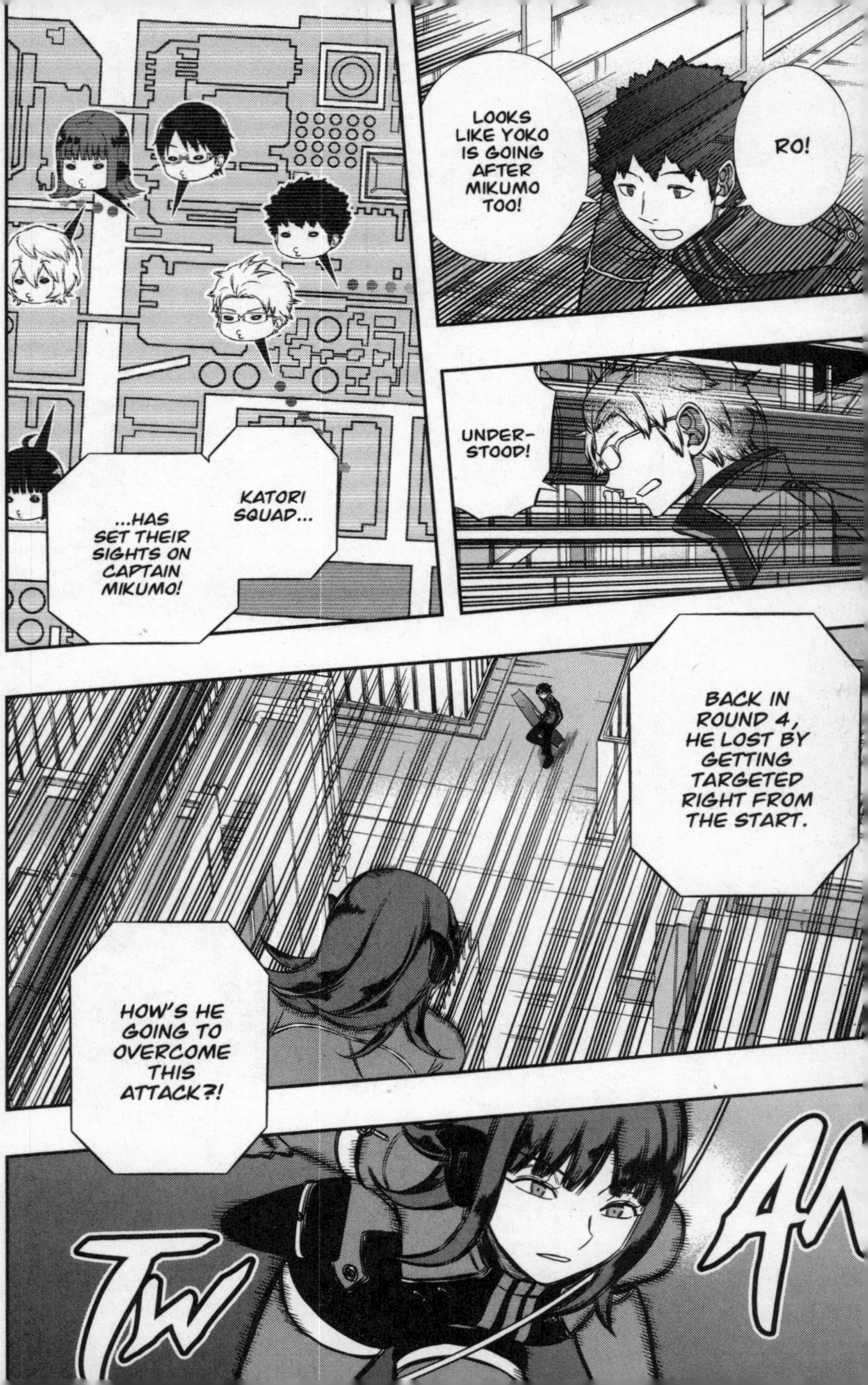
RO!
LOOKS LIKE YOKO IS GOING AFTER MIKUMO TOO!
UNDER-STOOD!
KATORI SQUAD...
...HAS SET THEIR SIGHTS ON CAPTAIN MIKUMO!
BACK IN ROUND 4, HE LOST BY GETTING TARGETED RIGHT FROM THE START.
HOW'S HE GOING TO OVERCOME THIS ATTACK?!

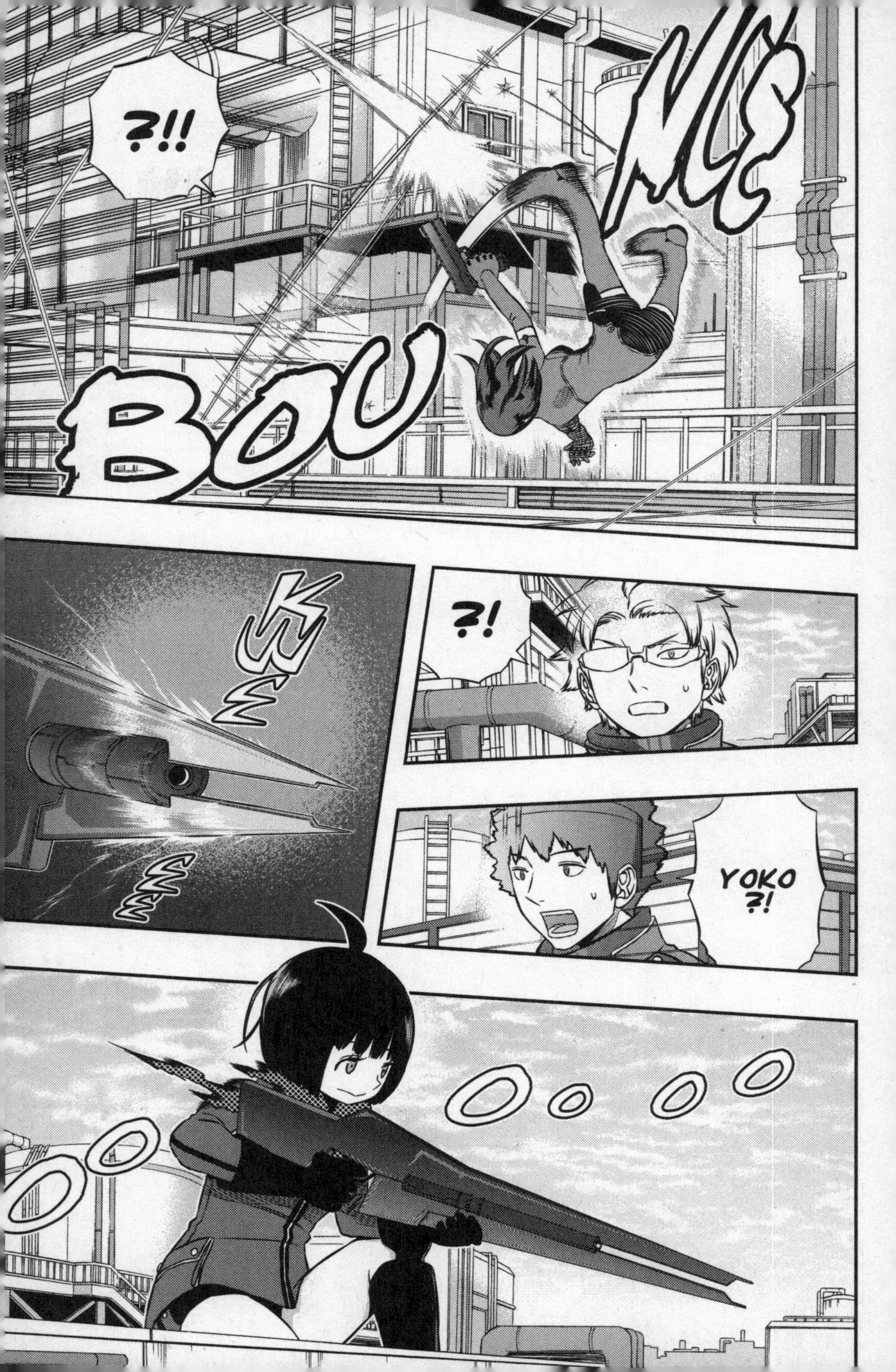
?!!
?!
YOKO ?!

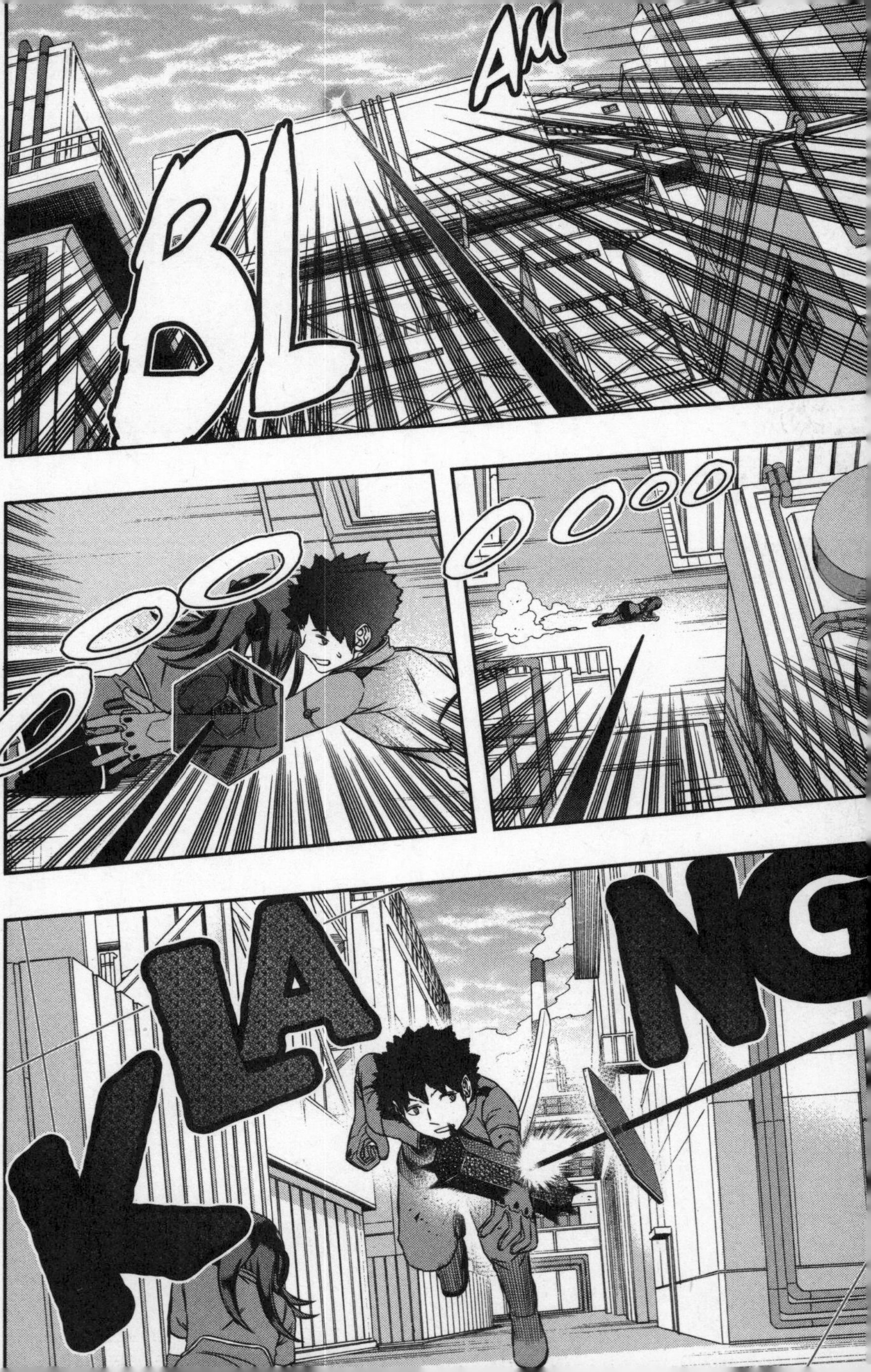
BLAM
KLANG

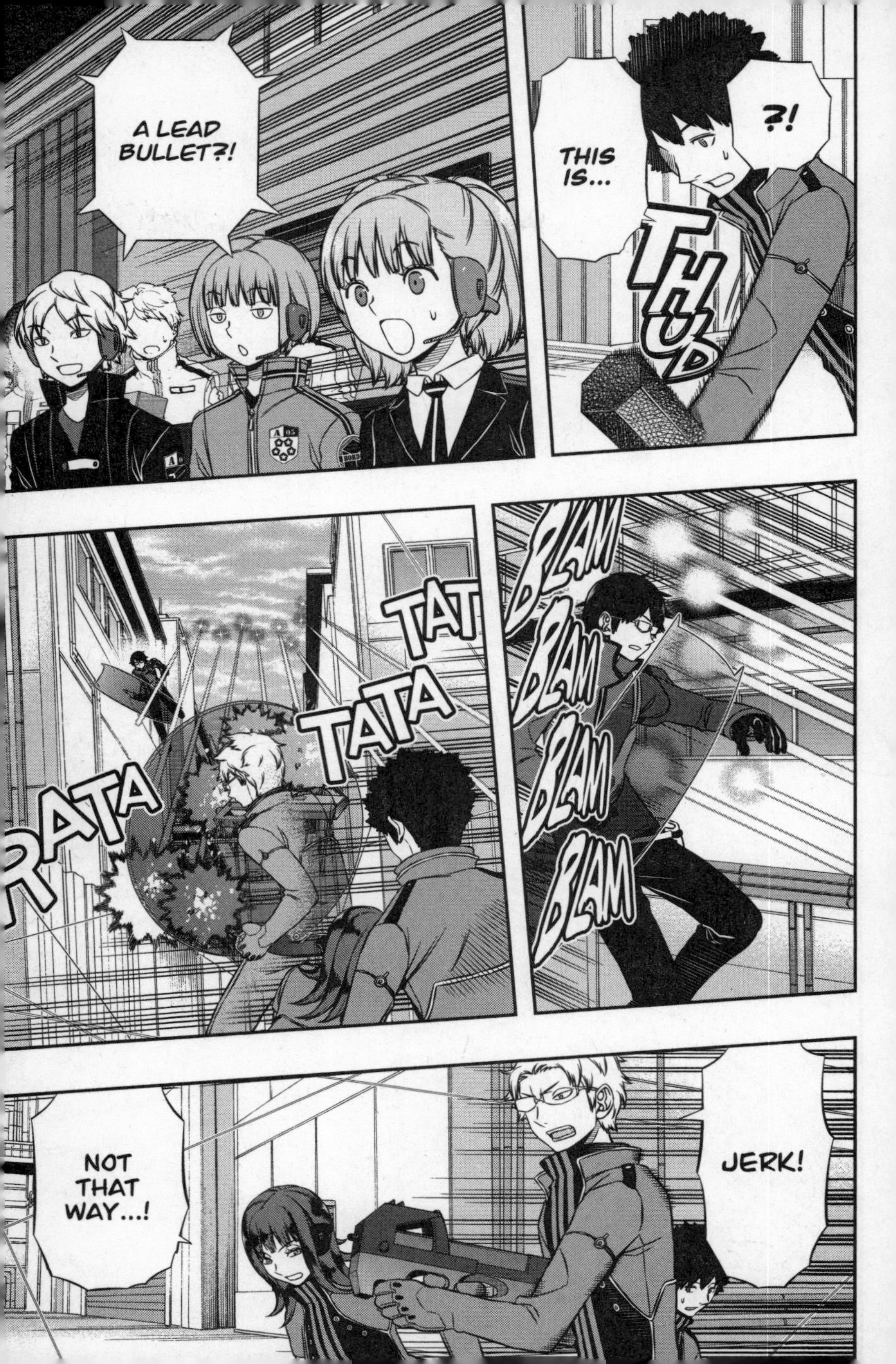
?!
THIS IS...
THUD
A LEAD BULLET?!
BLAM BLAM BLAM BLAM BLAM BLAM
TAT
TATA
RATA
JERK!
NOT THAT WAY...!

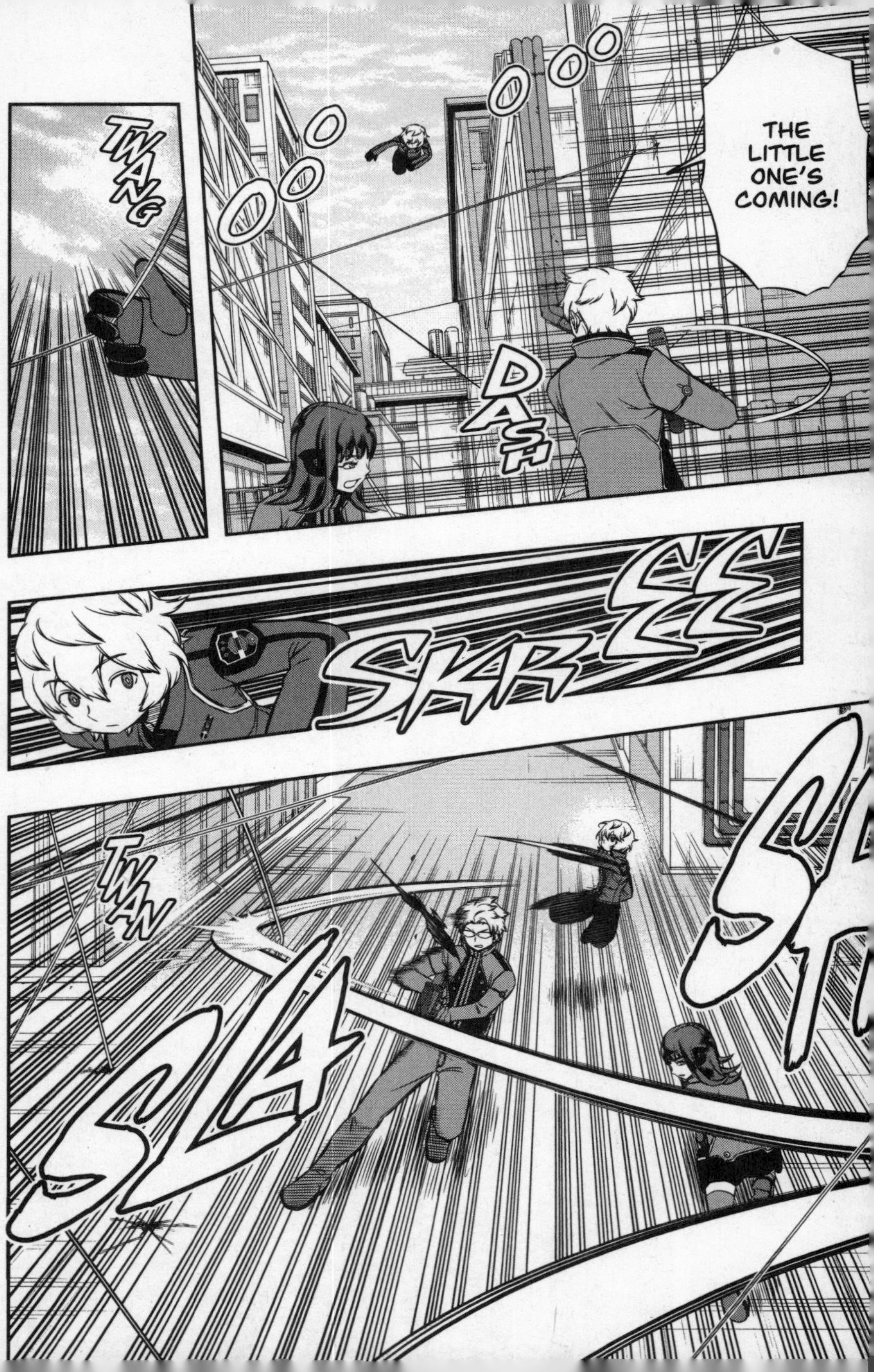
THE LITTLE ONE'S COMING!
DASH
TWANG
SKREEE
TWAN

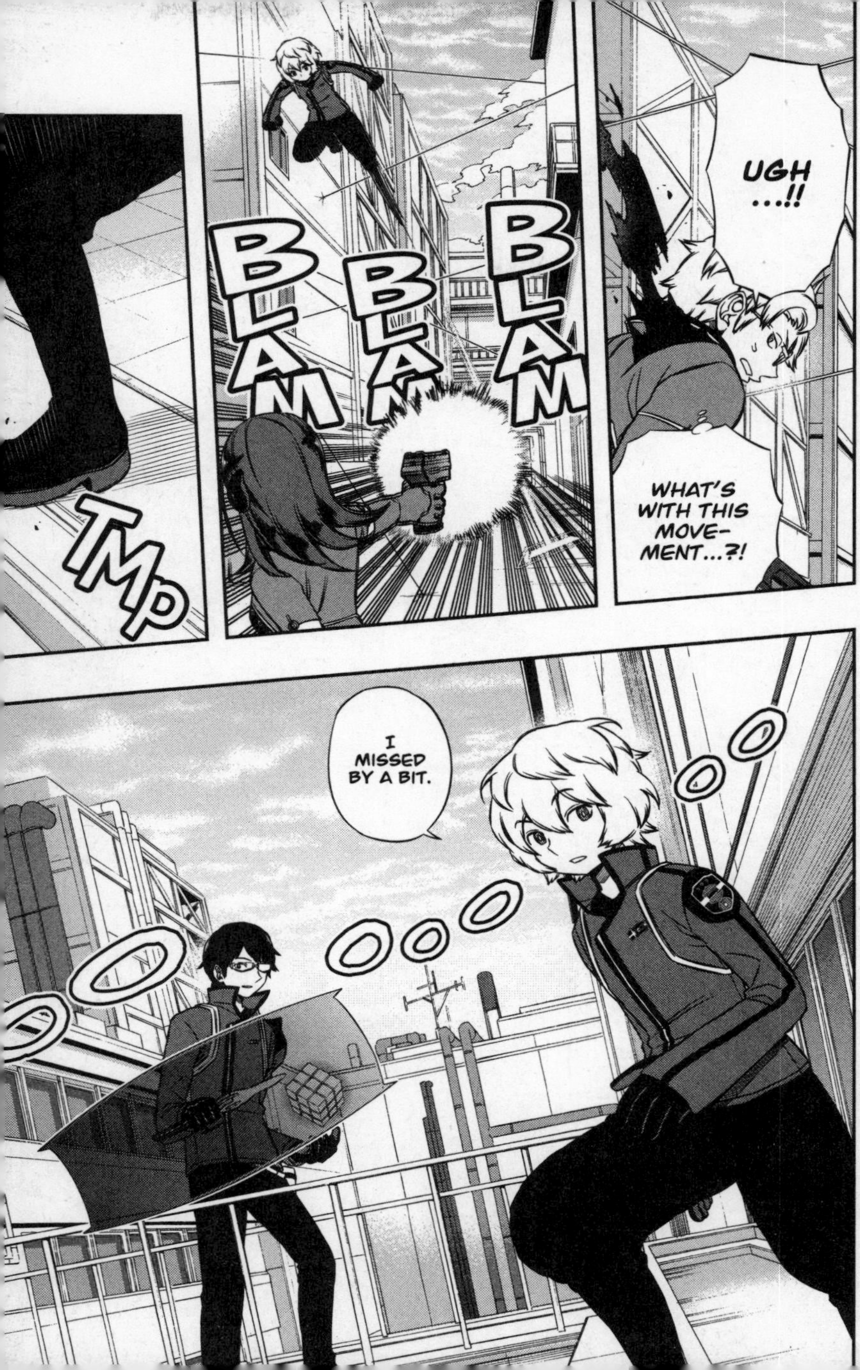

UGH ...!!
WHAT'S WITH THIS MOVE-MENT...?!
BLAM
BLAM
BLAM
TMP
I MISSED BY A BIT.

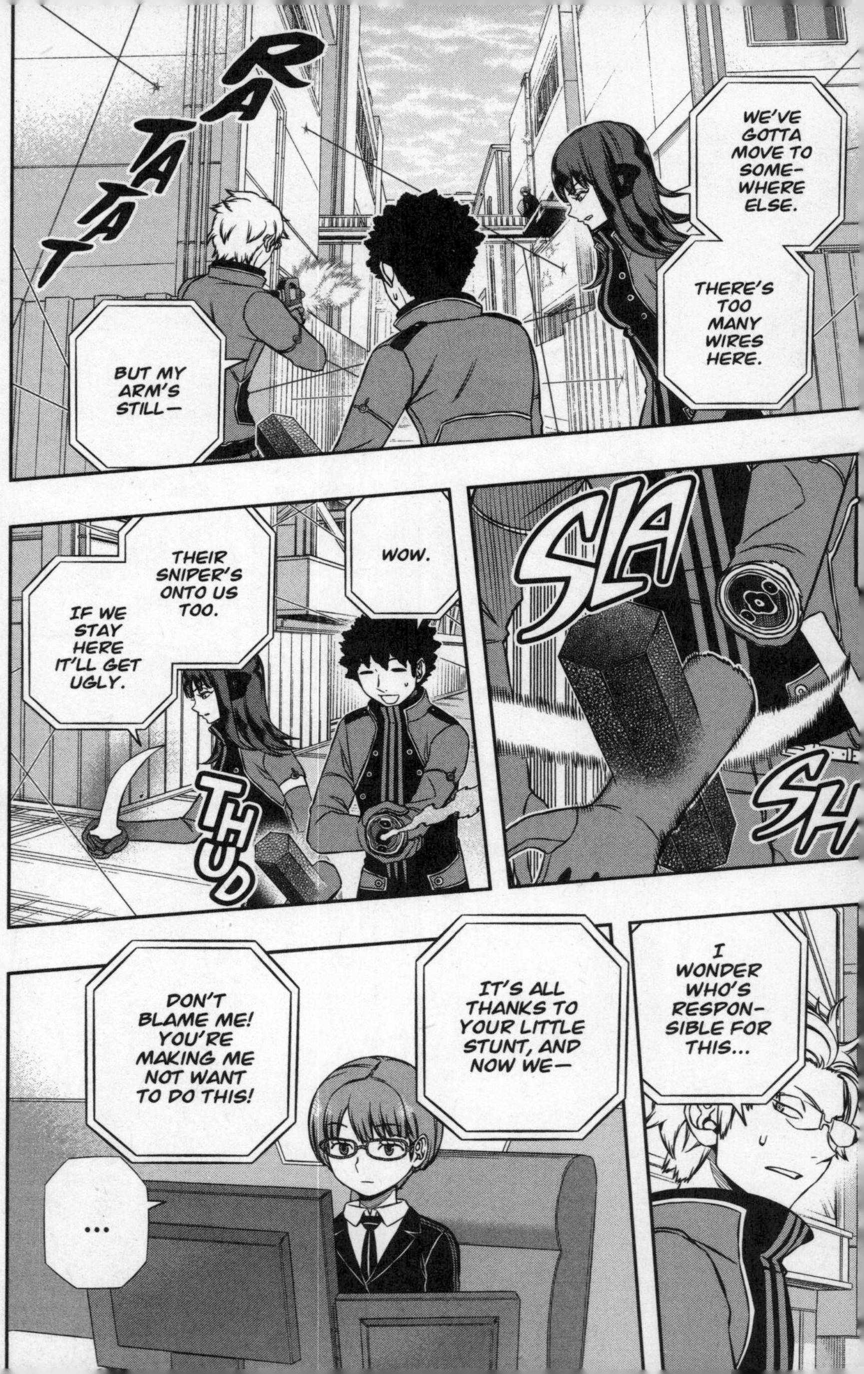
RATATAT
WE'VE GOTTA MOVE TO SOME-WHERE ELSE.
THERE'S TOO MANY WIRES HERE.
BUT MY ARM'S STILL—
SLA
SH
WOW.
THEIR SNIPER'S ONTO US TOO.
IF WE STAY HERE IT'LL GET UGLY.
THUD
I WONDER WHO'S RESPON-SIBLE FOR THIS...
IT'S ALL THANKS TO YOUR LITTLE STUNT, AND NOW WE—
DON'T BLAME ME! YOU'RE MAKING ME NOT WANT TO DO THIS!
...

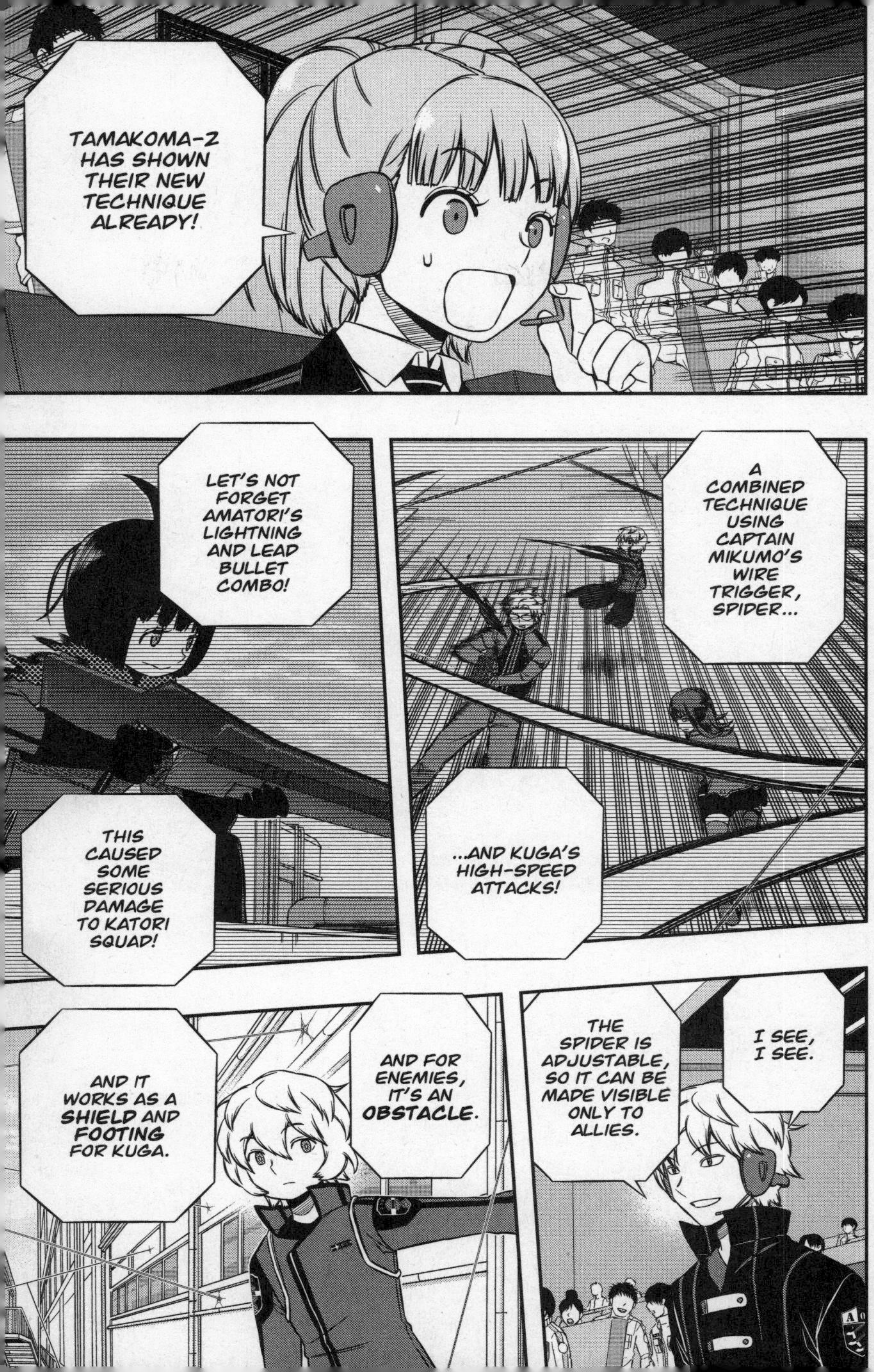

TAMAKOMA-2 HAS SHOWN THEIR NEW TECHNIQUE ALREADY!
A COMBINED TECHNIQUE USING CAPTAIN MIKUMO'S WIRE TRIGGER, SPIDER...
...AND KUGA'S HIGH-SPEED ATTACKS!
LET'S NOT FORGET AMATORI'S LIGHTNING AND LEAD BULLET COMBO!
THIS CAUSED SOME SERIOUS DAMAGE TO KATORI SQUAD!
I SEE, I SEE.
THE SPIDER IS ADJUSTABLE, SO IT CAN BE MADE VISIBLE ONLY TO ALLIES.
AND IT WORKS AS A **SHIELD AND FOOTING** FOR KUGA.
AND FOR ENEMIES, IT'S AN **OBSTACLE**.

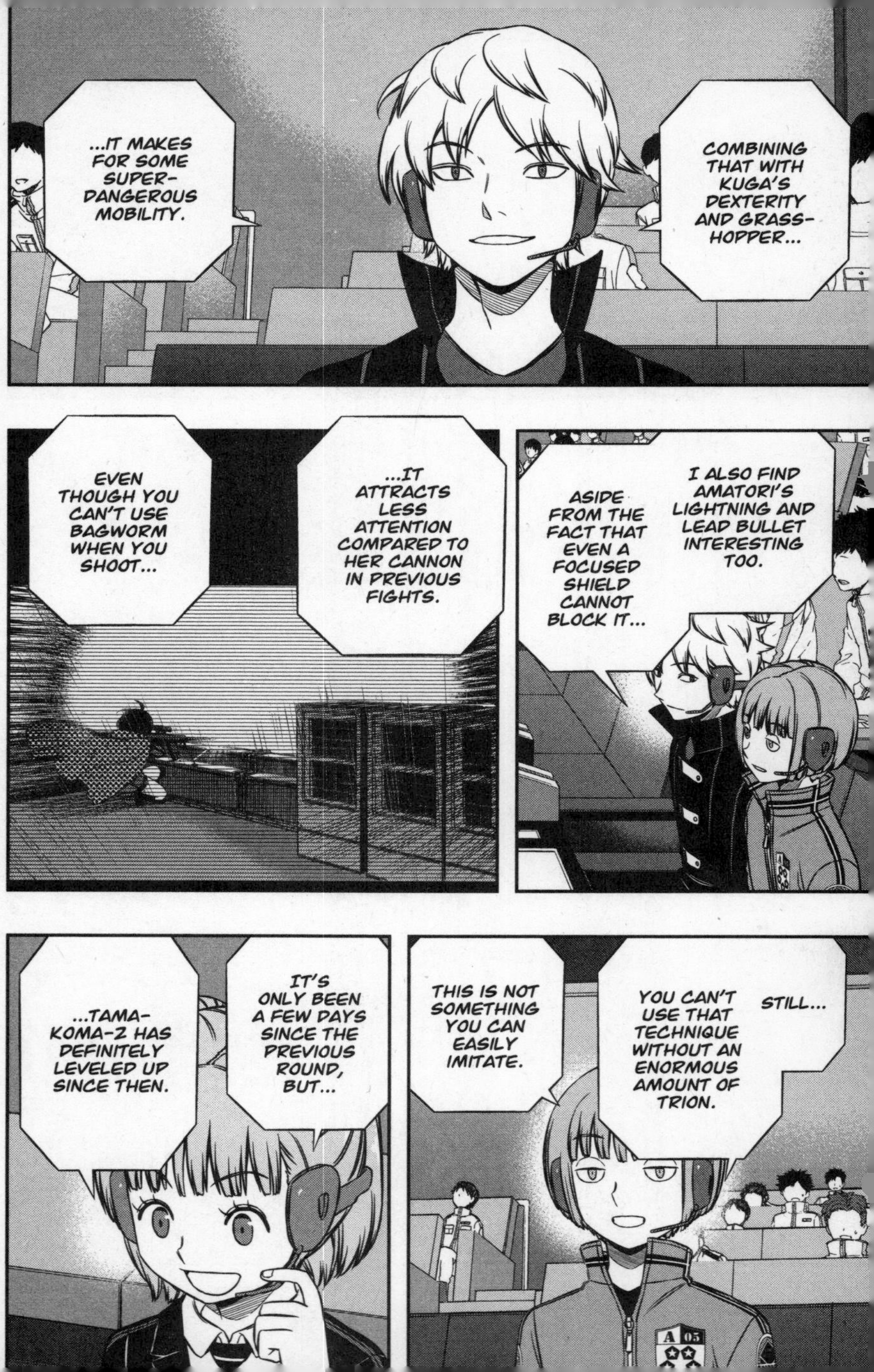
COMBINING THAT WITH KUGA'S DEXTERITY AND GRASS-HOPPER...
...IT MAKES FOR SOME SUPER-DANGEROUS MOBILITY.
I ALSO FIND AMATORI'S LIGHTNING AND LEAD BULLET INTERESTING TOO.
ASIDE FROM THE FACT THAT EVEN A FOCUSED SHIELD CANNOT BLOCK IT...
...IT ATTRACTS LESS ATTENTION COMPARED TO HER CANNON IN PREVIOUS FIGHTS.
EVEN THOUGH YOU CAN'T USE BAGWORM WHEN YOU SHOOT...
STILL...
YOU CAN'T USE THAT TECHNIQUE WITHOUT AN ENORMOUS AMOUNT OF TRION.
THIS IS NOT SOMETHING YOU CAN EASILY IMITATE.
IT'S ONLY BEEN A FEW DAYS SINCE THE PREVIOUS ROUND, BUT...
...TAMA-KOMA-2 HAS DEFINITELY LEVELED UP SINCE THEN.

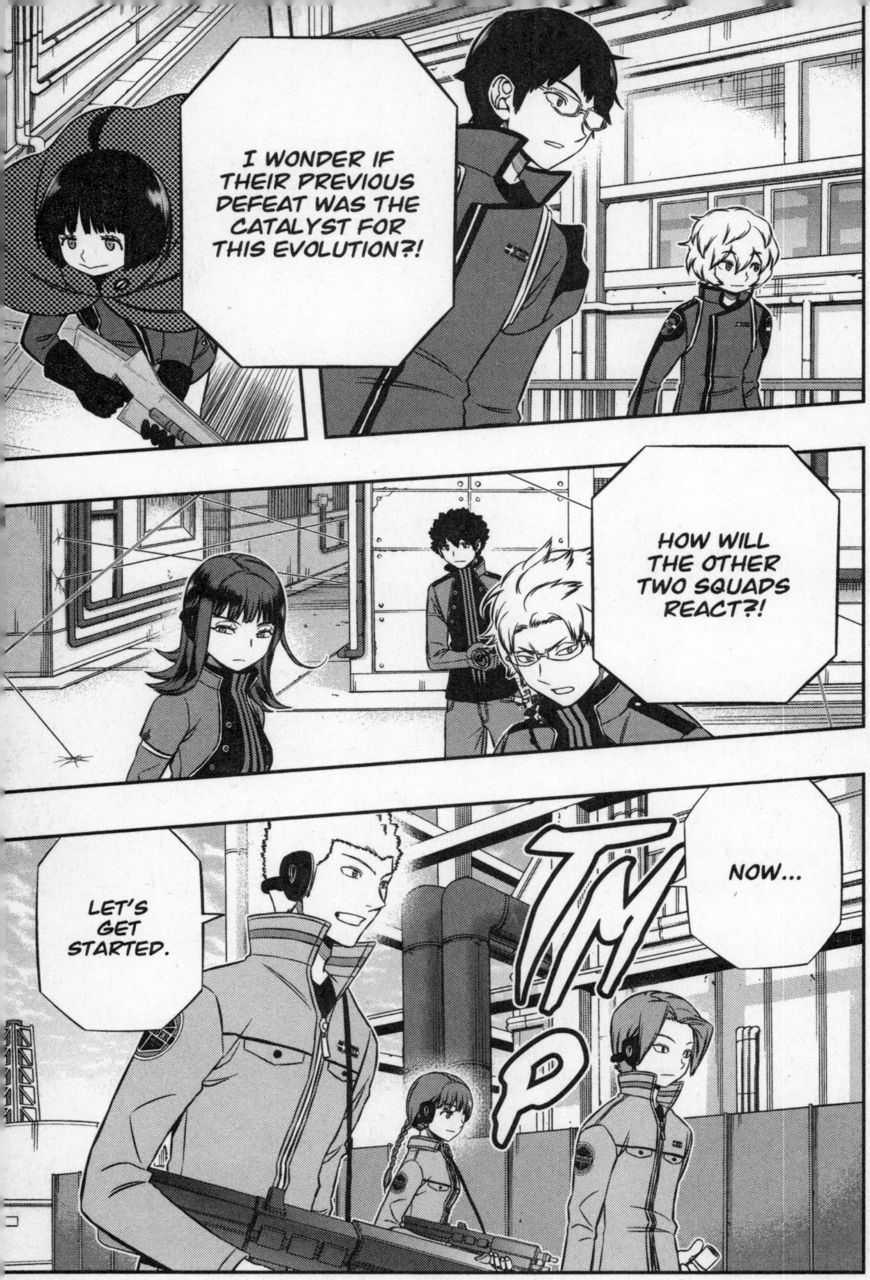
I WONDER IF THEIR PREVIOUS DEFEAT WAS THE CATALYST FOR THIS EVOLUTION?!
HOW WILL THE OTHER TWO SQUADS REACT?!
NOW...
TMP
LET'S GET STARTED.

WORLD TRIGGER

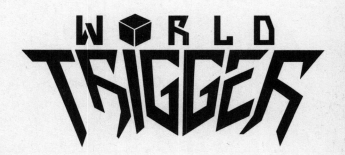

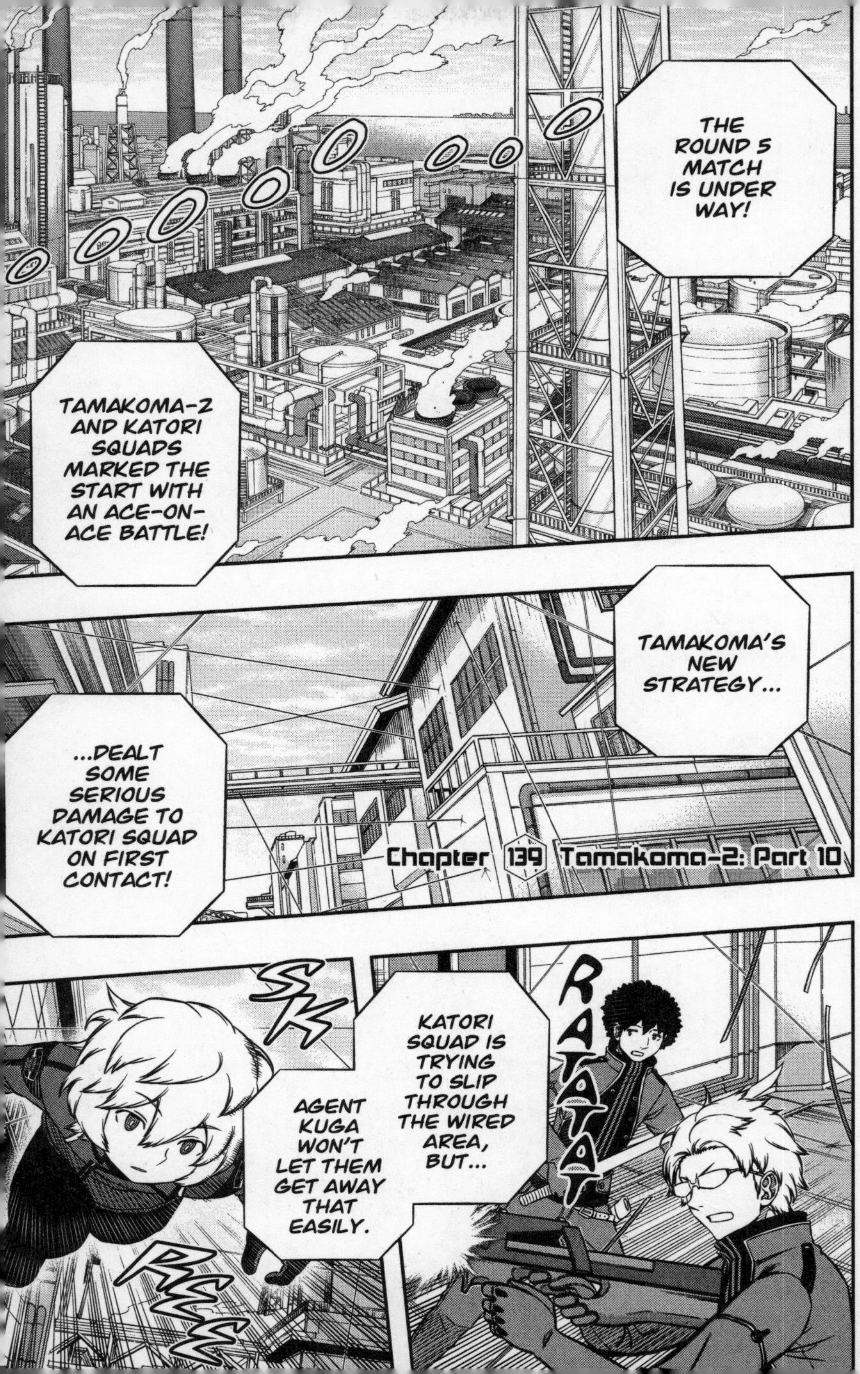
THE ROUND 5 MATCH IS UNDER WAY!
TAMAKOMA-2 AND KATORI SQUADS MARKED THE START WITH AN ACE-ON-ACE BATTLE!
TAMAKOMA'S NEW STRATEGY...
...DEALT SOME SERIOUS DAMAGE TO KATORI SQUAD ON FIRST CONTACT!
Chapter 139 Tamakoma-2: Part 10
RATATA
KATORI SQUAD IS TRYING TO SLIP THROUGH THE WIRED AREA, BUT...
AGENT KUGA WON'T LET THEM GET AWAY THAT EASILY.
SK

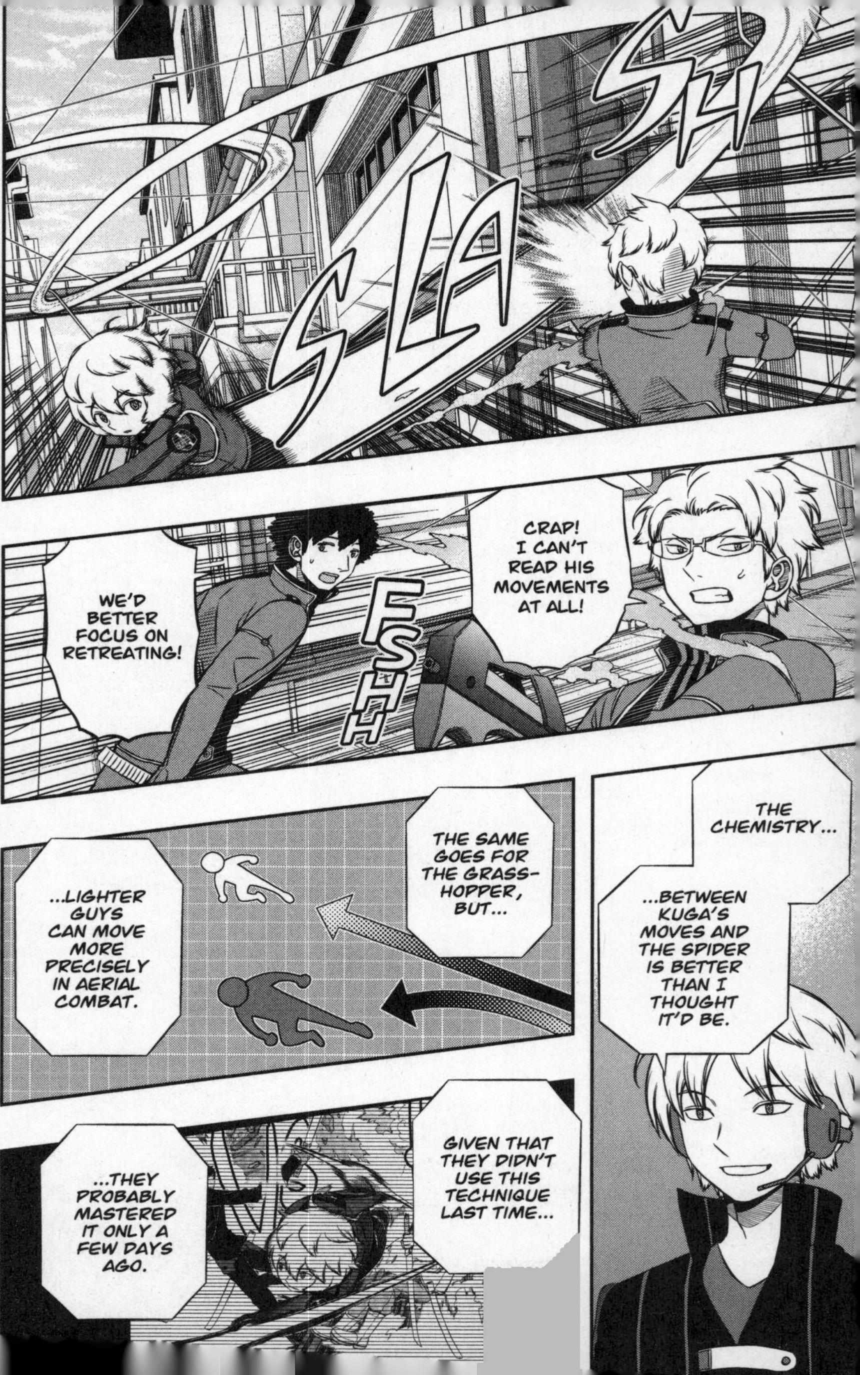
SLA
SH
CRAP! I CAN'T READ HIS MOVEMENTS AT ALL!
FSHHH
WE'D BETTER FOCUS ON RETREATING!
THE CHEMISTRY...
...BETWEEN KUGA'S MOVES AND THE SPIDER IS BETTER THAN I THOUGHT IT'D BE.
THE SAME GOES FOR THE GRASS-HOPPER, BUT...
...LIGHTER GUYS CAN MOVE MORE PRECISELY IN AERIAL COMBAT.
GIVEN THAT THEY DIDN'T USE THIS TECHNIQUE LAST TIME...
...THEY PROBABLY MASTERED IT ONLY A FEW DAYS AGO.

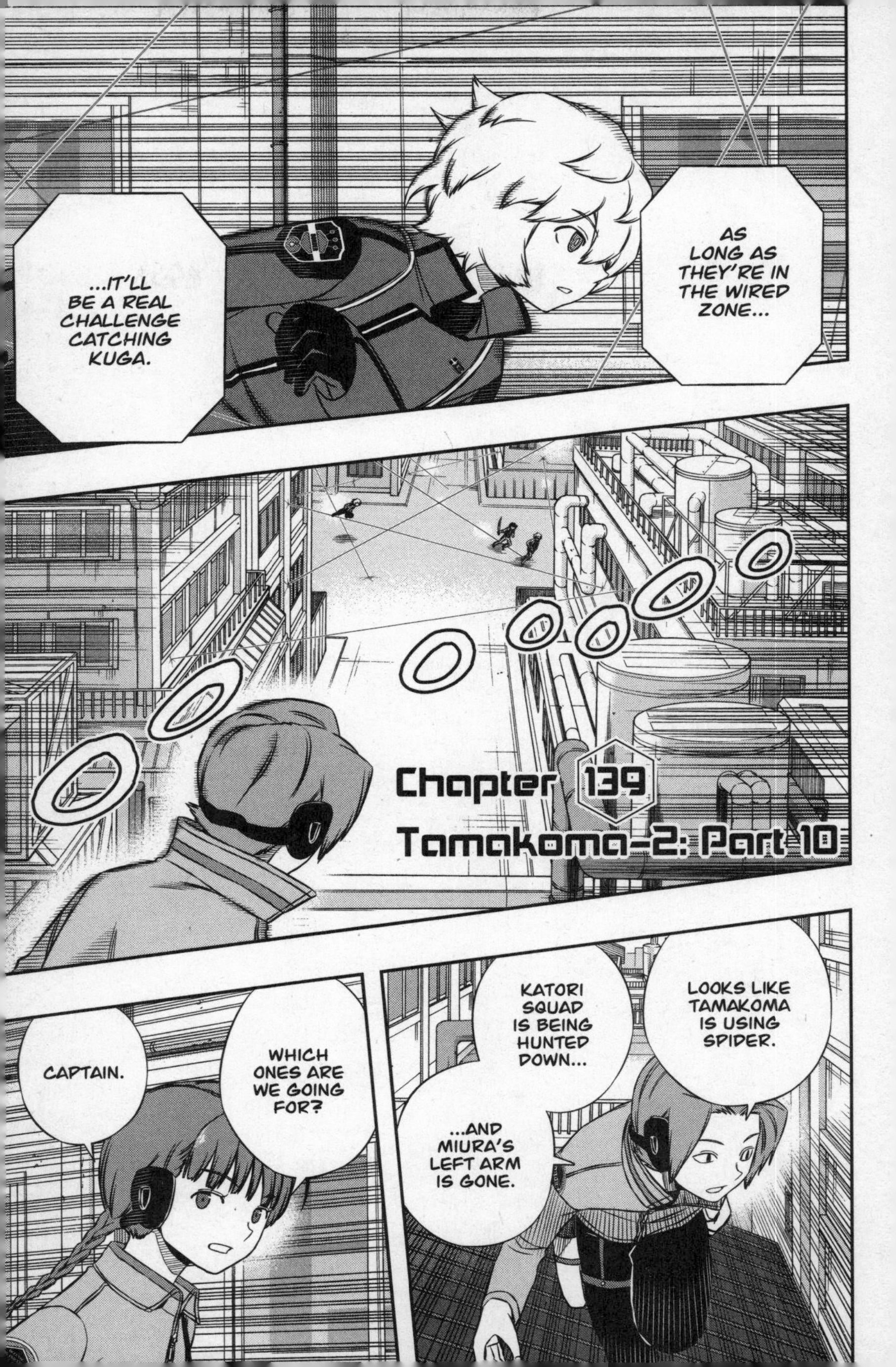
AS LONG AS THEY'RE IN THE WIRED ZONE...
...IT'LL BE A REAL CHALLENGE CATCHING KUGA.
Chapter 139
Tamakoma-2: Part 10
LOOKS LIKE TAMAKOMA IS USING SPIDER.
KATORI SQUAD IS BEING HUNTED DOWN...
...AND MIURA'S LEFT ARM IS GONE.
WHICH ONES ARE WE GOING FOR?
CAPTAIN.

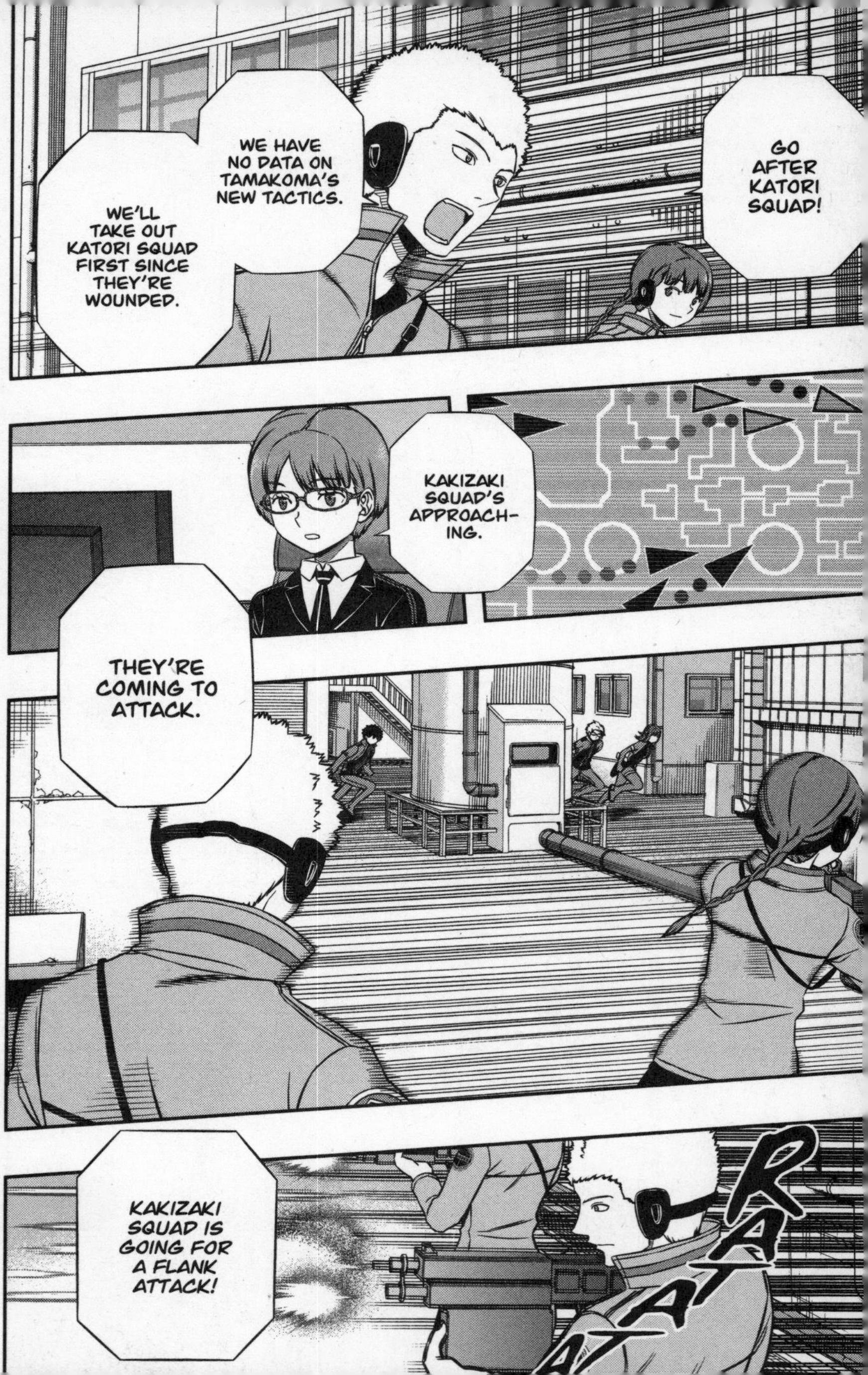
GO AFTER KATORI SQUAD!
WE HAVE NO DATA ON TAMAKOMA'S NEW TACTICS.
WE'LL TAKE OUT KATORI SQUAD FIRST SINCE THEY'RE WOUNDED.
KAKIZAKI SQUAD'S APPROACH-ING.
THEY'RE COMING TO ATTACK.
KAKIZAKI SQUAD IS GOING FOR A FLANK ATTACK!

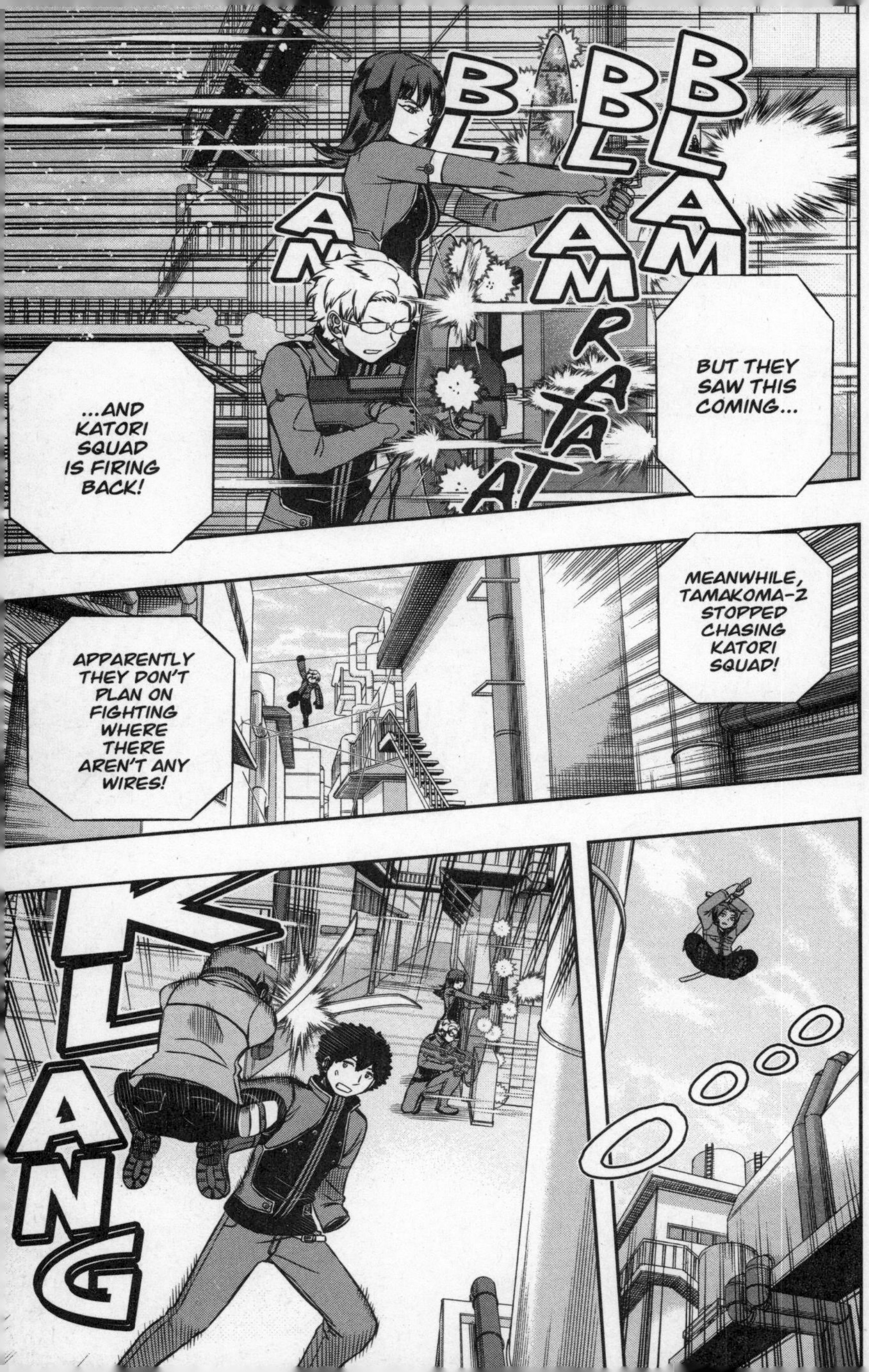
BLAM
BLAM
BLAM
RATATAT
BUT THEY SAW THIS COMING...
...AND KATORI SQUAD IS FIRING BACK!
MEANWHILE, TAMAKOMA-2 STOPPED CHASING KATORI SQUAD!
APPARENTLY THEY DON'T PLAN ON FIGHTING WHERE THERE AREN'T ANY WIRES!
OOOO
KLANG

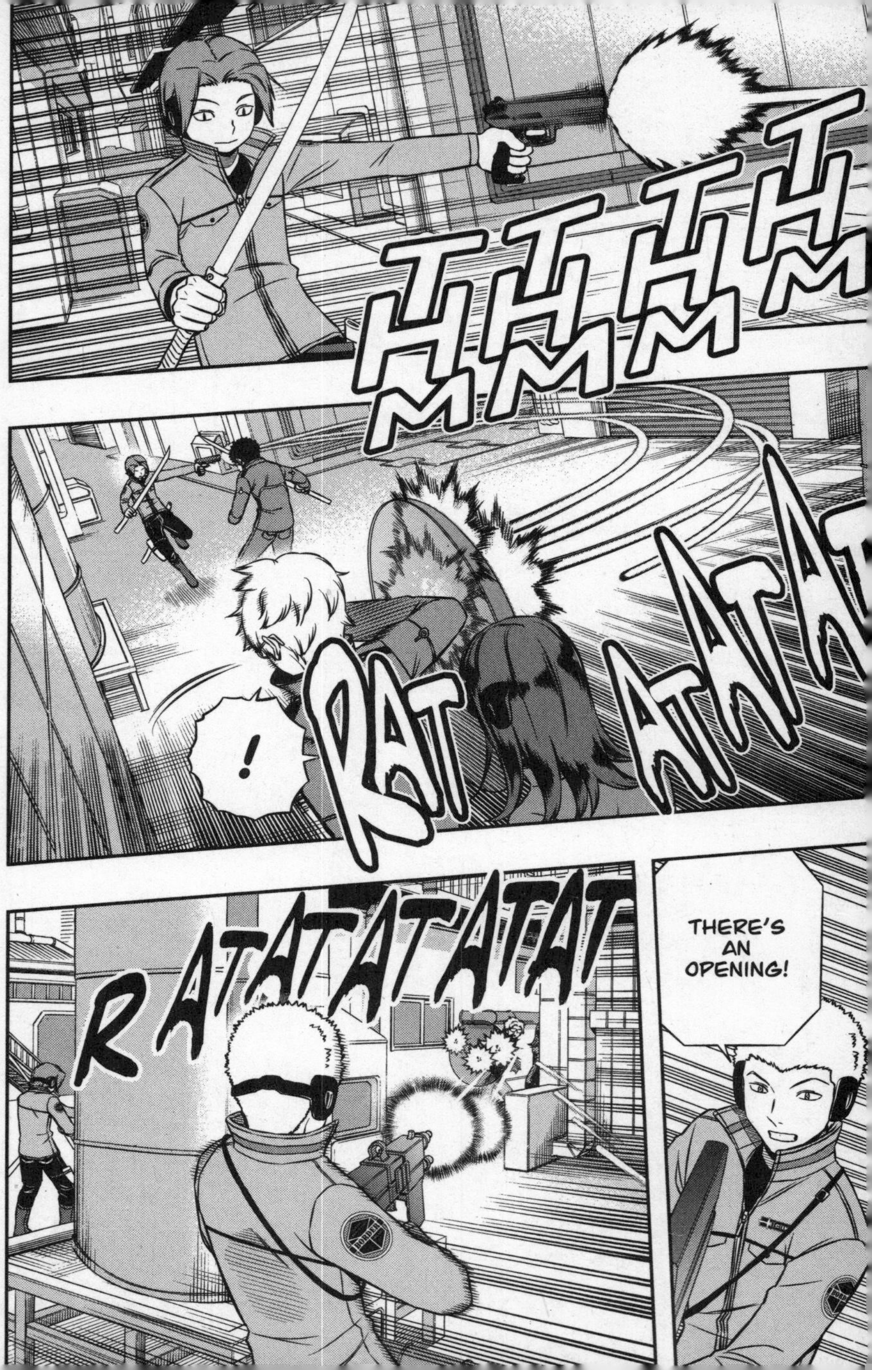
THHHHMMMM
RATATATAT
!
THERE'S AN OPENING!
RATATATATAT

TOMOE FROM KAKIZAKI SQUAD HAS BROKEN THROUGH THE ENEMY GUARD!

KLANG

KLANG
KLANG

UGH....!

ZIP

IT APPEARS MIURA LOSING AN ARM IS REALLY HURTING KATORI SQUAD.

KAKIZAKI SQUAD NOW HAS THE ADVANTAGE!

...KAKIZAKI SQUAD IS PROBABLY STRONGER.

DESPITE IT BEING TWO AGAINST THREE...

...TRIGGERS LIKE KOGETSU AND RAYGUST...

MAYBE A SCORPION COULD BE FINE, BUT...

...COULD BE HEAVY ENOUGH TO PUT YOU OFF-BALANCE.

RA TA TAT

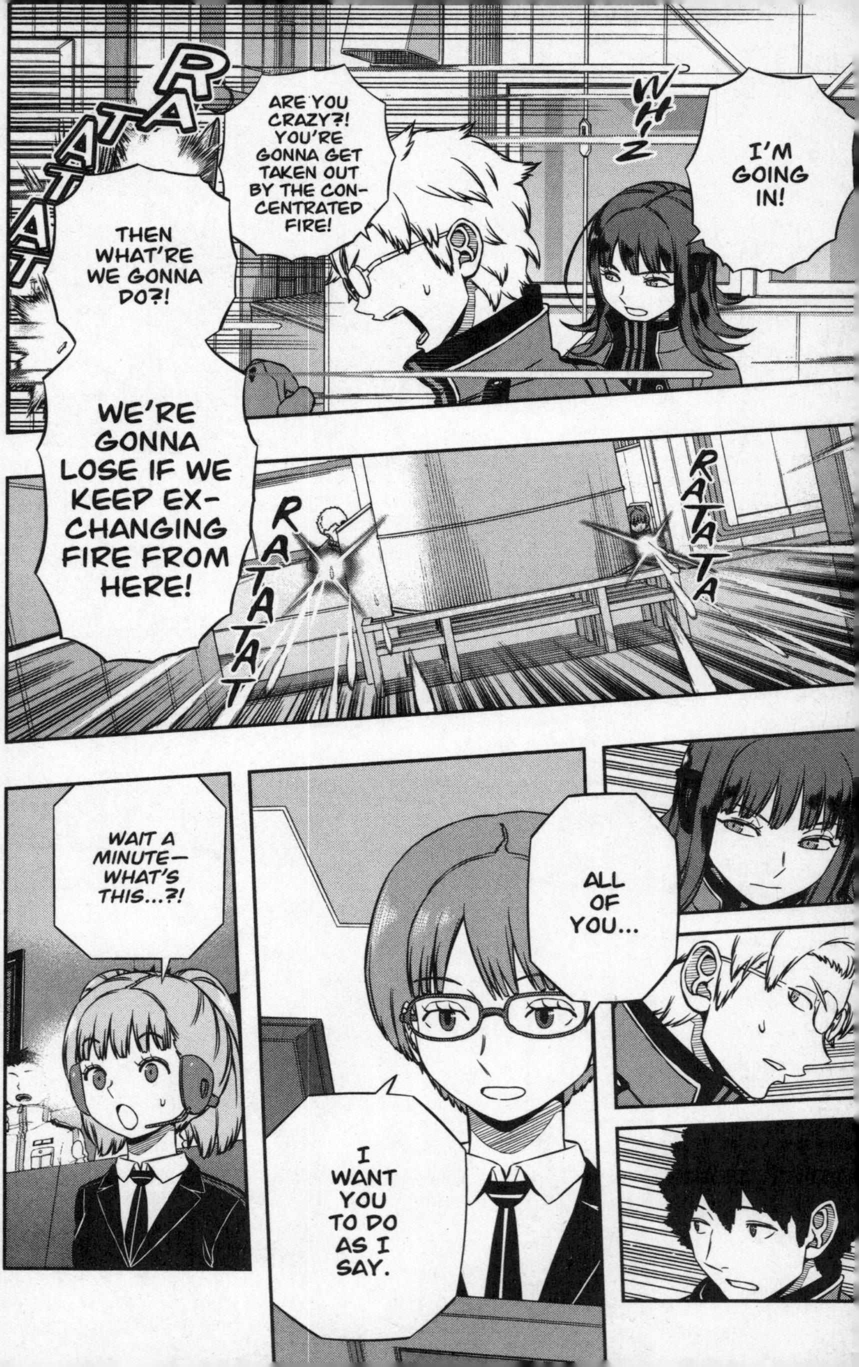

I'M GOING IN!
WHIZ
ARE YOU CRAZY?! YOU'RE GONNA GET TAKEN OUT BY THE CON-CENTRATED FIRE!
RATATAT
THEN WHAT'RE WE GONNA DO?!
WE'RE GONNA LOSE IF WE KEEP EX-CHANGING FIRE FROM HERE!
RATATA
RATATAT
ALL OF YOU...
I WANT YOU TO DO AS I SAY.
WAIT A MINUTE—WHAT'S THIS...?!

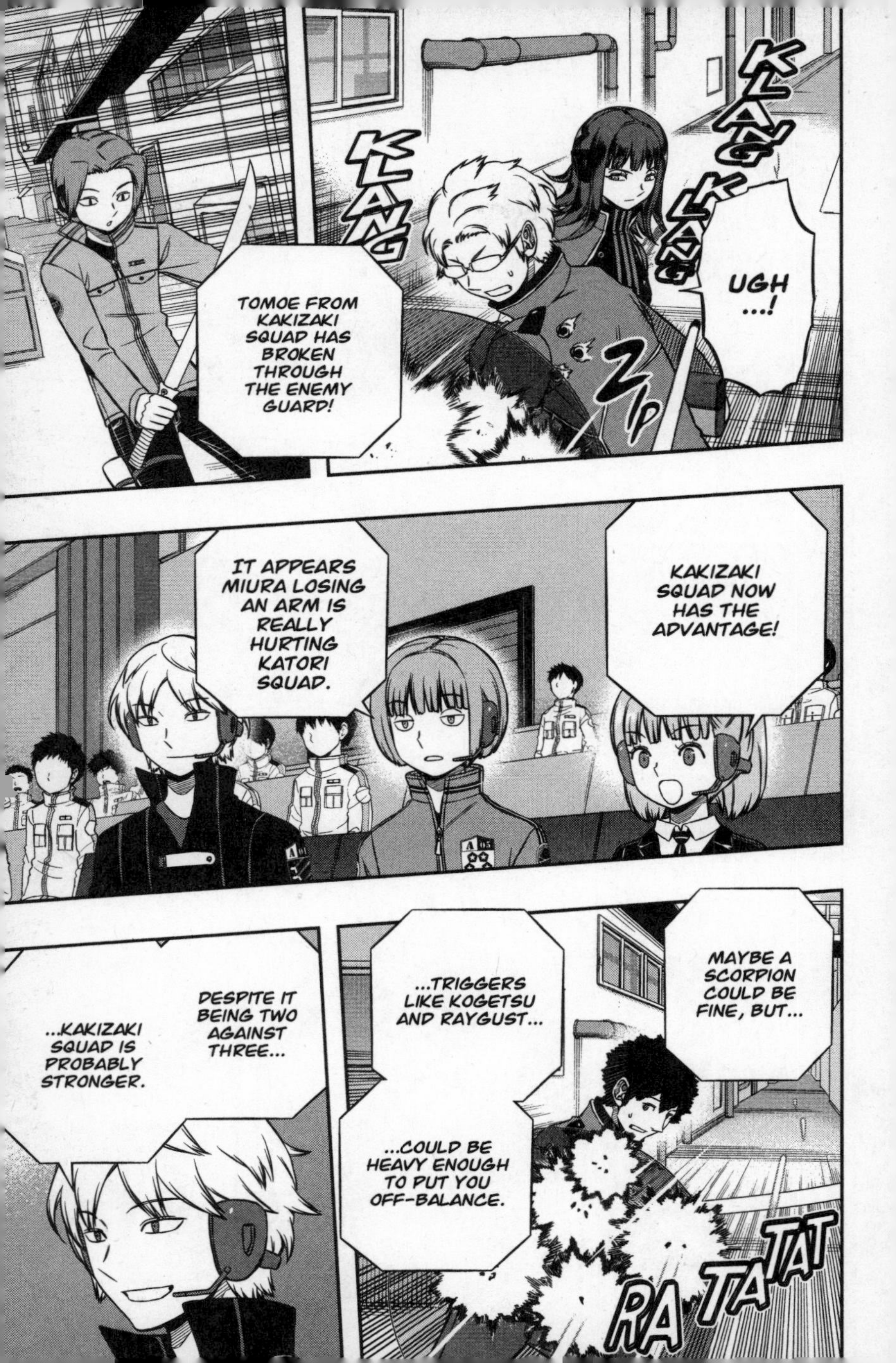
KLANG
KLANG
UGH ...!
KLANG
ZIP
TOMOE FROM KAKIZAKI SQUAD HAS BROKEN THROUGH THE ENEMY GUARD!
KAKIZAKI SQUAD NOW HAS THE ADVANTAGE!
IT APPEARS MIURA LOSING AN ARM IS REALLY HURTING KATORI SQUAD.
MAYBE A SCORPION COULD BE FINE, BUT...
...TRIGGERS LIKE KOGETSU AND RAYGUST...
...COULD BE HEAVY ENOUGH TO PUT YOU OFF-BALANCE.
RATATAT
DESPITE IT BEING TWO AGAINST THREE...
...KAKIZAKI SQUAD IS PROBABLY STRONGER.

RATATATAT

ARE YOU CRAZY?! YOU'RE GONNA GET TAKEN OUT BY THE CONCENTRATED FIRE!

WHIZ

I'M GOING IN!

THEN WHAT'RE WE GONNA DO?!

WE'RE GONNA LOSE IF WE KEEP EXCHANGING FIRE FROM HERE!

RATATAT

RATATA

WAIT A MINUTE— WHAT'S THIS...?!

ALL OF YOU...

I WANT YOU TO DO AS I SAY.

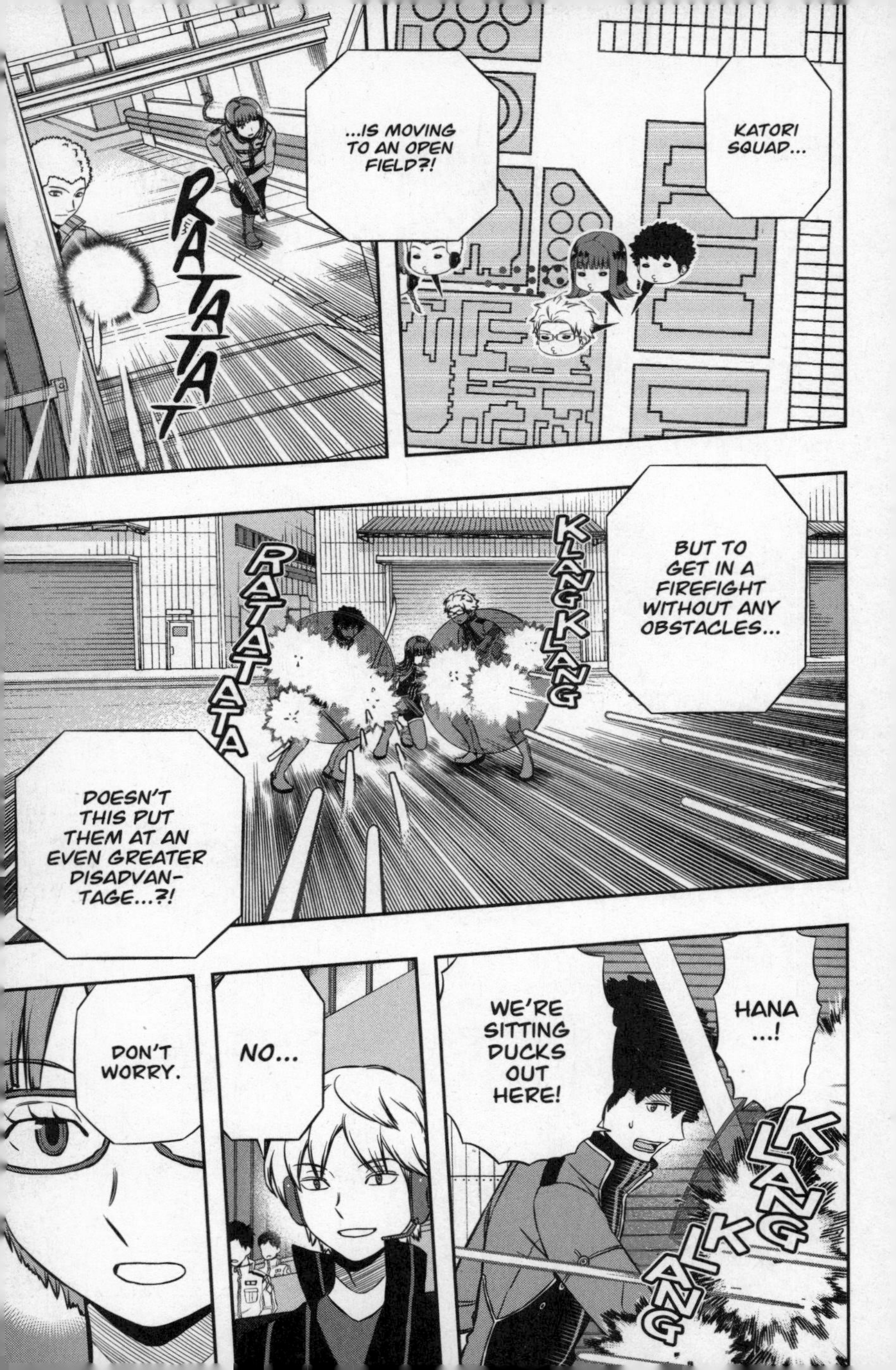
KATORI SQUAD...
...IS MOVING TO AN OPEN FIELD?!
RATATATAT
KLANGKLANG
BUT TO GET IN A FIREFIGHT WITHOUT ANY OBSTACLES...
RATATATA
DOESN'T THIS PUT THEM AT AN EVEN GREATER DISADVAN-TAGE...?!
HANA ...!
WE'RE SITTING DUCKS OUT HERE!
KLANG KLANG
NO...
DON'T WORRY.

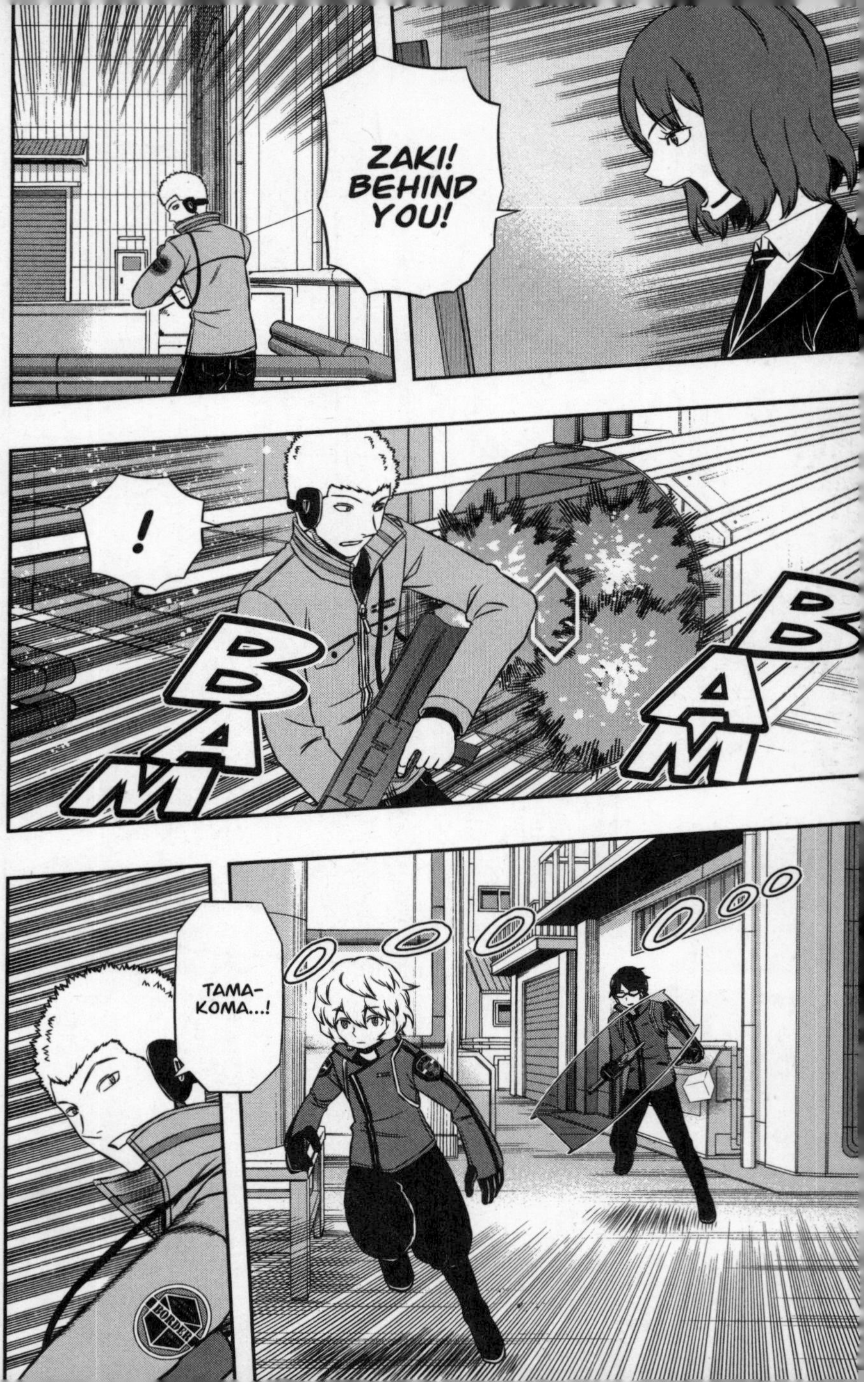
ZAKI! BEHIND YOU!
!
BAM
BAM
TAMA-KOMA...!

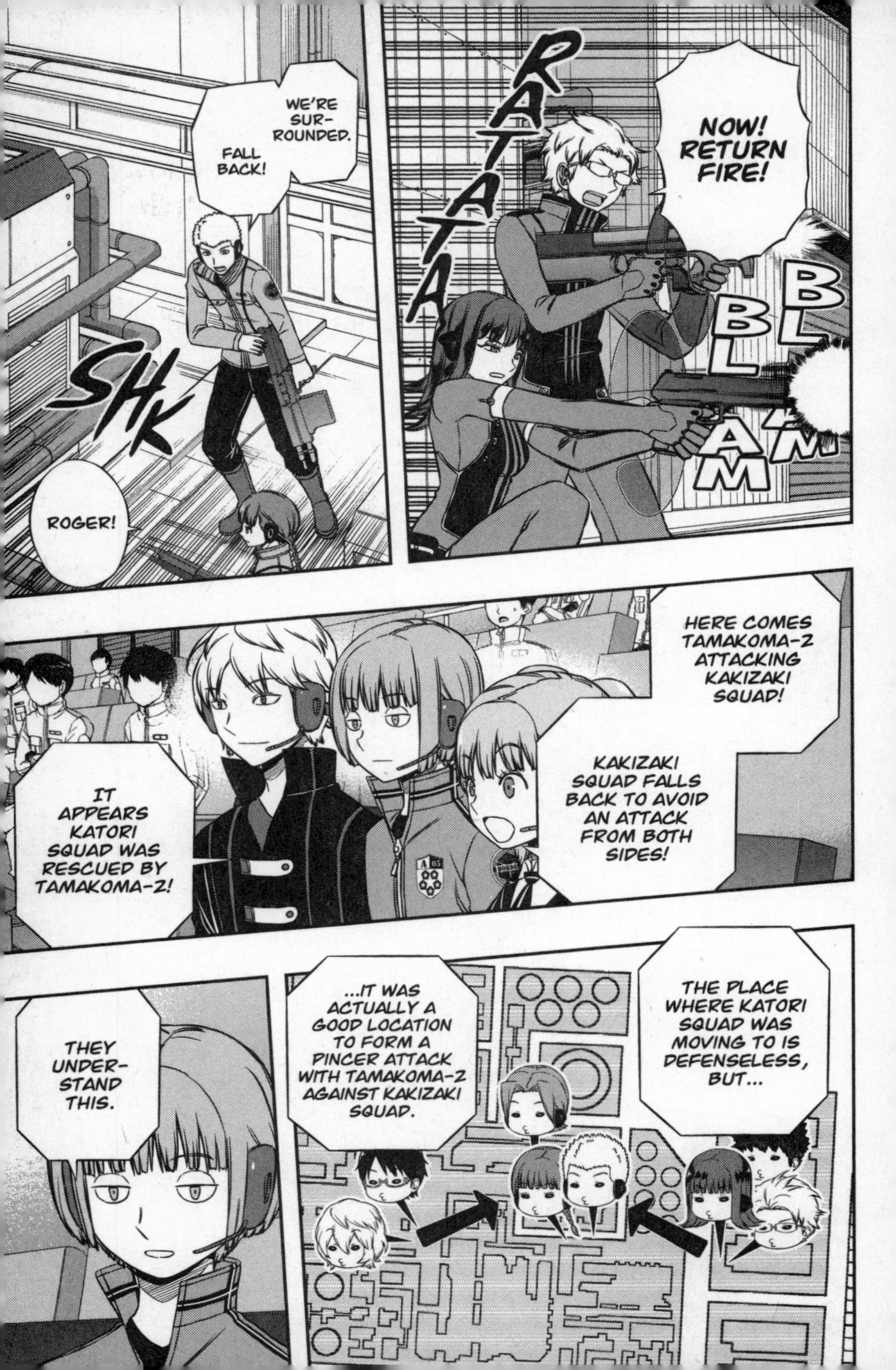

NOW! RETURN FIRE!
RATATATA
BLAM
BLAM
WE'RE SURROUNDED.
FALL BACK!
SHK
ROGER!
HERE COMES TAMAKOMA-2 ATTACKING KAKIZAKI SQUAD!
KAKIZAKI SQUAD FALLS BACK TO AVOID AN ATTACK FROM BOTH SIDES!
IT APPEARS KATORI SQUAD WAS RESCUED BY TAMAKOMA-2!
THE PLACE WHERE KATORI SQUAD WAS MOVING TO IS DEFENSELESS, BUT...
...IT WAS ACTUALLY A GOOD LOCATION TO FORM A PINCER ATTACK WITH TAMAKOMA-2 AGAINST KAKIZAKI SQUAD.
THEY UNDERSTAND THIS.

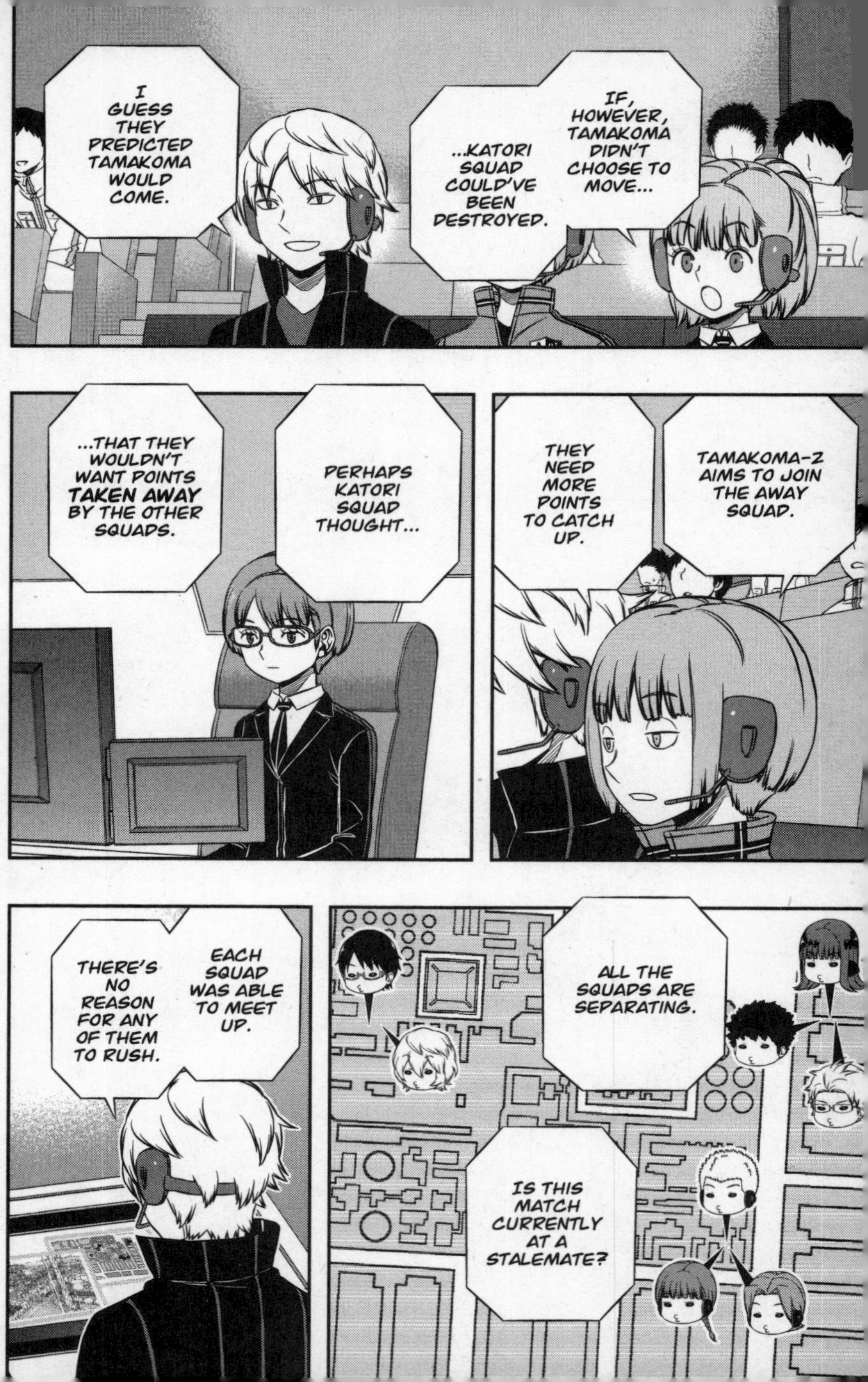
IF, HOWEVER, TAMAKOMA DIDN'T CHOOSE TO MOVE...
...KATORI SQUAD COULD'VE BEEN DESTROYED.
I GUESS THEY PREDICTED TAMAKOMA WOULD COME.
TAMAKOMA-2 AIMS TO JOIN THE AWAY SQUAD.
THEY NEED MORE POINTS TO CATCH UP.
PERHAPS KATORI SQUAD THOUGHT...
...THAT THEY WOULDN'T WANT POINTS TAKEN AWAY BY THE OTHER SQUADS.
ALL THE SQUADS ARE SEPARATING.
IS THIS MATCH CURRENTLY AT A STALEMATE?
EACH SQUAD WAS ABLE TO MEET UP.
THERE'S NO REASON FOR ANY OF THEM TO RUSH.

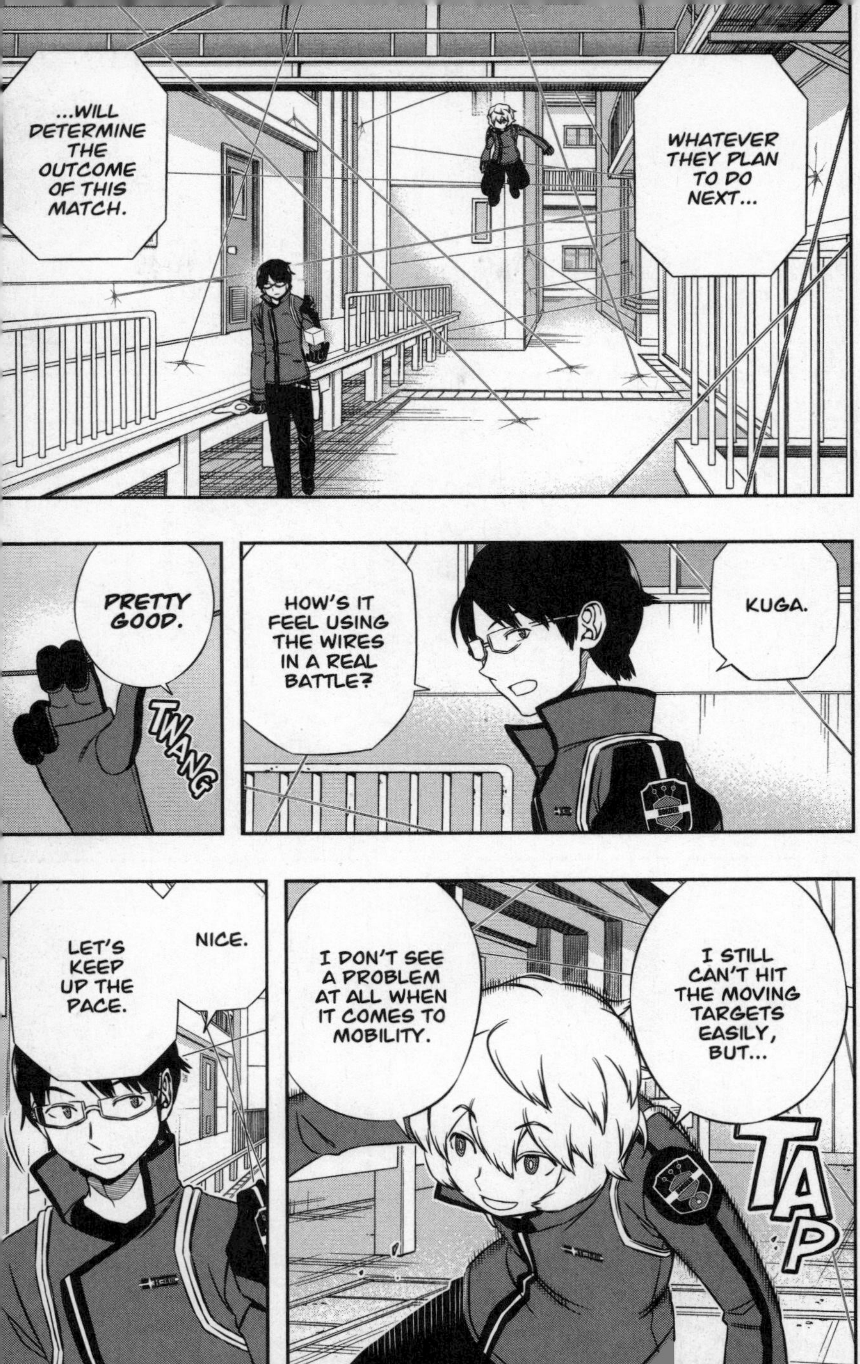
WHATEVER THEY PLAN TO DO NEXT...
...WILL DETERMINE THE OUTCOME OF THIS MATCH.
KUGA.
HOW'S IT FEEL USING THE WIRES IN A REAL BATTLE?
PRETTY GOOD.
TWANG
I STILL CAN'T HIT THE MOVING TARGETS EASILY, BUT...
I DON'T SEE A PROBLEM AT ALL WHEN IT COMES TO MOBILITY.
TAP
NICE.
LET'S KEEP UP THE PACE.

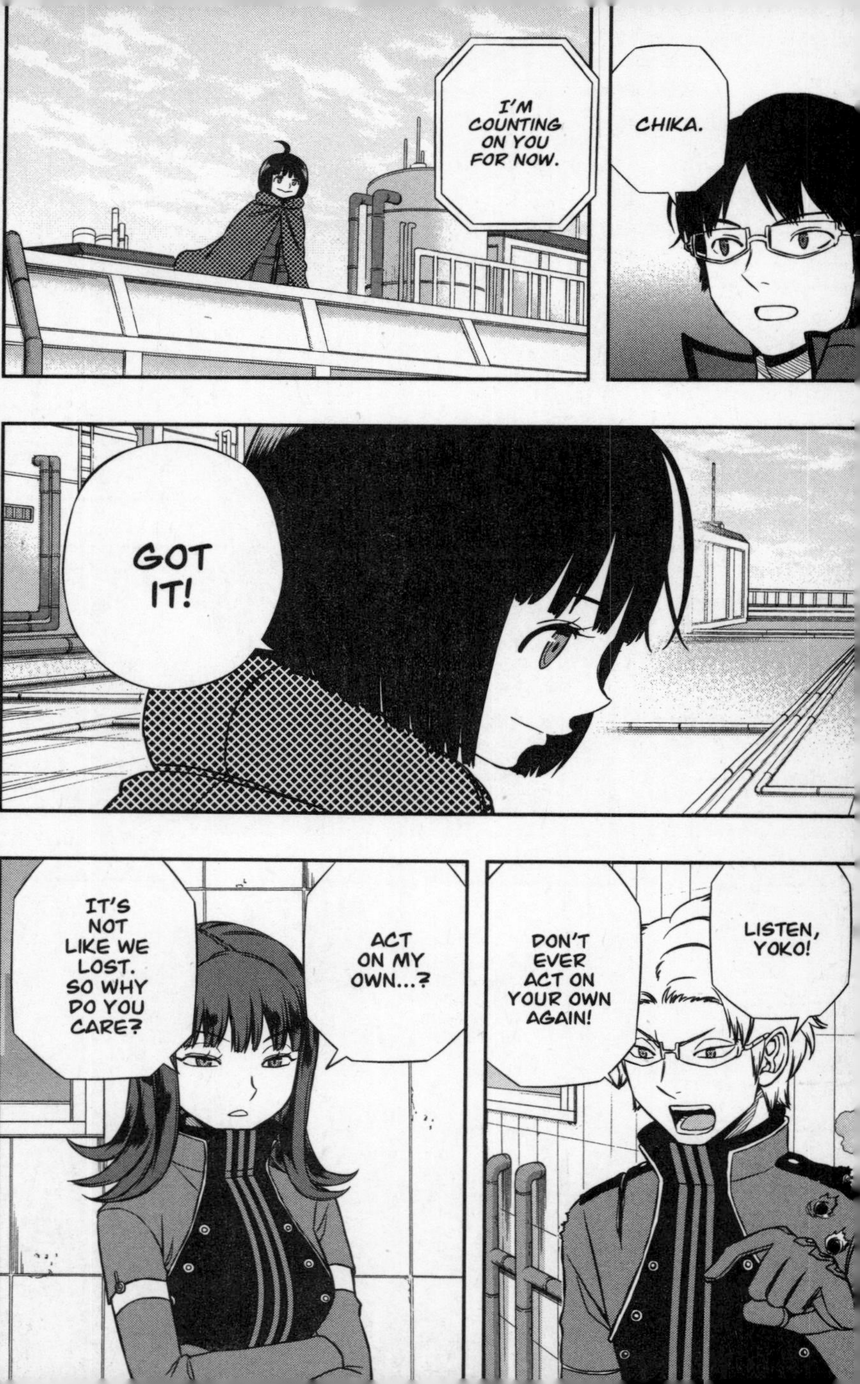
CHIKA.
I'M COUNTING ON YOU FOR NOW.
GOT IT!
LISTEN, YOKO!
DON'T EVER ACT ON YOUR OWN AGAIN!
ACT ON MY OWN...?
IT'S NOT LIKE WE LOST. SO WHY DO YOU CARE?

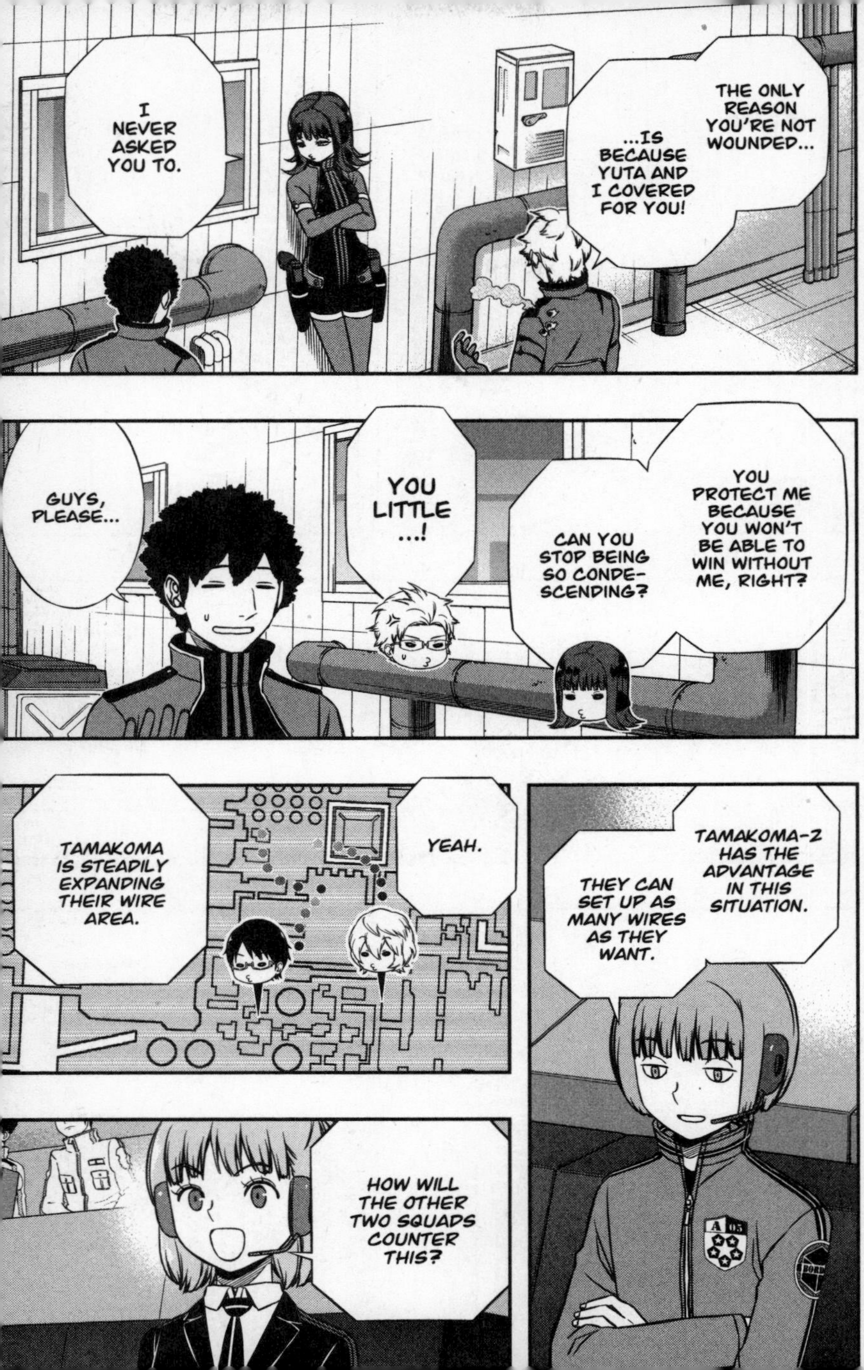
THE ONLY REASON YOU'RE NOT WOUNDED...
...IS BECAUSE YUTA AND I COVERED FOR YOU!
I NEVER ASKED YOU TO.
YOU PROTECT ME BECAUSE YOU WON'T BE ABLE TO WIN WITHOUT ME, RIGHT?
CAN YOU STOP BEING SO CONDE-SCENDING?
YOU LITTLE ...!
GUYS, PLEASE...
TAMAKOMA-2 HAS THE ADVANTAGE IN THIS SITUATION.
THEY CAN SET UP AS MANY WIRES AS THEY WANT.
YEAH.
TAMAKOMA IS STEADILY EXPANDING THEIR WIRE AREA.
HOW WILL THE OTHER TWO SQUADS COUNTER THIS?

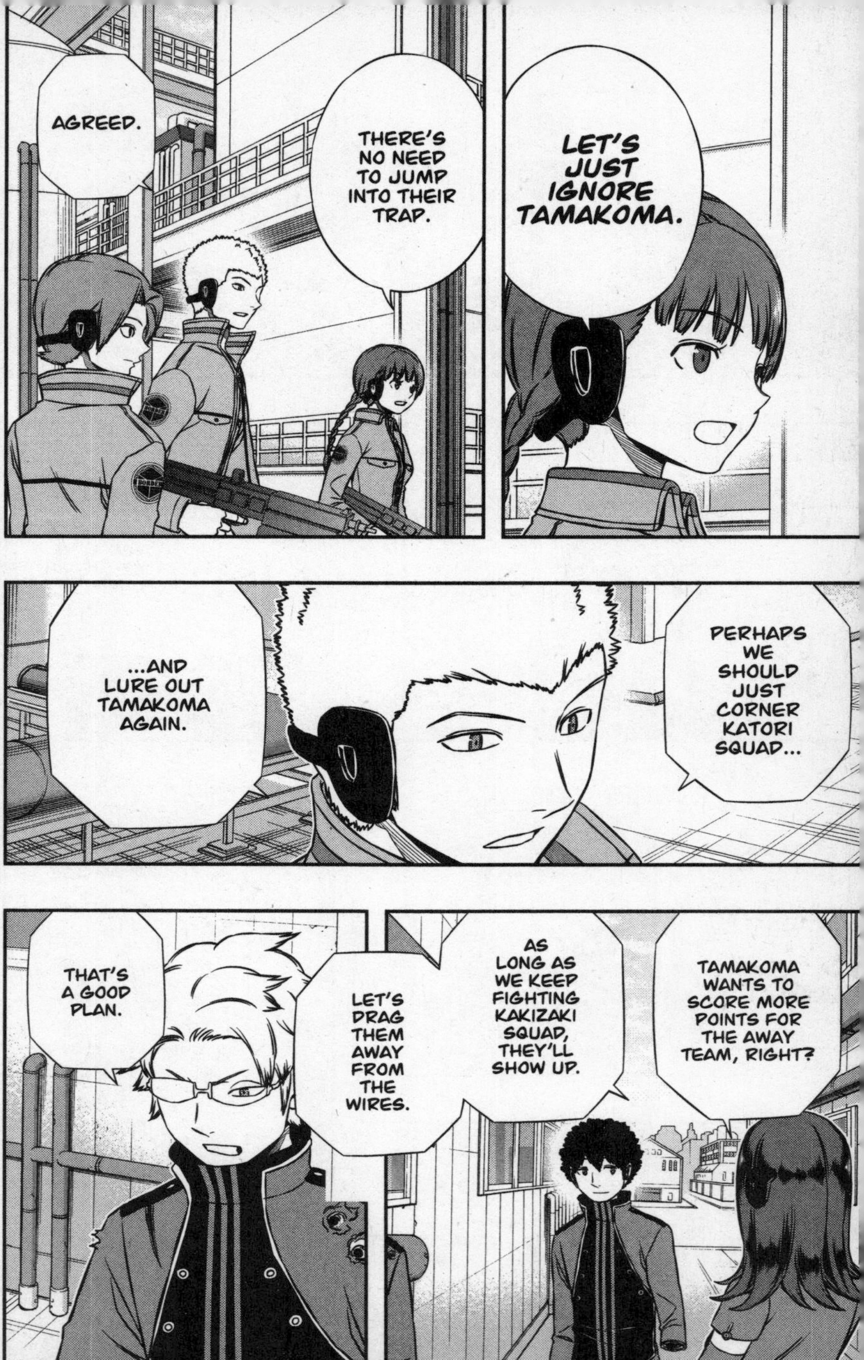

LET'S JUST IGNORE TAMAKOMA.
THERE'S NO NEED TO JUMP INTO THEIR TRAP.
AGREED.
PERHAPS WE SHOULD JUST CORNER KATORI SQUAD...
...AND LURE OUT TAMAKOMA AGAIN.
TAMAKOMA WANTS TO SCORE MORE POINTS FOR THE AWAY TEAM, RIGHT?
AS LONG AS WE KEEP FIGHTING KAKIZAKI SQUAD, THEY'LL SHOW UP.
LET'S DRAG THEM AWAY FROM THE WIRES.
THAT'S A GOOD PLAN.

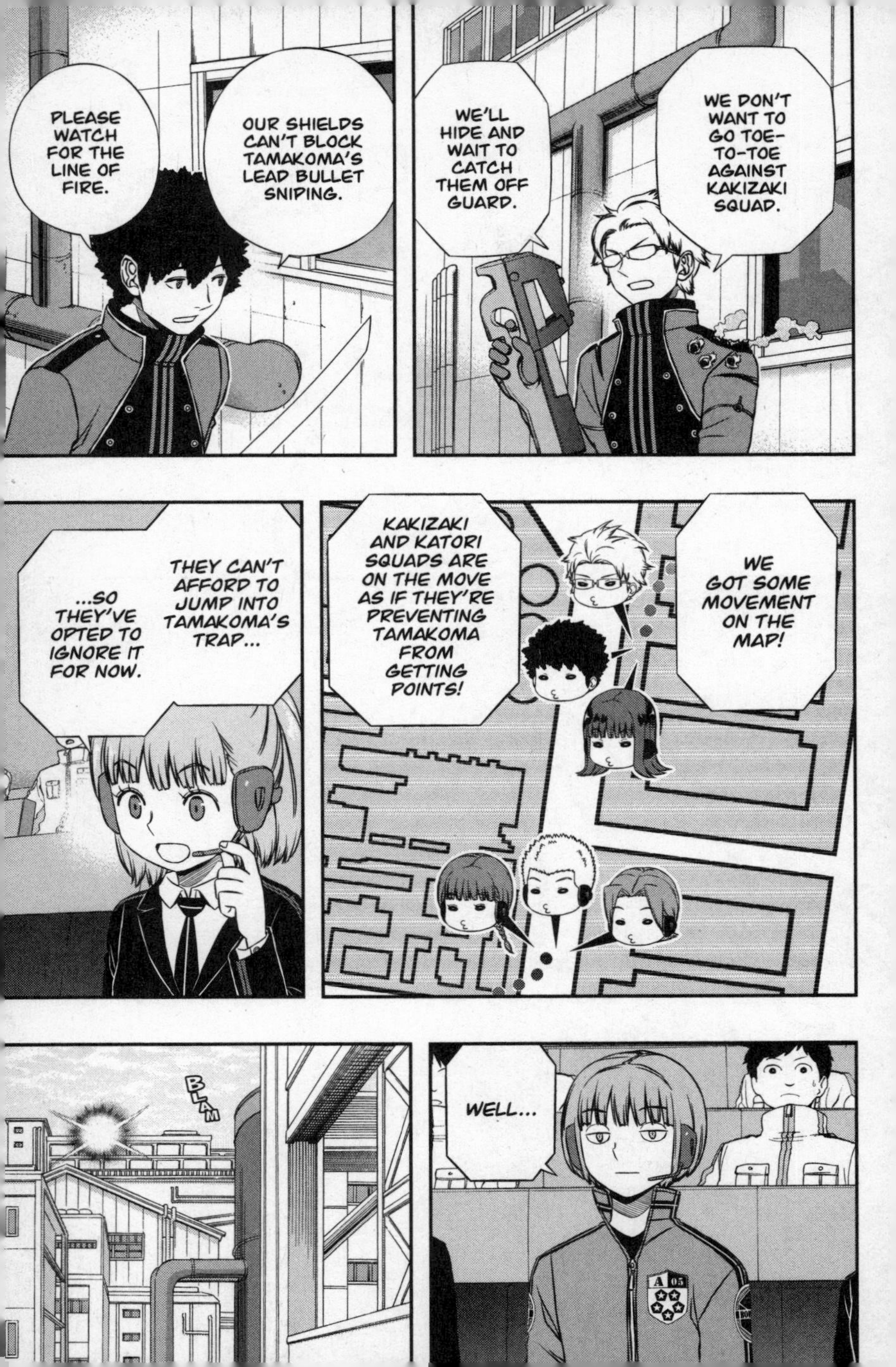

WE DON'T WANT TO GO TOE-TO-TOE AGAINST KAKIZAKI SQUAD.
WE'LL HIDE AND WAIT TO CATCH THEM OFF GUARD.
OUR SHIELDS CAN'T BLOCK TAMAKOMA'S LEAD BULLET SNIPING.
PLEASE WATCH FOR THE LINE OF FIRE.
WE GOT SOME MOVEMENT ON THE MAP!
KAKIZAKI AND KATORI SQUADS ARE ON THE MOVE AS IF THEY'RE PREVENTING TAMAKOMA FROM GETTING POINTS!
THEY CAN'T AFFORD TO JUMP INTO TAMAKOMA'S TRAP...
...SO THEY'VE OPTED TO IGNORE IT FOR NOW.
WELL...
BLAM

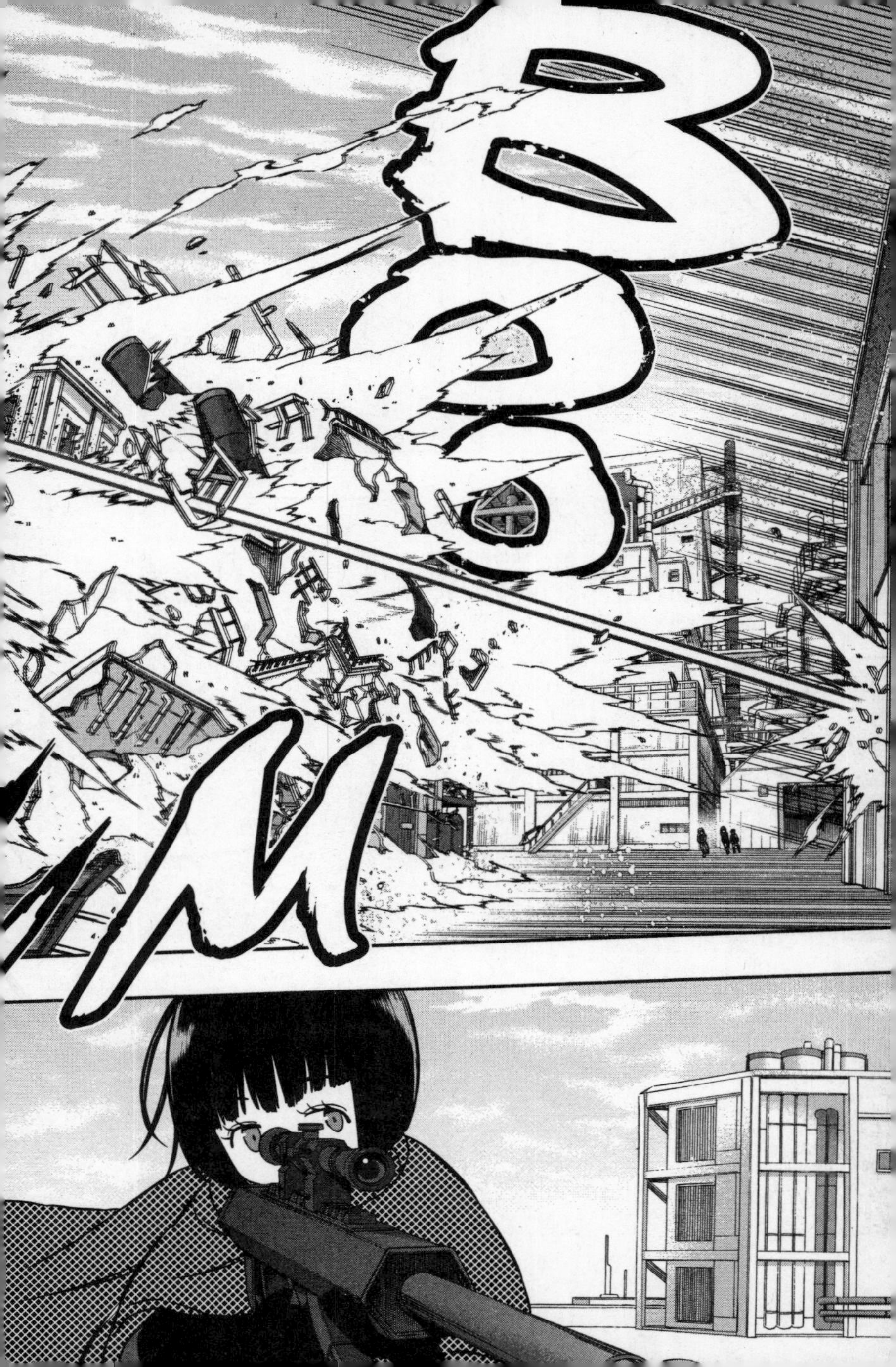
BOOM

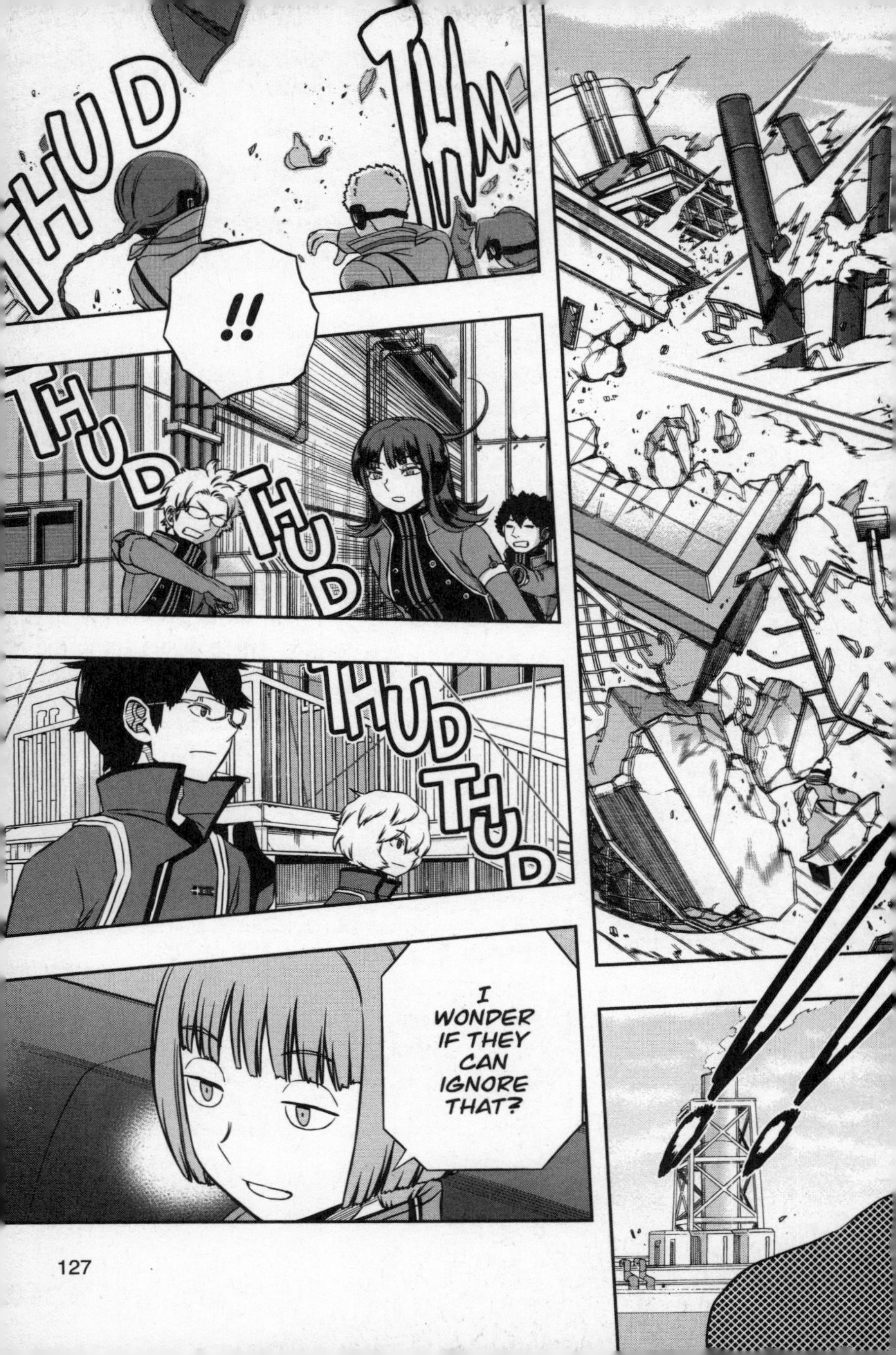
THM
THUD
!!
THUD
THUD
THUD
THUD
I WONDER IF THEY CAN IGNORE THAT?

Katori Squad

Border HQ B-Rank #9

B-009

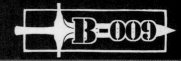

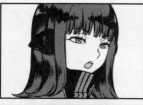

Yoko Katori

Captain, All-Rounder

■16 years old
(High school student)
■Born Oct. 18

■Luna Falcata
Blood type O
■Height: 5'2"
■Likes: Video games, rice crackers, friends, winning

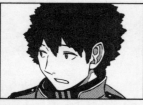

Yuta Miura

Attacker

■17 years old
(High school student)
■Born Sept. 3

■Lupus
Blood type B
■Height: 5'9"
■Likes: Peace, oranges, tsukemen, Yoko in a good mood

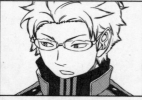

Rokuro Wakamura

Gunner

■17 years old
(High school student)
■Born April 16

■Falco
Blood type B
■Height: 5'8"
■Likes: Egg sandwiches, chicken, Hana when she's studying.

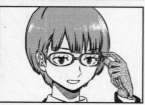

Hana Somei

Operator

■16 years old
(High school student)
■Born July 1

■Gladius
Blood type AB
■Height: 5'1"
■Likes: Working through problems, hot chocolate, friends

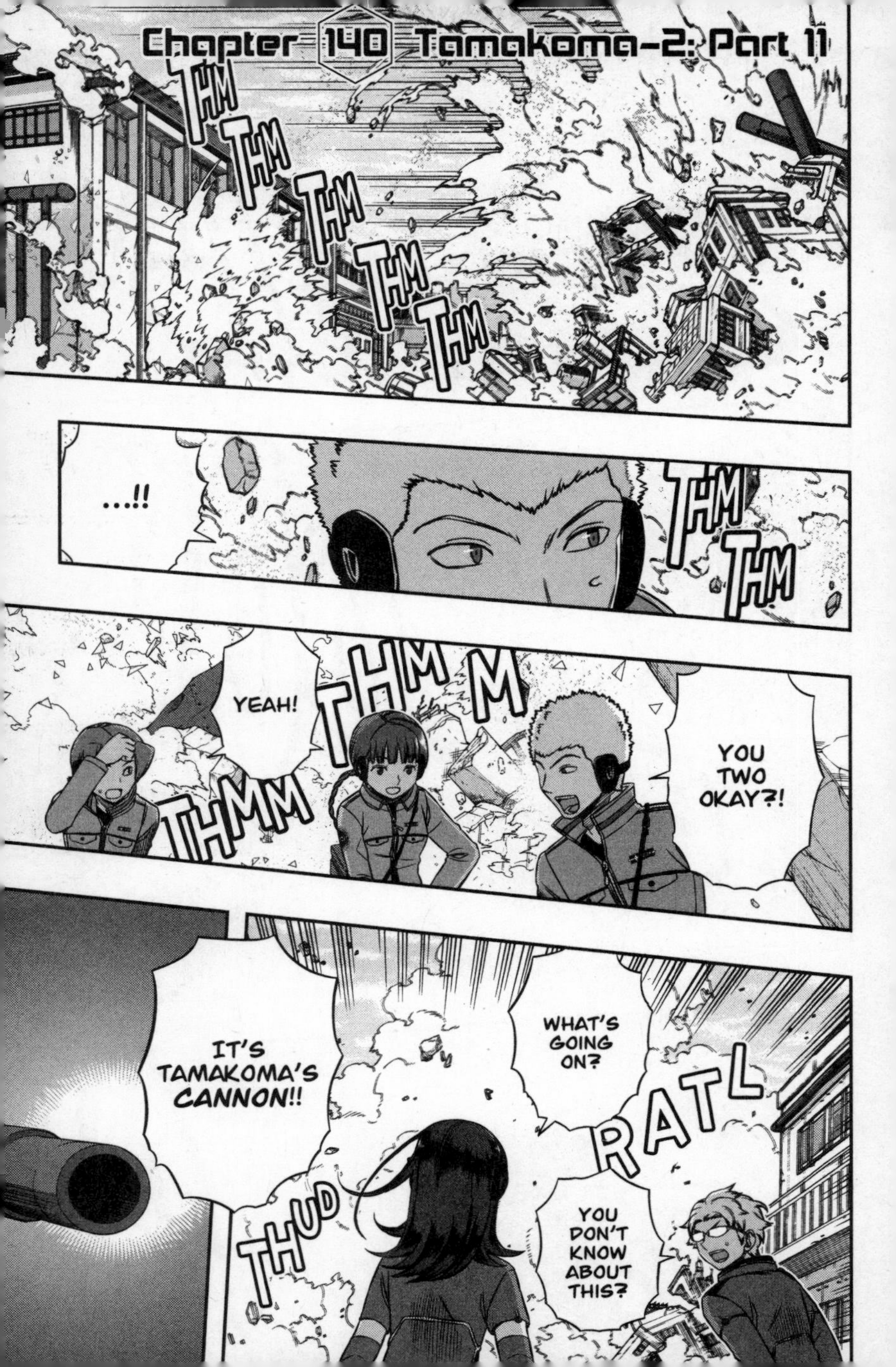
Chapter 140 Tamakoma-2: Part 11
THM
THM
THM
THM
THM
THM
THM
...!!
YOU TWO OKAY?!
THM M
YEAH!
THMM
WHAT'S GOING ON?
IT'S TAMAKOMA'S CANNON!!
RATL
YOU DON'T KNOW ABOUT THIS?
THUD

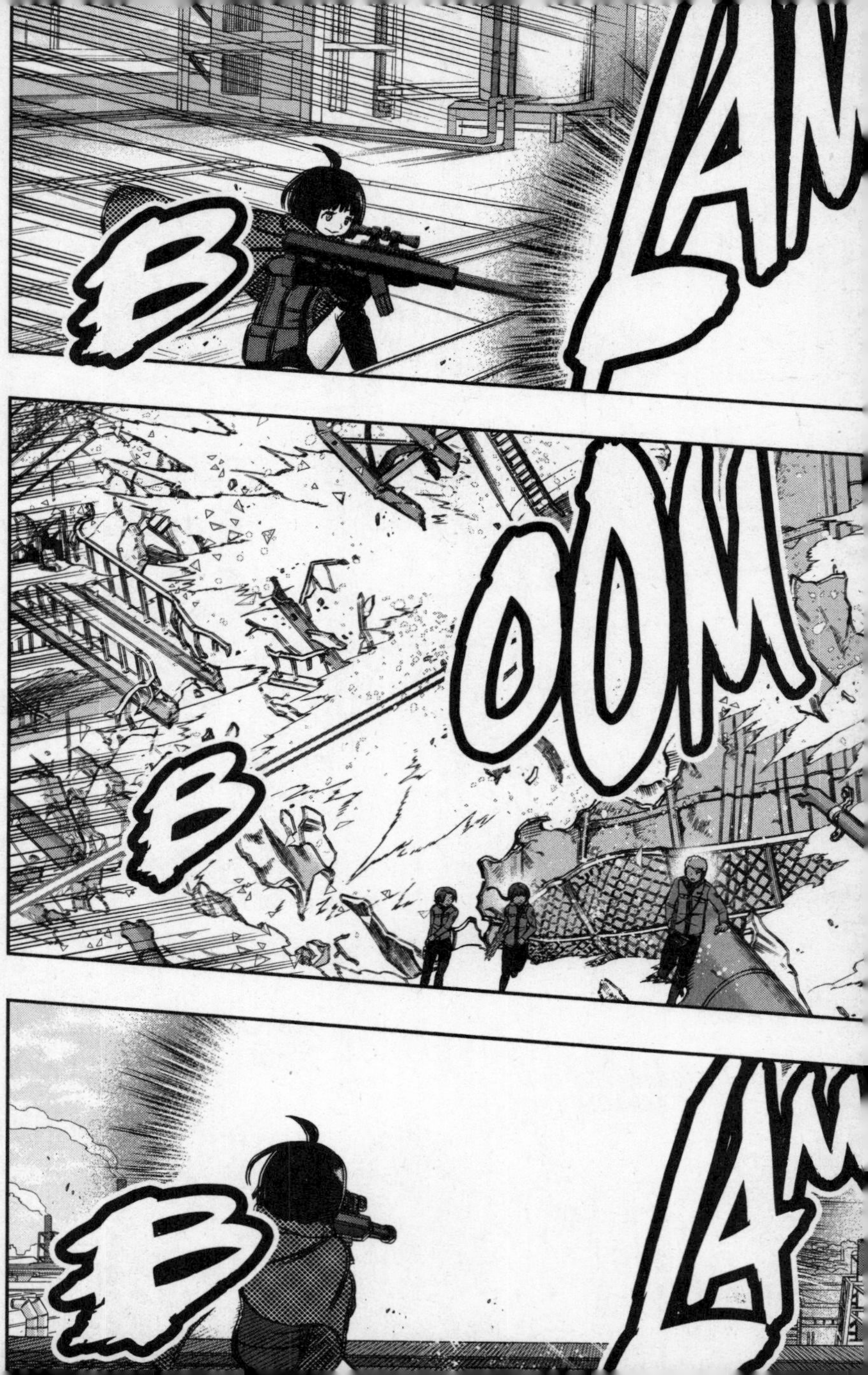
BLAM
BOOM
BLAM

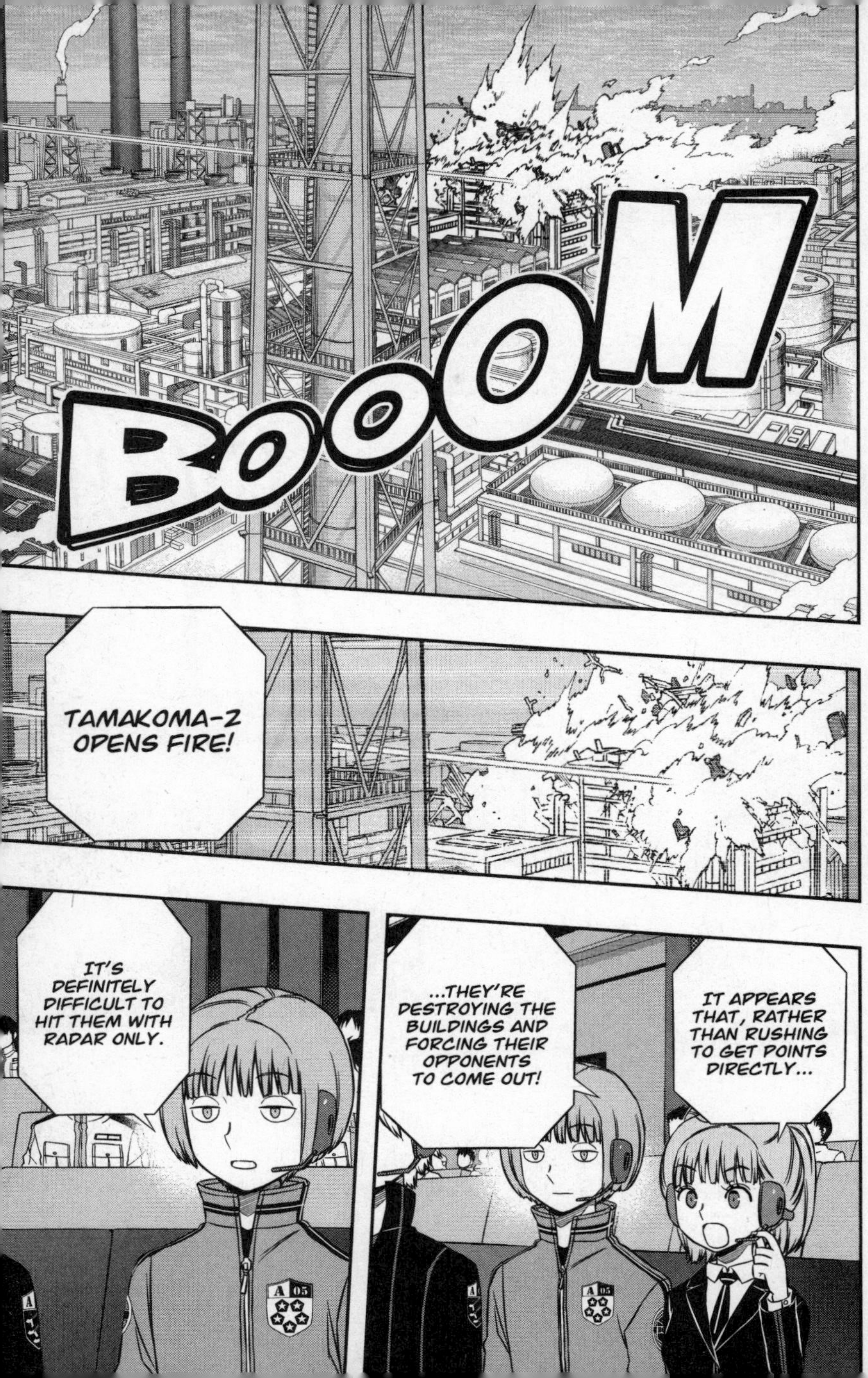
BOOOM
TAMAKOMA-2 OPENS FIRE!
IT APPEARS THAT, RATHER THAN RUSHING TO GET POINTS DIRECTLY...
...THEY'RE DESTROYING THE BUILDINGS AND FORCING THEIR OPPONENTS TO COME OUT!
IT'S DEFINITELY DIFFICULT TO HIT THEM WITH RADAR ONLY.

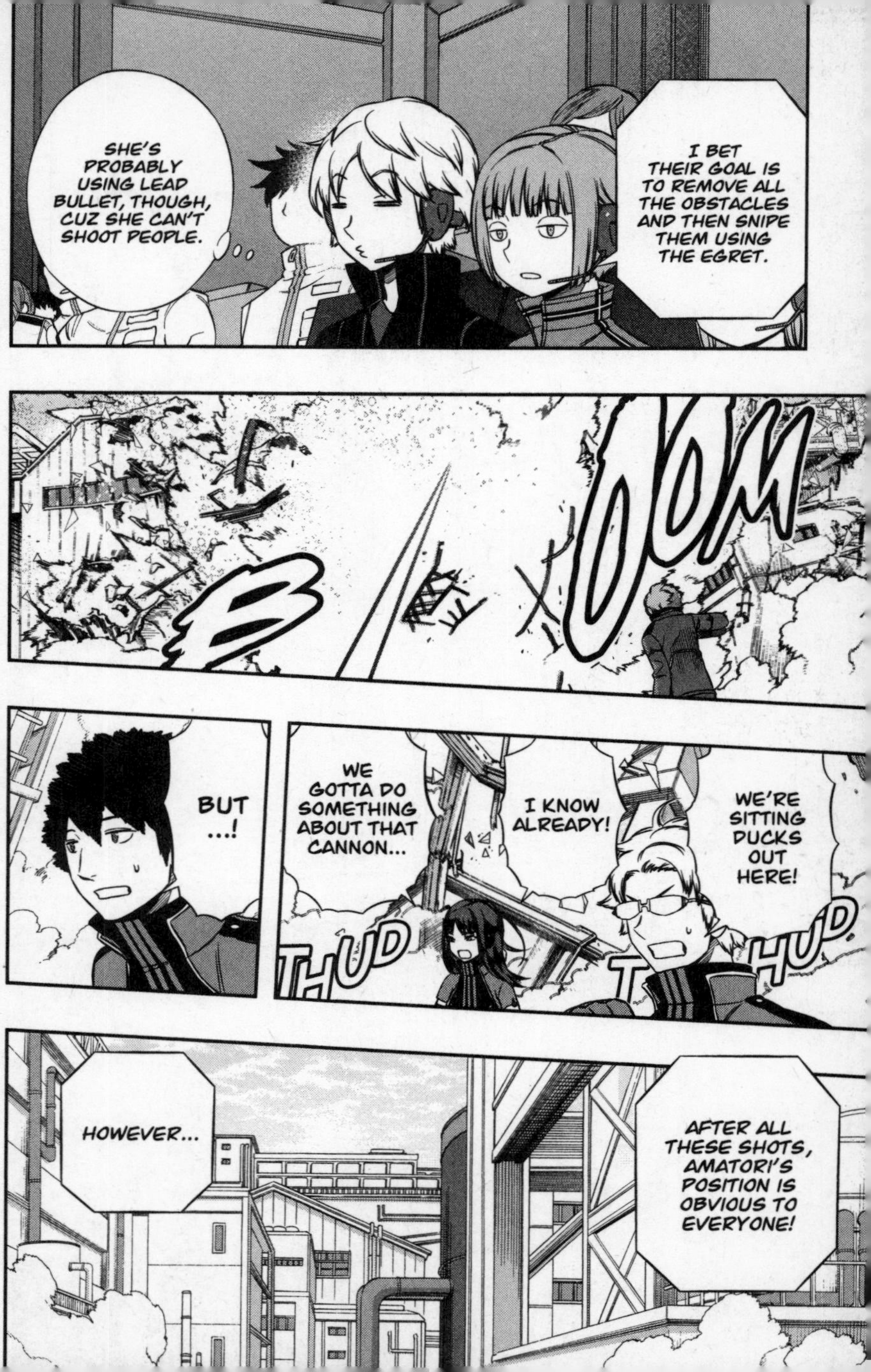
I BET THEIR GOAL IS TO REMOVE ALL THE OBSTACLES AND THEN SNIPE THEM USING THE EGRET.
SHE'S PROBABLY USING LEAD BULLET, THOUGH, CUZ SHE CAN'T SHOOT PEOPLE.
BOOM
WE'RE SITTING DUCKS OUT HERE!
I KNOW ALREADY!
WE GOTTA DO SOMETHING ABOUT THAT CANNON...
THUD
THUD
BUT ...!
AFTER ALL THESE SHOTS, AMATORI'S POSITION IS OBVIOUS TO EVERYONE!
HOWEVER...

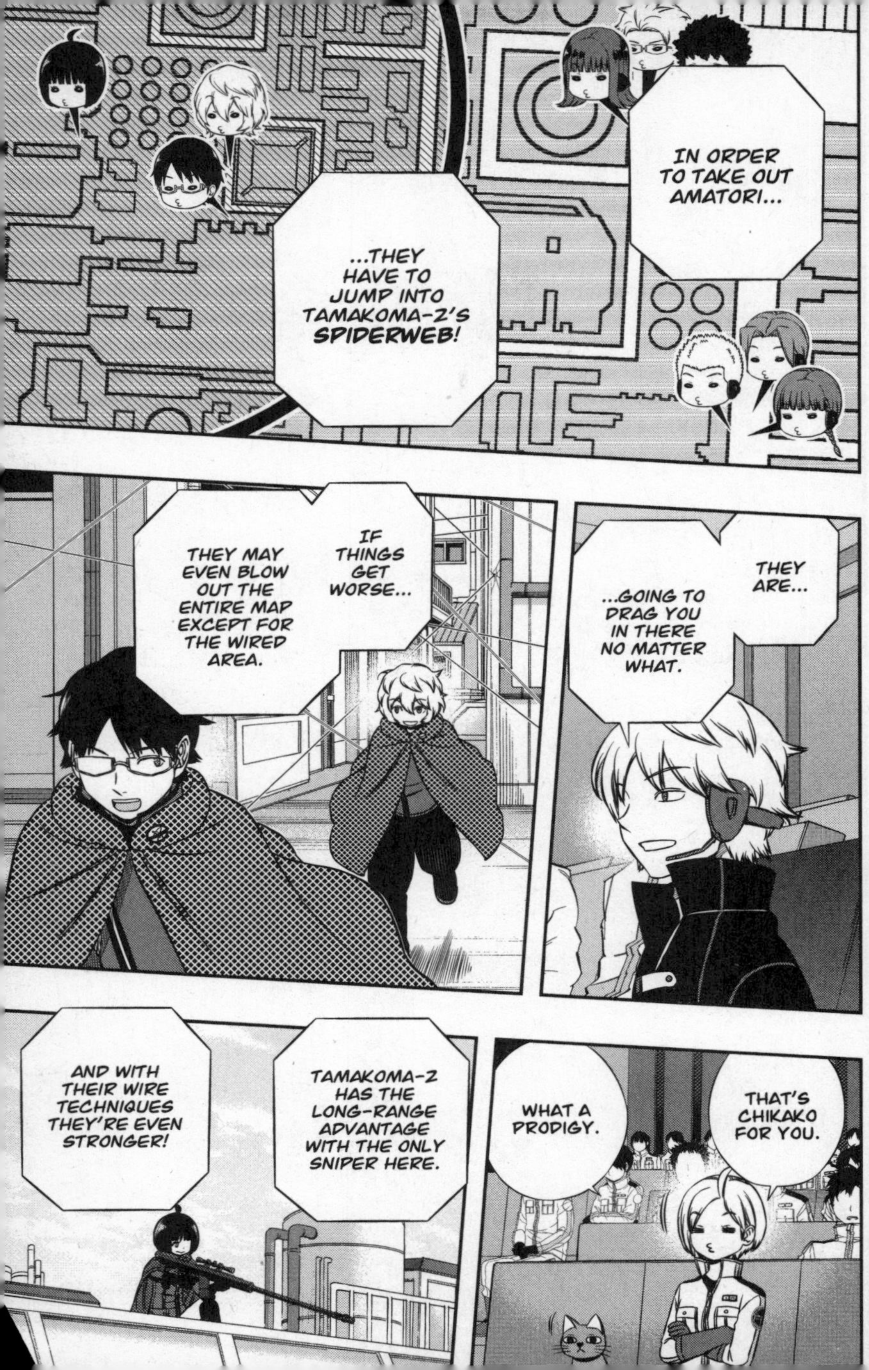
IN ORDER TO TAKE OUT AMATORI...
...THEY HAVE TO JUMP INTO TAMAKOMA-2'S SPIDERWEB!
THEY ARE...
...GOING TO DRAG YOU IN THERE NO MATTER WHAT.
IF THINGS GET WORSE...
THEY MAY EVEN BLOW OUT THE ENTIRE MAP EXCEPT FOR THE WIRED AREA.
THAT'S CHIKAKO FOR YOU.
WHAT A PRODIGY.
TAMAKOMA-2 HAS THE LONG-RANGE ADVANTAGE WITH THE ONLY SNIPER HERE.
AND WITH THEIR WIRE TECHNIQUES THEY'RE EVEN STRONGER!

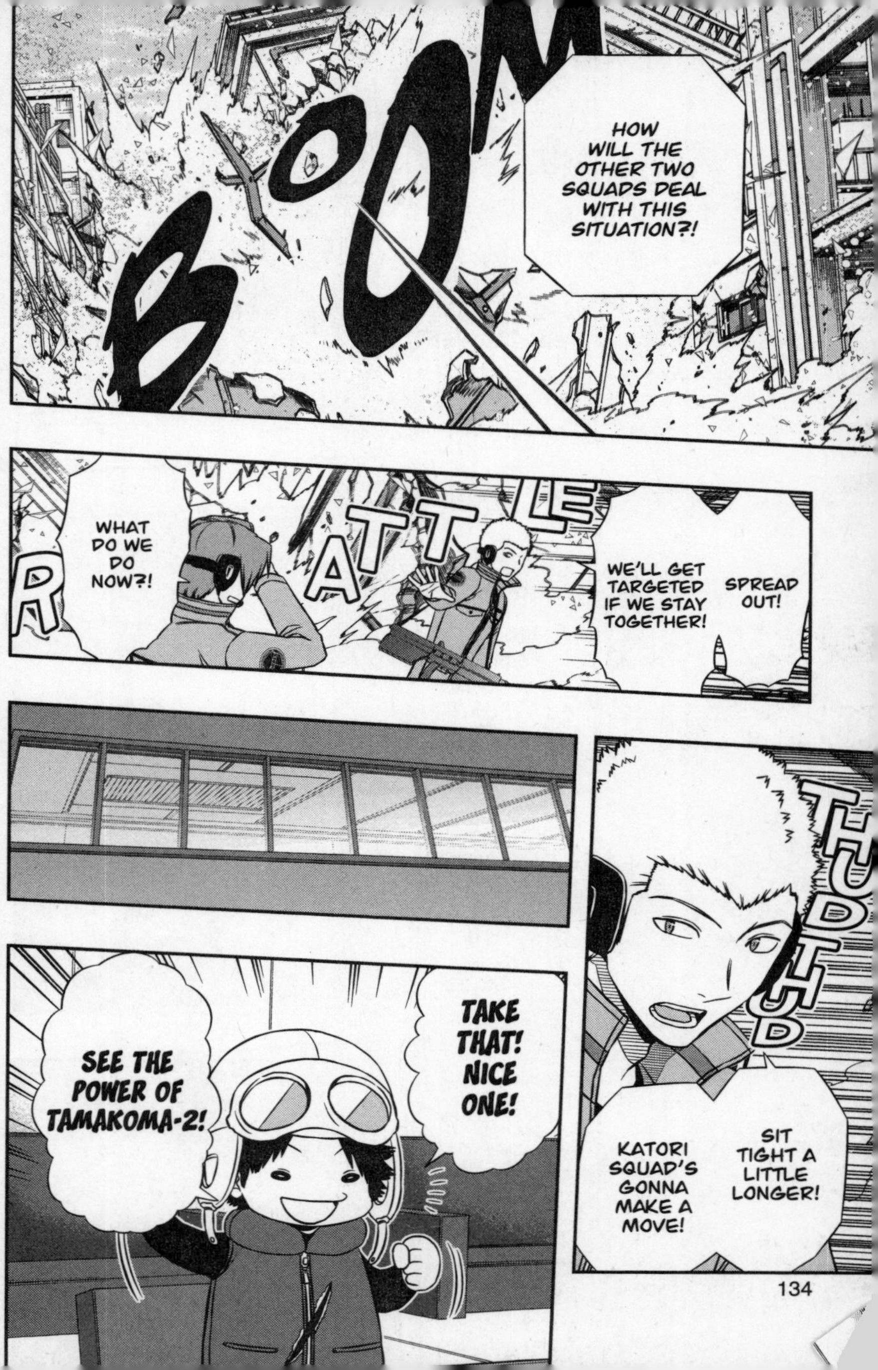
BOOM
HOW WILL THE OTHER TWO SQUADS DEAL WITH THIS SITUATION?!
SPREAD OUT!
WE'LL GET TARGETED IF WE STAY TOGETHER!
RATTLE
WHAT DO WE DO NOW?!
THUD THUD
SIT TIGHT A LITTLE LONGER!
KATORI SQUAD'S GONNA MAKE A MOVE!
TAKE THAT! NICE ONE!
SEE THE POWER OF TAMAKOMA-2!

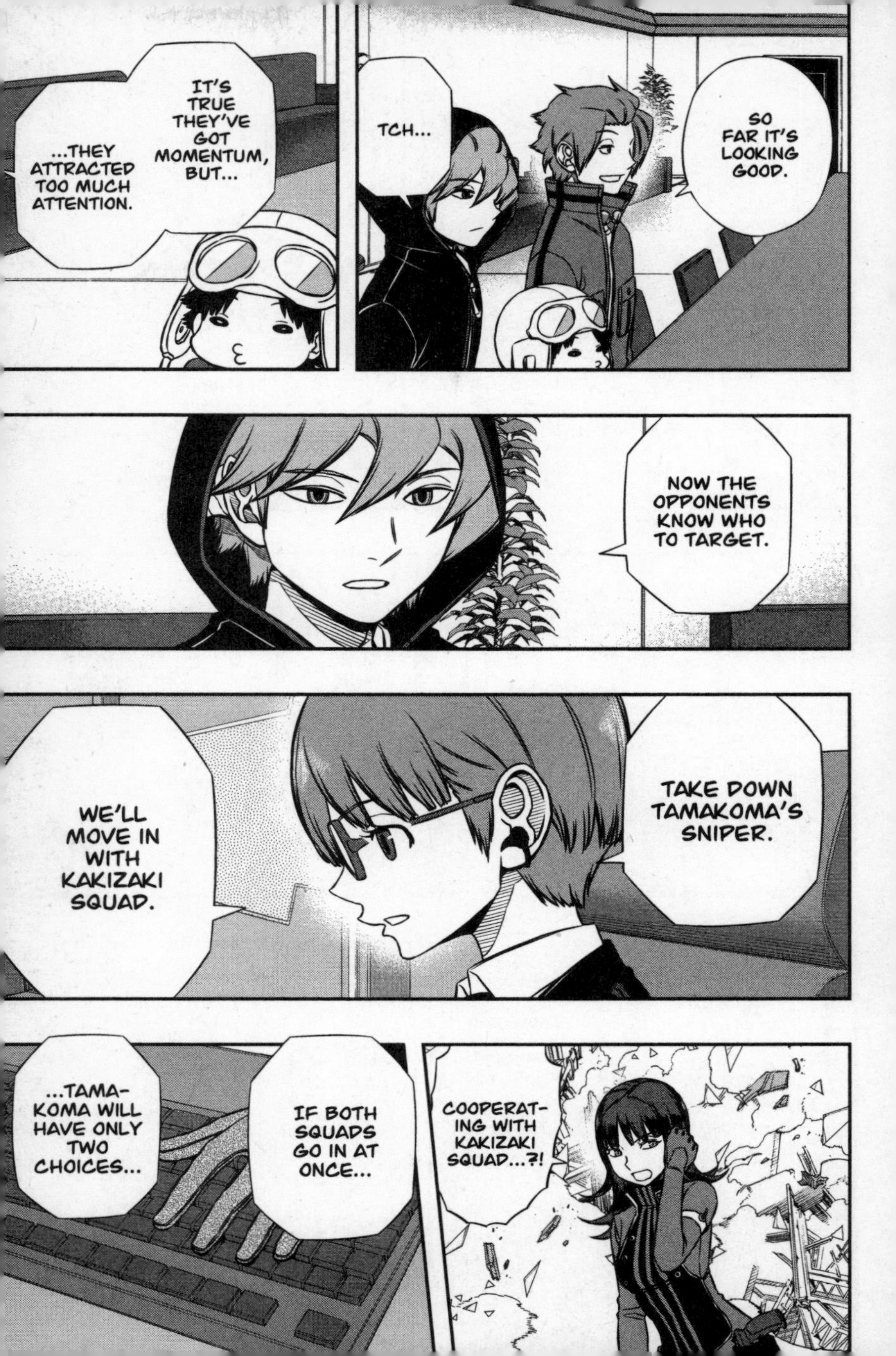
SO FAR IT'S LOOKING GOOD.
TCH...
IT'S TRUE THEY'VE GOT MOMENTUM, BUT...
...THEY ATTRACTED TOO MUCH ATTENTION.
NOW THE OPPONENTS KNOW WHO TO TARGET.
TAKE DOWN TAMAKOMA'S SNIPER.
WE'LL MOVE IN WITH KAKIZAKI SQUAD.
COOPERAT-ING WITH KAKIZAKI SQUAD...?!
IF BOTH SQUADS GO IN AT ONCE...
...TAMA-KOMA WILL HAVE ONLY TWO CHOICES...

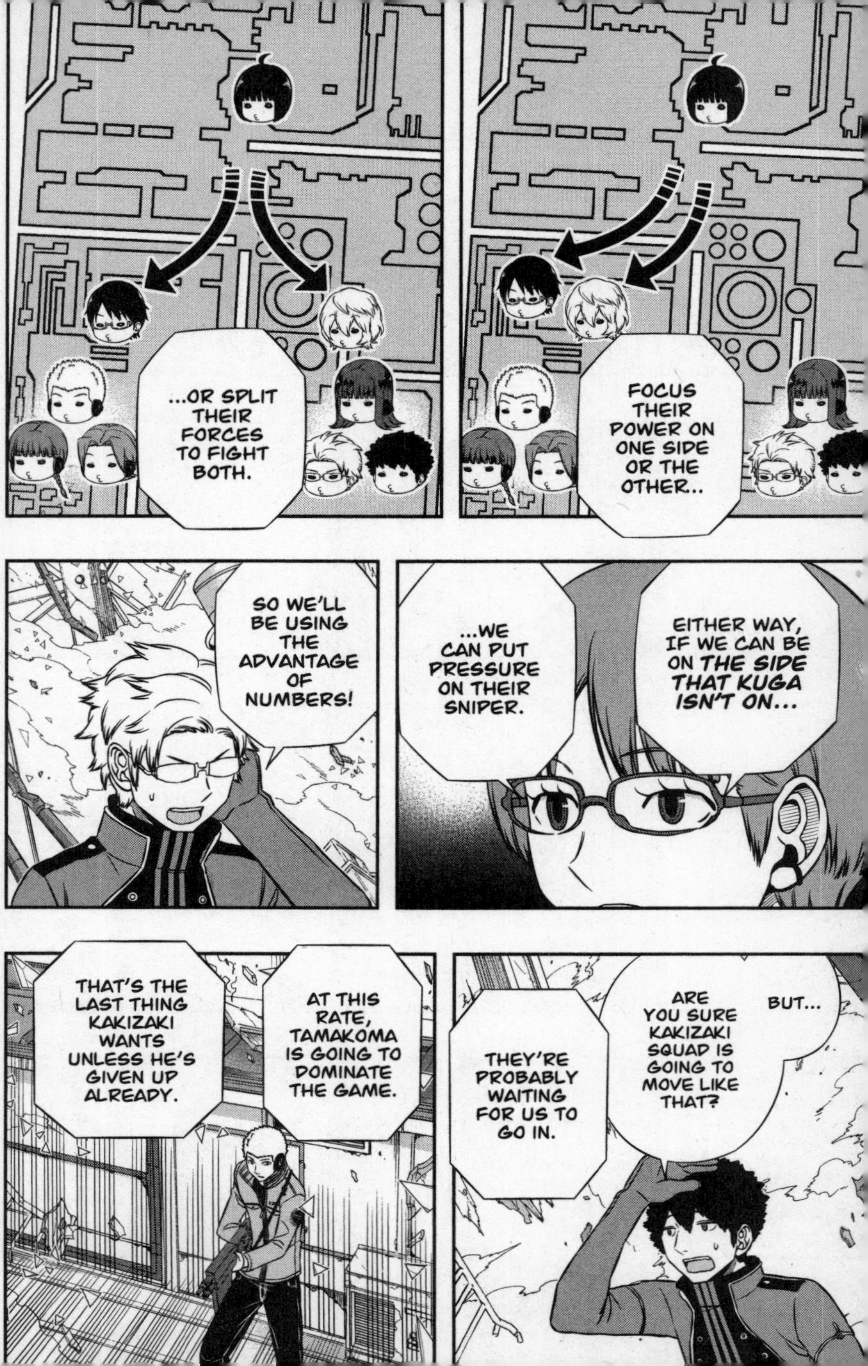
FOCUS THEIR POWER ON ONE SIDE OR THE OTHER...
...OR SPLIT THEIR FORCES TO FIGHT BOTH.
EITHER WAY, IF WE CAN BE ON *THE SIDE THAT KUGA ISN'T ON*...
...WE CAN PUT PRESSURE ON THEIR SNIPER.
SO WE'LL BE USING THE ADVANTAGE OF NUMBERS!
BUT...
ARE YOU SURE KAKIZAKI SQUAD IS GOING TO MOVE LIKE THAT?
THEY'RE PROBABLY WAITING FOR US TO GO IN.
AT THIS RATE, TAMAKOMA IS GOING TO DOMINATE THE GAME.
THAT'S THE LAST THING KAKIZAKI WANTS UNLESS HE'S GIVEN UP ALREADY.

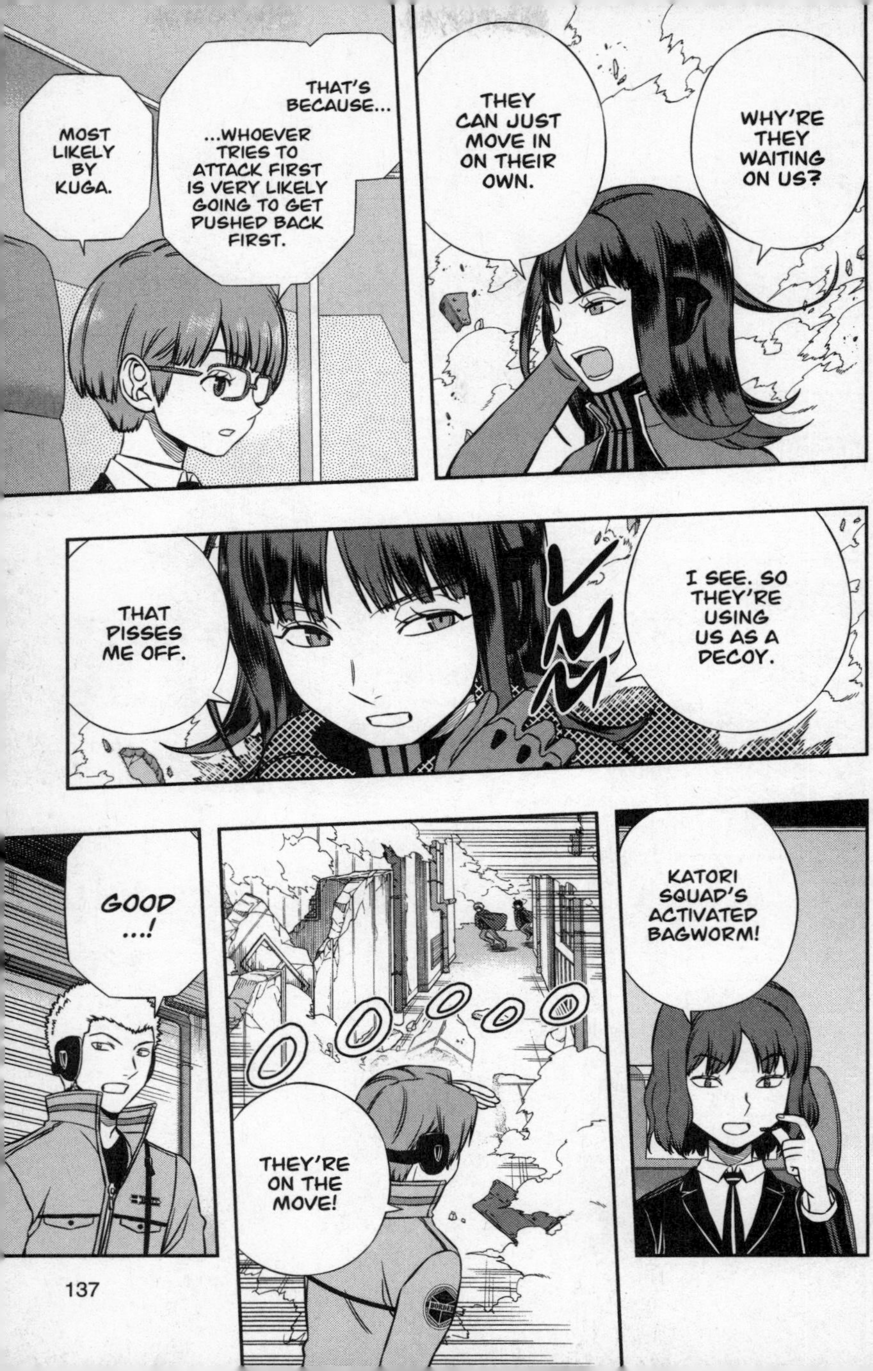
WHY'RE THEY WAITING ON US?
THEY CAN JUST MOVE IN ON THEIR OWN.
THAT'S BECAUSE...
...WHOEVER TRIES TO ATTACK FIRST IS VERY LIKELY GOING TO GET PUSHED BACK FIRST.
MOST LIKELY BY KUGA.
I SEE. SO THEY'RE USING US AS A DECOY.
THAT PISSES ME OFF.
KATORI SQUAD'S ACTIVATED BAGWORM!
THEY'RE ON THE MOVE!
GOOD ...!

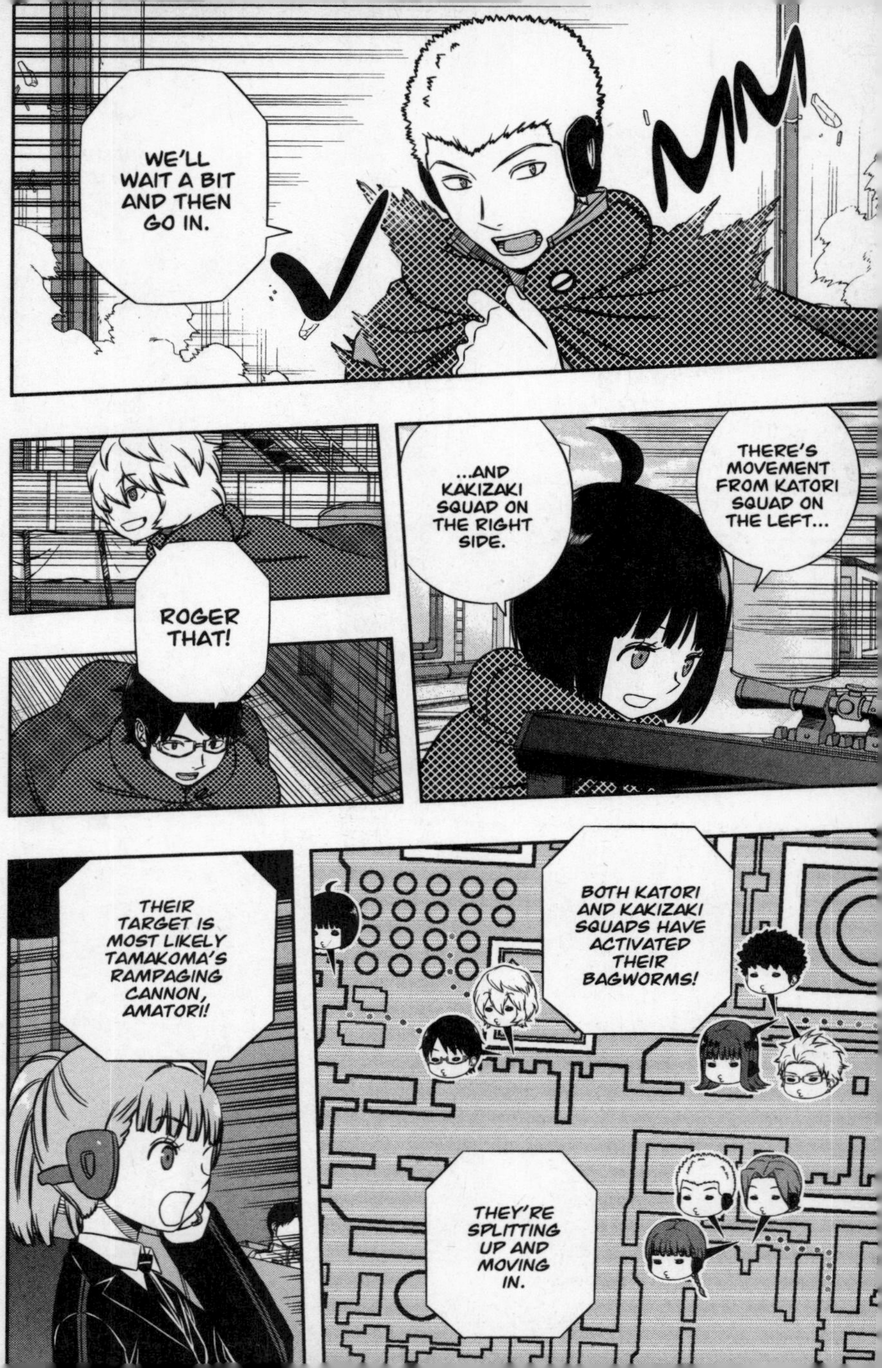
WE'LL WAIT A BIT AND THEN GO IN.
MM
THERE'S MOVEMENT FROM KATORI SQUAD ON THE LEFT...
...AND KAKIZAKI SQUAD ON THE RIGHT SIDE.
ROGER THAT!
BOTH KATORI AND KAKIZAKI SQUADS HAVE ACTIVATED THEIR BAGWORMS!
THEY'RE SPLITTING UP AND MOVING IN.
THEIR TARGET IS MOST LIKELY TAMAKOMA'S RAMPAGING CANNON, AMATORI!

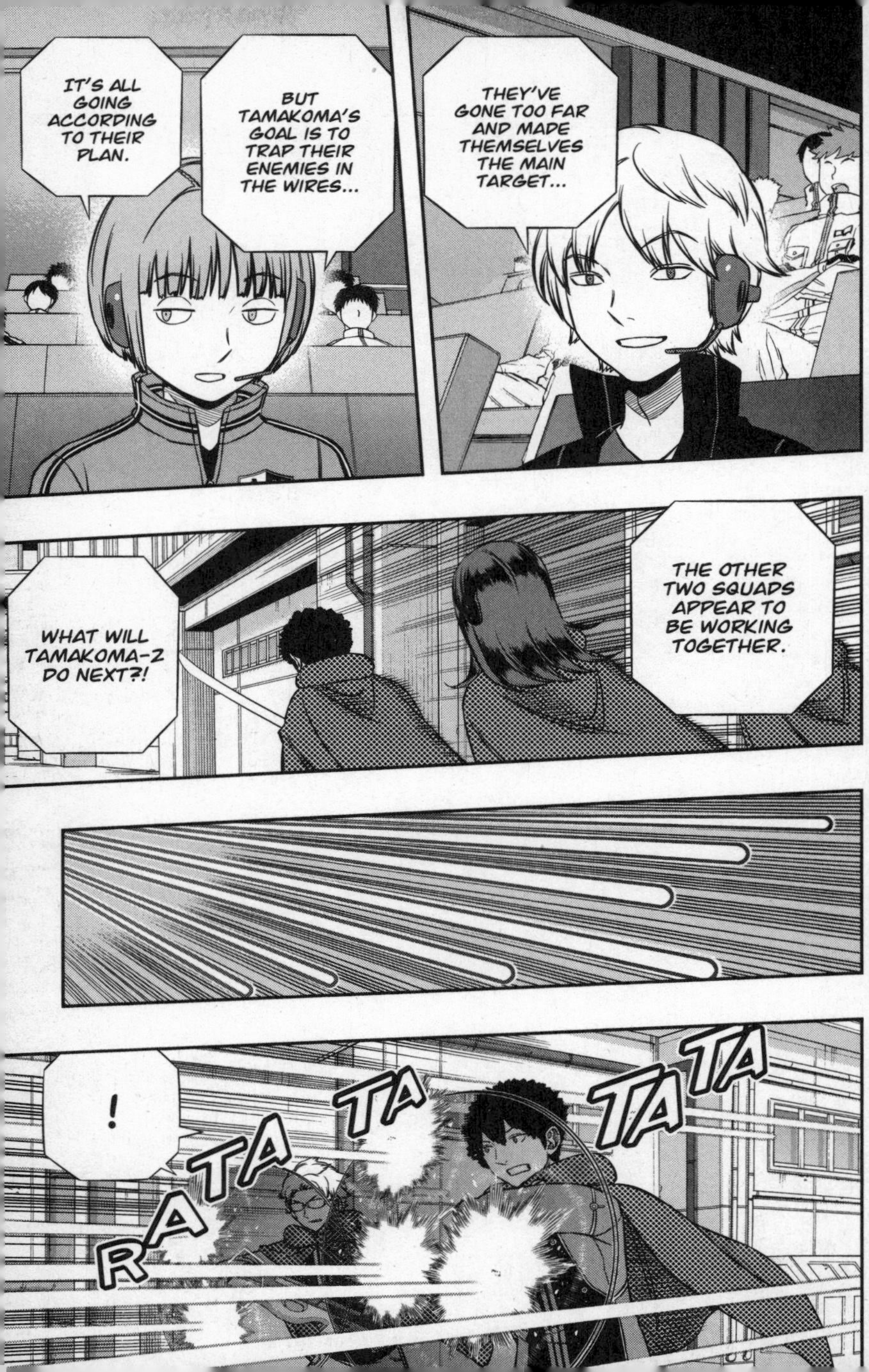
THEY'VE GONE TOO FAR AND MADE THEMSELVES THE MAIN TARGET...
BUT TAMAKOMA'S GOAL IS TO TRAP THEIR ENEMIES IN THE WIRES...
IT'S ALL GOING ACCORDING TO THEIR PLAN.
THE OTHER TWO SQUADS APPEAR TO BE WORKING TOGETHER.
WHAT WILL TAMAKOMA-2 DO NEXT?!
TATA
!
RATATA

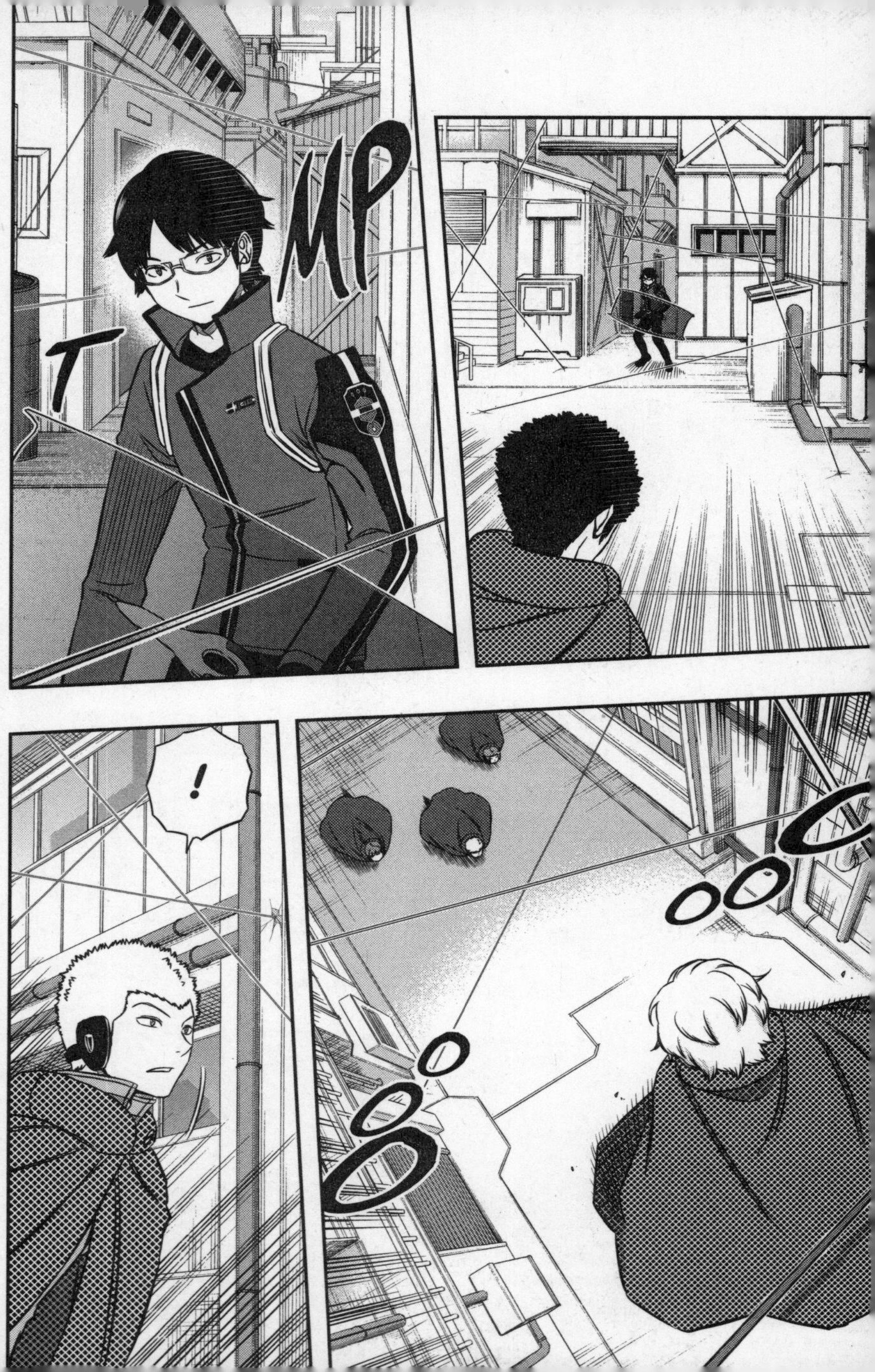
TMP
!

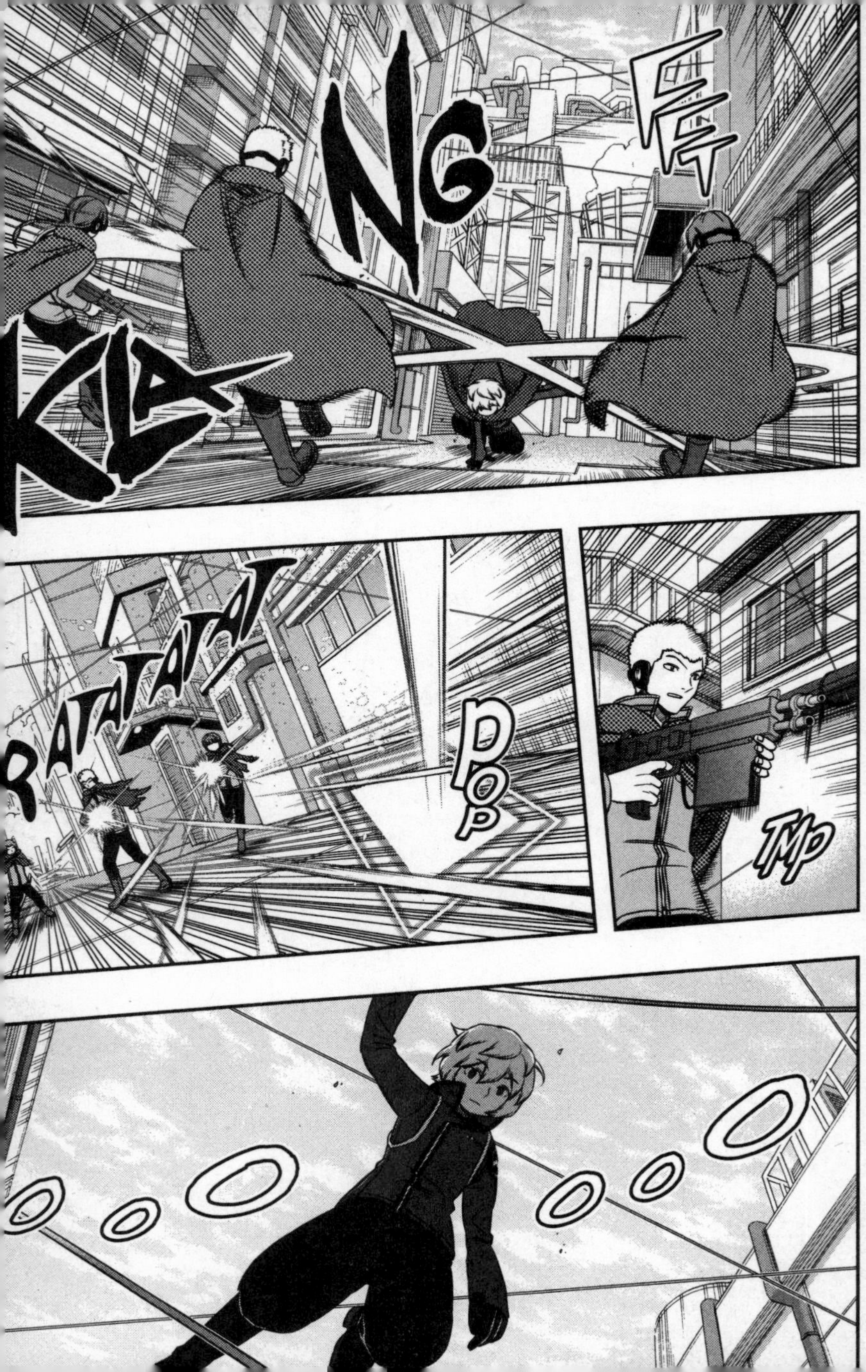
FFFT
KLANG
TMP
POP
POP
RATATATATAT

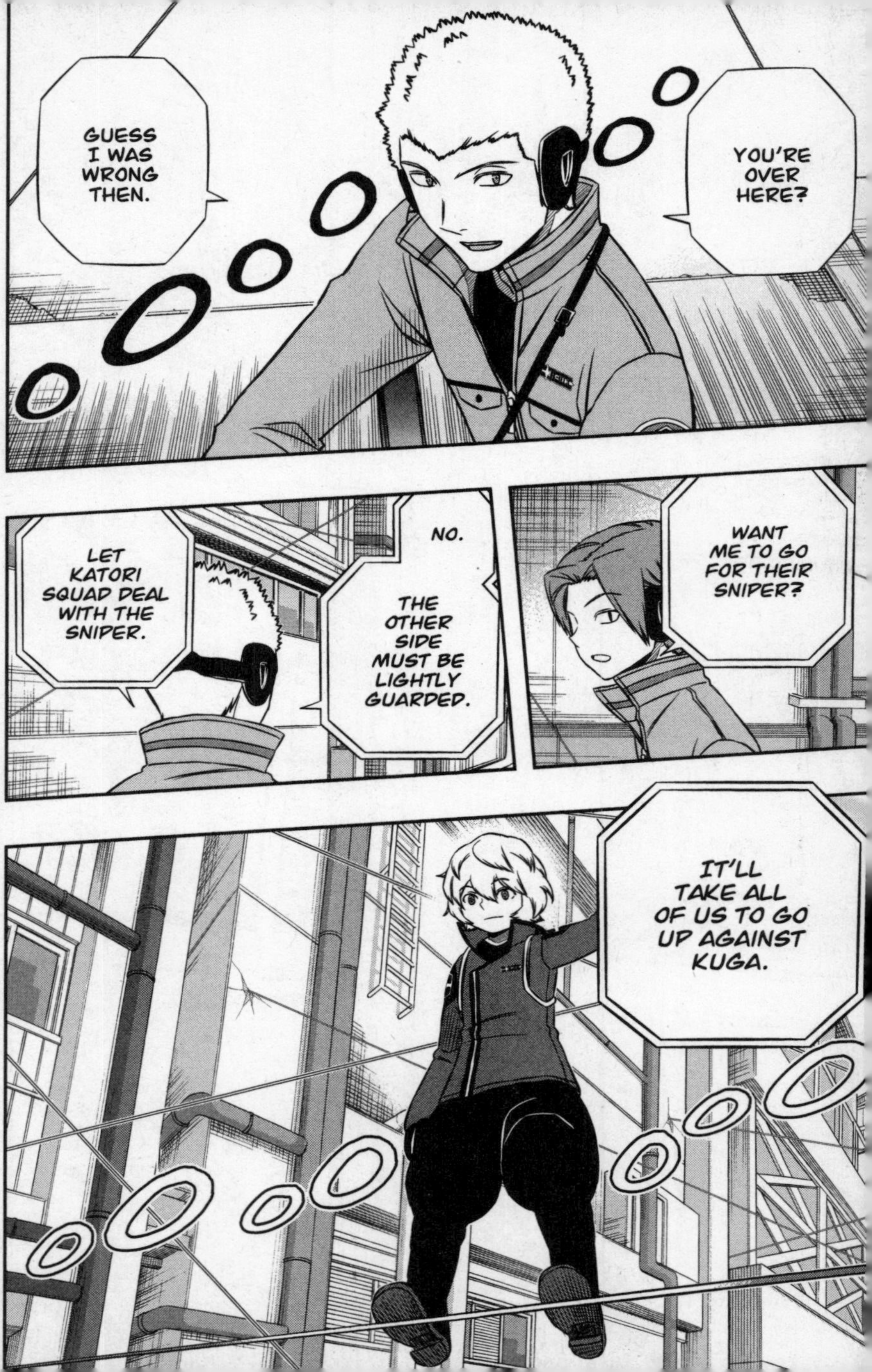
YOU'RE OVER HERE?
GUESS I WAS WRONG THEN.
WANT ME TO GO FOR THEIR SNIPER?
NO.
THE OTHER SIDE MUST BE LIGHTLY GUARDED.
LET KATORI SQUAD DEAL WITH THE SNIPER.
IT'LL TAKE ALL OF US TO GO UP AGAINST KUGA.

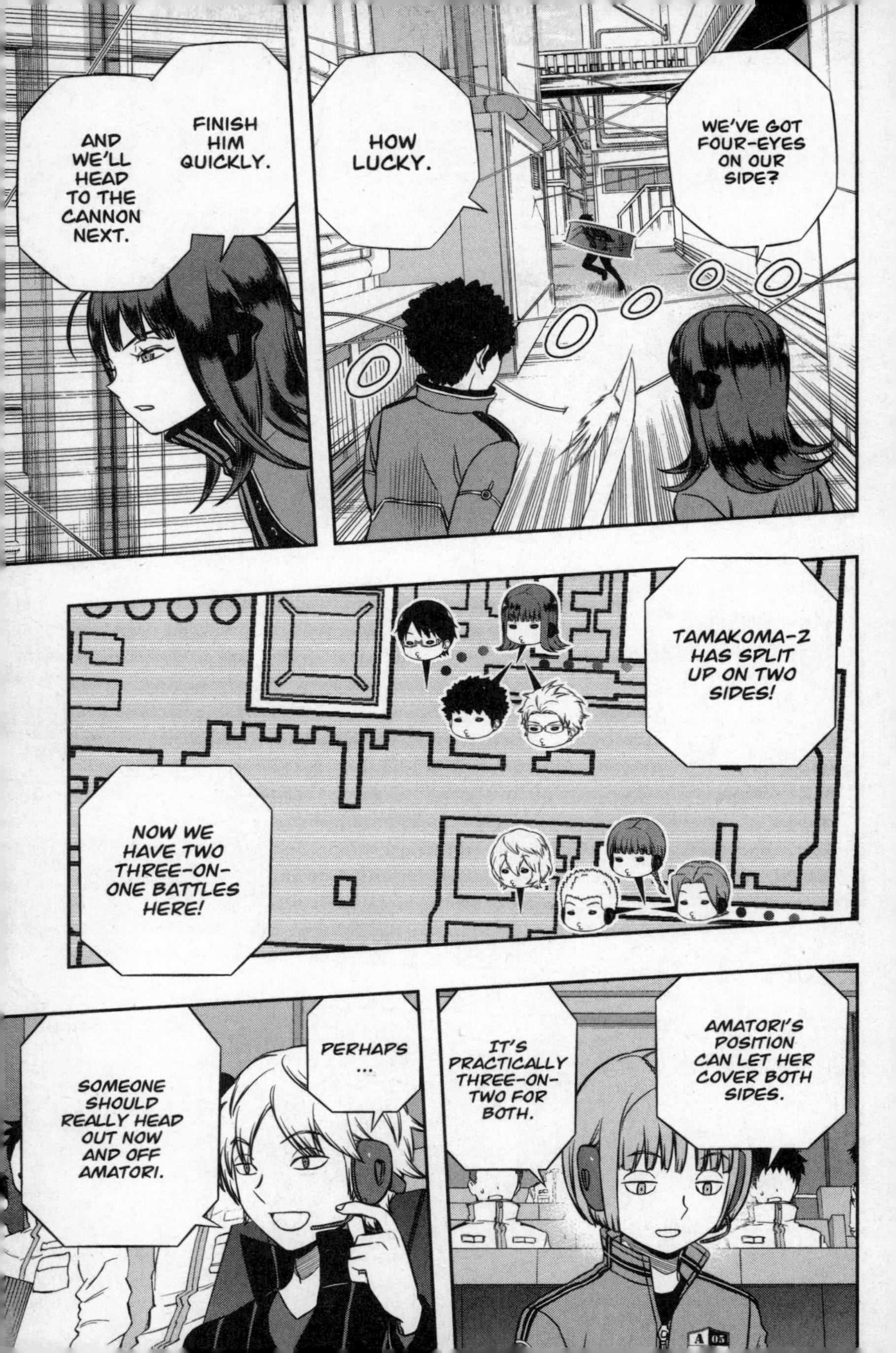
WE'VE GOT FOUR-EYES ON OUR SIDE?
HOW LUCKY.
FINISH HIM QUICKLY.
AND WE'LL HEAD TO THE CANNON NEXT.
TAMAKOMA-2 HAS SPLIT UP ON TWO SIDES!
NOW WE HAVE TWO THREE-ON-ONE BATTLES HERE!
AMATORI'S POSITION CAN LET HER COVER BOTH SIDES.
IT'S PRACTICALLY THREE-ON-TWO FOR BOTH.
PERHAPS...
SOMEONE SHOULD REALLY HEAD OUT NOW AND OFF AMATORI.

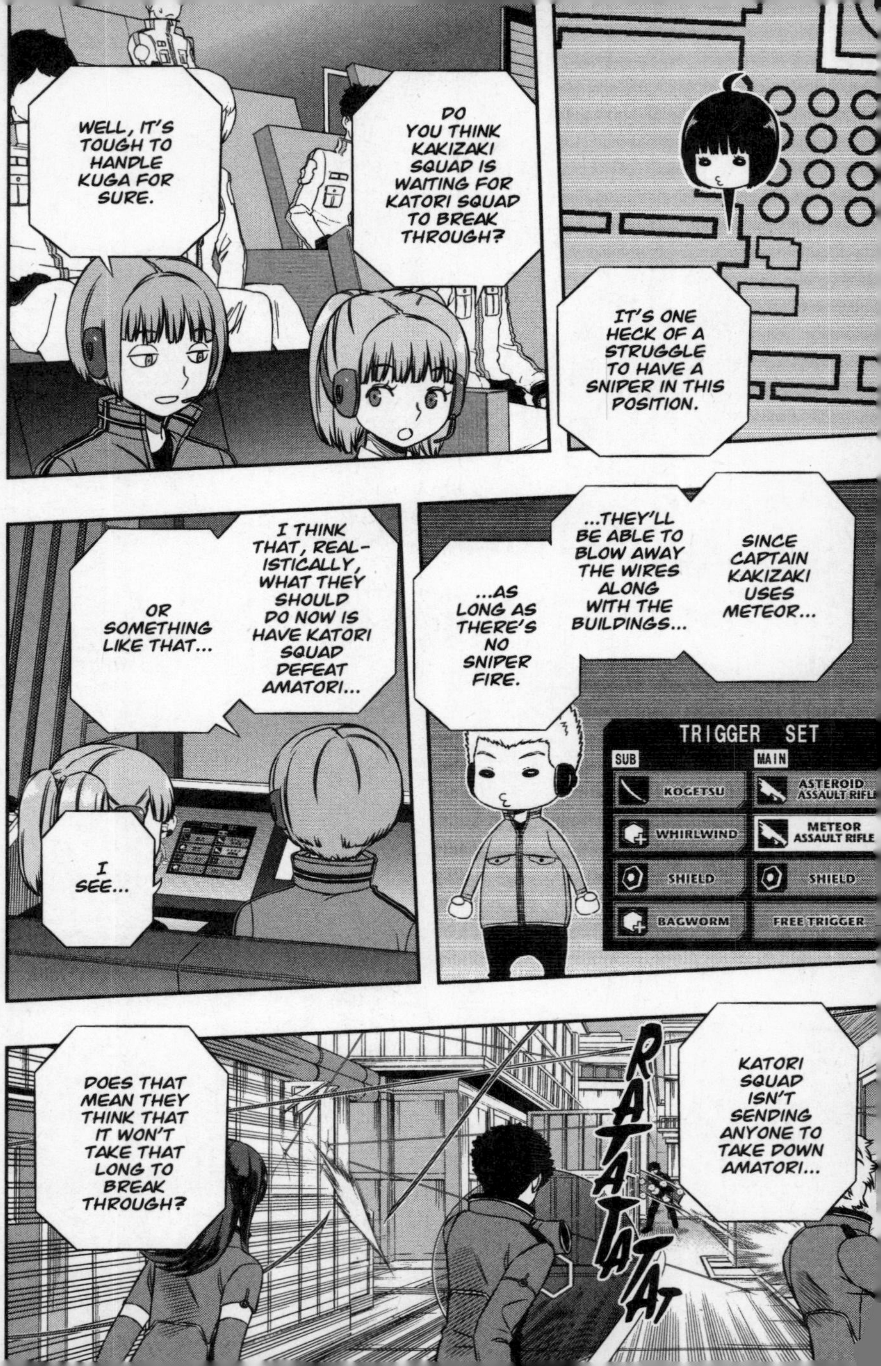
IT'S ONE HECK OF A STRUGGLE TO HAVE A SNIPER IN THIS POSITION.
DO YOU THINK KAKIZAKI SQUAD IS WAITING FOR KATORI SQUAD TO BREAK THROUGH?
WELL, IT'S TOUGH TO HANDLE KUGA FOR SURE.
SINCE CAPTAIN KAKIZAKI USES METEOR...
...THEY'LL BE ABLE TO BLOW AWAY THE WIRES ALONG WITH THE BUILDINGS...
...AS LONG AS THERE'S NO SNIPER FIRE.
TRIGGER SET
SUB
MAIN
KOGETSU
ASTEROID ASSAULT RIFL
WHIRLWIND
METEOR ASSAULT RIFLE
SHIELD
SHIELD
BAGWORM
FREE TRIGGER
I THINK THAT, REAL-ISTICALLY, WHAT THEY SHOULD DO NOW IS HAVE KATORI SQUAD DEFEAT AMATORI...
OR SOMETHING LIKE THAT...
I SEE...
KATORI SQUAD ISN'T SENDING ANYONE TO TAKE DOWN AMATORI...
RATATATAT
DOES THAT MEAN THEY THINK THAT IT WON'T TAKE THAT LONG TO BREAK THROUGH?

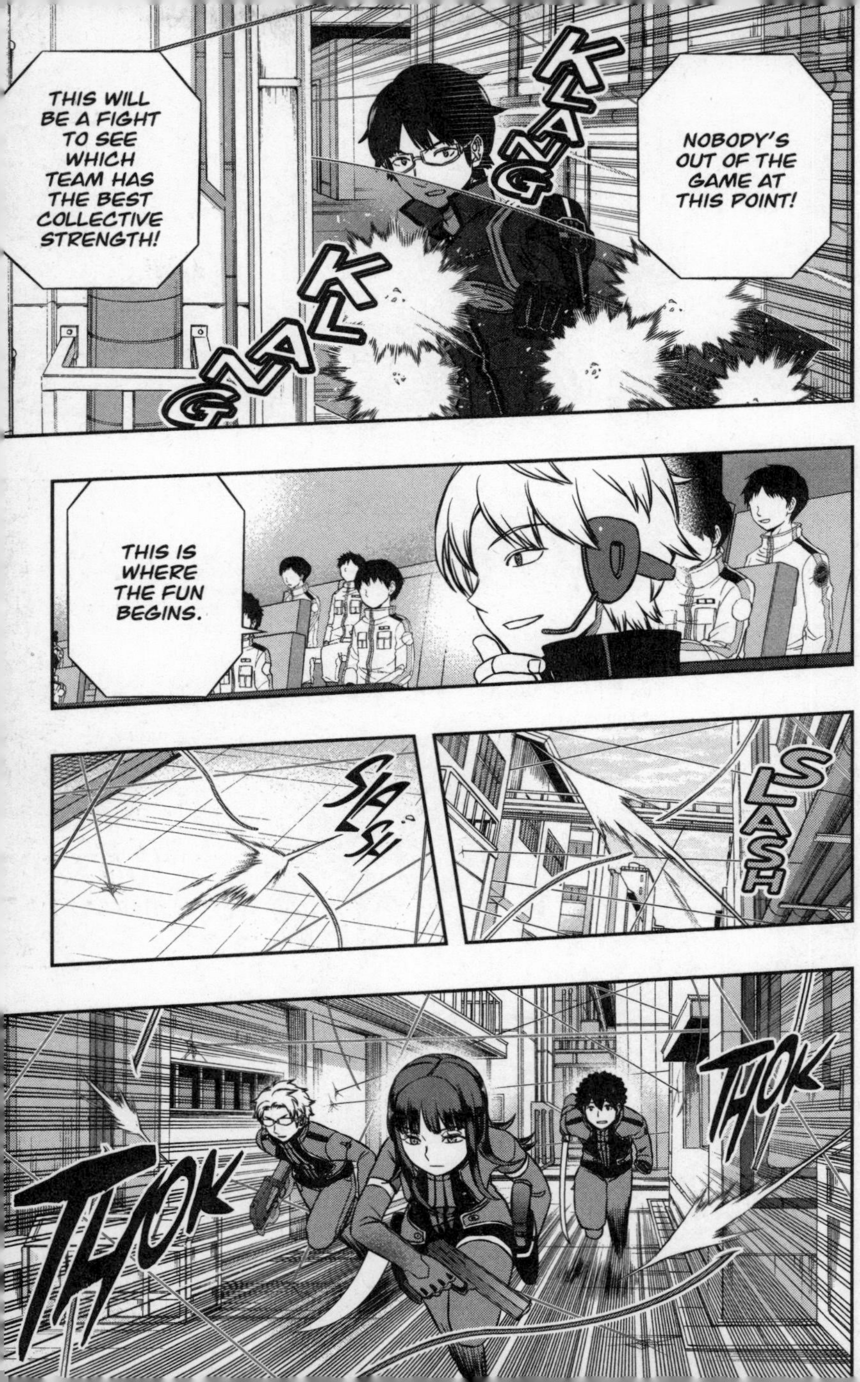
NOBODY'S OUT OF THE GAME AT THIS POINT!
KLANG
KLANG
THIS WILL BE A FIGHT TO SEE WHICH TEAM HAS THE BEST COLLECTIVE STRENGTH!
THIS IS WHERE THE FUN BEGINS.
SLASH
SLASH
THOK
THOK

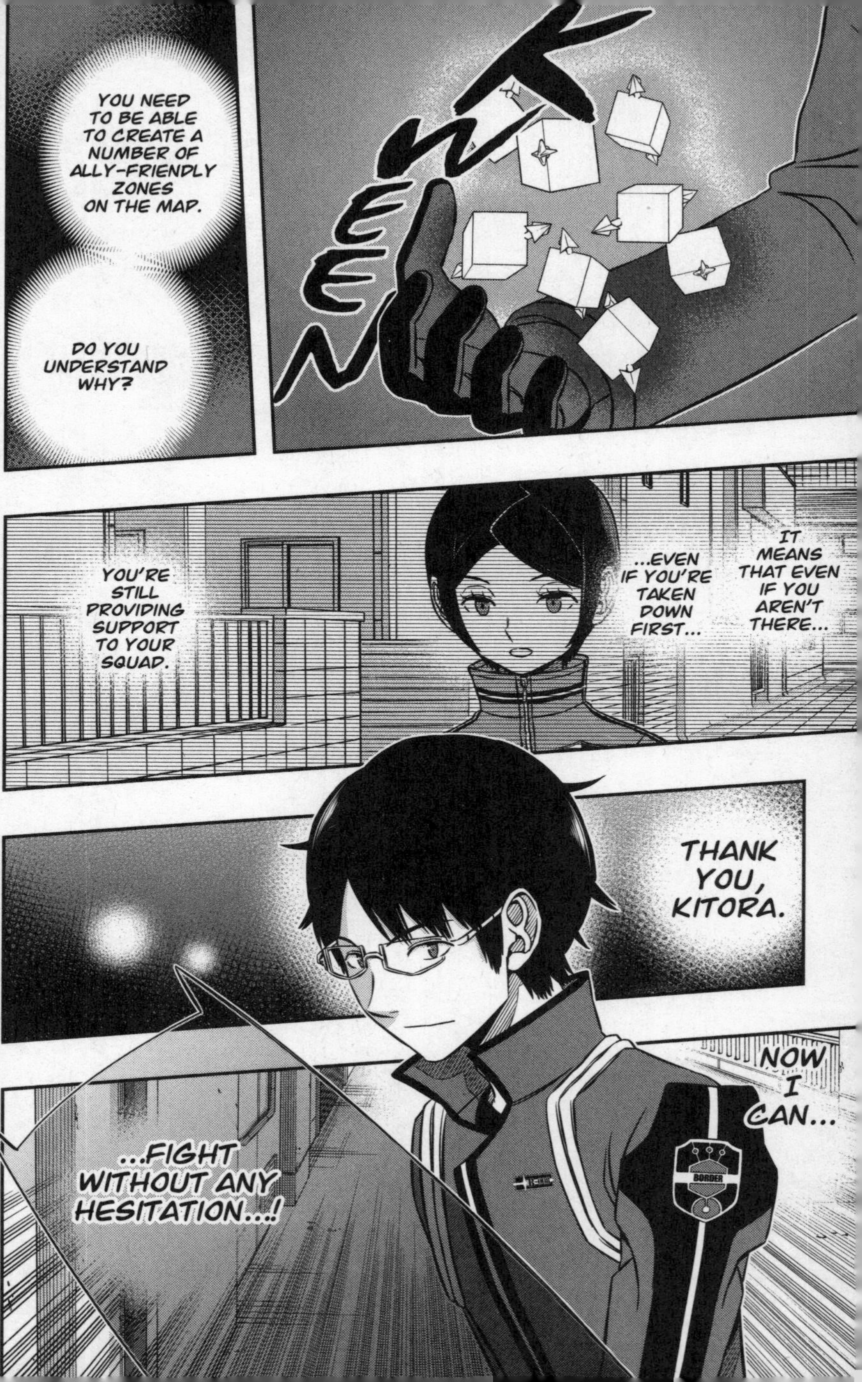
KWEEN
YOU NEED TO BE ABLE TO CREATE A NUMBER OF ALLY-FRIENDLY ZONES ON THE MAP.
DO YOU UNDERSTAND WHY?
IT MEANS THAT EVEN IF YOU AREN'T THERE...
...EVEN IF YOU'RE TAKEN DOWN FIRST...
YOU'RE STILL PROVIDING SUPPORT TO YOUR SQUAD.
THANK YOU, KITORA.
NOW I CAN...
...FIGHT WITHOUT ANY HESITATION...!

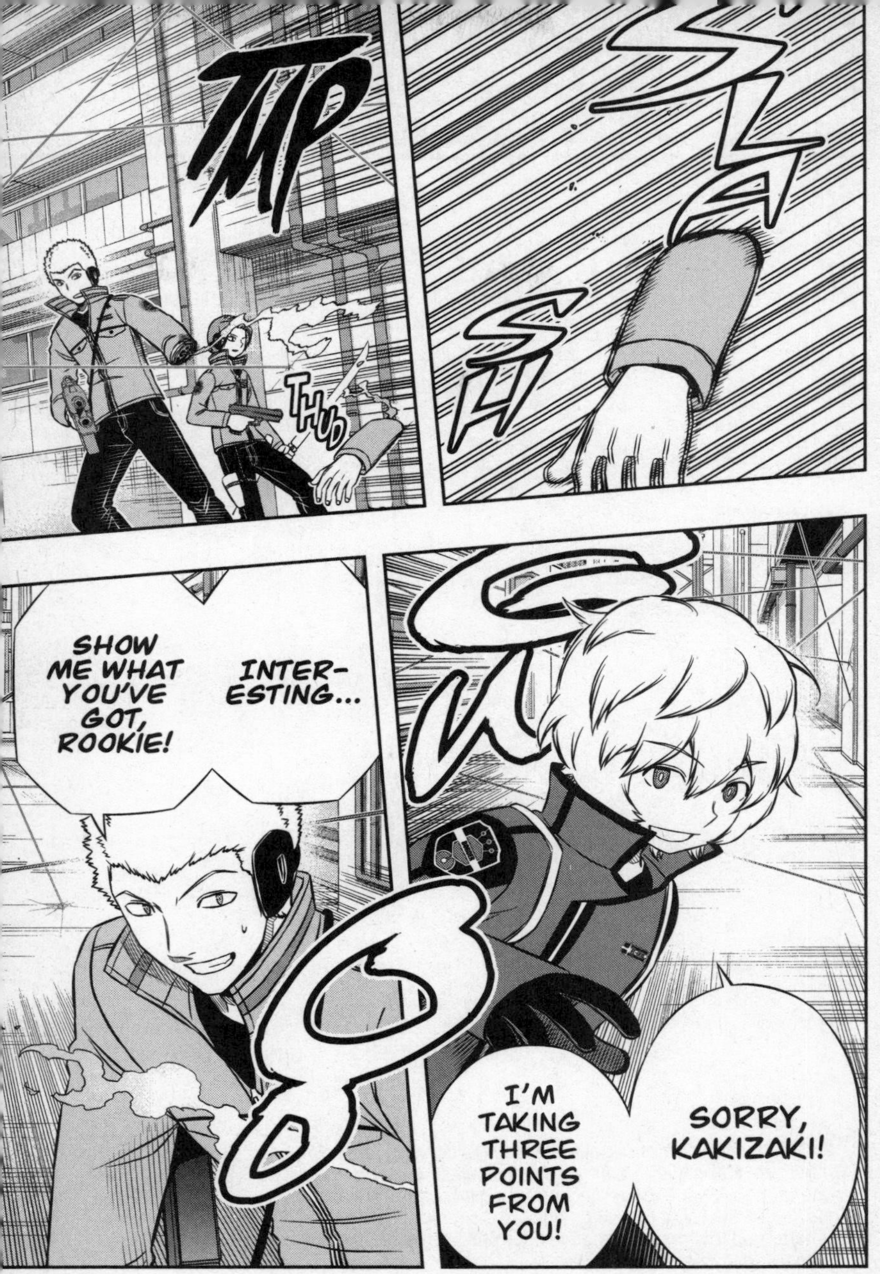
SHA
SH
TMP
THUD
SORRY, KAKIZAKI!
I'M TAKING THREE POINTS FROM YOU!
INTERESTING...
SHOW ME WHAT YOU'VE GOT, ROOKIE!

Katori Squad Strategy Room

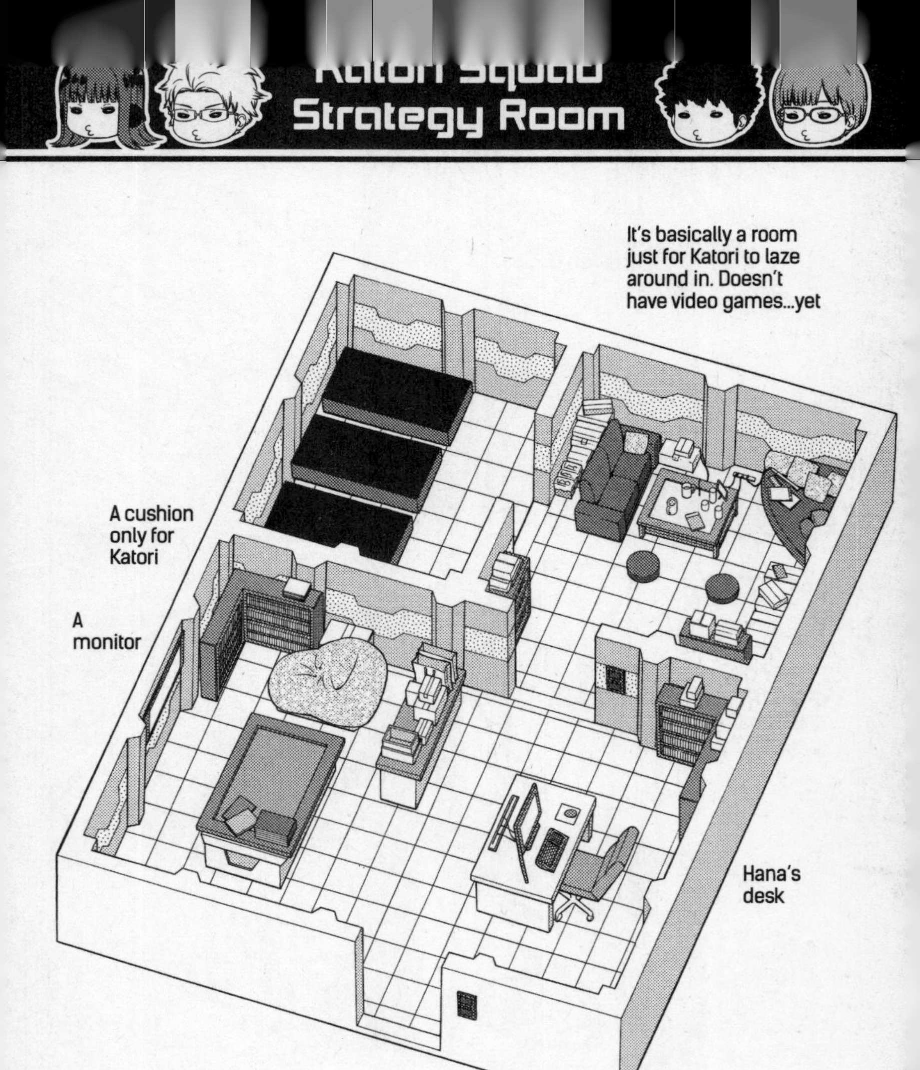
It's basically a room just for Katori to laze around in. Doesn't have video games...yet
A cushion only for Katori
A monitor
Hana's desk

Katori Squad's room is pretty much Katori's domain. Aside from Hana's desk, the boys are only allowed to use the area around the operator desk and the circular chairs in the small room in the back. Somehow, the room is pretty messy. At one point, Katori was determined to remove all the video games from the room, but her plan failed thanks to mobile games.

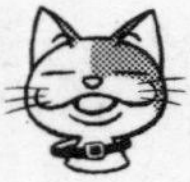

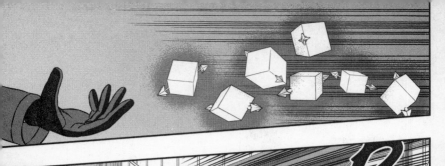

Chapter 141
Tamakoma-2: Part 12

FORGET THE WIRES!

ONCE MY EYES ADJUST, I CAN SEE THEM!

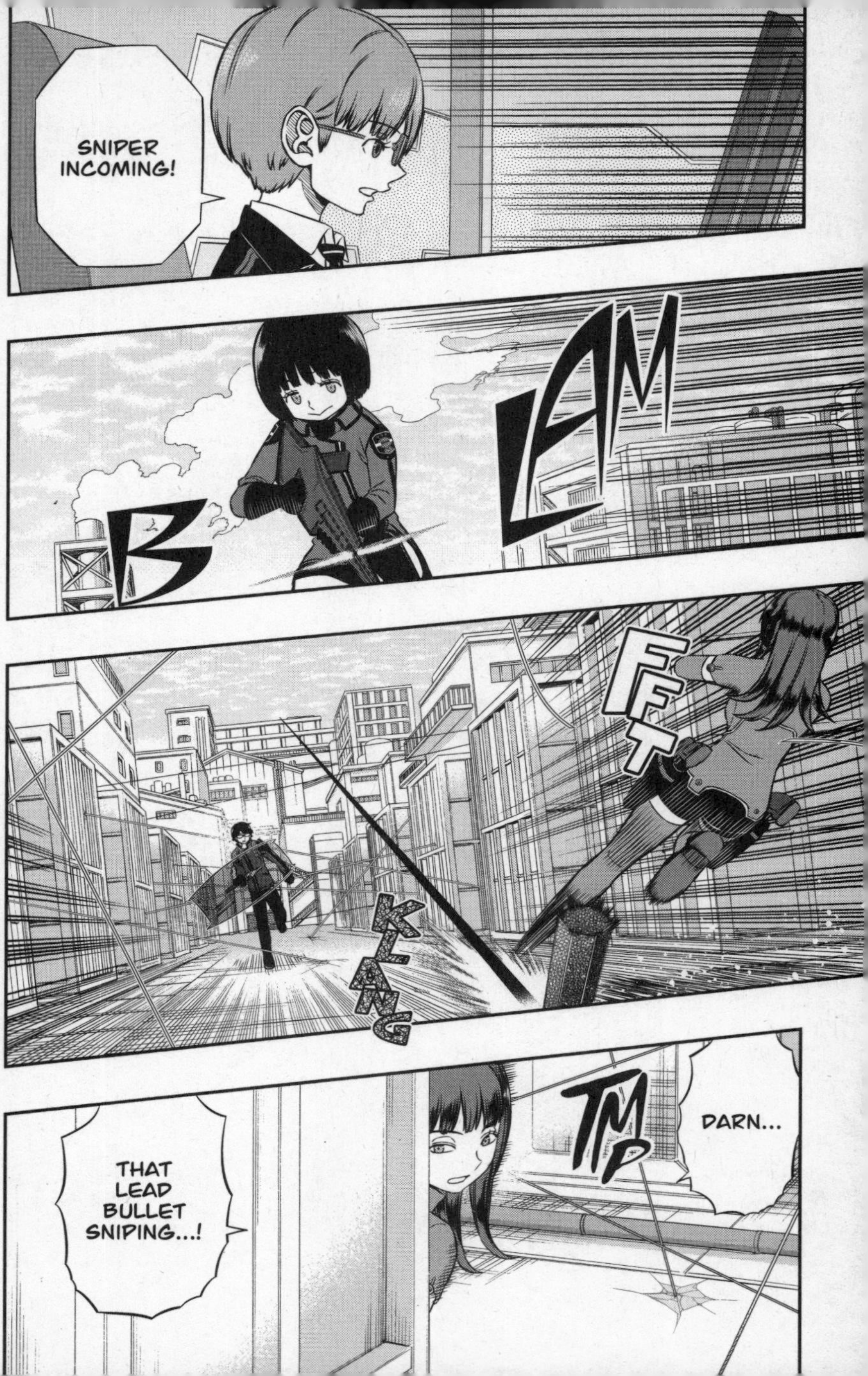
SNIPER INCOMING!
BLAM
FFT
KLANG
DARN...
TMP
THAT LEAD BULLET SNIPING...!

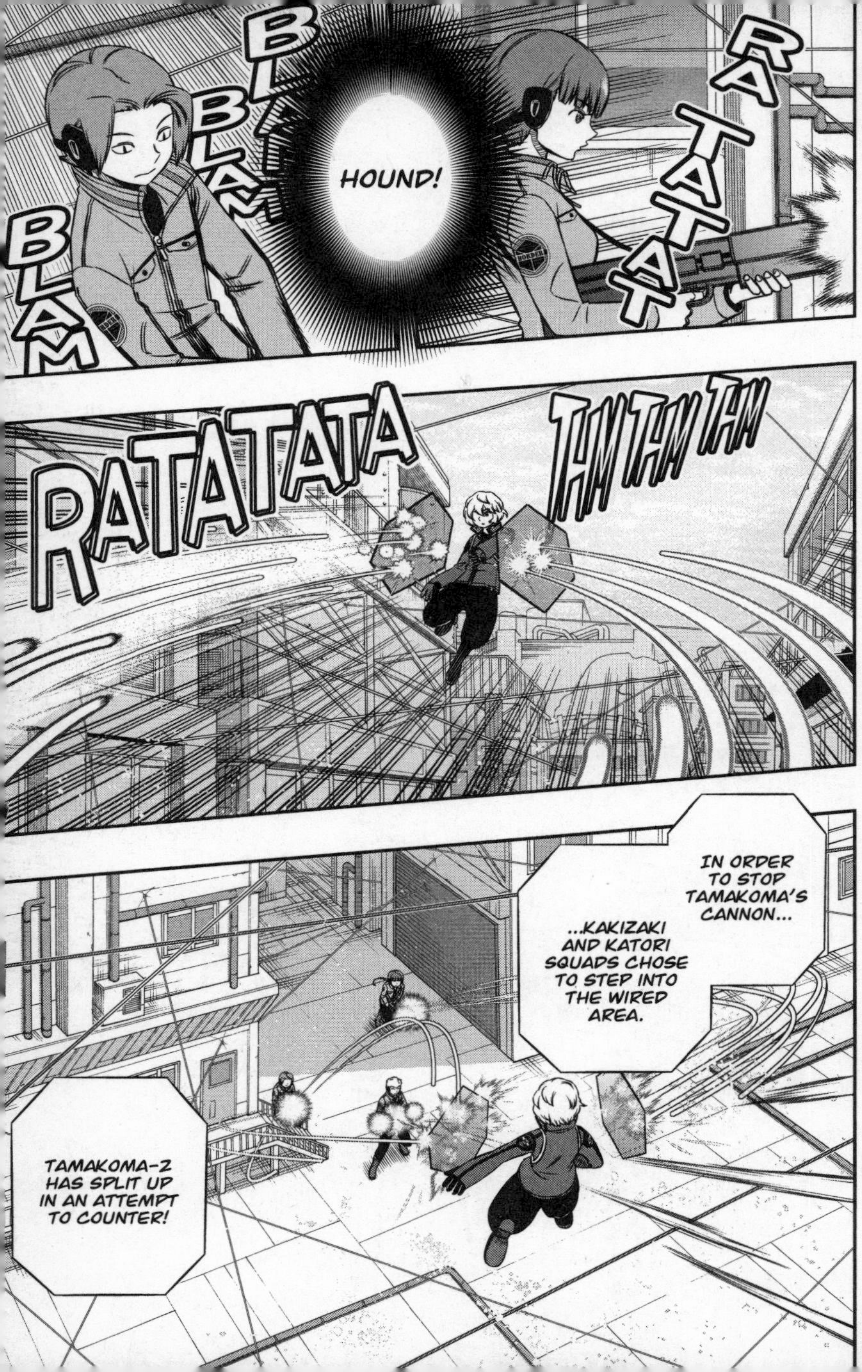
RATATAT
HOUND!
BLAM
BLAM
BLAM
THM THM THM
RATATATA
IN ORDER TO STOP TAMAKOMA'S CANNON...
...KAKIZAKI AND KATORI SQUADS CHOSE TO STEP INTO THE WIRED AREA.
TAMAKOMA-2 HAS SPLIT UP IN AN ATTEMPT TO COUNTER!

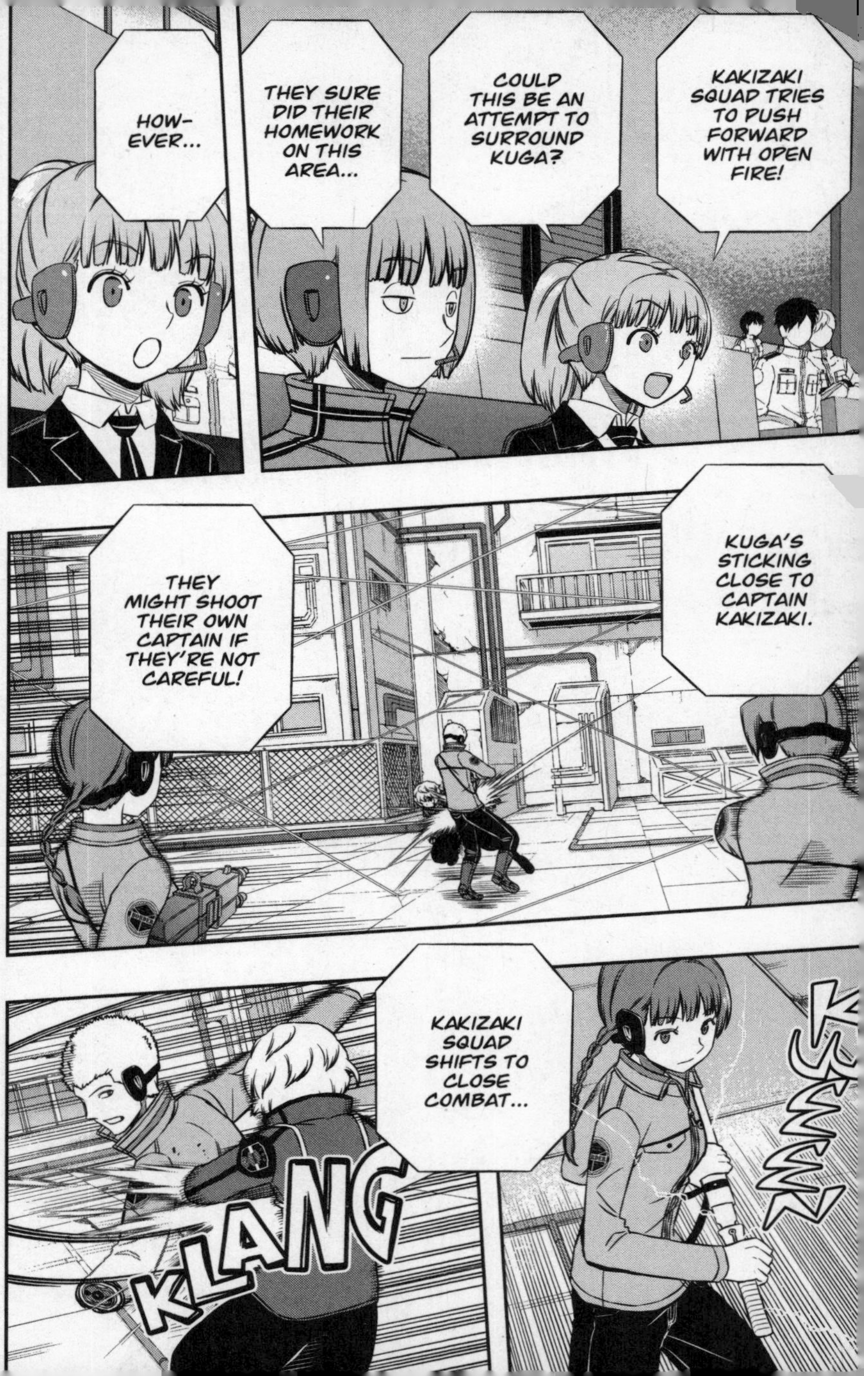
KAKIZAKI SQUAD TRIES TO PUSH FORWARD WITH OPEN FIRE!
COULD THIS BE AN ATTEMPT TO SURROUND KUGA?
THEY SURE DID THEIR HOMEWORK ON THIS AREA...
HOW-EVER...
KUGA'S STICKING CLOSE TO CAPTAIN KAKIZAKI.
THEY MIGHT SHOOT THEIR OWN CAPTAIN IF THEY'RE NOT CAREFUL!
KAKIZAKI SQUAD SHIFTS TO CLOSE COMBAT...
KLANG

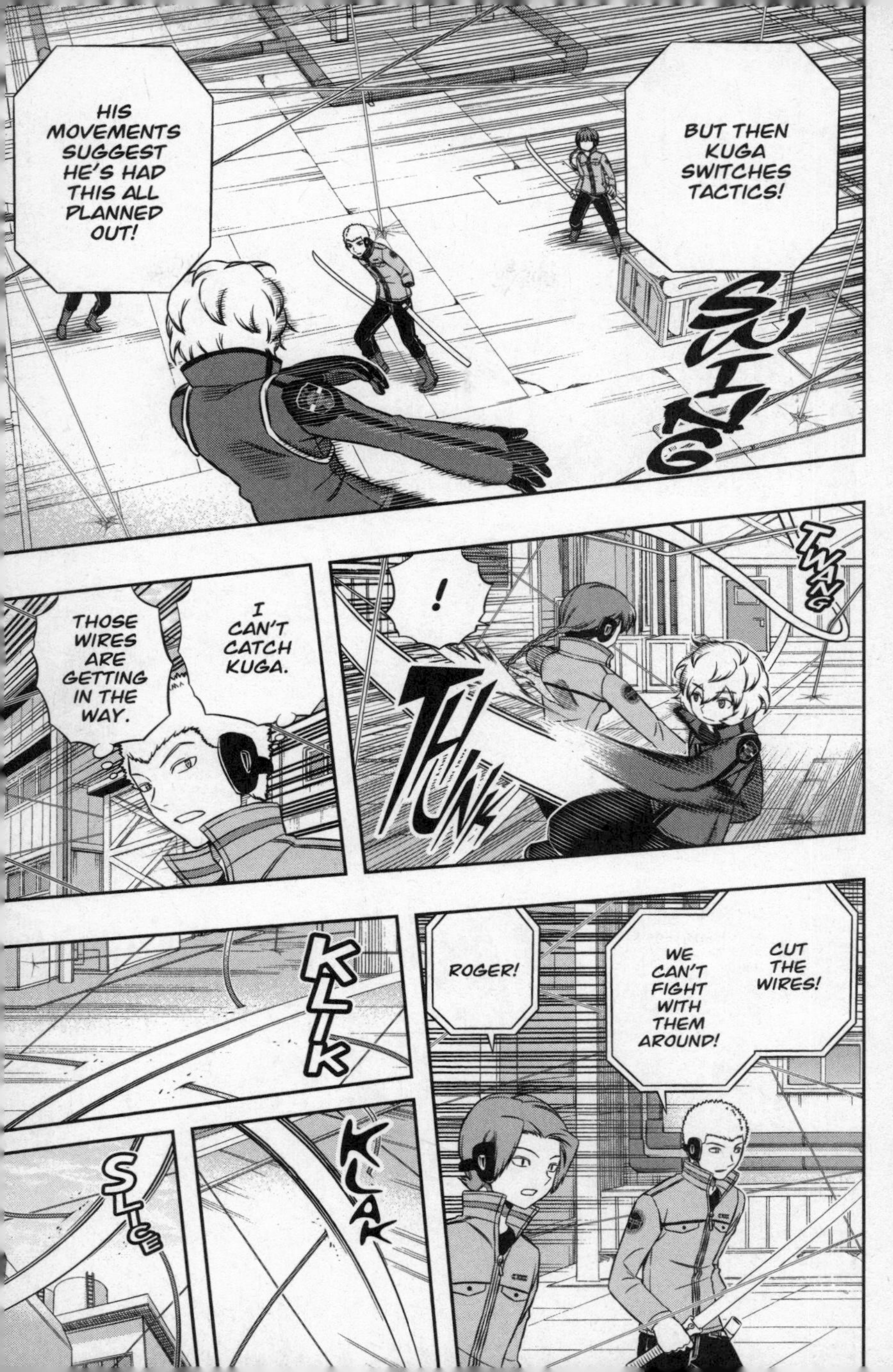
BUT THEN KUGA SWITCHES TACTICS!
HIS MOVEMENTS SUGGEST HE'S HAD THIS ALL PLANNED OUT!
SWING
TWANG
!
THUNK
I CAN'T CATCH KUGA.
THOSE WIRES ARE GETTING IN THE WAY.
CUT THE WIRES!
WE CAN'T FIGHT WITH THEM AROUND!
ROGER!
KLIK
KLAK
SLICE

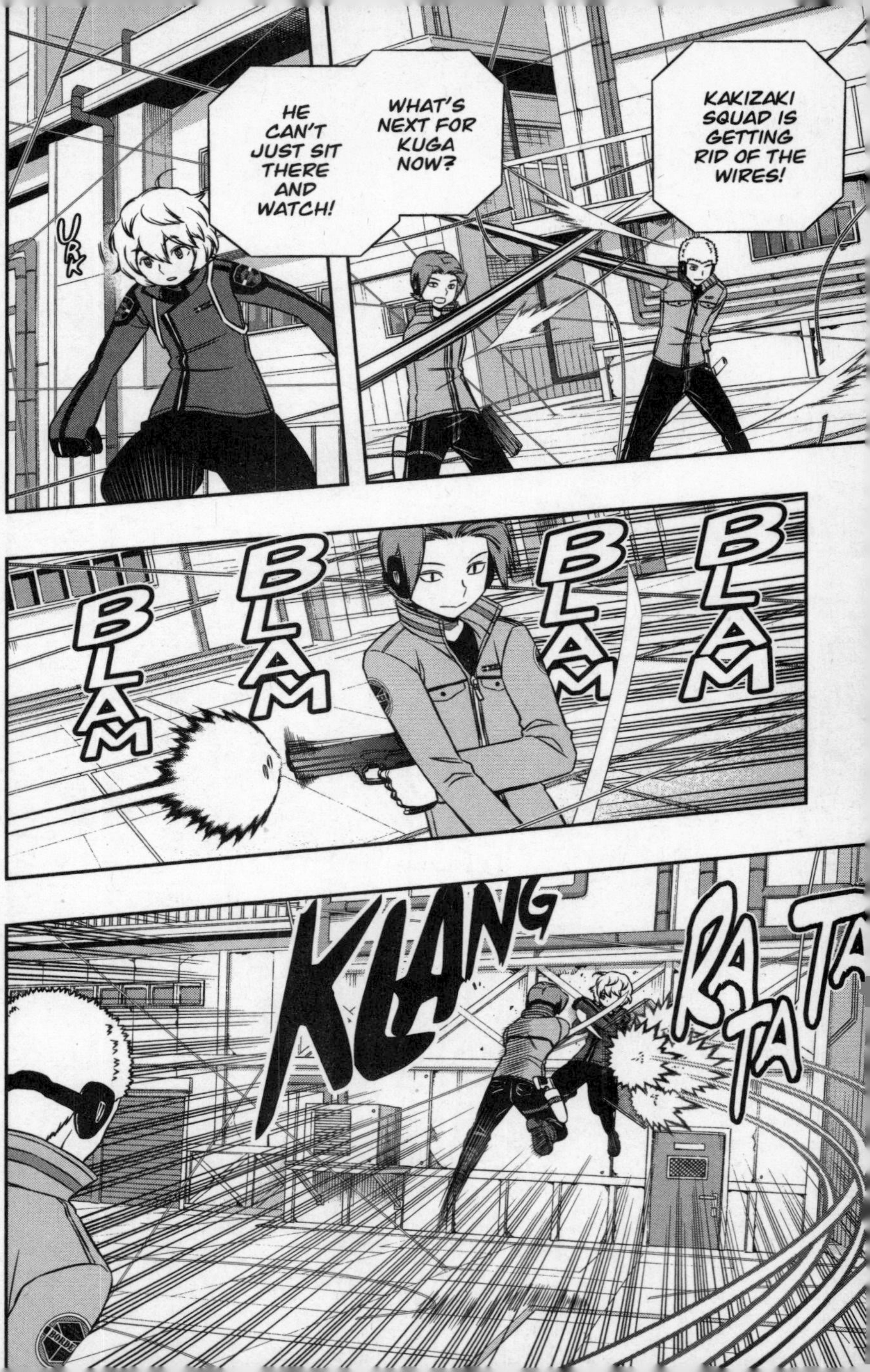
KAKIZAKI SQUAD IS GETTING RID OF THE WIRES!
WHAT'S NEXT FOR KUGA NOW?
HE CAN'T JUST SIT THERE AND WATCH!
URK
BLAM
BLAM
BLAM
BLAM
RATATA
KLANG

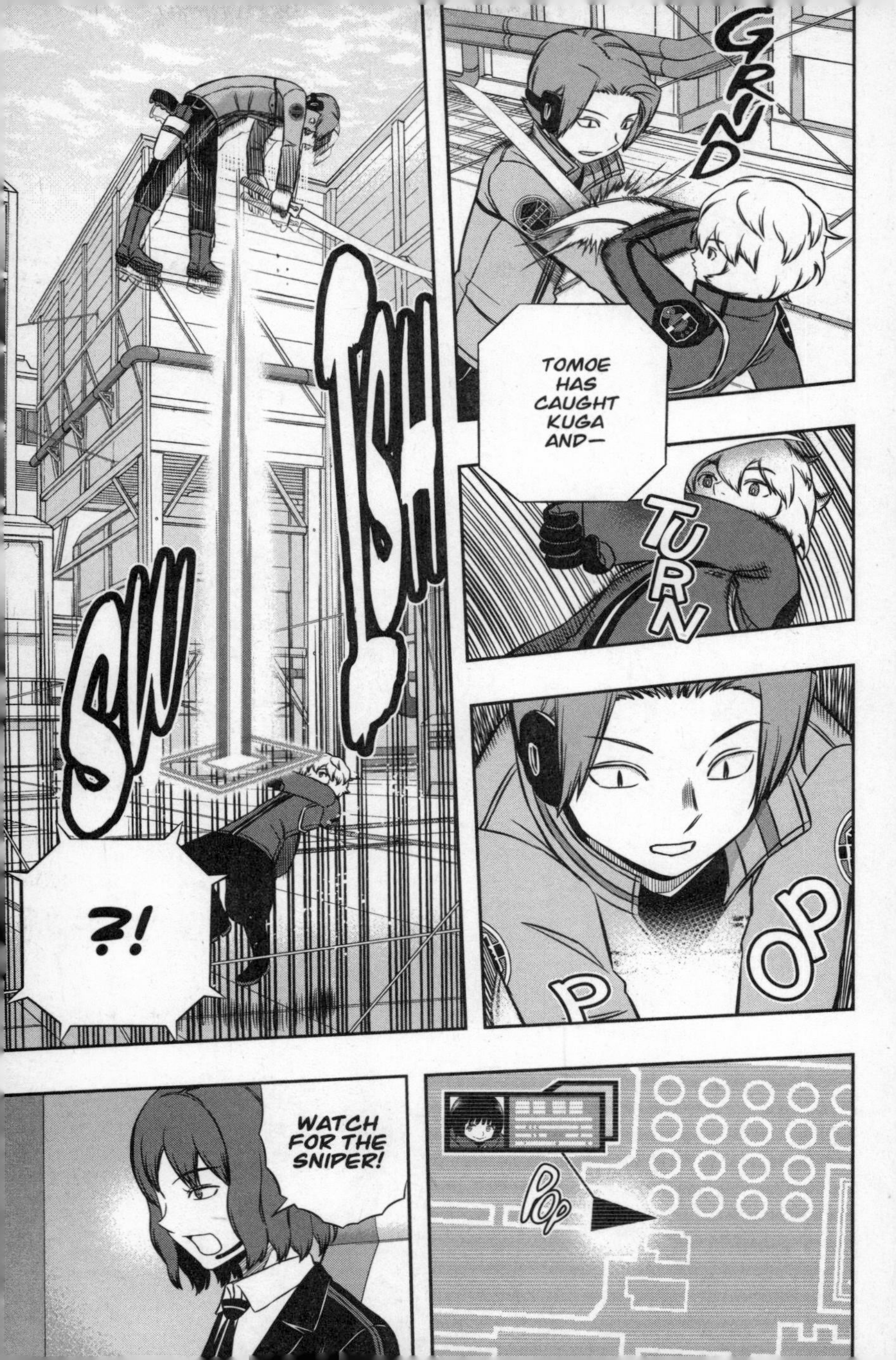
GRIND
TOMOE HAS CAUGHT KUGA AND—
TURN
POP
TSH
SWH
?!
Pop
WATCH FOR THE SNIPER!

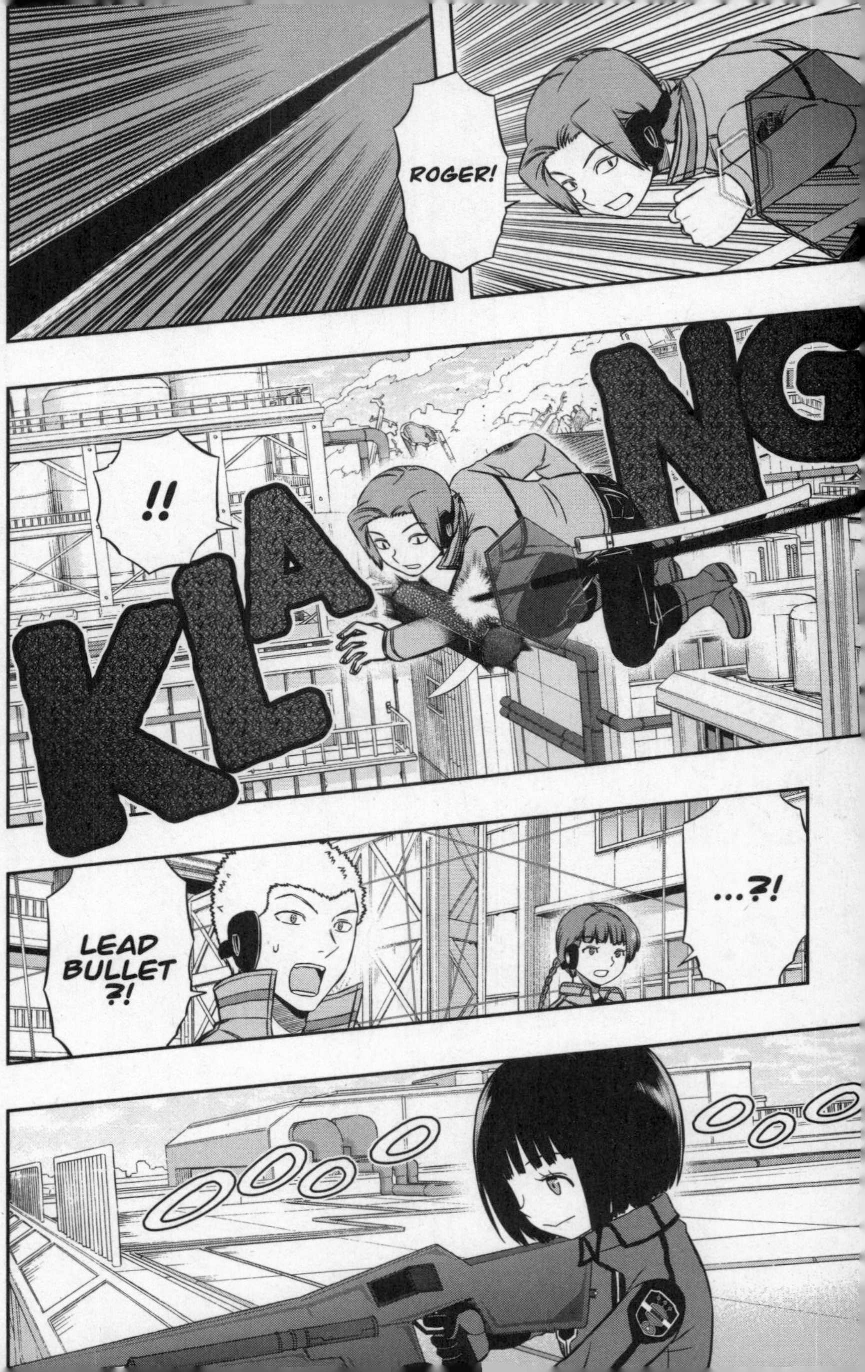
ROGER!
!!
KLANG
...?!
LEAD BULLET ?!

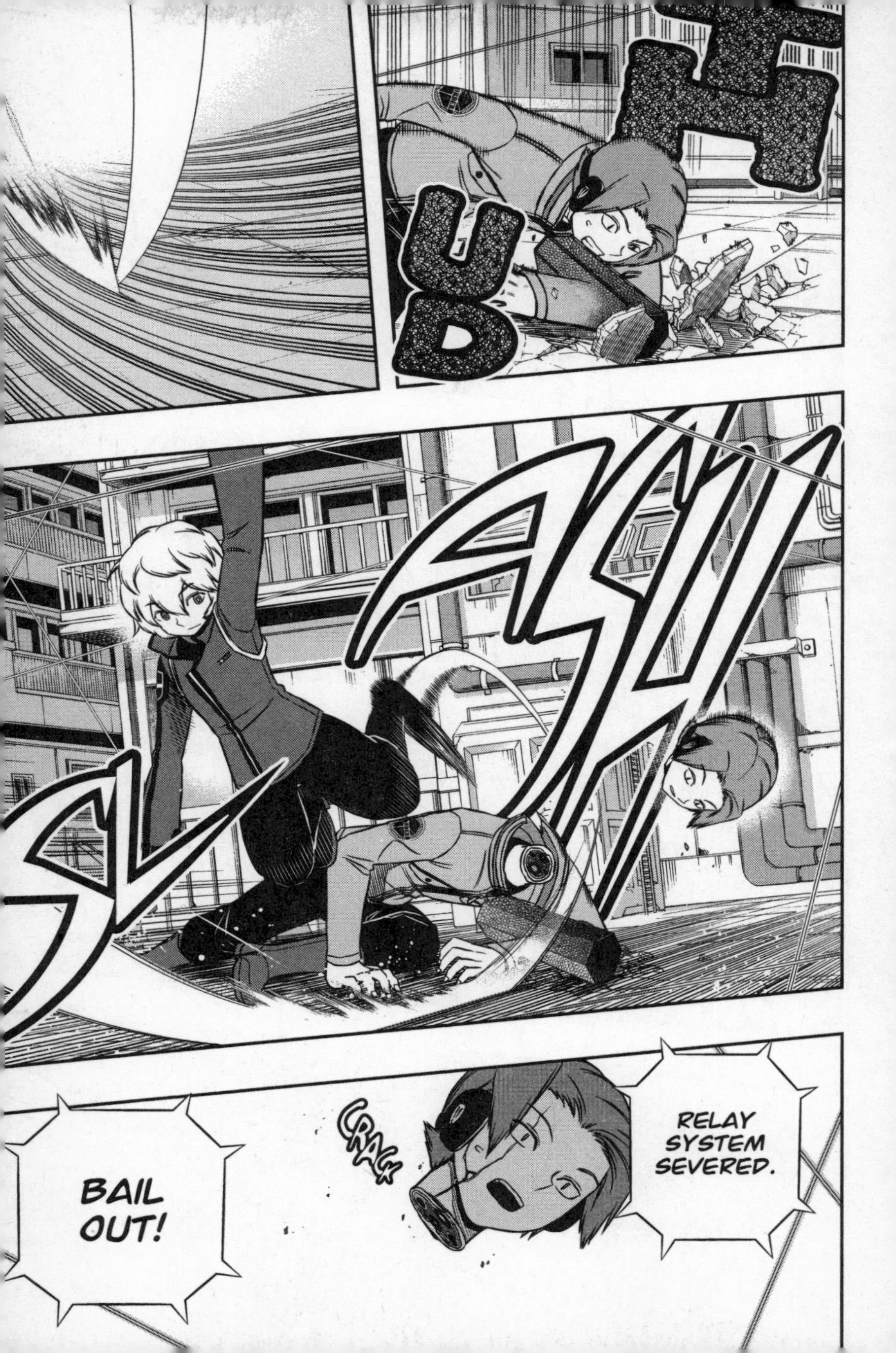
RELAY SYSTEM SEVERED.
CRACK
BAIL OUT!

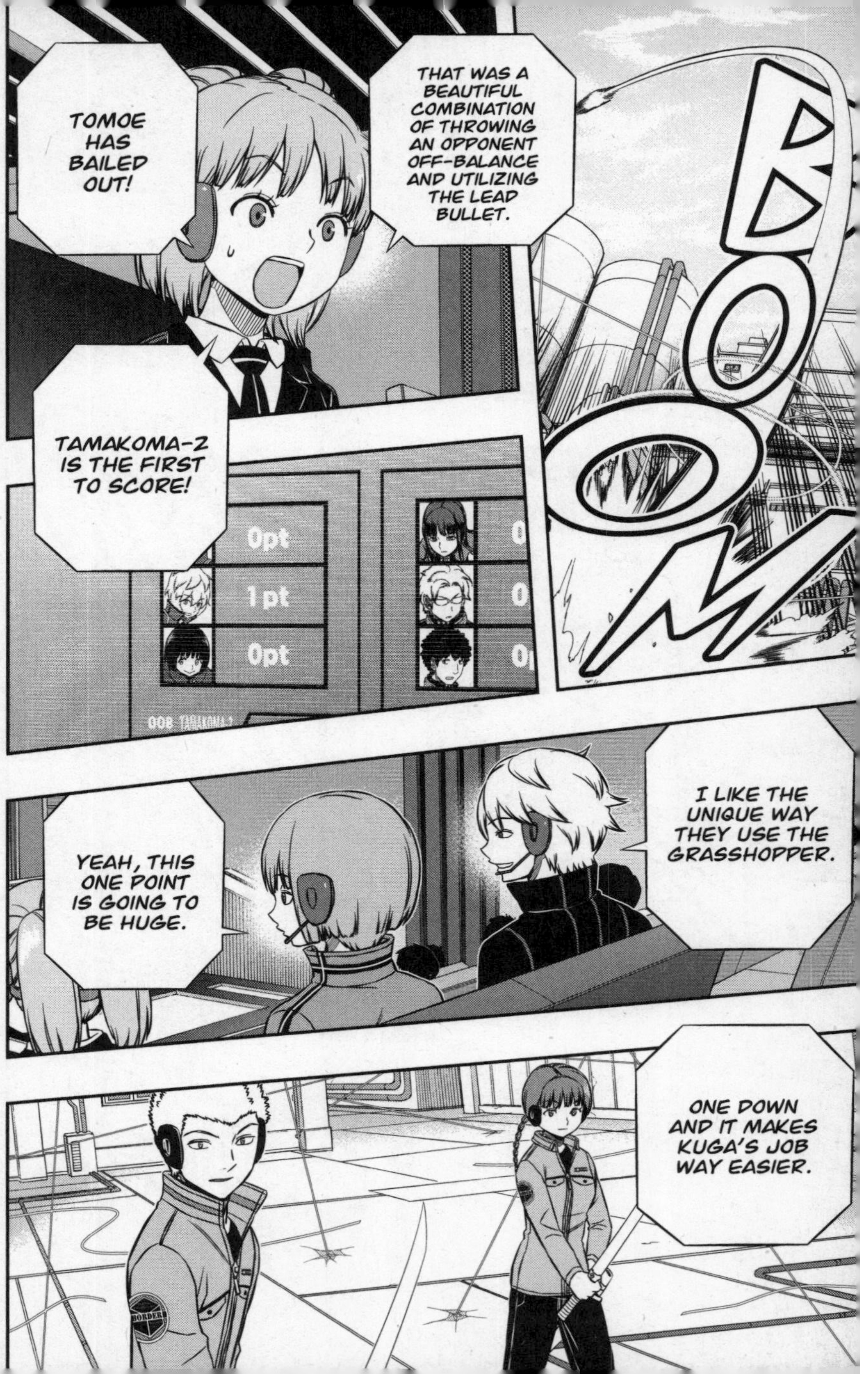
BOOM
THAT WAS A BEAUTIFUL COMBINATION OF THROWING AN OPPONENT OFF-BALANCE AND UTILIZING THE LEAD BULLET.
TOMOE HAS BAILED OUT!
TAMAKOMA-2 IS THE FIRST TO SCORE!
0pt
1pt
0pt
I LIKE THE UNIQUE WAY THEY USE THE GRASSHOPPER.
YEAH, THIS ONE POINT IS GOING TO BE HUGE.
ONE DOWN AND IT MAKES KUGA'S JOB WAY EASIER.

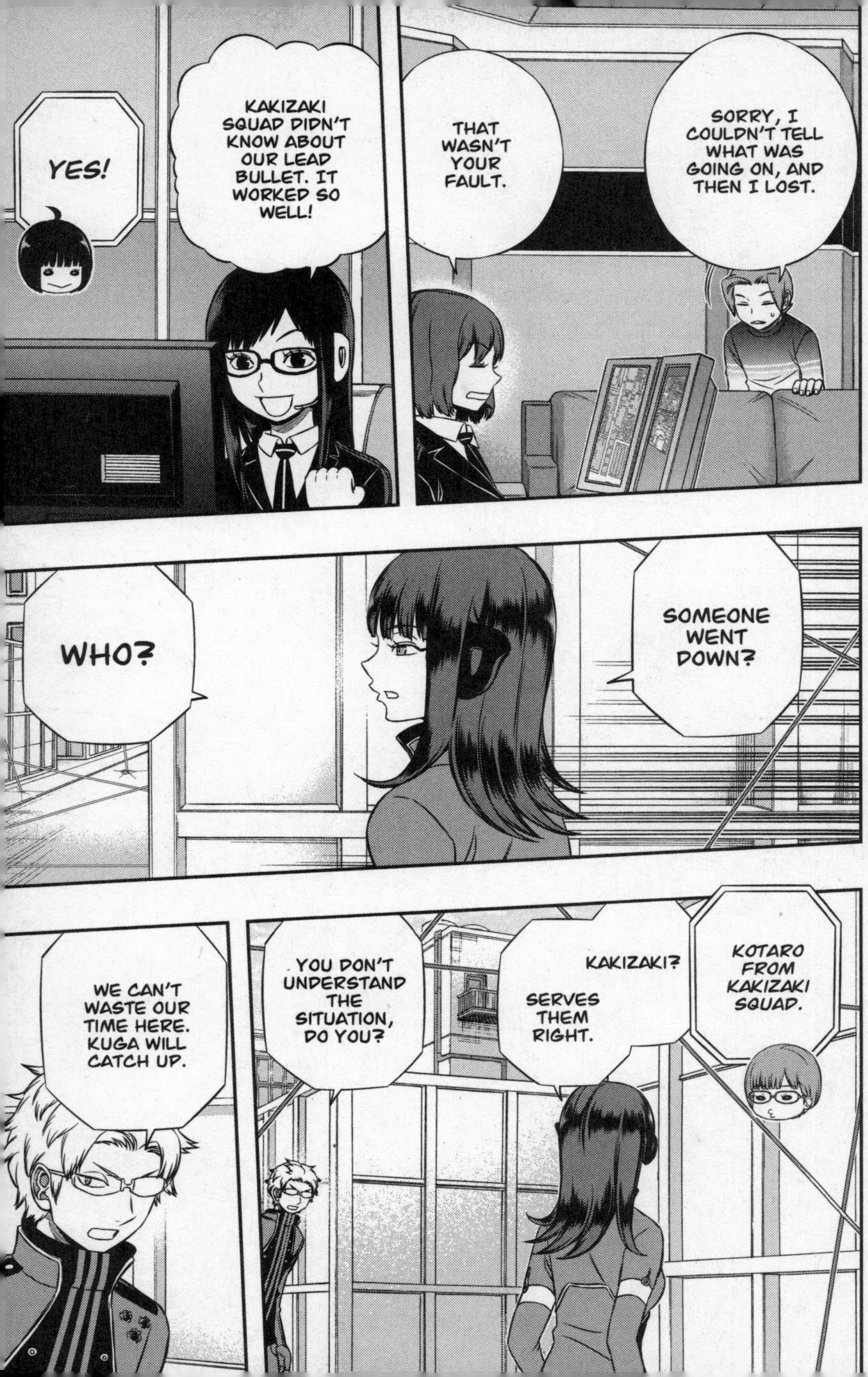
SORRY, I COULDN'T TELL WHAT WAS GOING ON, AND THEN I LOST.
THAT WASN'T YOUR FAULT.
KAKIZAKI SQUAD DIDN'T KNOW ABOUT OUR LEAD BULLET. IT WORKED SO WELL!
YES!
SOMEONE WENT DOWN?
WHO?
KOTARO FROM KAKIZAKI SQUAD.
KAKIZAKI?
SERVES THEM RIGHT.
YOU DON'T UNDERSTAND THE SITUATION, DO YOU?
WE CAN'T WASTE OUR TIME HERE. KUGA WILL CATCH UP.

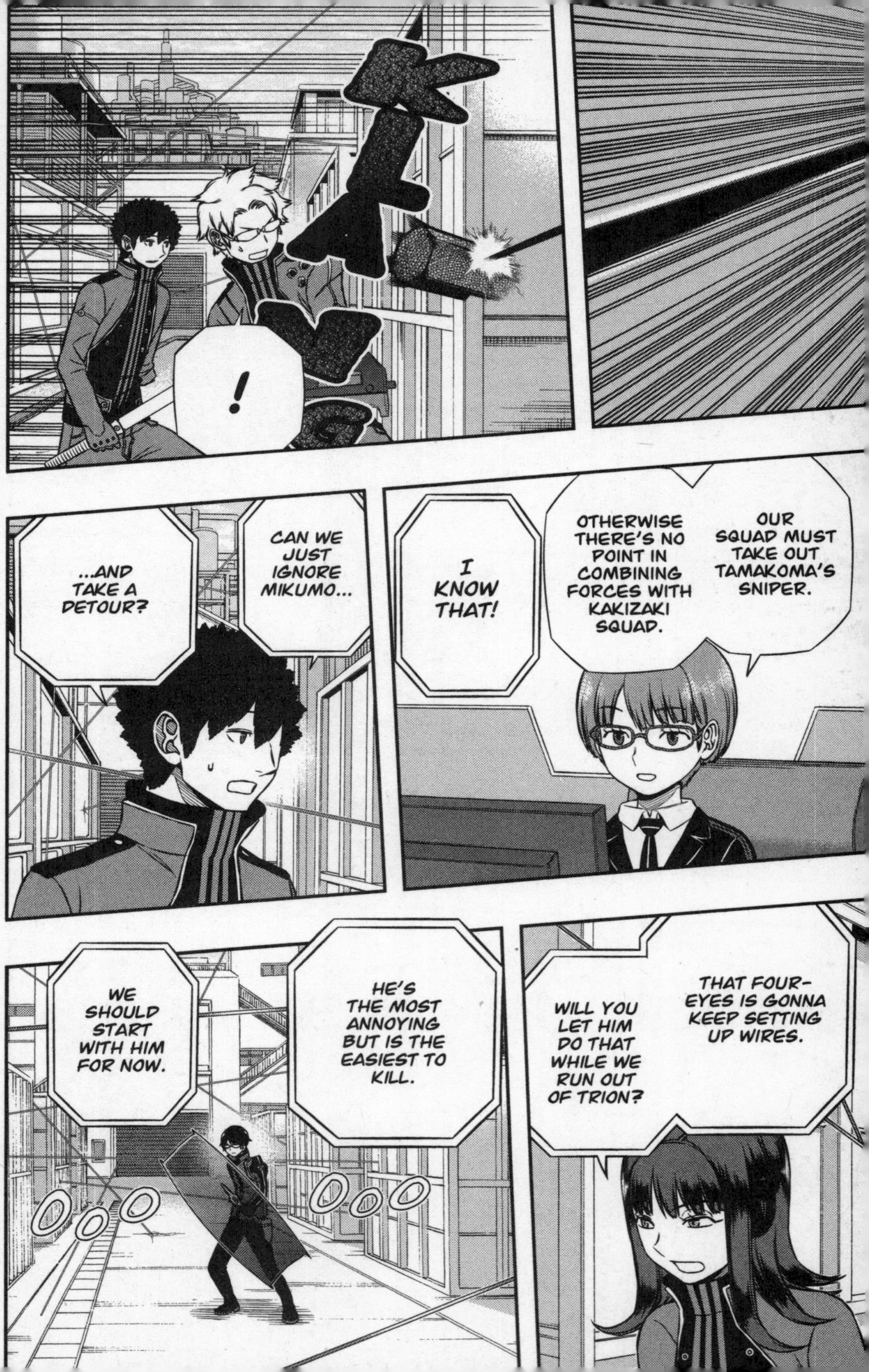
!
OUR SQUAD MUST TAKE OUT TAMAKOMA'S SNIPER.
OTHERWISE THERE'S NO POINT IN COMBINING FORCES WITH KAKIZAKI SQUAD.
I KNOW THAT!
CAN WE JUST IGNORE MIKUMO...
...AND TAKE A DETOUR?
THAT FOUR-EYES IS GONNA KEEP SETTING UP WIRES.
WILL YOU LET HIM DO THAT WHILE WE RUN OUT OF TRION?
HE'S THE MOST ANNOYING BUT IS THE EASIEST TO KILL.
WE SHOULD START WITH HIM FOR NOW.

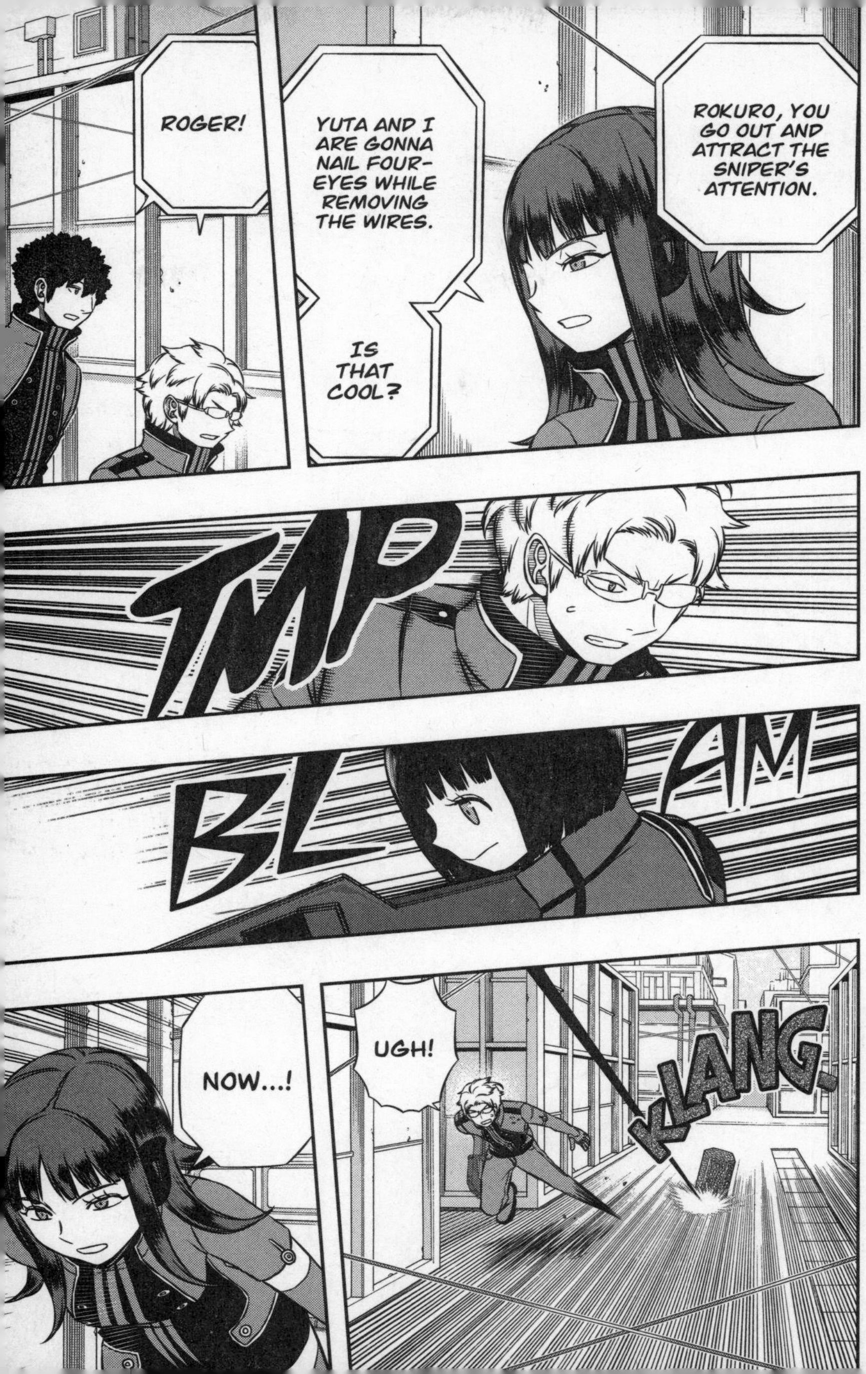
ROKURO, YOU GO OUT AND ATTRACT THE SNIPER'S ATTENTION.
YUTA AND I ARE GONNA NAIL FOUR-EYES WHILE REMOVING THE WIRES.
IS THAT COOL?
ROGER!
TMP
BLAM
KLANG.
UGH!
NOW...!

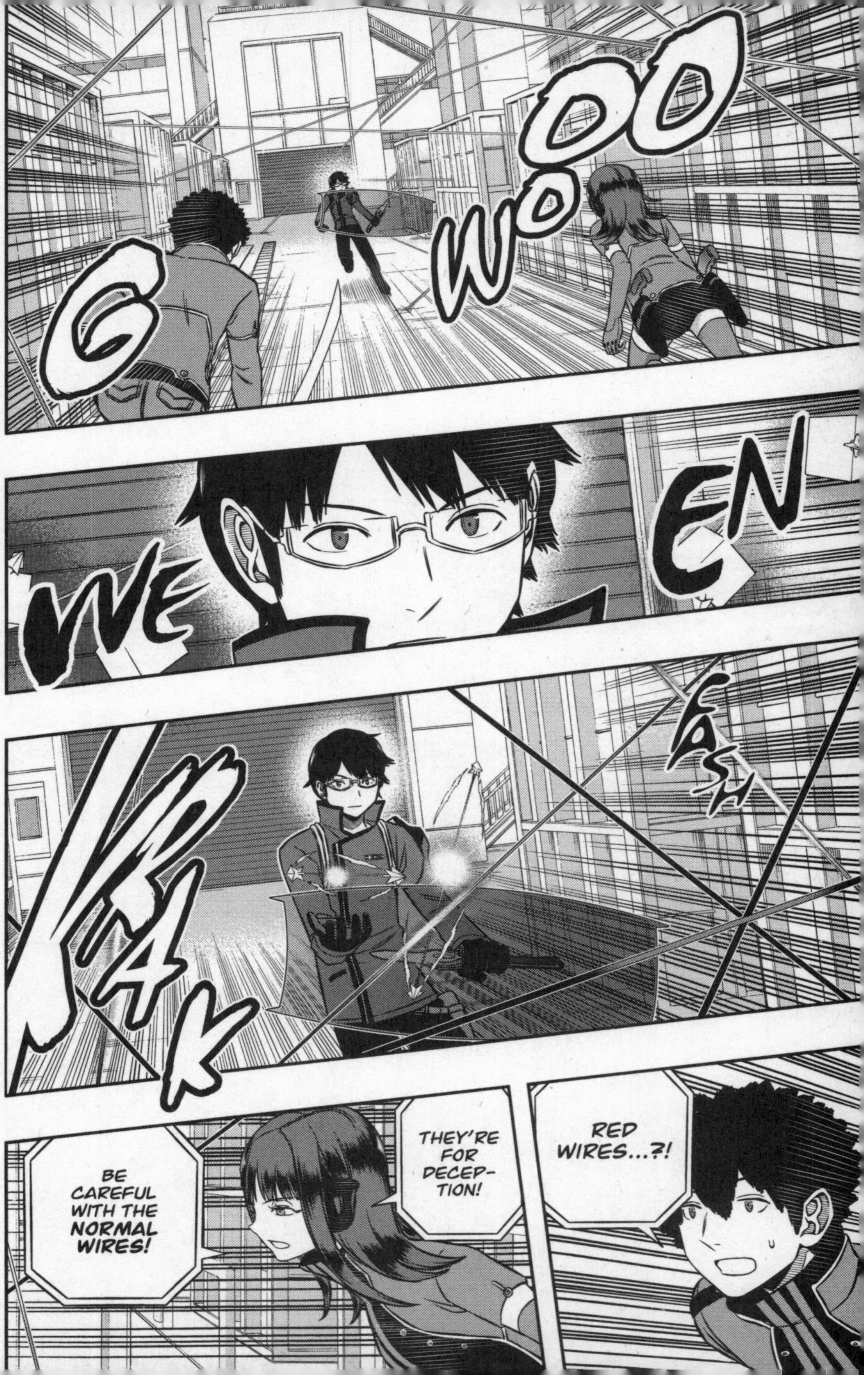
GWOOO
VVEEN
FASH
KRAK
RED WIRES...?!
THEY'RE FOR DECEP-TION!
BE CAREFUL WITH THE **NORMAL** WIRES!

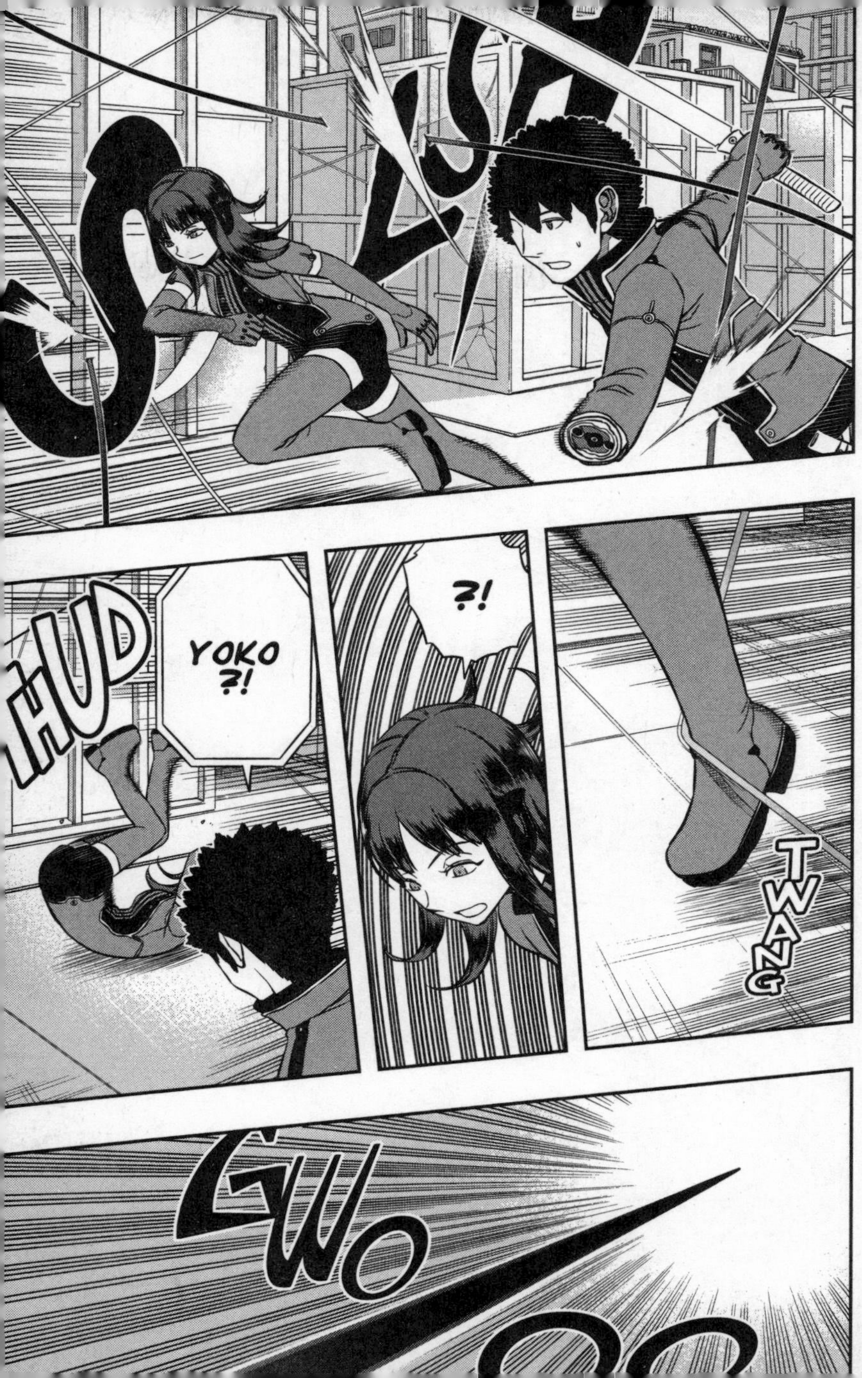

TWANG
?!
YOKO ?!

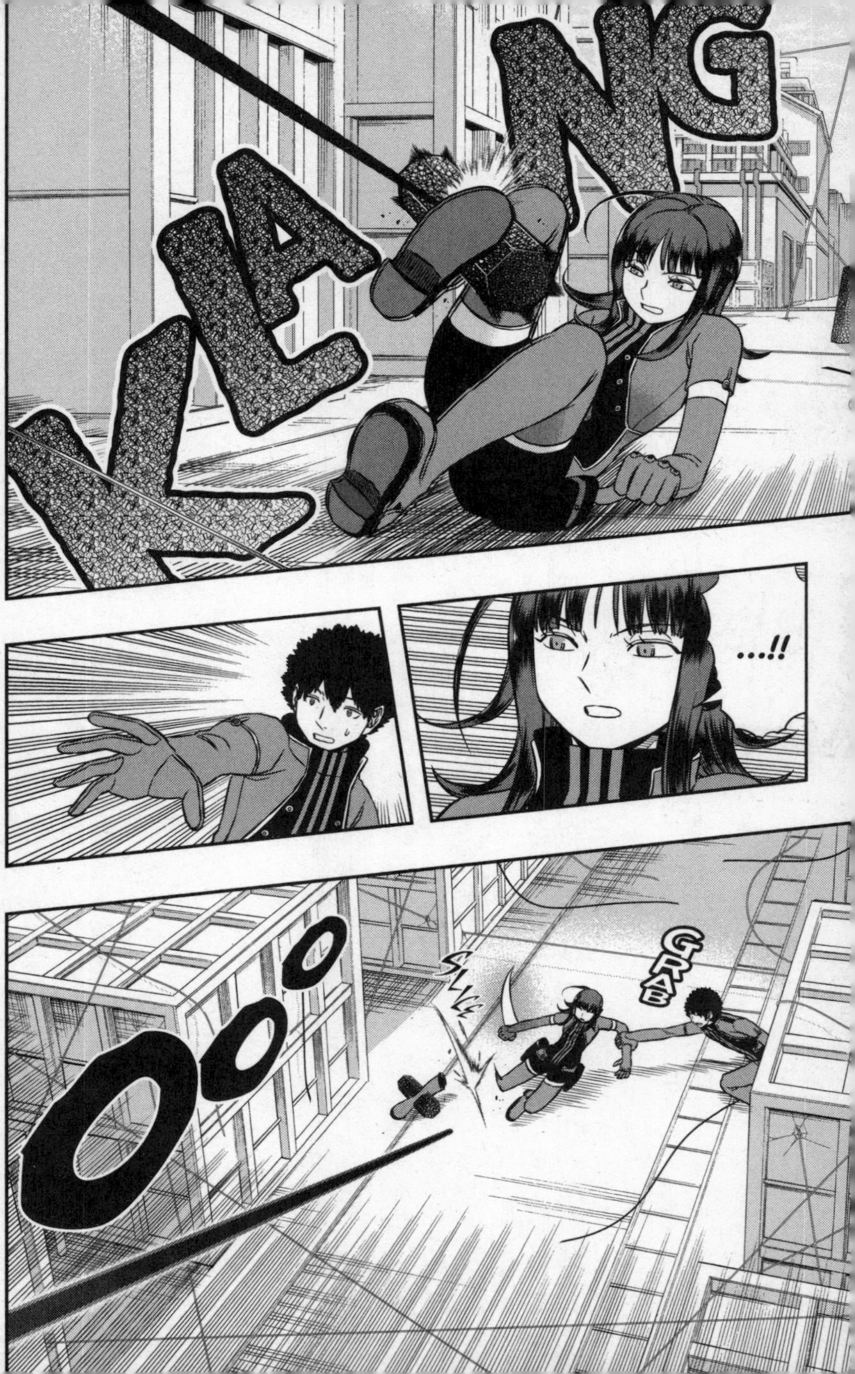
KLANG
...!!
GRAB
SLICE
OOO

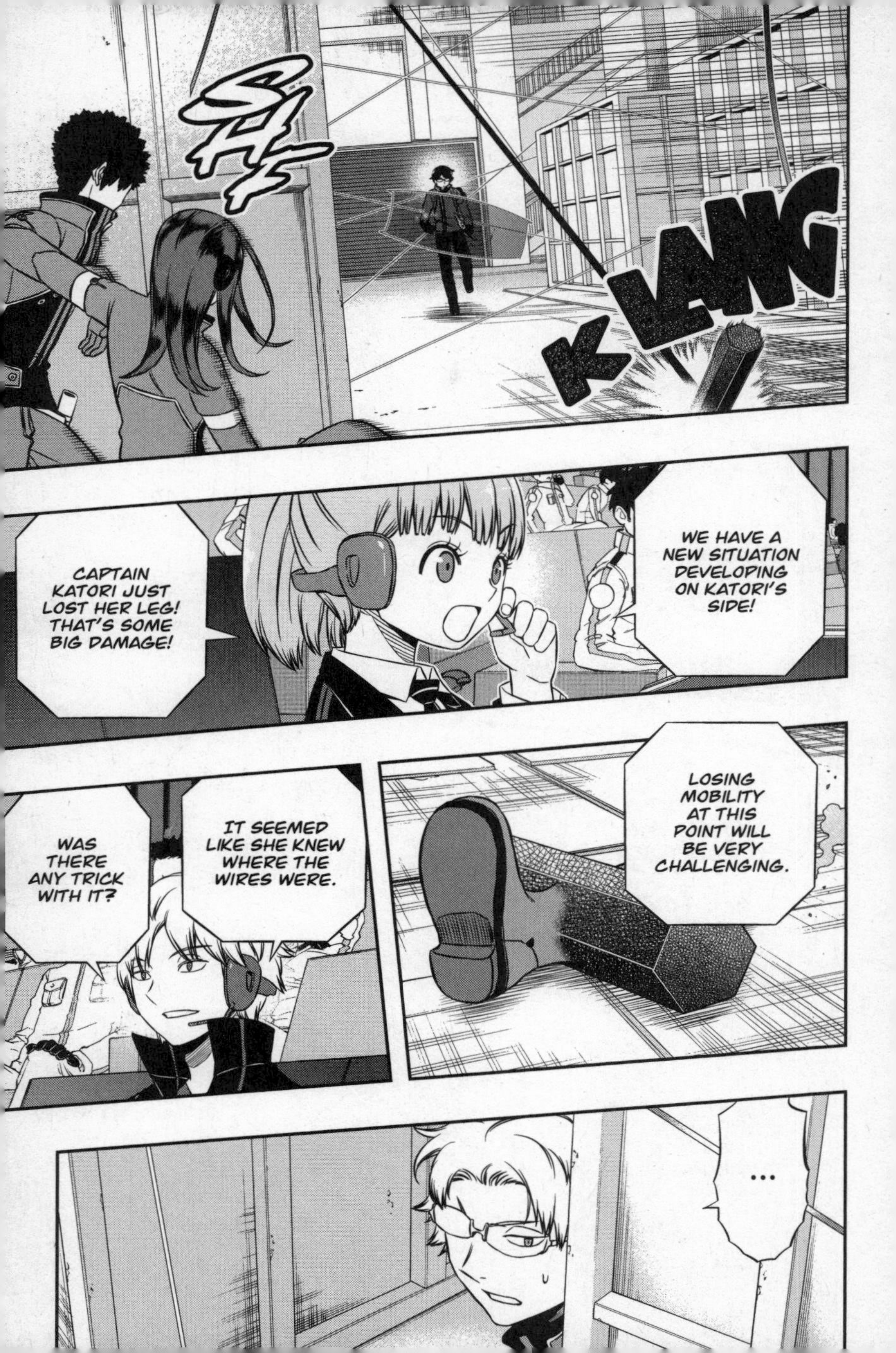
KLANG
SHF
WE HAVE A NEW SITUATION DEVELOPING ON KATORI'S SIDE!
CAPTAIN KATORI JUST LOST HER LEG! THAT'S SOME BIG DAMAGE!
LOSING MOBILITY AT THIS POINT WILL BE VERY CHALLENGING.
IT SEEMED LIKE SHE KNEW WHERE THE WIRES WERE.
WAS THERE ANY TRICK WITH IT?
...

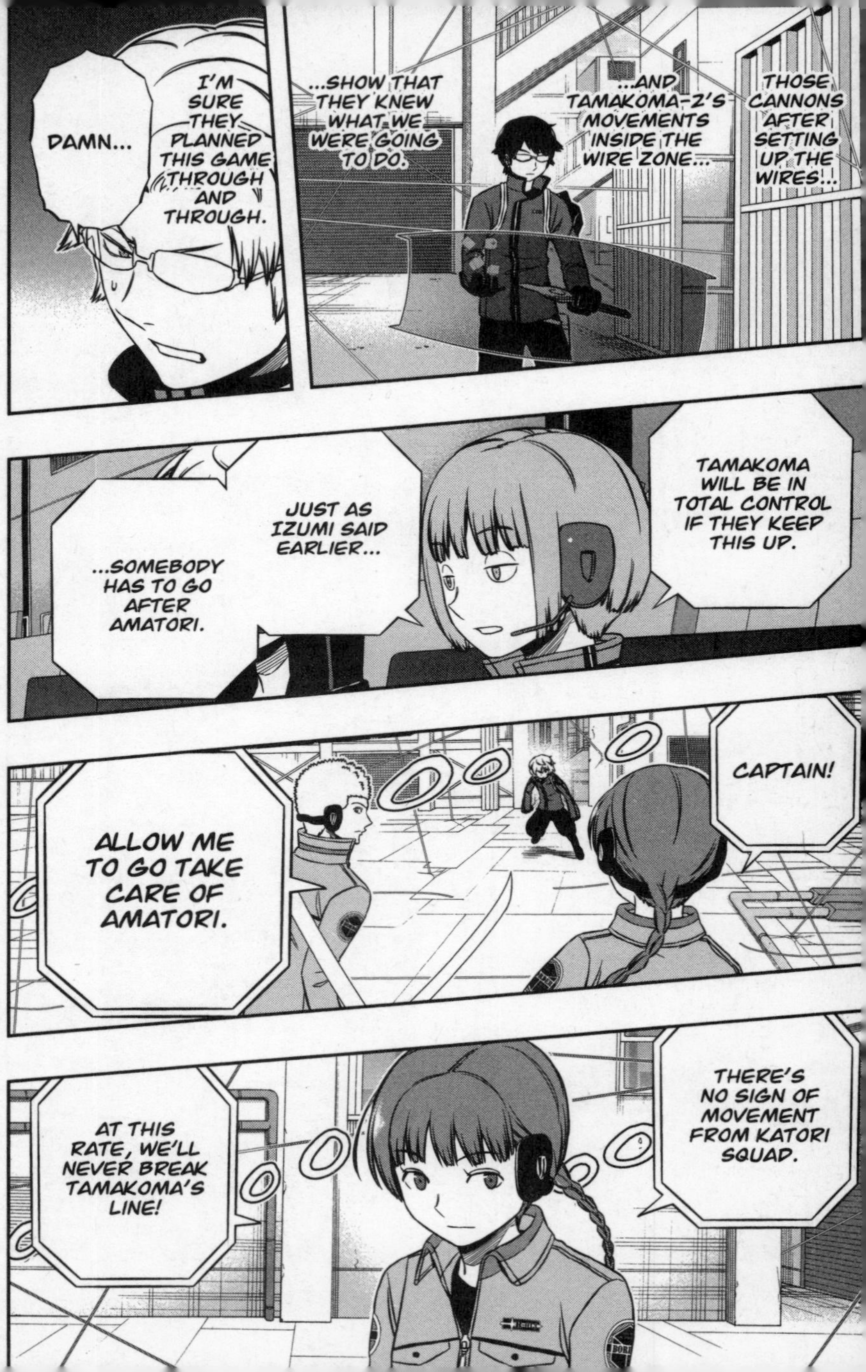
THOSE CANNONS AFTER SETTING UP THE WIRES...
...AND TAMAKOMA-2'S MOVEMENTS INSIDE THE WIRE ZONE...
...SHOW THAT THEY KNEW WHAT WE WERE GOING TO DO.
I'M SURE THEY PLANNED THIS GAME THROUGH AND THROUGH.
DAMN...
TAMAKOMA WILL BE IN TOTAL CONTROL IF THEY KEEP THIS UP.
JUST AS IZUMI SAID EARLIER...
...SOMEBODY HAS TO GO AFTER AMATORI.
CAPTAIN!
ALLOW ME TO GO TAKE CARE OF AMATORI.
THERE'S NO SIGN OF MOVEMENT FROM KATORI SQUAD.
AT THIS RATE, WE'LL NEVER BREAK TAMAKOMA'S LINE!

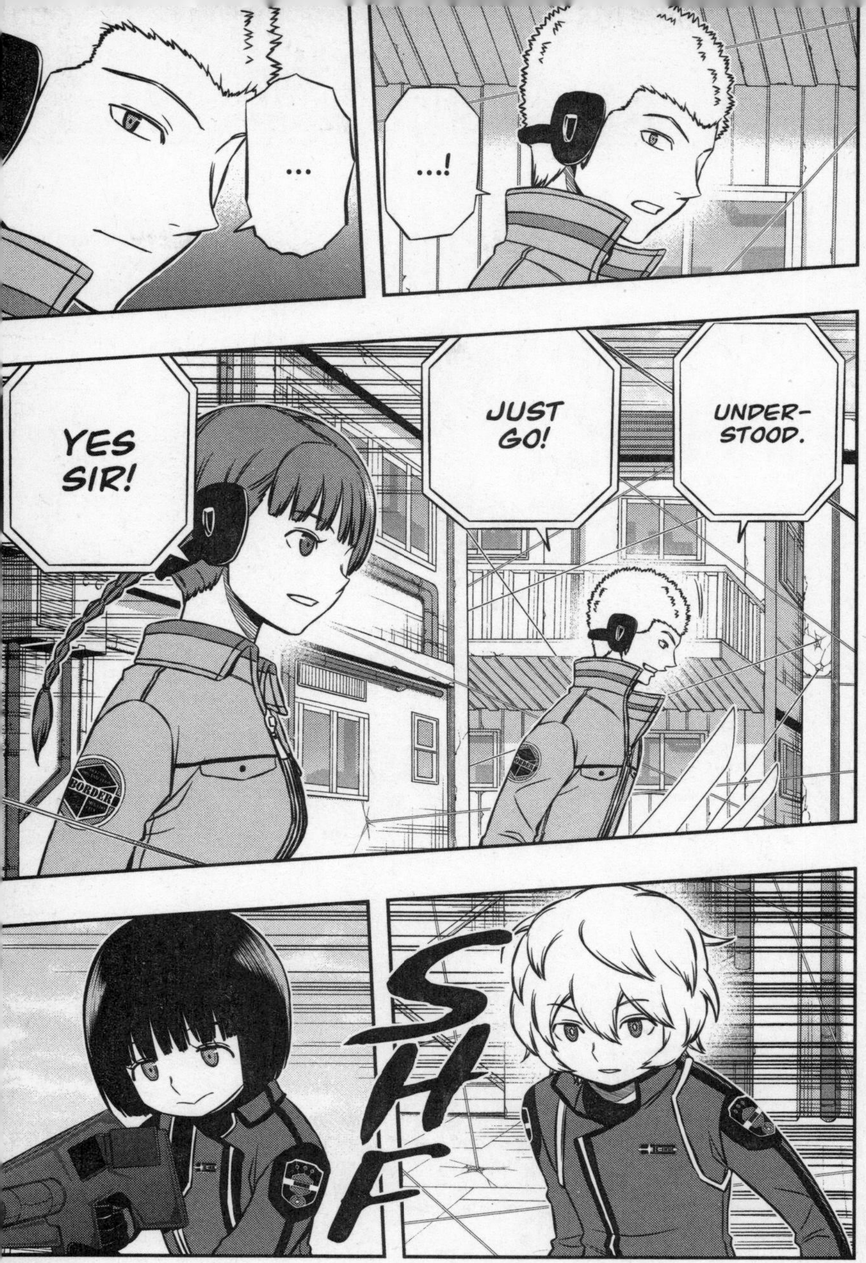
...!
...
UNDER-STOOD.
JUST GO!
YES SIR!
SHF

Kakizaki Squad Strategy Room

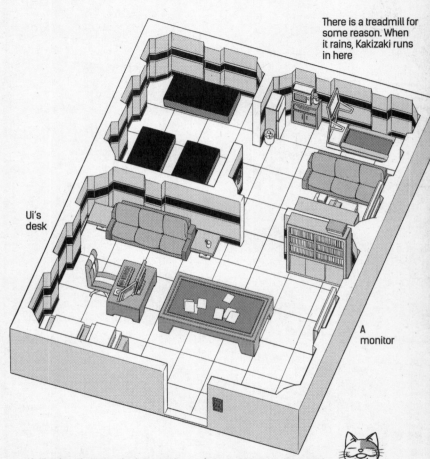

There is a treadmill for some reason. When it rains, Kakizaki runs in here

Ui's desk

A monitor

Unlike the other squads, they use the room for legitimate training and operation-planning purposes, rather than a room to relax. That's why it's so tidy. On his days off, Kakizaki goes outside to play sports. The other three members stay in this room to check the logs or eat snacks. It's got a serious "ready for anything" atmosphere.

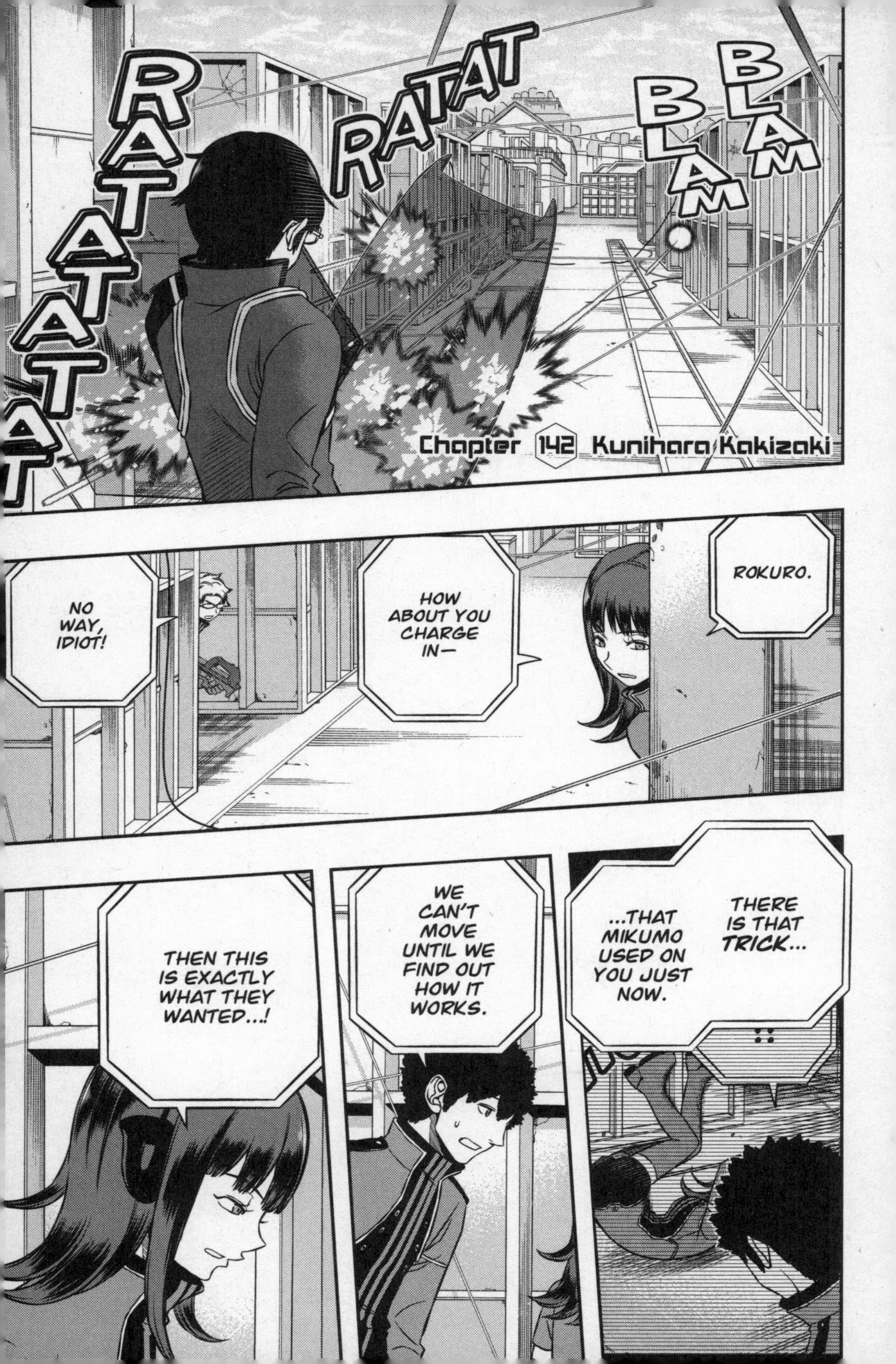
BLAM BLAM
RATAT
RATATATAT
Chapter 142 Kunihara Kakizaki
ROKURO.
HOW ABOUT YOU CHARGE IN—
NO WAY, IDIOT!
THERE IS THAT TRICK...
...THAT MIKUMO USED ON YOU JUST NOW.
WE CAN'T MOVE UNTIL WE FIND OUT HOW IT WORKS.
THEN THIS IS EXACTLY WHAT THEY WANTED...!

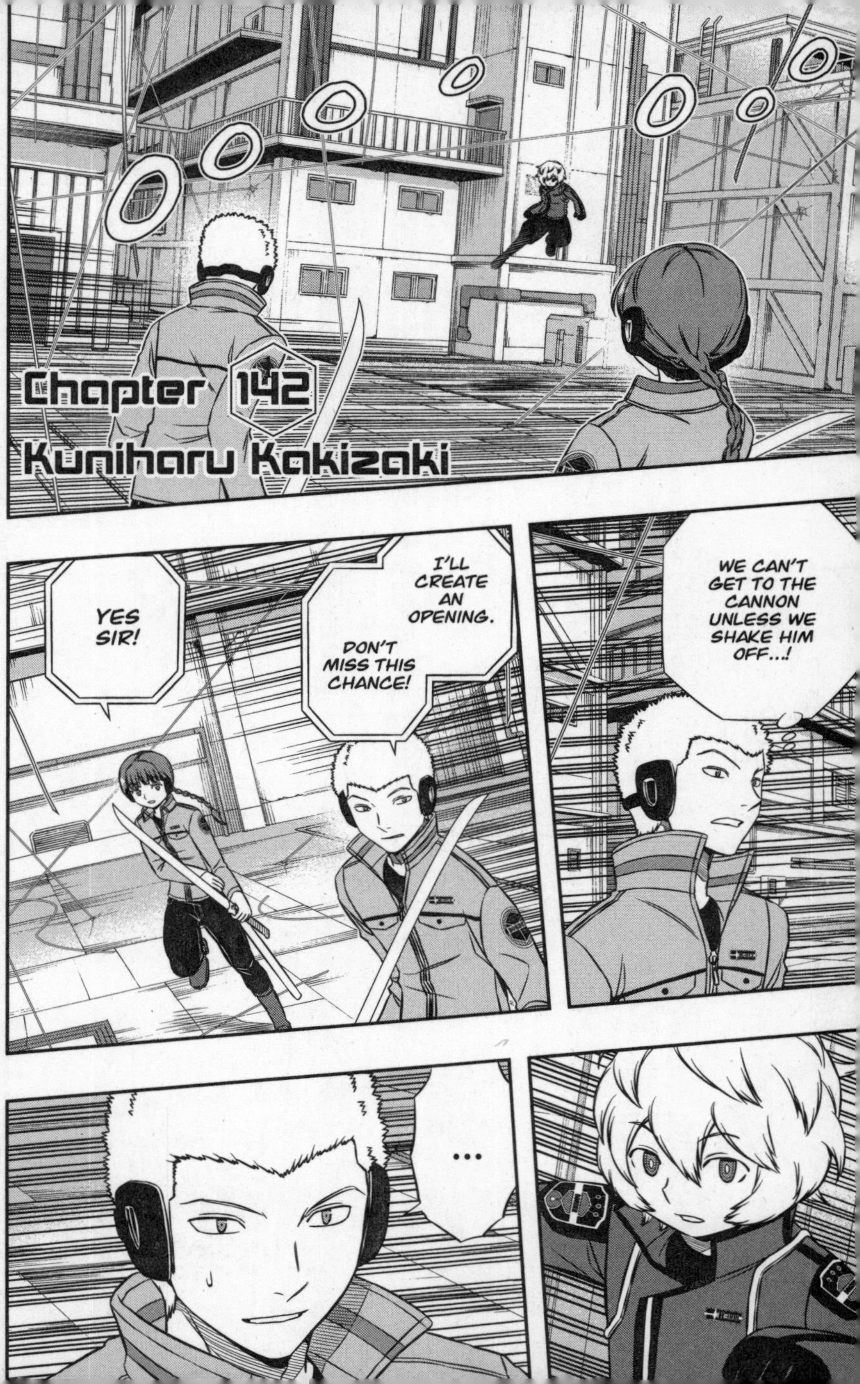
Chapter 142
Kuniharu Kakizaki
WE CAN'T GET TO THE CANNON UNLESS WE SHAKE HIM OFF...!
I'LL CREATE AN OPENING.
DON'T MISS THIS CHANCE!
YES SIR!
...

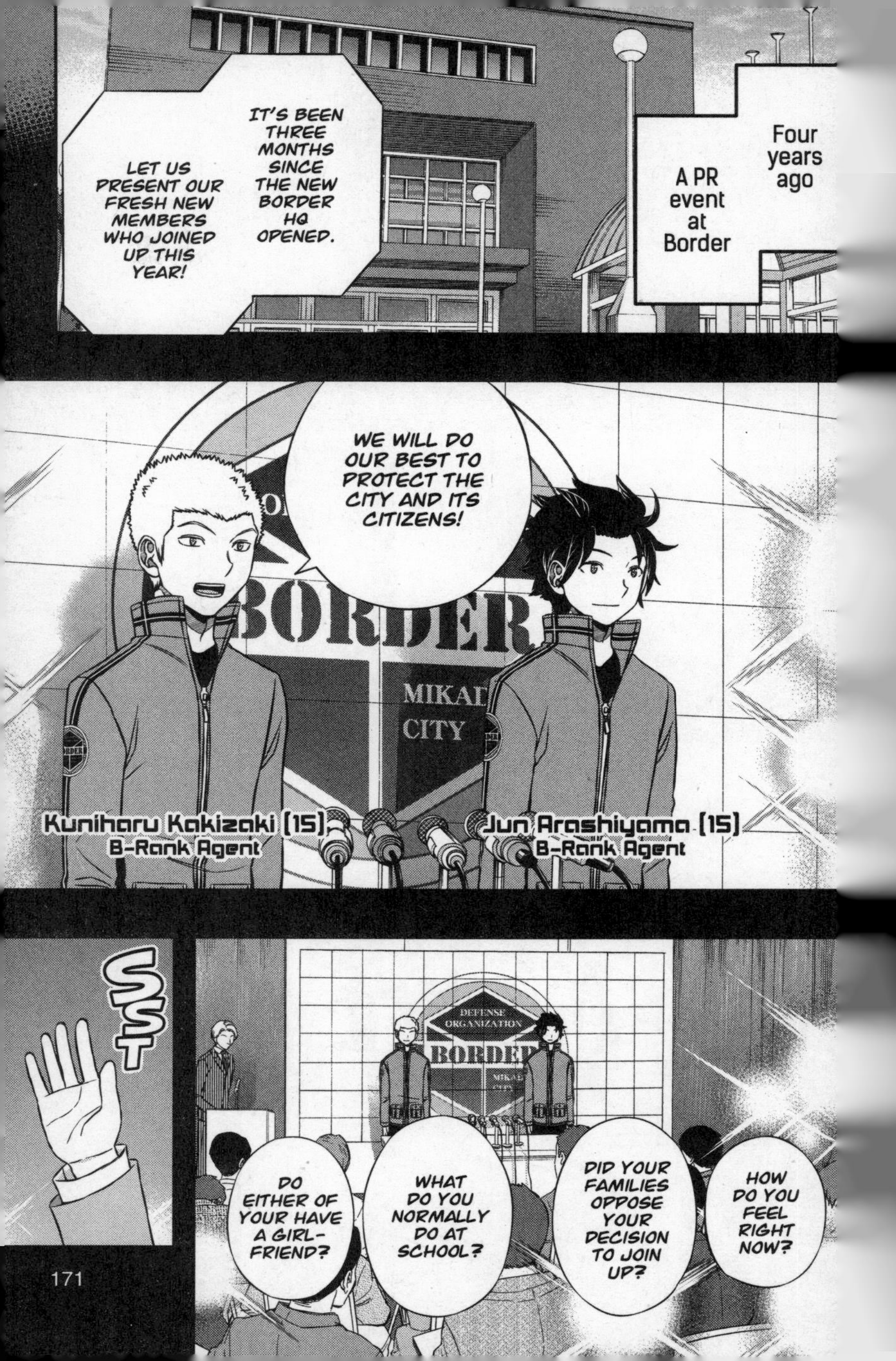
Four years ago
A PR event at Border
IT'S BEEN THREE MONTHS SINCE THE NEW BORDER HQ OPENED.
LET US PRESENT OUR FRESH NEW MEMBERS WHO JOINED UP THIS YEAR!
WE WILL DO OUR BEST TO PROTECT THE CITY AND ITS CITIZENS!
BORDER
MIKAD
CITY
Jun Arashiyama (15)
B-Rank Agent
Kuniharu Kakizaki (15)
B-Rank Agent
DEFENSE ORGANIZATION
BORDER
HOW DO YOU FEEL RIGHT NOW?
DID YOUR FAMILIES OPPOSE YOUR DECISION TO JOIN UP?
WHAT DO YOU NORMALLY DO AT SCHOOL?
DO EITHER OF YOUR HAVE A GIRL-FRIEND?
SST

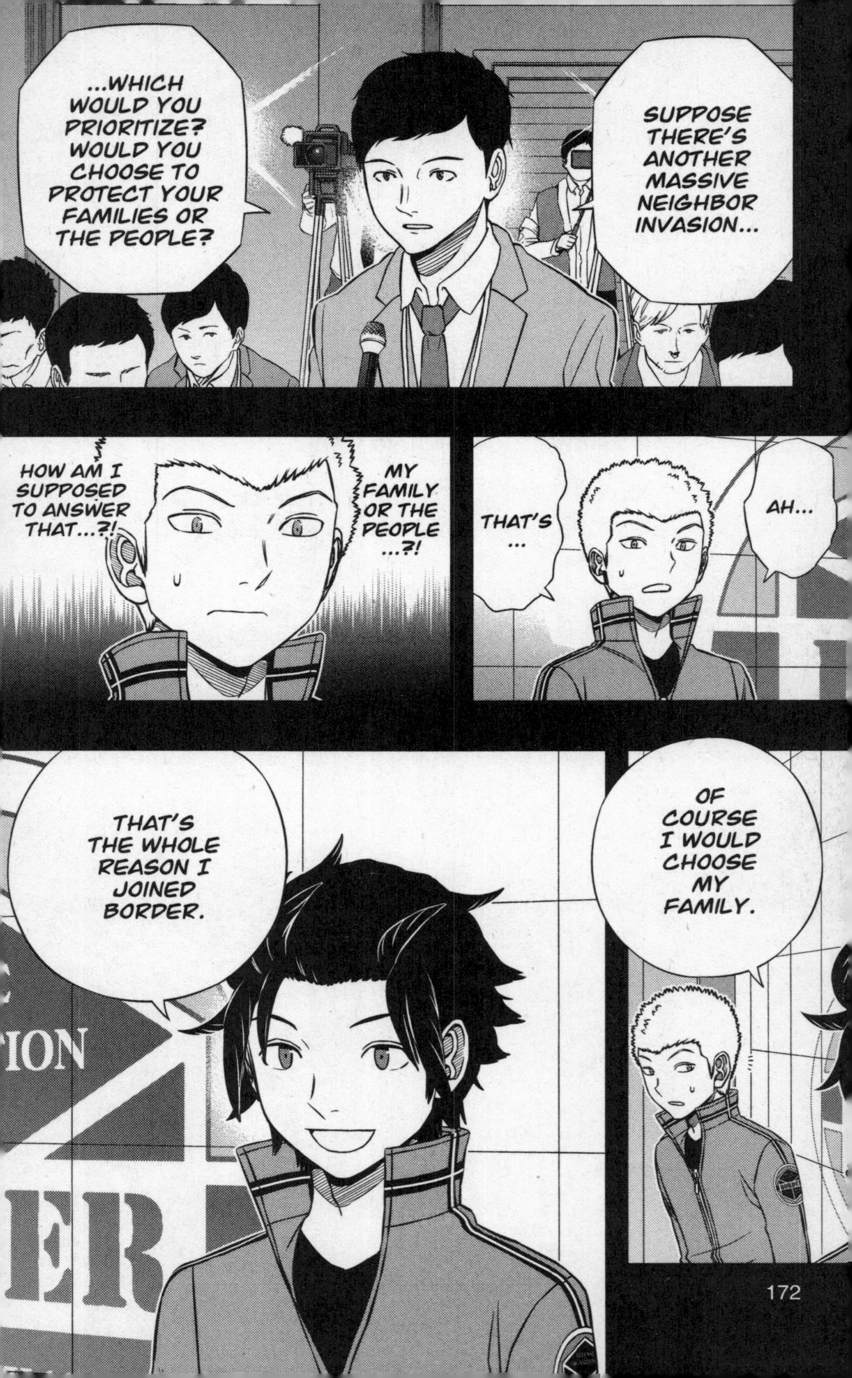
SUPPOSE THERE'S ANOTHER MASSIVE NEIGHBOR INVASION...
...WHICH WOULD YOU PRIORITIZE? WOULD YOU CHOOSE TO PROTECT YOUR FAMILIES OR THE PEOPLE?
AH...
THAT'S ...
MY FAMILY OR THE PEOPLE ...?!
HOW AM I SUPPOSED TO ANSWER THAT...?!
OF COURSE I WOULD CHOOSE MY FAMILY.
THAT'S THE WHOLE REASON I JOINED BORDER.

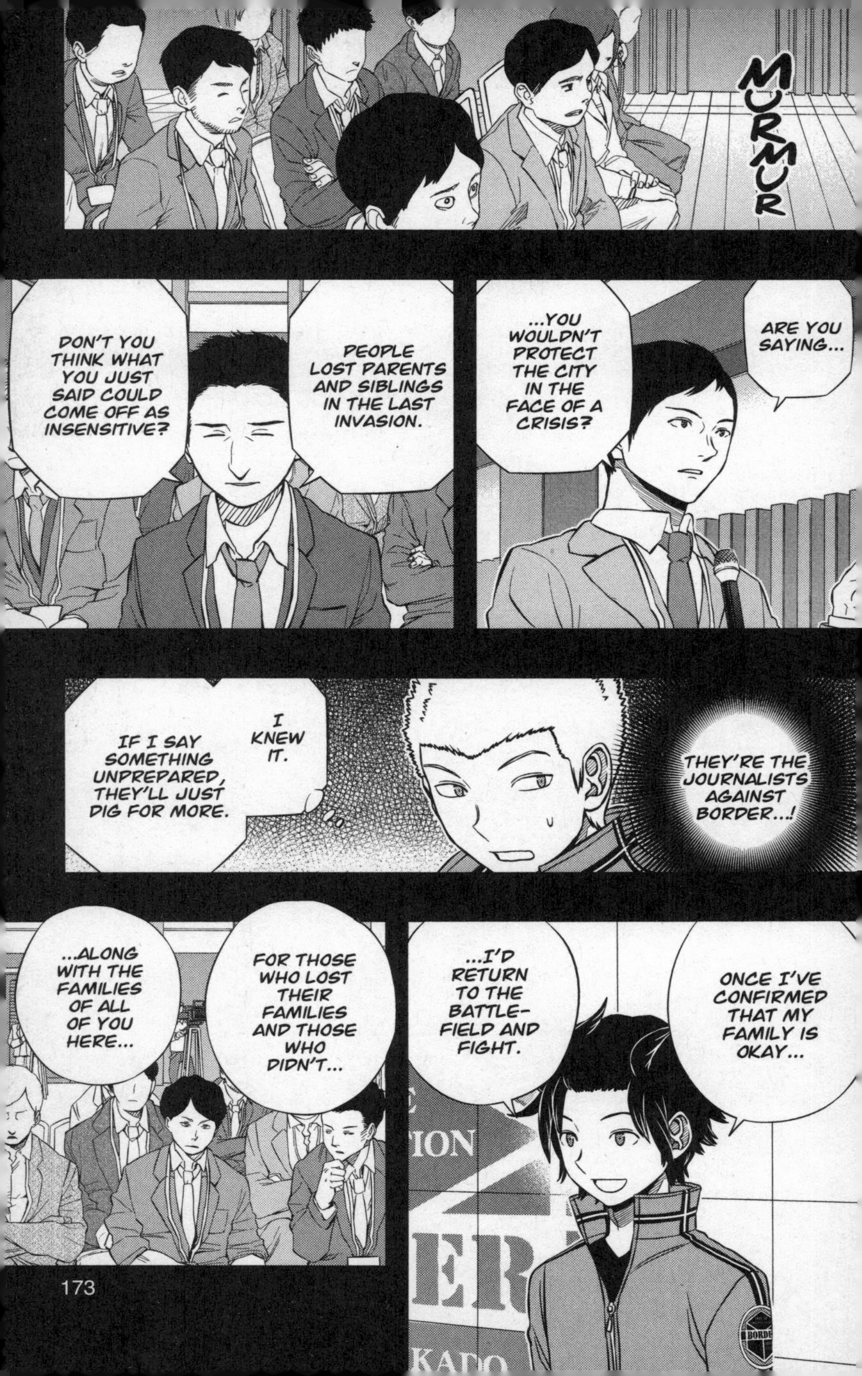
MURMUR
ARE YOU SAYING...
...YOU WOULDN'T PROTECT THE CITY IN THE FACE OF A CRISIS?
PEOPLE LOST PARENTS AND SIBLINGS IN THE LAST INVASION.
DON'T YOU THINK WHAT YOU JUST SAID COULD COME OFF AS INSENSITIVE?
THEY'RE THE JOURNALISTS AGAINST BORDER...!
I KNEW IT.
IF I SAY SOMETHING UNPREPARED, THEY'LL JUST DIG FOR MORE.
ONCE I'VE CONFIRMED THAT MY FAMILY IS OKAY...
...I'D RETURN TO THE BATTLE-FIELD AND FIGHT.
FOR THOSE WHO LOST THEIR FAMILIES AND THOSE WHO DIDN'T...
...ALONG WITH THE FAMILIES OF ALL OF YOU HERE...

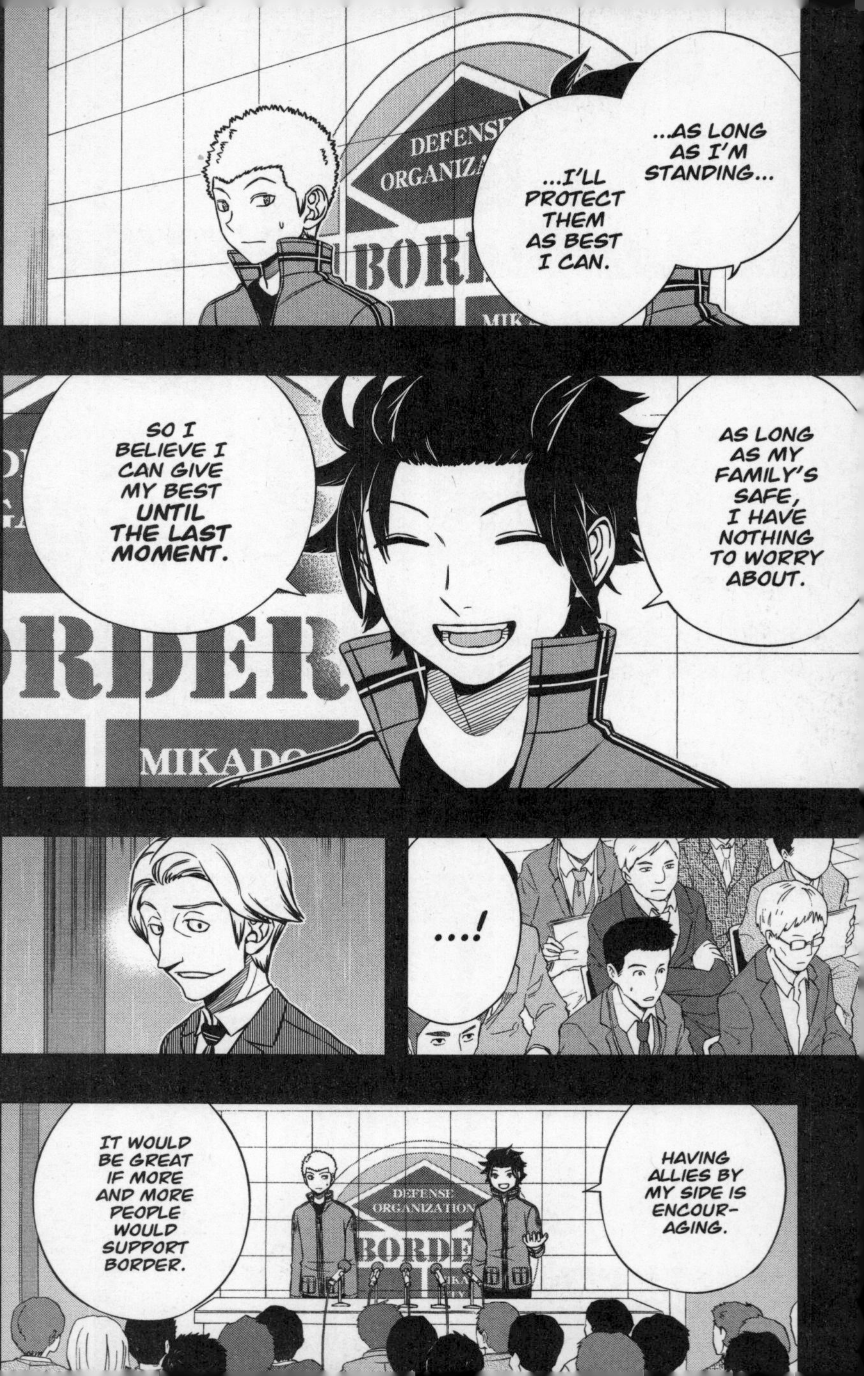
...AS LONG AS I'M STANDING...
...I'LL PROTECT THEM AS BEST I CAN.
AS LONG AS MY FAMILY'S SAFE, I HAVE NOTHING TO WORRY ABOUT.
SO I BELIEVE I CAN GIVE MY BEST UNTIL THE LAST MOMENT.
...!
HAVING ALLIES BY MY SIDE IS ENCOUR-AGING.
DEFENSE ORGANIZATION
IT WOULD BE GREAT IF MORE AND MORE PEOPLE WOULD SUPPORT BORDER.

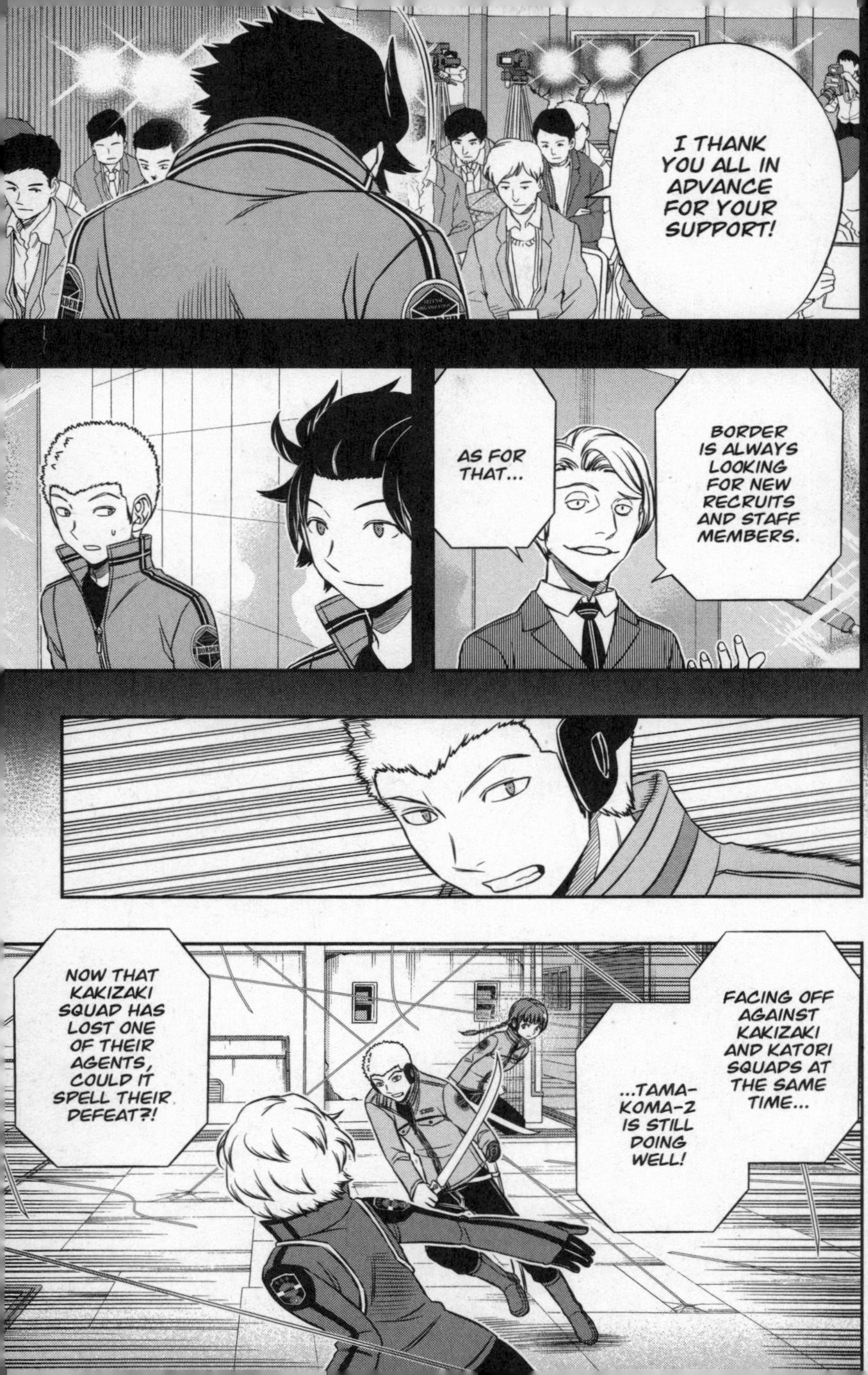
I THANK YOU ALL IN ADVANCE FOR YOUR SUPPORT!
BORDER IS ALWAYS LOOKING FOR NEW RECRUITS AND STAFF MEMBERS.
AS FOR THAT...
FACING OFF AGAINST KAKIZAKI AND KATORI SQUADS AT THE SAME TIME...
...TAMA-KOMA-2 IS STILL DOING WELL!
NOW THAT KAKIZAKI SQUAD HAS LOST ONE OF THEIR AGENTS, COULD IT SPELL THEIR DEFEAT?!

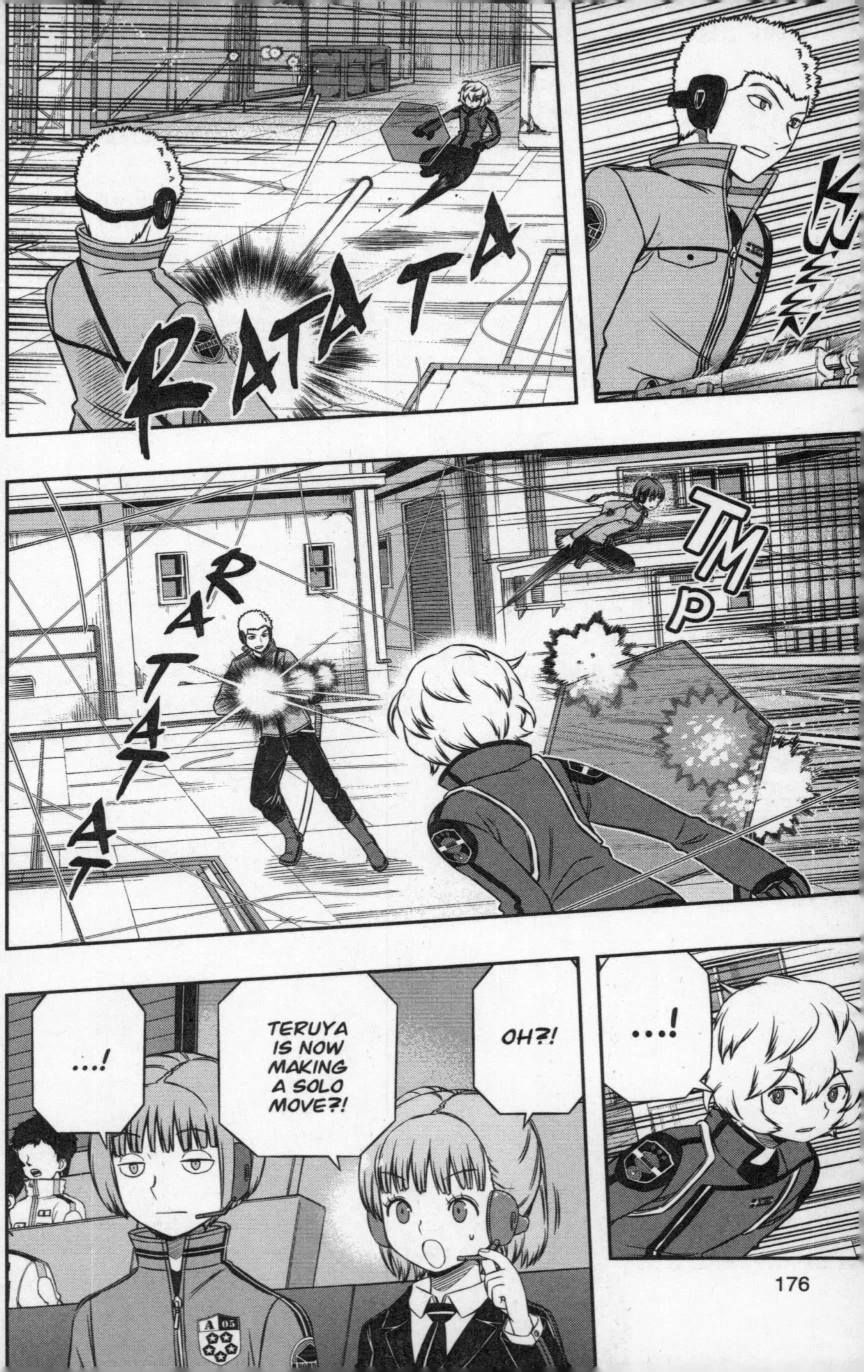
RATATA
TMP
RATATAT
...!
OH?!
TERUYA IS NOW MAKING A SOLO MOVE?!
...!

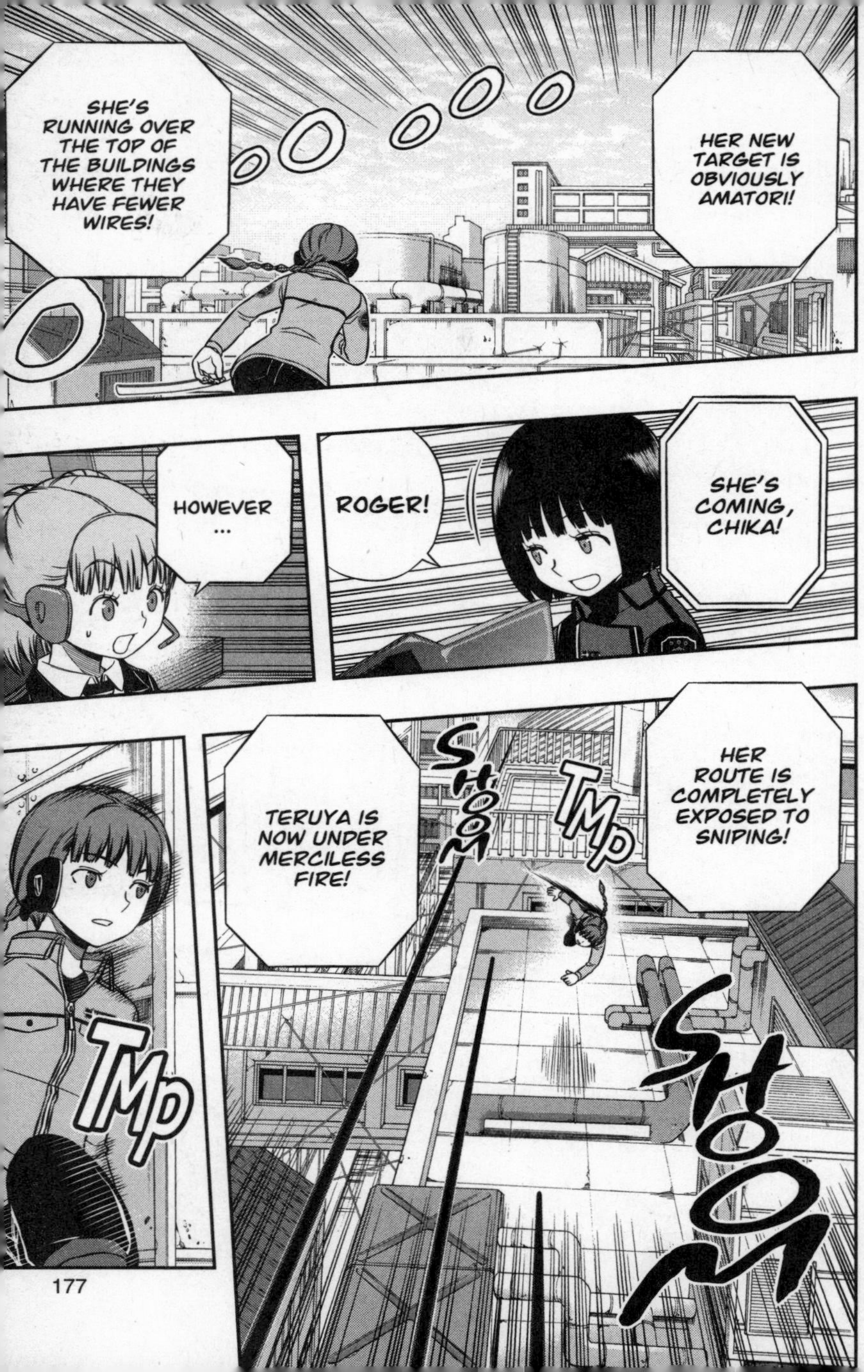
HER NEW TARGET IS OBVIOUSLY AMATORI!
SHE'S RUNNING OVER THE TOP OF THE BUILDINGS WHERE THEY HAVE FEWER WIRES!
SHE'S COMING, CHIKA!
ROGER!
HOWEVER ...
HER ROUTE IS COMPLETELY EXPOSED TO SNIPING!
TMP
SHOOM
TERUYA IS NOW UNDER MERCILESS FIRE!
SHOOM
TMP

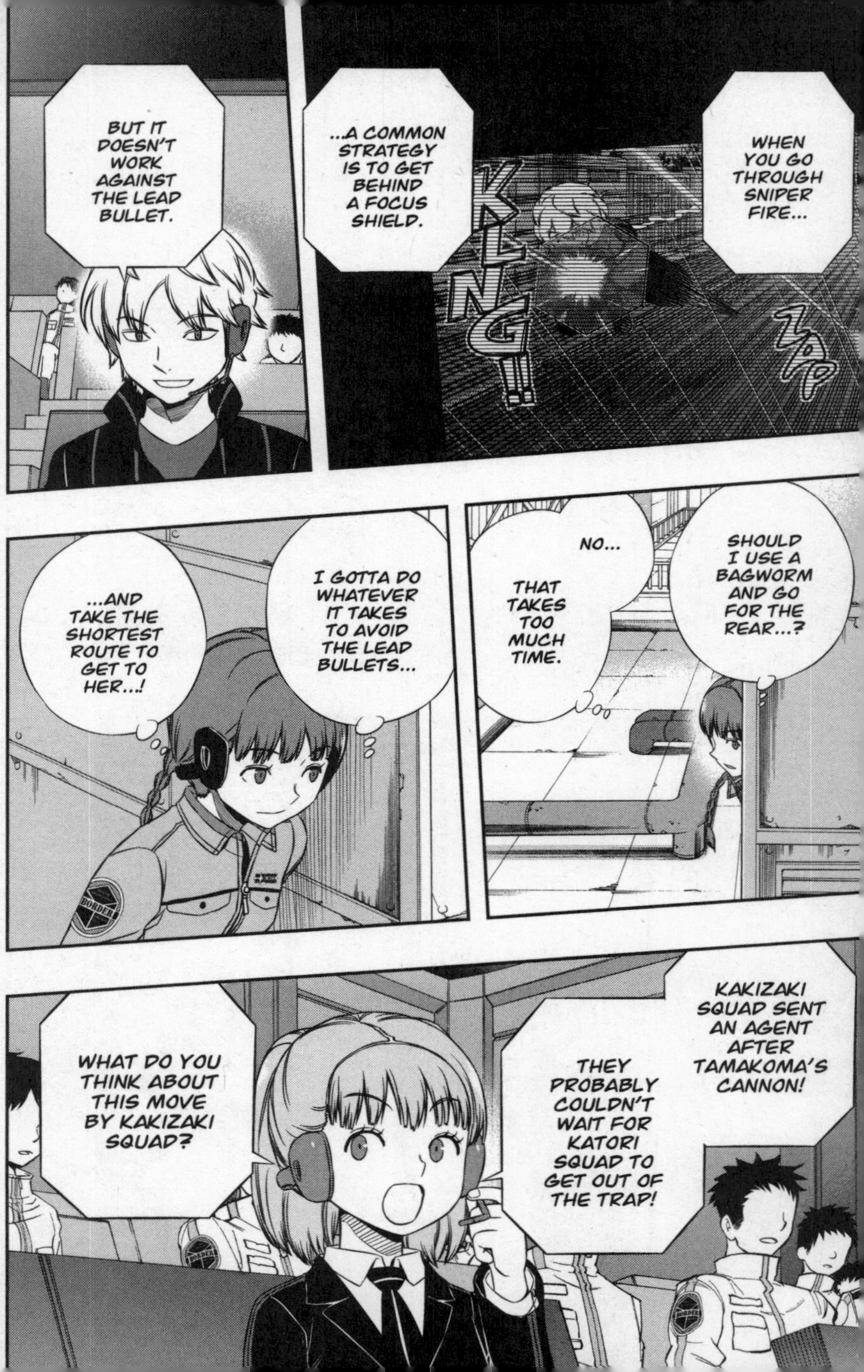
WHEN YOU GO THROUGH SNIPER FIRE...
...A COMMON STRATEGY IS TO GET BEHIND A FOCUS SHIELD.
KLNG!!
BUT IT DOESN'T WORK AGAINST THE LEAD BULLET.
SHOULD I USE A BAGWORM AND GO FOR THE REAR...?
NO...
THAT TAKES TOO MUCH TIME.
I GOTTA DO WHATEVER IT TAKES TO AVOID THE LEAD BULLETS...
...AND TAKE THE SHORTEST ROUTE TO GET TO HER...!
KAKIZAKI SQUAD SENT AN AGENT AFTER TAMAKOMA'S CANNON!
THEY PROBABLY COULDN'T WAIT FOR KATORI SQUAD TO GET OUT OF THE TRAP!
WHAT DO YOU THINK ABOUT THIS MOVE BY KAKIZAKI SQUAD?

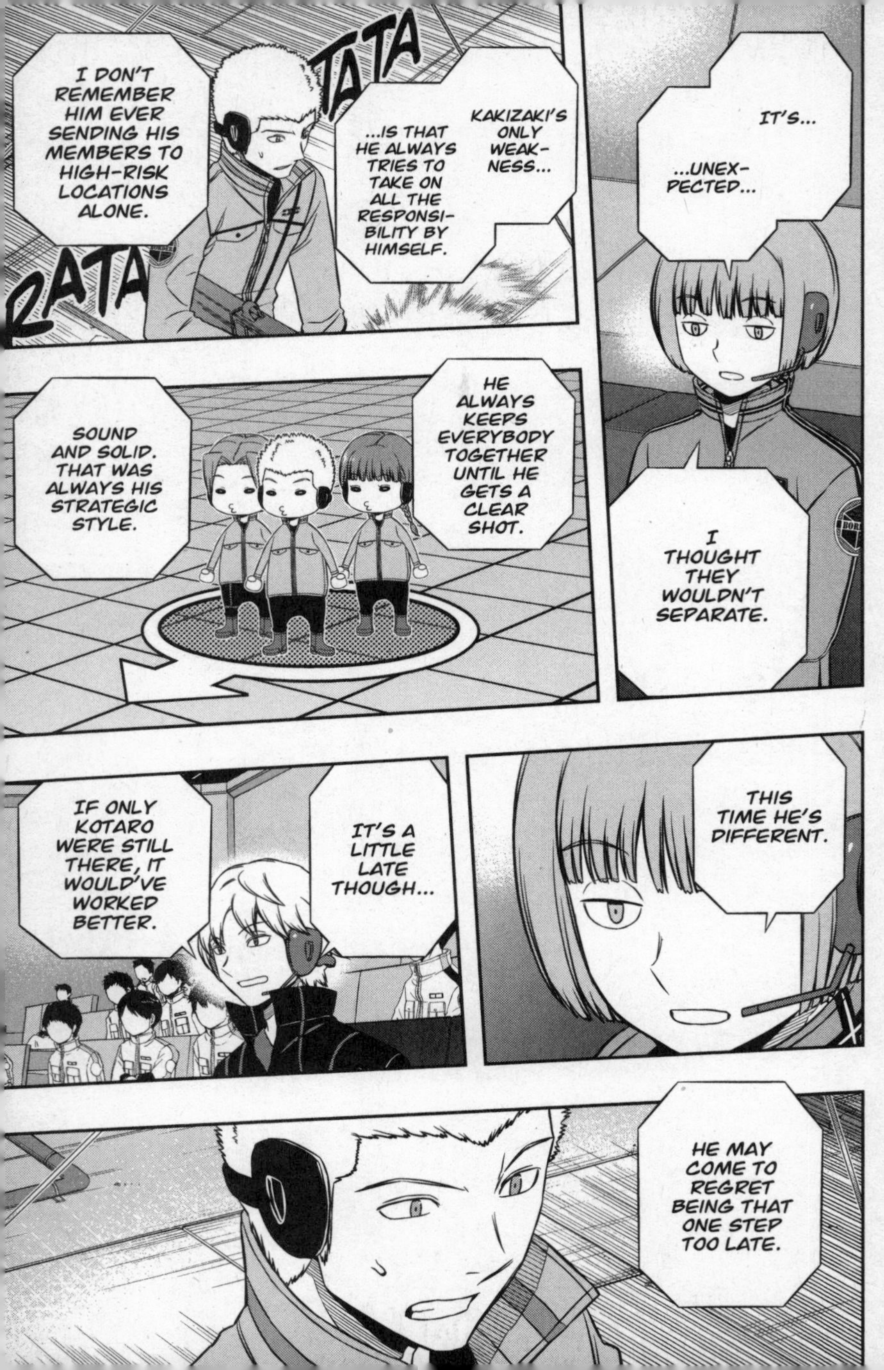
IT'S...
...UNEX-PECTED...
I THOUGHT THEY WOULDN'T SEPARATE.
TATA
KAKIZAKI'S ONLY WEAK-NESS...
...IS THAT HE ALWAYS TRIES TO TAKE ON ALL THE RESPONSI-BILITY BY HIMSELF.
I DON'T REMEMBER HIM EVER SENDING HIS MEMBERS TO HIGH-RISK LOCATIONS ALONE.
RATA
HE ALWAYS KEEPS EVERYBODY TOGETHER UNTIL HE GETS A CLEAR SHOT.
SOUND AND SOLID. THAT WAS ALWAYS HIS STRATEGIC STYLE.
THIS TIME HE'S DIFFERENT.
IT'S A LITTLE LATE THOUGH...
IF ONLY KOTARO WERE STILL THERE, IT WOULD'VE WORKED BETTER.
HE MAY COME TO REGRET BEING THAT ONE STEP TOO LATE.

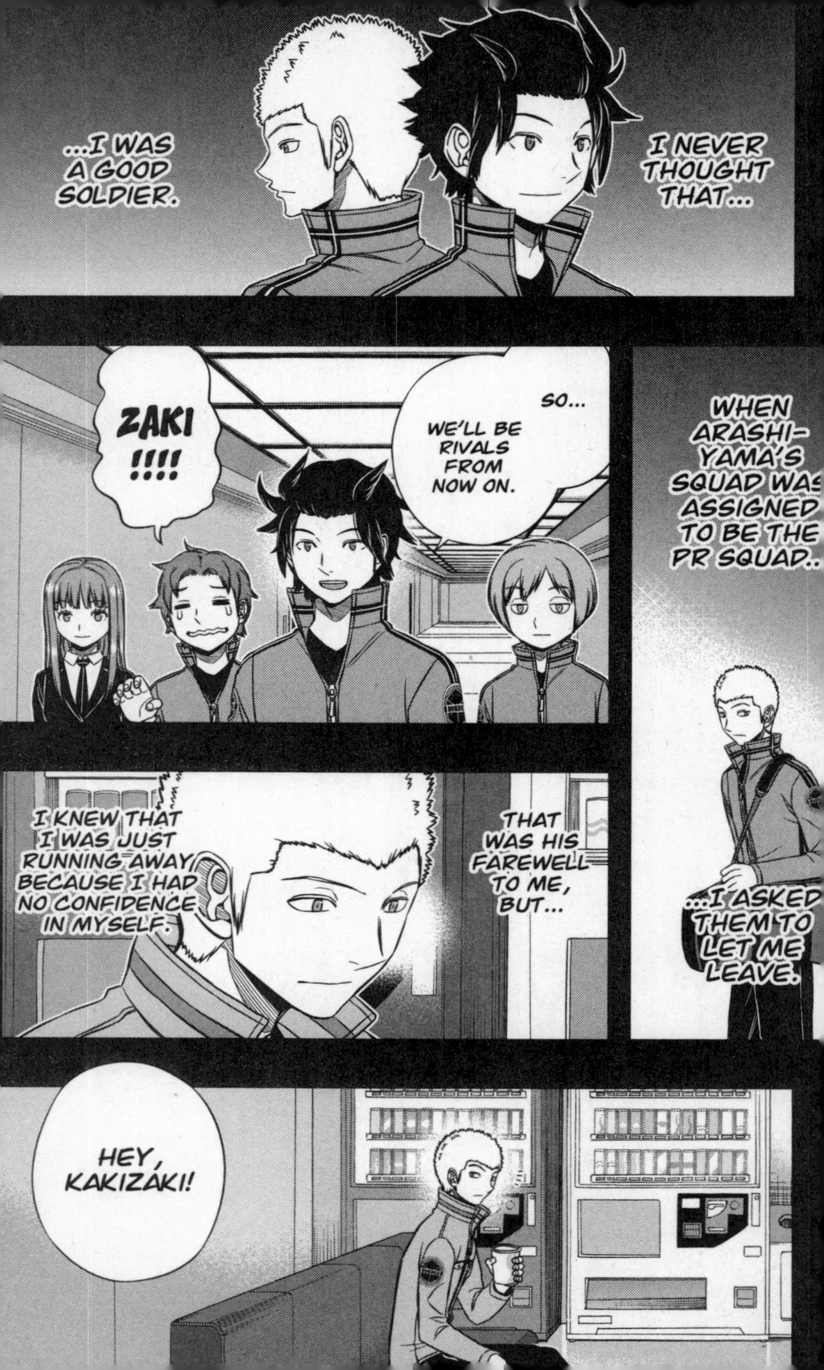

I NEVER THOUGHT THAT...
...I WAS A GOOD SOLDIER.
WHEN ARASHI-YAMA'S SQUAD WAS ASSIGNED TO BE THE PR SQUAD...
...I ASKED THEM TO LET ME LEAVE.
SO... WE'LL BE RIVALS FROM NOW ON.
ZAKI!!!!
THAT WAS HIS FAREWELL TO ME, BUT...
I KNEW THAT I WAS JUST RUNNING AWAY BECAUSE I HAD NO CONFIDENCE IN MYSELF.
HEY, KAKIZAKI!

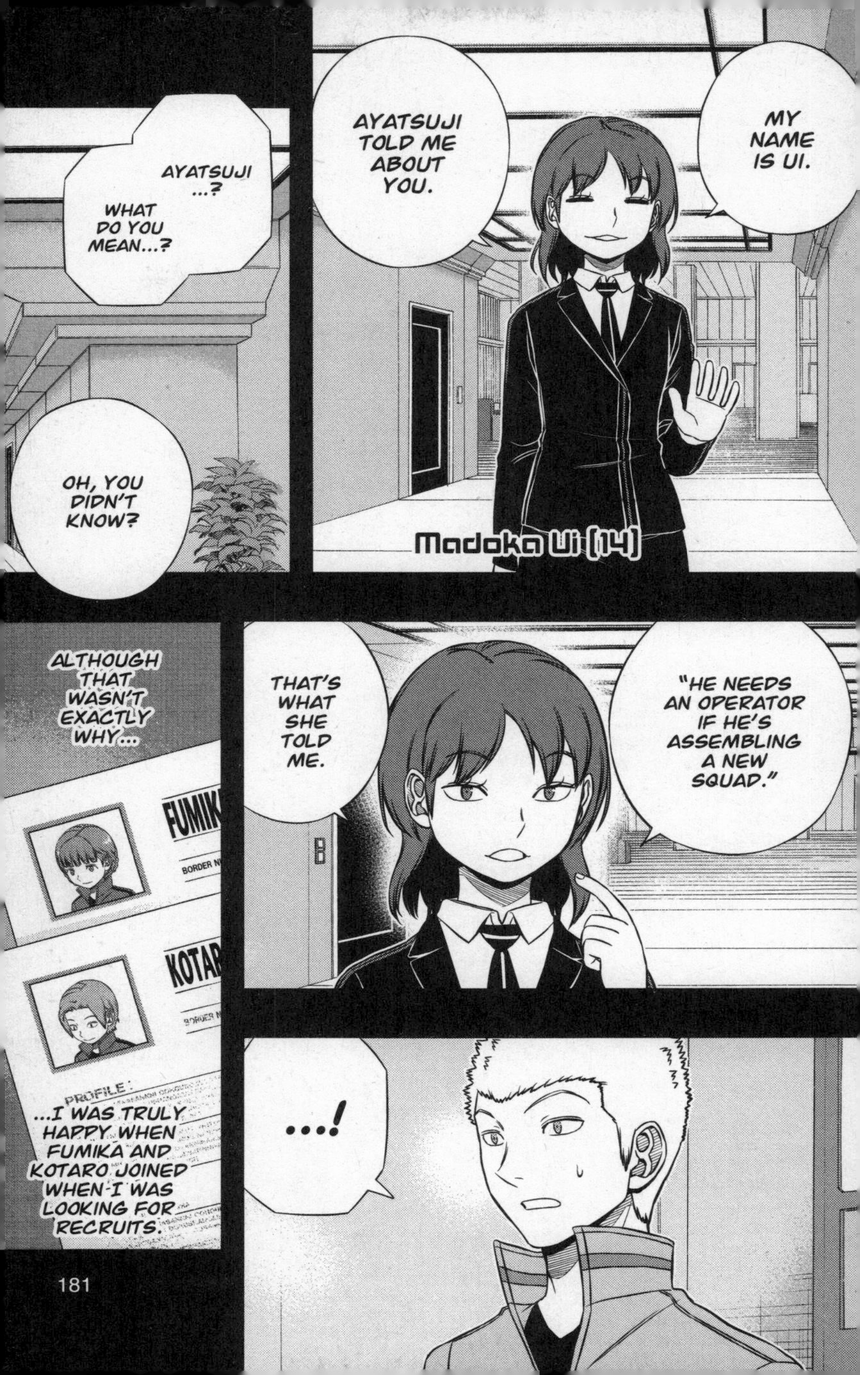
MY NAME IS UI.
AYATSUJI TOLD ME ABOUT YOU.
Madoka Ui (14)
AYATSUJI ...?
WHAT DO YOU MEAN...?
OH, YOU DIDN'T KNOW?
"HE NEEDS AN OPERATOR IF HE'S ASSEMBLING A NEW SQUAD."
THAT'S WHAT SHE TOLD ME.
...!
ALTHOUGH THAT WASN'T EXACTLY WHY...
PROFILE:
...I WAS TRULY HAPPY WHEN FUMIKA AND KOTARO JOINED WHEN I WAS LOOKING FOR RECRUITS.

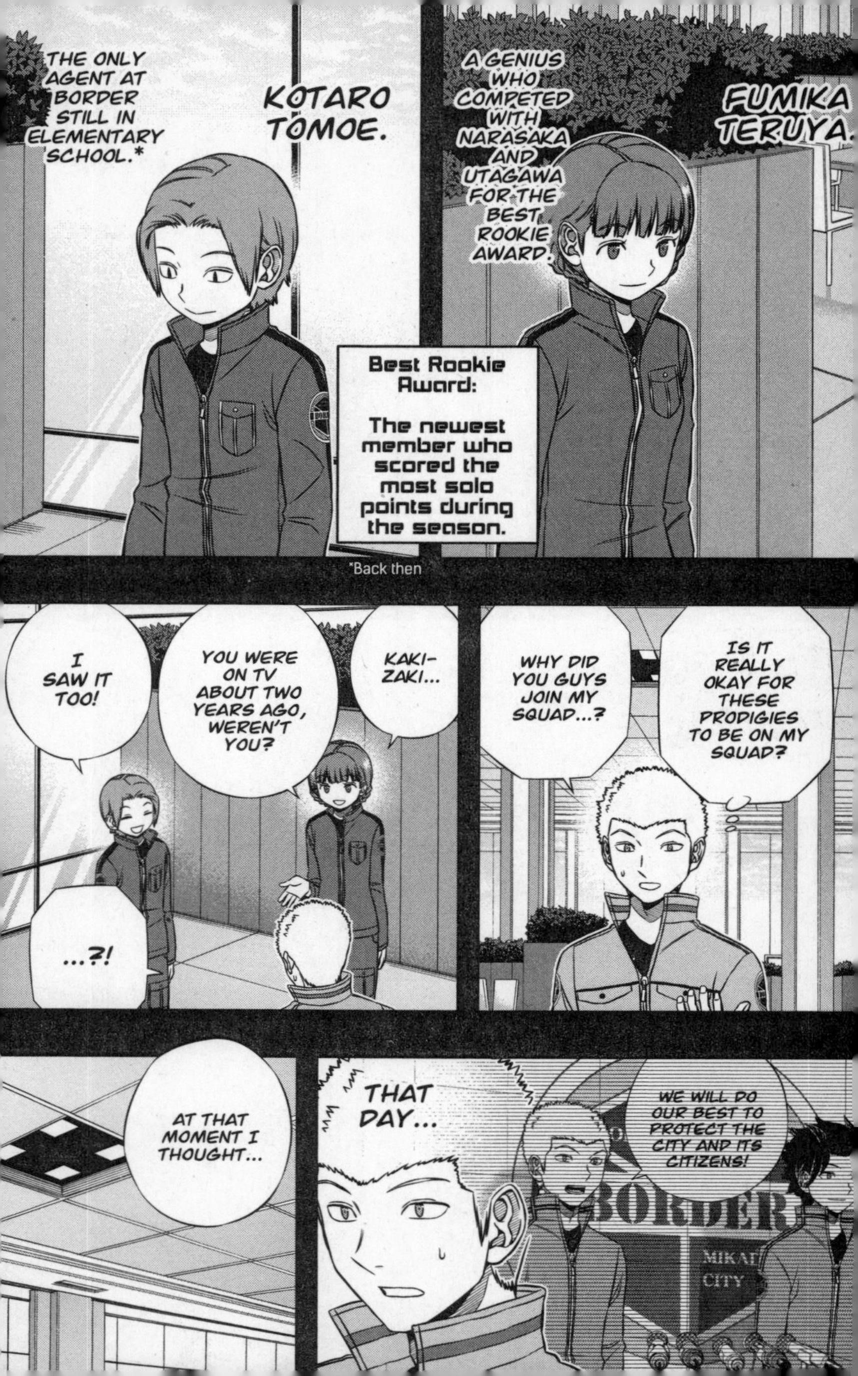
A GENIUS WHO COMPETED WITH NARASAKA AND UTAGAWA FOR THE BEST ROOKIE AWARD.
FUMIKA TERUYA.
Best Rookie Award: The newest member who scored the most solo points during the season.
THE ONLY AGENT AT BORDER STILL IN ELEMENTARY SCHOOL.*
KOTARO TOMOE.
IS IT REALLY OKAY FOR THESE PRODIGIES TO BE ON MY SQUAD?
WHY DID YOU GUYS JOIN MY SQUAD...?
KAKI-ZAKI...
YOU WERE ON TV ABOUT TWO YEARS AGO, WEREN'T YOU?
I SAW IT TOO!
...?!
WE WILL DO OUR BEST TO PROTECT THE CITY AND ITS CITIZENS!
THAT DAY...
BORDER
AT THAT MOMENT I THOUGHT...

*Back then

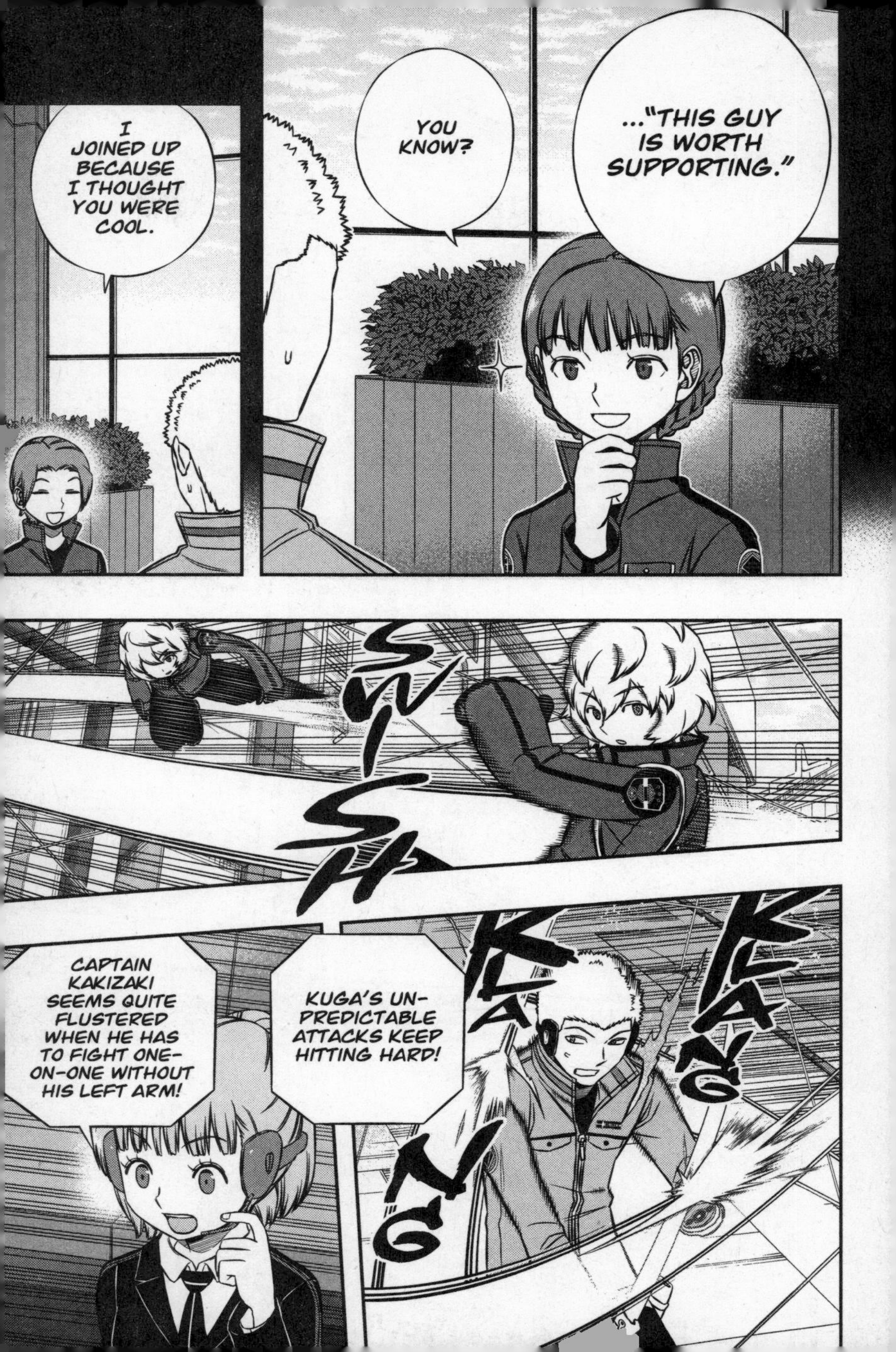
..."THIS GUY IS WORTH SUPPORTING."
YOU KNOW?
I JOINED UP BECAUSE I THOUGHT YOU WERE COOL.
SWISH
KLANG
KLANG
KUGA'S UN-PREDICTABLE ATTACKS KEEP HITTING HARD!
CAPTAIN KAKIZAKI SEEMS QUITE FLUSTERED WHEN HE HAS TO FIGHT ONE-ON-ONE WITHOUT HIS LEFT ARM!

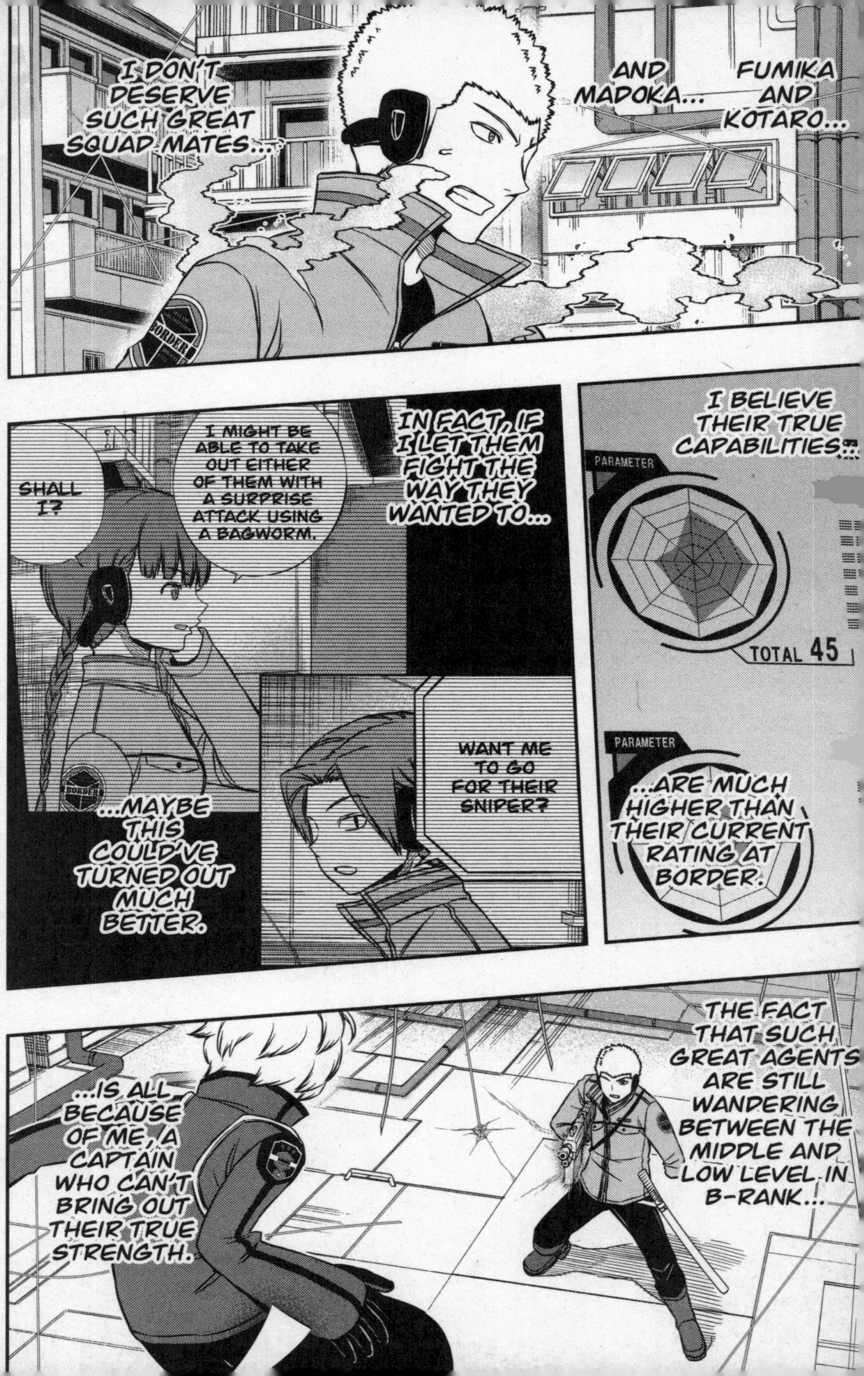
FUMIKA AND KOTARO...
AND MADOKA...
I DON'T DESERVE SUCH GREAT SQUAD MATES...
I BELIEVE THEIR TRUE CAPABILITIES...
PARAMETER
TOTAL 45
PARAMETER
...ARE MUCH HIGHER THAN THEIR CURRENT RATING AT BORDER.
IN FACT, IF I LET THEM FIGHT THE WAY THEY WANTED TO...
I MIGHT BE ABLE TO TAKE OUT EITHER OF THEM WITH A SURPRISE ATTACK USING A BAGWORM.
SHALL I?
WANT ME TO GO FOR THEIR SNIPER?
...MAYBE THIS COULD'VE TURNED OUT MUCH BETTER.
THE FACT THAT SUCH GREAT AGENTS ARE STILL WANDERING BETWEEN THE MIDDLE AND LOW LEVEL IN B-RANK...
...IS ALL BECAUSE OF ME, A CAPTAIN WHO CAN'T BRING OUT THEIR TRUE STRENGTH.

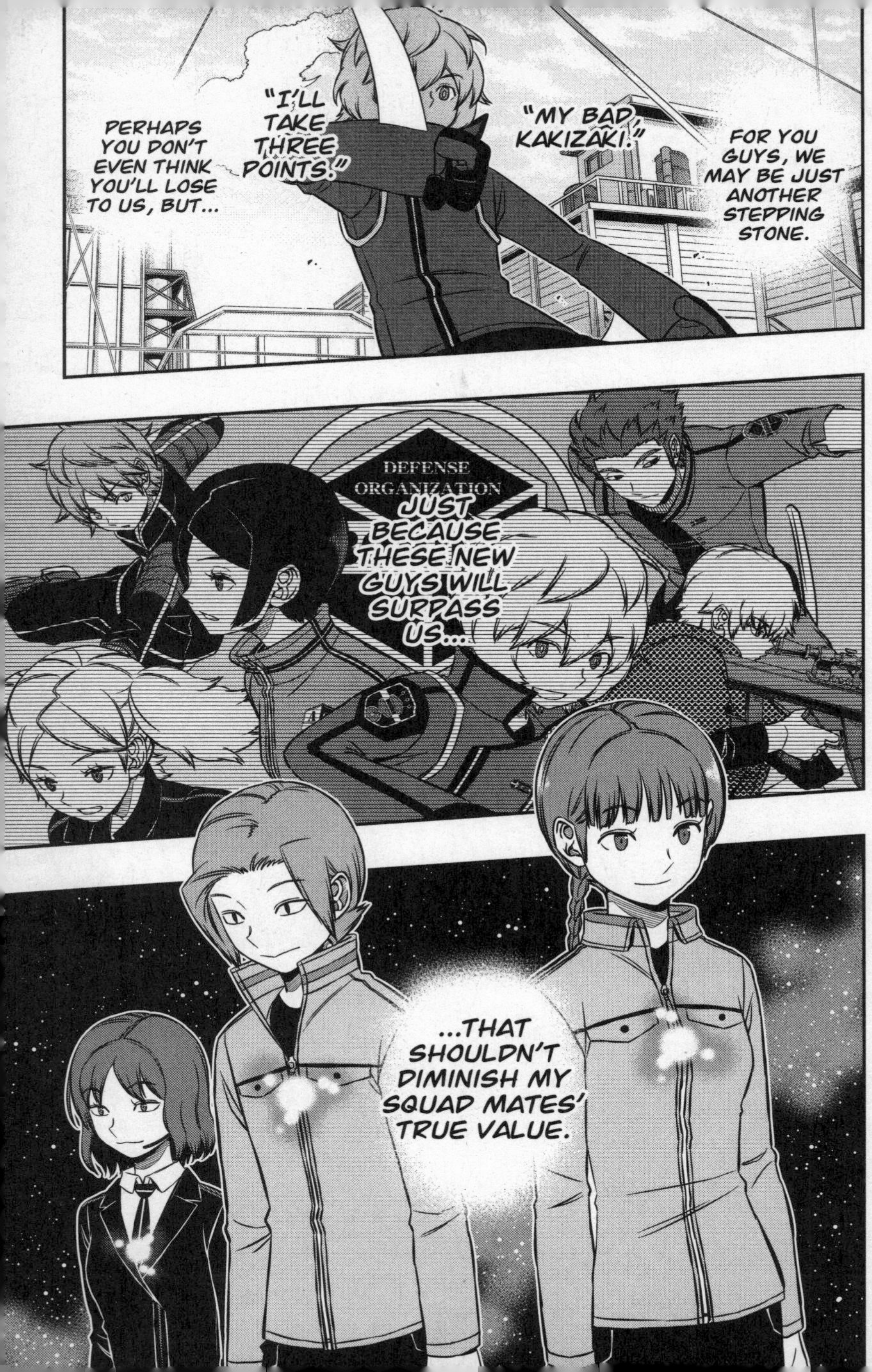
FOR YOU GUYS, WE MAY BE JUST ANOTHER STEPPING STONE.
"MY BAD, KAKIZAKI."
"I'LL TAKE THREE POINTS."
PERHAPS YOU DON'T EVEN THINK YOU'LL LOSE TO US, BUT...
DEFENSE ORGANIZATION
JUST BECAUSE THESE NEW GUYS WILL SURPASS US...
...THAT SHOULDN'T DIMINISH MY SQUAD MATES' TRUE VALUE.

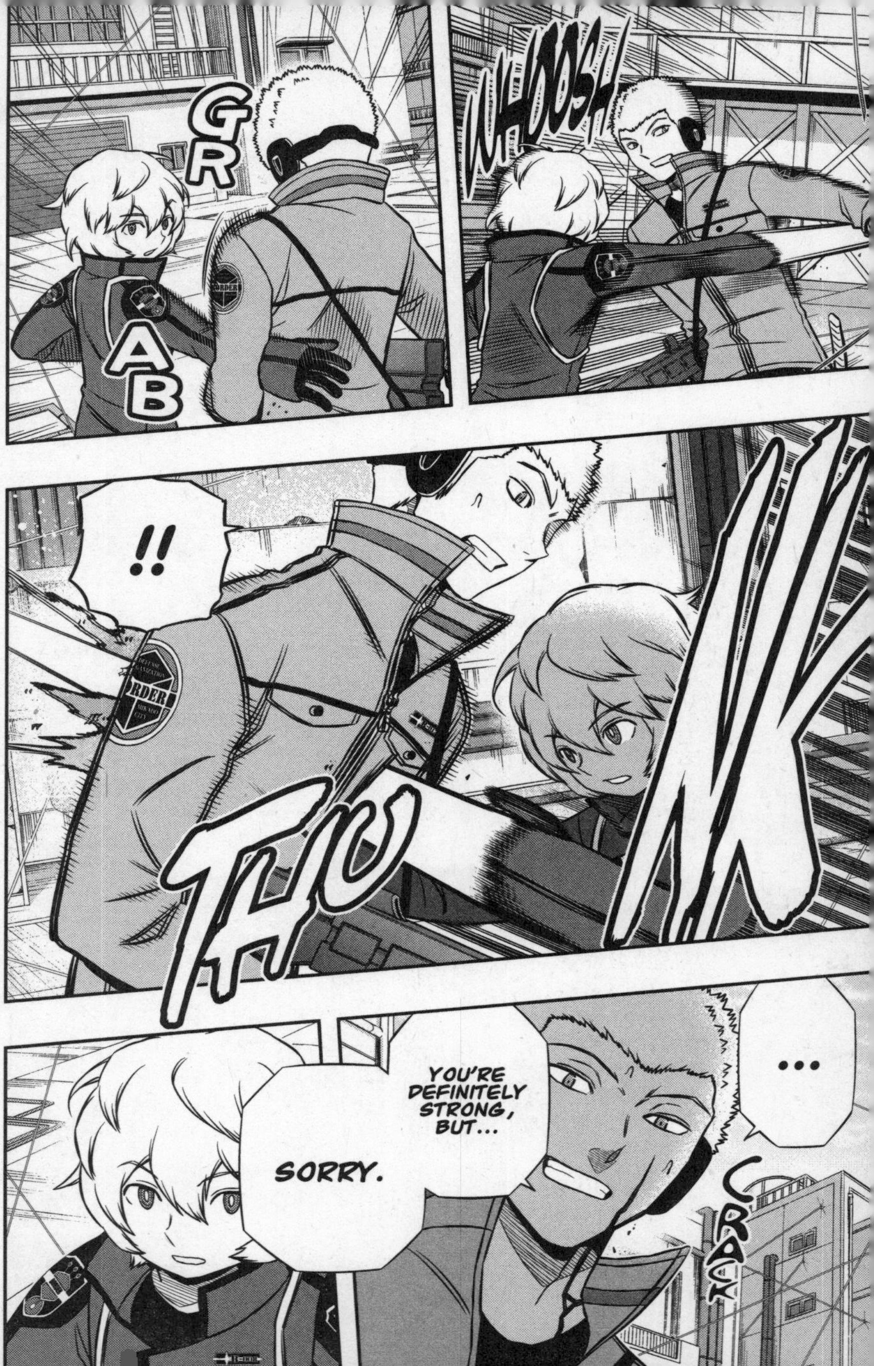
WHOOSH!
GRAB
!!
THUNK
...
CRACK
YOU'RE DEFINITELY STRONG, BUT...
SORRY.

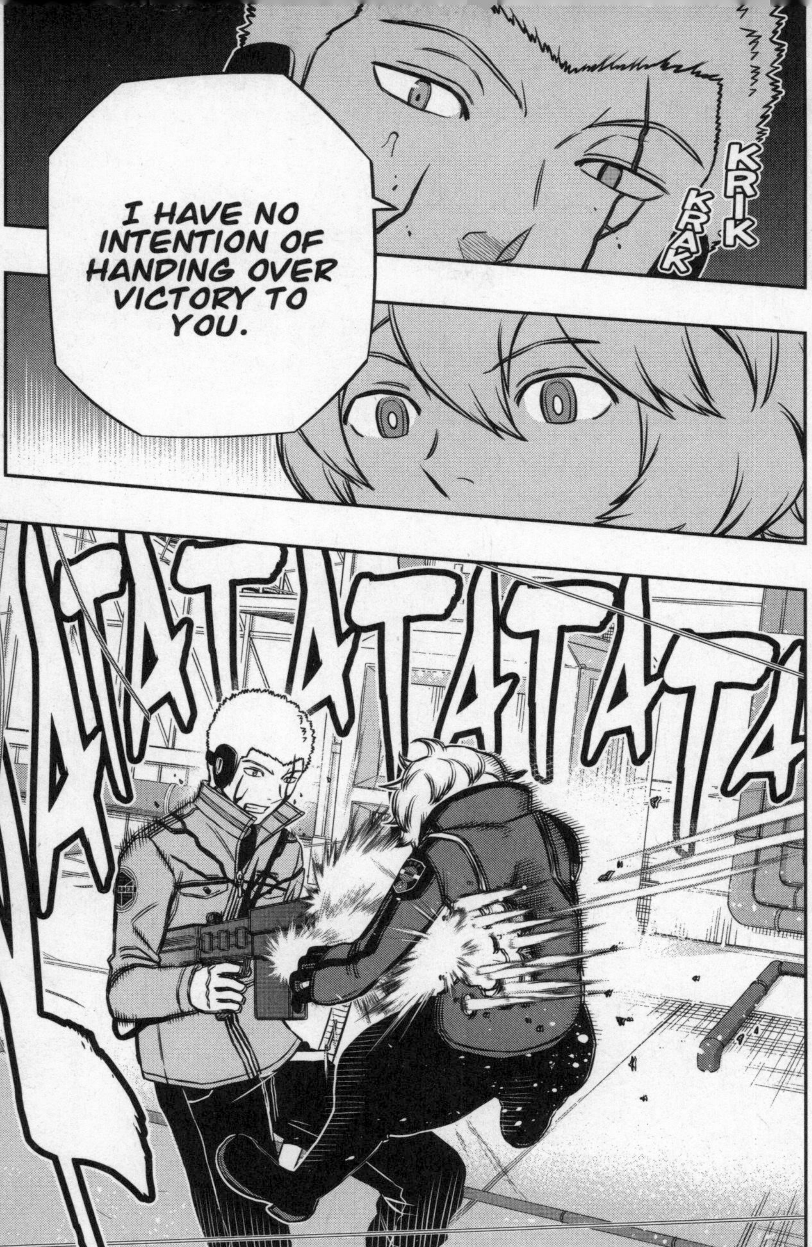
I HAVE NO INTENTION OF HANDING OVER VICTORY TO YOU.
KRIK KRAK

To Be Continued In ***World Trigger*** 17!

Kanoya
Japanese-style confection store

Endnote bonus Mikado City Tour

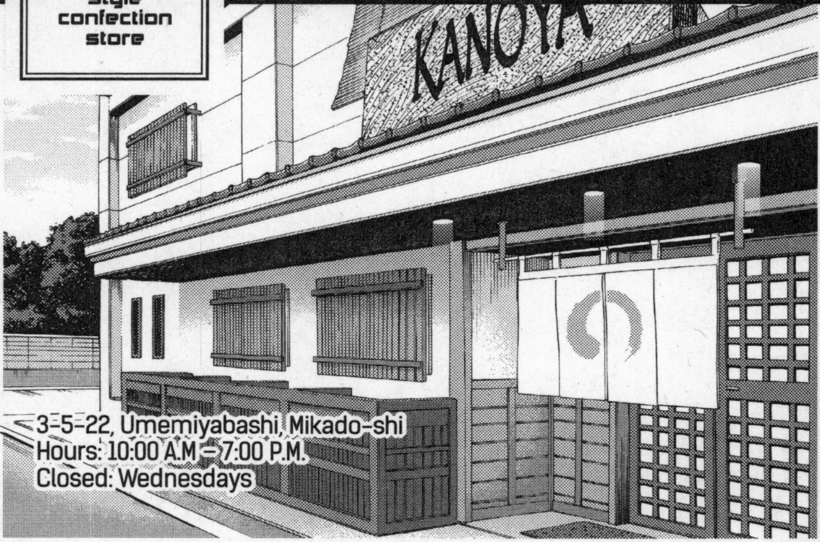
KANOYA
3-5-22, Umemiyabashi, Mikado-shi
Hours: 10:00 A.M – 7:00 P.M.
Closed: Wednesdays

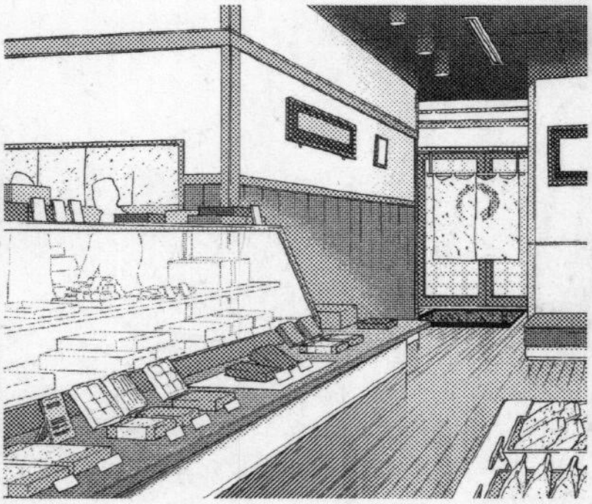

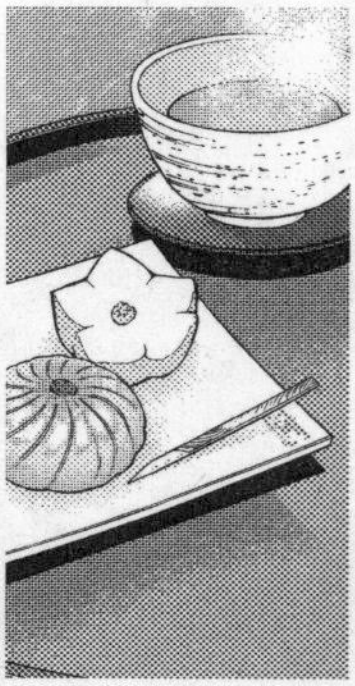

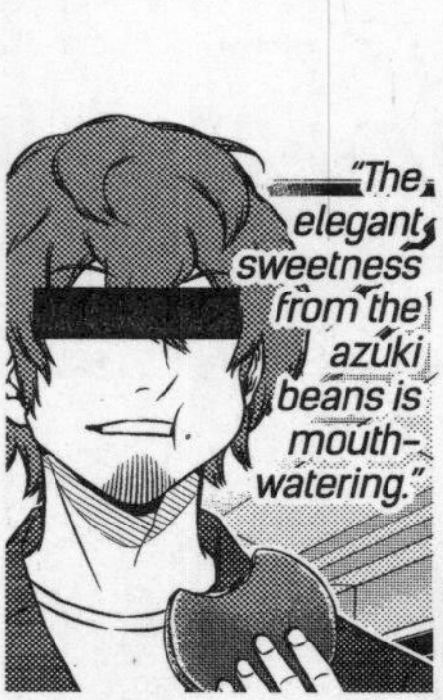
"The elegant sweetness from the azuki beans is mouth-watering."

It's a store that has very classy *dorayaki*. This place is famous among the girls at Border thanks to Tsukimi, who loves Japanese pastries. It's a little expensive, but it's nice to indulge sometimes.

This famous store in Higashi Mikado, once lost in the first large-scale invasion, is back in business at a new location in Umemiyabashi. While it may be a new location, the soul of the store remains the same. There is a space to sit and have tea and pastries.

Takeout available.

Here stands the old house

Jujuen
Char-grilled barbecue

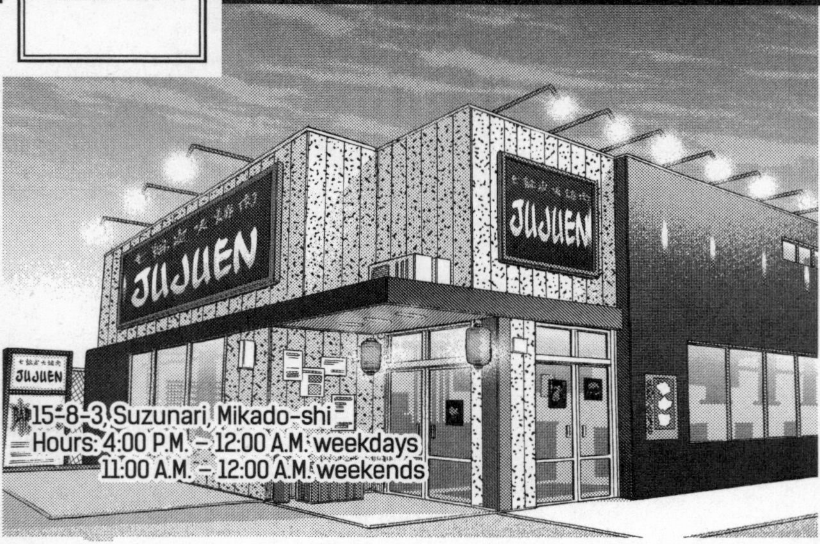
JUJUEN
JUJUEN
JUJUEN
15-8-3, Suzunari, Mikado-shi
Hours: 4:00 P.M. – 12:00 A.M. weekdays
11:00 A.M. – 12:00 A.M. weekends

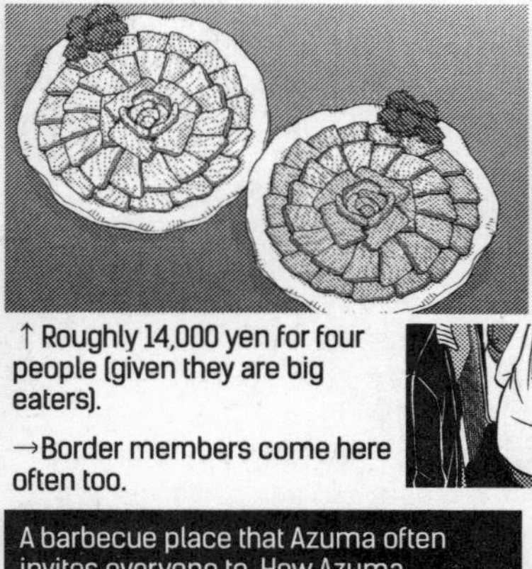

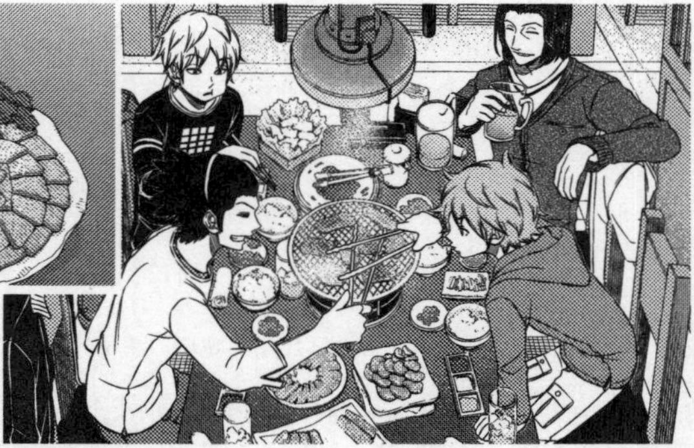

↑ Roughly 14,000 yen for four people (given they are big eaters).

→Border members come here often too.

A barbecue place that Azuma often invites everyone to. How Azuma always affords to pay for everyone is a big mystery. Both Ninomiya and Miwa grew up nice and strong thanks to the meat from this place. Since it's close to the Suzunari branch, Kuruma Squad may come here too. All hail barbecue.

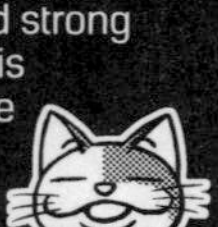

It's a store with incredible luck—surviving two Neighbor invasions without any damage, despite being close to the evacuation zones. For this reason, it's said that eating here keeps people safe from Neighbors. Border agents frequent this place.

For the common folk

WORLD TRIGGER

Bonus Character Pages

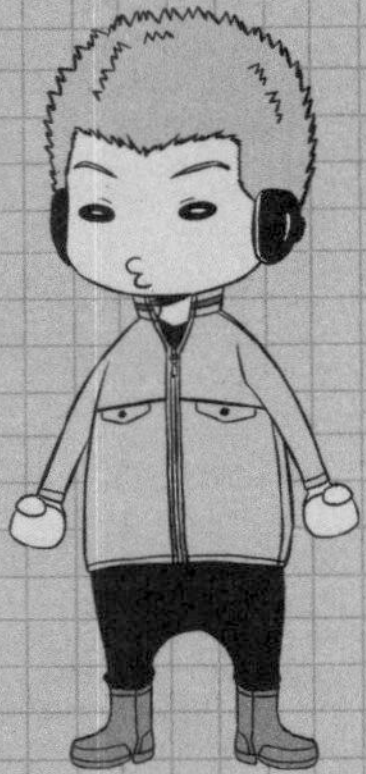

ZAKI

Angsty Normie

Even though he was busy trying to portray himself as a weak man in the flashback scenes, he's actually really popular with his friends and juniors and even plays basketball with Utagawa and Kuma on his days off. He's basically an athletic dude living the good life. He appears to be the most low-browed man amongst all the characters, but his hair is actually long in the front. Most people just don't notice. He's one of the few 19-year-olds with common sense and is good at problem solving. Age of death...92.

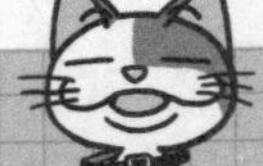

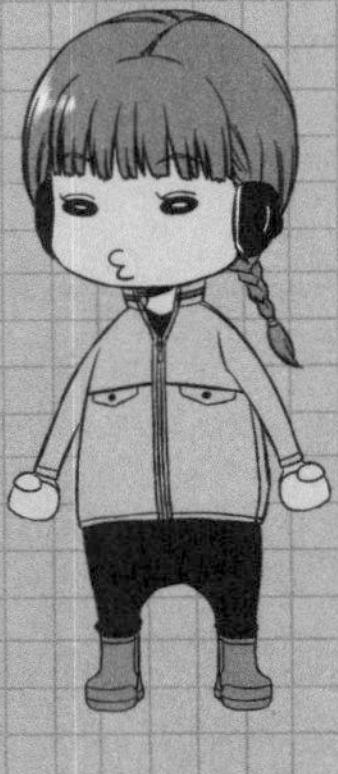

TERUYA

Courageous Stalker Waifu

A highly skilled, too-good-for-you lady from a preppy girls' school. This lofty-dream-girl has a habit of taking care of weaklings and (abridged for space) has some balls to indirectly say "I'm here to look after you cuz you suck," which comes from her slightly sadistic side. But she can't handle ghosts. In a haunted house in an amusement park, she beat the crap out of a ghost doll actor and she got away with it thanks to her dad's money. All hail the power of money!

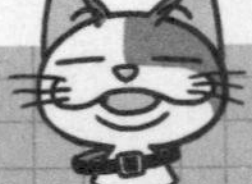

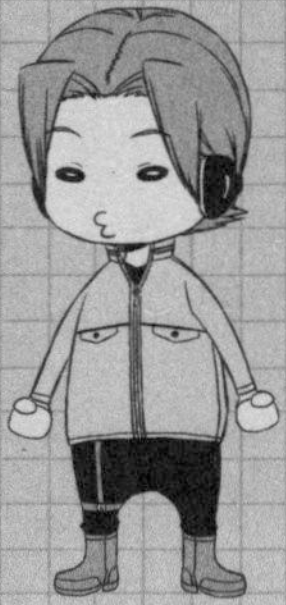

KOTARO

Well-Trained Puppy

A very precious puppy whose loyalty didn't fade even after his captain turned out to be super lame. While he claims to respect Kakizaki, his hair is styled after Jin's. What the heck is wrong with you, kid?! Anyway, thanks to his obedient and respectful personality, he's idolized as a mascot...particularly by his female seniors. Here's another dude who's living the good life!

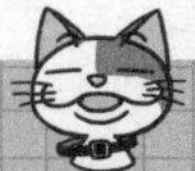

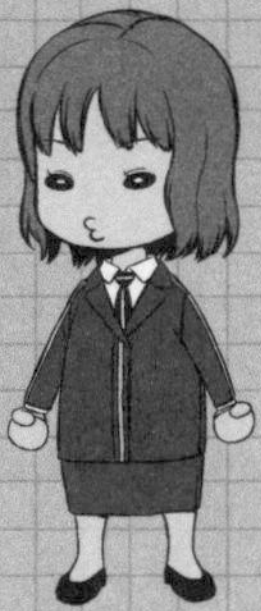

UI

Shadow Boss

A realist operator who maintains a cohesive team by whipping her flaky captain's butt into gear. Her personality is as refreshing as cold somen noodles in the summer—a stark contrast to the normies on her squad. She lives in temporary housing in Mikado City, but is saving up to live with her family in a place that allows cats. A B-cup girl whose eyes look similar to Izumi's and Arafune's, but is not related to either of them.

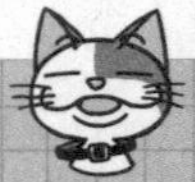

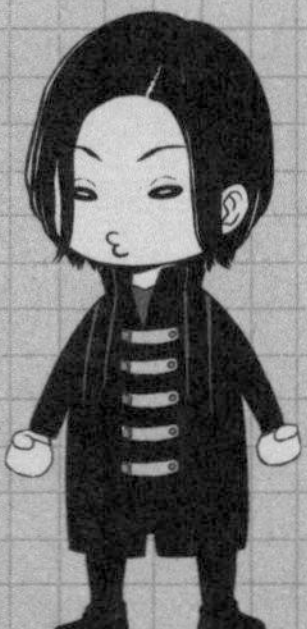

YUIGA

Protagonist's Rival

A-Rank No. 1 and a scion of a large enterprise. The rival/senior to Four-Eyes. What a juicy position! His position and title alone should be good enough to get him a ton of fans...*aaaand* I hear cicadas in my office, in the walls, making weird sounds...and now I'm scared. I was okay with bugs when I was little. Why am I scared of them now that I'm older? They're still chirping...

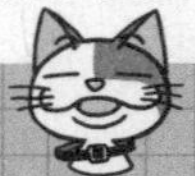

YOU'RE READING THE WRONG WAY!

World Trigger reads from right to left, starting in the upper-right corner. Japanese is read from right to left, meaning that action, sound effects, and word-balloon order are completely reversed from the English order.

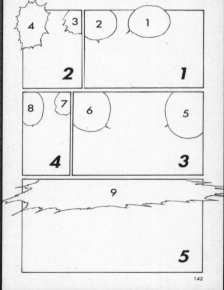